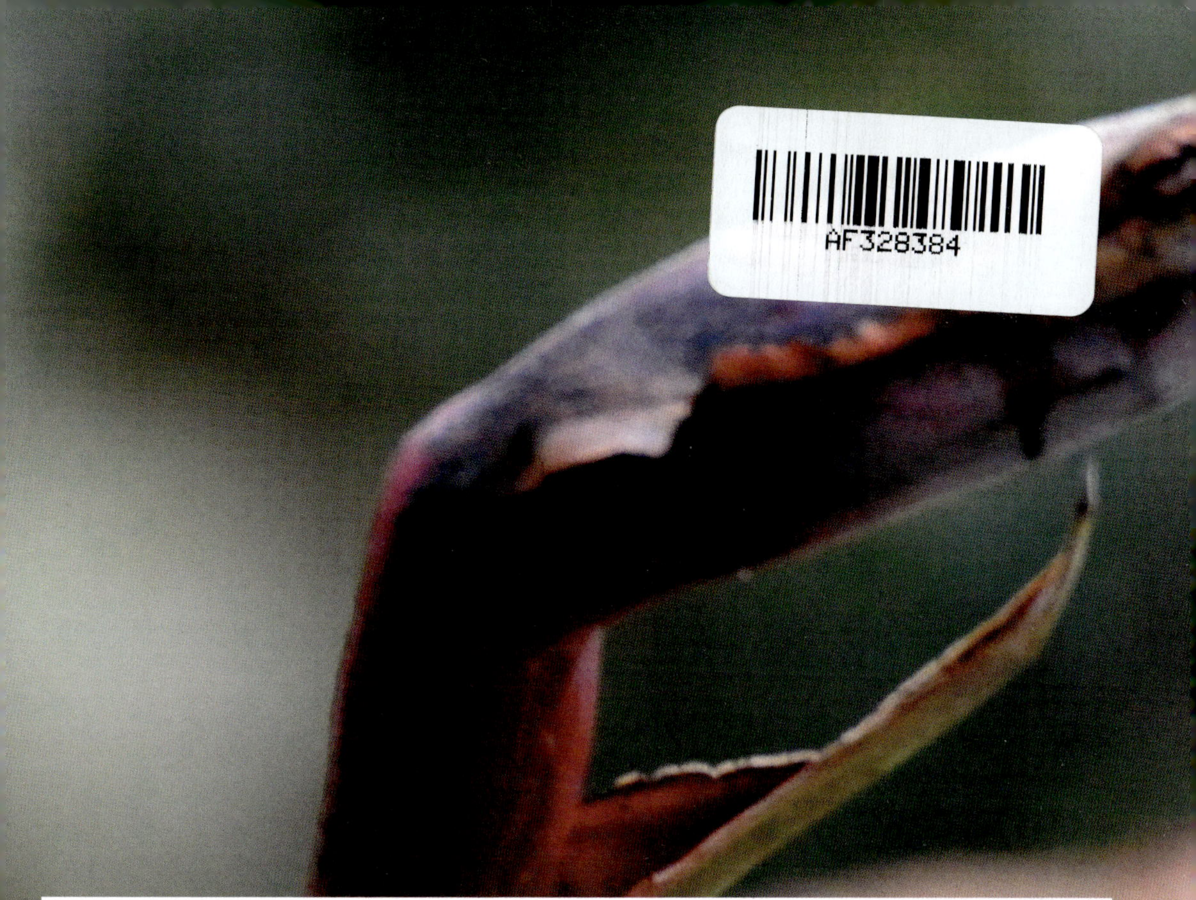

Bring nature back to the city

How to conduct urban nature conservation

Ernst Wohlitz
N Dip (Nature Conservation and Management)
B Agric (Animal Production)

Published by
BRIZA PUBLICATIONS
CK/1990/011690/23

www.briza.co.za

P O Box 11050, Queenswood 0121
Pretoria
South Africa

First edition, first impression 2016

ISBN 978-1-920217-61-7

Project manager: Johan Steenkamp
Language editor: Johan Steenkamp
Illustrations: Linette Ferreira
Printed and bound by ABC Press, Epping, Cape Town

TABLE OF CONTENTS

PREFACE

Most of the facts and issues raised in this book are not new and were already put forward in the late 1990s. Many issues stayed dormant until early 2000. It was the countries with the least natural open space that realised that something had to be done to focus on the importance of urban conservation. However, conservation services are often still not regarded as essential municipal services.

Awareness of global warming and climate change highlighted the need for ecological infrastructure in the urban environment. The services this infrastructure supplied became clearer and it was realised that the natural urban environment will be the only way to make cities resilient to climate change.

In 2004, the author started looking for information on urban nature conservation. Few publications and a limited amount of research material were available at the time. The only book on the subject published by then was the one by Toney Kendle & Stephen Forbes (published in 1997 by E & FN Spon, an imprint of Thomson Professional, 2-6 Boundry Row, London, SE1 8HN, UK). It is sad to report that the author could only obtain a second-hand copy from a library in the USA that wanted to get rid of it because of poor interest in the subject.

The lack of information on this subject prompted the writing of this book. Initially, the idea was to compile a document that students could use to increase their knowledge on the subject. Nature conservation students are trained in conservation principles focused on nature reserves, game farming and biodiversity management. Urban nature conservation is a specialised field. One needs the standard basic knowledge of conservation principles with additional urban nature conservation principles.

The author spent most of his life working for a metro city concentrating on urban nature conservation. Most of the principles implemented were gained through experience as well as trial and error management. It was therefore important to start recording the information and pass it on to newcomers. After consultation with stakeholders, it became clear that more than an informal document was needed and that a book on the subject would be more realistic. It also became clear that such a publication would have to reach a wider audience than merely students. Information must be available to a broad spectrum of readers, from the local resident to the specialist birder, the town planner, engineer and postgraduate student, among others.

Readers are advised to start with the chapters that interest them the most. The early chapters are less technical than those towards the end of the book.

Ernst Wohlitz
March 2016

ACKNOWLEDGEMENTS

The author wants to thank the following people who contributed to the writing of this book:
- Dr Marthinus Jordaan, who assisted with the technical input and guidance to publish this book.
- Rose Correia, who helped with the language editing.
- All staff at Tshwane Nature Conservation who contributed information and offered input and support.
- Thinus Prinsloo, colleague and friend.
- David Boshoff and Hencke Marais, who gave practical advice on the chapter on wildlife management in a city.
- Phillip de Beer for permission to use one of his photographs on the front cover.
- Jaco Ackerman for valuable guidance on the best approach to be followed during the writing of this book.
- Sas Kloppers who helped to initiate the writing process.

Briza Publications and Ernst Wohlitz express OUR sincere gratitude to the sponsors:

E OPPENHEIMER AND SON, SOUTH AFRICA and
WESTAIR AVIATION, NAMIBIA

as well as contributors

VAN HUYSSTEENS COMMERCIAL ATTORNEYS, PRETORIA, SOUTH AFRICA and
DR BASIE SPIES, CANADA

Special thanks to Nicky and Strilli Oppenheimer of E Oppenheimer & Son for their support of this book.

E Oppenheimer & Son is the investment holding company of the Oppenheimer Family interests, founders of the global mining company Anglo American, and managing shareholders of De Beers (the world's leading diamond company), until its acquisition by Anglo American.

The Oppenheimer Family has a rich history and association with conservation work in South Africa, having long been supporters of biodiversity conservation and research in natural sciences and wildlife administration.

These conservation efforts are inspired by the Oppenheimer Family's passion for the preservation of South Africa's natural heritage: Nicky and Strilli Oppenheimer were joint recipients of the *World Wildlife Fund's Lonmin Award* for environmental conservation in 2007, in recognition of their outstanding contribution to conservation. Active research centres occur on four of their properties, Tswalu Kalahari Reserve, Telperion, Shangani Ranch and Wakefield, with numerous research projects conducted on the properties annually.

E Oppenheimer & Son remains a dedicated custodian of South Africa's unique urban ecological heritage.

Dr Duncan MacFadyen
Manager: Research & Conservation

WESTAIR
A V I A T I O N
Flights tailored to suit your needs
Corporate VIP Charters
Charters & Fly-In Safaris
Emergency Medical Air Evacuation
www.westair.com.na
reservations@westair.com.na
+264 83 937 8247 | +264 81 124 6813

EXECUTIVE SUMMARY

Following the preface, executive summary and glossary of terms, **Chapter 1** starts with the perceptions people have on urban nature conservation. Challenges are highlighted, as well as the way forward to change perceptions for the better.

Chapter 2 lists most of the functions of urban green areas. It highlights the principles of how urban nature functions and how humans can participate to fit in.

Chapter 3 is focused on local residents. It highlights urban nature in their gardens (mammals, birds, reptiles, and insects). Then it analyses how humans used to think and how they need to synchronise their lifestyles to make urban nature more sustainable. It also addresses capacity-building and the importance of spreading the correct message.

Chapter 4 looks at wildlife management in a city. It focuses on tools and methods to create and maintain suitable habitats for wildlife in an urban environment. Then it pays attention to bird hides, the hobby of birdwatching and attracting and feeding birds. The chapter finally addresses problems that residents often experience with mammals and reptiles in an urban environment.

Chapter 5 deals with information on Red Data species. Guidance on protected species is highlighted. Reasons why some species need special protection are given, and the dangers for species that are prone to extinction are described.

Chapter 6 explains the roles and responsibilities of local governments towards open spaces and the management thereof. Open space principles and networks are explained. There is a full description of green, blue, brown, grey and red nodes and ways.

Chapter 7 deals with ecosystem services. It describes the threat to the environment (fragmentation, habitat loss, etc.) and then it shows how an evaluation of an urban nature area can be conducted. It also provides a template for an ecological management plan. The last part of the chapter deals with biodiversity and ecosystem restoration for sustainable development. Examples of habitat and species action plans are explained.

Chapter 8 supplies information on alien invasive plants and defines invader species, as well as control methods to be used. Different categories of alien plants are also explained, with reasons why it is so important to address the threats.

Chapter 9 highlights all the important information needed for wetlands and watercourses. The first part deals with hydrology, soils and vegetation of wetlands in the urban environment. The chapter then raises all issues related to watercourses and the management of watercourses and their riparian zones. It ends with buffer zones, a very important subject.

Chapter 10 describes mountains and ridges in the urban environment. There are guidelines on ways to control development in and around mountainous areas.

Ridges as biodiversity hotspots are explained, as well as the importance of ridges for Red Data species and their contribution to urban ecological infrastructure.

Chapter 11 focuses on the impact of industries and technological development on urban nature areas. Then it tackles storm water pollution issues and ways to address these problems.

Chapter 12 explains the procedure and implementation of environmental impact assessments (EIAs). It highlights the impact of development on biodiversity. There is a section on grasslands, wetlands and coasts, with an explanation of the EIA process for each of these habitats.

Chapter 13 is about the impact of utilisation on urban nature areas. It also deals with sustainable utilisation of urban nature areas. Visitor carrying capacity is highlighted, as well as ways to determine visitor numbers. The chapter finally focuses on recreational facilities within urban nature areas, visitor activities themselves and how they should synchronise with the urban environment.

Chapter 14 is an academic approach to urban nature conservation. It focuses on the specialist issues of urban nature conservation. Ecological corridors are the main drive to link up all urban nature areas and safeguard biodiversity by maintaining genetic diversity. It also looks at social needs and enrichment.

Chapter 15 describes the history, functioning and contribution of friends groups and how such groups can enhance urban nature areas. The role of the Wildlife and Environmental Society of South Africa (WESSA) in running friends groups and the necessary tools to operate a friends group are also discussed.

Chapter 16 considers the future approach to urban nature. It explains the previous approach to nature conservation where pockets of nature areas were protected without addressing the role of ecological corridors. It highlights the change to an approach of conserving an ecological function (including the ecological corridors). It shows the links between biodiversity and climate change and then highlights the issues that should be addressed in a biodiversity management system.

Chapter 17 explains what ecological infrastructure means, why it is important to invest in ecological infrastructure and how it should be dealt with. It also highlights the importance of mainstreaming this responsibility in all sectors of society.

Chapter 18 presents a very interesting activist story by Thierry Revert, who tells what really happened during the first Earth Summit in Rio de Janeiro in June, 1992.

The book concludes with a literature list, addenda, abbreviations and an index.

GLOSSARY OF TERMS

A

Adaptation: The adjustment of an organism to its environment or the process by which it enhances such fitness.

Agenda 21: A comprehensive plan of action to be taken globally, nationally and locally by organisations of the United Nations, governments and major groups in every area in which human activity has an impact on the environment. www.un.org/esa/sustdev/documents/agenda21/index.htm.

Alien species: A plant or animal species introduced from elsewhere, neither endemic nor indigenous.

B

Biodiversity: The diversity of genes, species and ecosystems on Earth, and the ecological and evolutionary processes that maintain this diversity. Biodiversity (diversity of species) is an indicator of the health of an ecosystem.

Biome: A major biotic community characterised by dominant forms of plant life and the prevailing climate, e.g. grassland, savannah, and forest.

Biodiversity assets: Species, ecosystems and other biodiversity-related resources that generate ecosystem services, support livelihoods, and provide a basis for economic growth, social development and human well-being.

Buffer: A strip of land surrounding a wetland or riparian area in which activities are controlled or restricted, in order to reduce the impact of adjacent land uses on the wetland or riparian area.

C

Carbon sequestration: A biochemical process through which atmospheric carbon is absorbed and stored by living organisms, including plants and soil micro-organisms, and involving the storage of carbon in soils, with the potential to reduce atmospheric carbon dioxide levels.

Catchment : An area contributing to run-off at a particular point in a river system.

Carrying-capacity: The number of animal units per year that the ecosystem can support without undergoing detrimental change.

Climate change: Long-term changes in the weather patterns of the Earth, including temperature, wind and rainfall, especially as a result of the increase in temperature of the Earth's atmosphere, resulting from the increased concentration of certain gasses.

Climate change adaptation: Initiatives and measures to reduce the vulnerability of natural and human systems to the actual or expected effects of climate change. Adaptation can be of several different types.

Conservation: The preservation of biological units such as genes, species, populations and ecosystems to prevent their extinction.

Conservancy: A contractually legitimised co-management entity, involving two or more recognised land and resource authorities, formed for the use and conservation of natural resources on land under their jurisdiction.

C-Plan: Conservation plan focusing on the mapping and management of biodiversity priority areas. The C-Plan includes protected areas, irreplaceable and important sites owing to the presence of Red Data species, endemic species and potential habitat for these species.

Critically endangered: Relating to a taxon that is facing an extremely high risk of extinction in the wild in the immediate future.

Cultivated: Related to an area that is still perceived as predominantly 'green' but no longer in its natural state and developed by human intervention, care and use.

D

Degradation: A process of loss of quality of the environment, leading to a reduction in ecosystem function and loss of ecosystem services.

Development: A process for improving human well-being through a relocation of resources that involves some modification of the environment. It addresses basic needs, equity and the redistribution of wealth. Its focus is on the quality of life rather than the quantity of economic activity.

Dichlorodiphenyltrichloroethane (DDT): A chemical for insecticidal treatment discovered by the Swiss chemist Paul Hermann in 1939. It was used during World War II to control malaria and typhus among civilians and troops. After the war it was used in the agriculture sector. Because of inappropriate usage of this chemical, insects developed a resistance against it, reversing early successes against malaria mosquitoes.

Disturbance: A general term used in ecology to describe a range of factors that cause change in an ecosystem or that disrupt ecosystem functioning. Disturbances may be natural (e.g. natural fires, floods) or artificial (e.g. ploughing, clearing of vegetation for building, etc.).

Diversity: The sum total of a variety of biological units at various scales, be it genes, species, populations or ecosystems.

E

Ecological cycles: A variety of processes, driven ultimately by solar energy that maintains ecosystems by sustaining life and replenishing renewable resources. They include nutrient, carbon, nitrogen, oxygen and water cycles.

Ecological corridors: Roadways of natural habitat providing connectivity of various patches of native habitats, along or through which faunal species may travel without any obstructions.

Ecological footprint: Human impact in terms of the amount of land that is required to sustain an individual, city, country, etc. For example, the ecological footprint of a city is usually many times larger than the geographical area it takes up. This is because cities make use of resources from outside their boundaries and dispose of waste outside their boundaries.

Ecological sensitivity: Sensitivity of vegetation habitat types based on the following criteria:
- Red Data species habitat
- Percentage disturbance
- Species diversity
- Percentage of alien infestation
- Local importance
- Regional importance

Ecological value: Non-monetary assessment of ecosystem integrity, health or resilience, all of which are important indicators to determine critical thresholds and minimum requirements for ecosystem service provision.

Ecosystem: An assemblage of living organisms, the interactions between them and with their physical environment. Each ecosystem is characterised by its composition (the living and non-living components of which it is made), its structure (how the components are organised in time and space) and the ecological processes.

Ecosystem-based adaptation: The use of biodiversity and ecosystem services as part of an overall strategy to help people adapt to the adverse effects of climate change. Ecosystem-based adaptation involves maintaining ecosystems in a natural, near-natural or functioning state, or restoring ecosystems, where necessary, to support human adaptation to climate change.

Ecosystem approach: A strategy for the integrated management of land, water and living resources that promotes conservation and sustainable use in an equitable way. The ecosystem approach recognises that humans are an integral part of ecosystems and stresses the need for integrated and holistic environmental decision-making.

Ecosystem health: An ecosystem is considered stable or healthy if it returns to its original state after a disturbance, exhibits low temporal variability over time, or does not change dramatically in the face of disturbance.

Ecological infrastructure: Natural biodiversity, ecosystems and resources that provide a flow of essential ecosystem services to human communities, and that support livelihoods and economic activities. Networks of ecological infrastructure may take the form of large tracts of natural land, or small remaining patches or corridors embedded in production landscapes. If ecological infrastructure is degraded or lost, the flow of ecosystem services will be diminished.

Ecological processes: All the processes that result from the relationships and interactions within and between ecosystems. These processes operate at various scales and include, for example, nutrient cycles, energy flow, soil formation, nitrogen fixation, carbon storage, predator-prey interactions, fire cycles, seasonal migrations of species, and pollination. Ecological processes are sometimes interchangeably referred to as ecosystem processes or ecosystem functions.

Ecosystem resilience: The ability of an ecosystem to maintain its functions (biological, chemical and physical) in the face of disturbance or to recover from external pressures. A climate-resilient ecosystem would retain its functions in the face of climate change. Ecosystem-based adaptation will require measures to maintain the resilience of ecosystems under new climatic conditions, so that they can continue to supply essential services.

Ecosystem services: The benefits that people obtain from ecosystems, including provisioning services (such as food and water), regulating services (such as flood control), cultural services (such as recreational benefits), and supporting services (such as nutrient cycling, carbon storage) that maintain the conditions for life on Earth.

Ecotourism: Travel undertaken to visit natural sites or regions without harming them.

Endangered: Related to a taxon that is critically endangered but is facing a very high risk of extinction in the wild in the near future.

Endemic: Restricted or exclusive to a particular geographic area, occurring nowhere else. Endemism refers to the occurrence of endemic species.

Environment: The surroundings within which humans exist and that are made up of:
- The land, water and the atmosphere of the Earth.
- Micro-organisms, plant and animal life.
- Any part or combination of the above and the interrelationships among and between them.
- The physical, chemical, aesthetic and cultural properties and conditions of the foregoing that influence human health and well-being.

Environmental goods and services: Such goods and services include:
- Benefits obtained from ecosystems such as food, fuel, fibre and genetic resources.
- Benefits from the regulation of ecosystem processes such as climate regulation, disease, flood control and detoxification.
- Cultural non-material benefits obtained from ecosystems, such as benefits of a spiritual, recreational, aesthetic, inspirational, educational, community and symbolic nature.

Extinct: Relating to a species that is no longer represented by living individuals.

F

Flood attenuation: The natural or man-made processes or structures that reduce the severity of potential flooding.

Floodplain: A relatively level alluvial (sand or gravel) area lying adjacent to a river channel that has been constructed by the present river in its existing regime.

Foot slope: The lowest portion of a hill-slope.

Fragmentation (of habitat or ecosystems): Development (urbanisation, agriculture, etc.) that takes place on land where natural ecosystems occur and that results in those ecosystems being split up into smaller pieces. Such fragmentation may have a serious impact on the ability of the ecosystem to function.

G

Groundwater: Subsurface water in the saturated zone below the water table.

H

Habitat: In relation to a specific species, a place or type of site where such a species naturally occurs.

Hydrology: The study of the occurrence, distribution and movement of water over, on and under the land surface.

Hydromorphic: A term used to describe soils that are associated with bogs, marshes, swamps and other poorly drained areas; these soils undergo protracted periods of being waterlogged and usually comprise an upper layer containing decaying plants or organic matter and a lower layer of clay.

I

Indigenous species: In relation to a specific area, a species that occurs, or has historically occurred naturally in a free state in nature within that specific area, but excluding a species introduced in that area as a result of human activity.

Incentives: Specific inducements designed and implemented to influence government bodies, businesses, non-government organisations, or local people to conserve biological diversity or to use its components in a sustainable manner. Incentive measures usually take the form of a new policy, law or economic or social programme.

Invasive/invader: Usually described at the species level. An invasive species (invader) is any plant or animal species whose establishment and spread outside of its natural range threatens (or has the potential to threaten) natural ecosystems, habitats or other species. Invasive species may cause economic or environmental harm, or even harm to human health. Invasive species are often, but not exclusively, species that have been introduced (by man) from elsewhere.

K

Kyoto Protocol: An international agreement linked to the United Nations Framework Convention on Climate Change, which sets binding targets for industrialised and developing countries to reduce greenhouse gas emissions.

M

Marsh: An herbaceous wetland dominated by emergent herbaceous vegetation (usually taller than 1 m), such as the common reed (*Phragmites australis*), which may be seasonally wet, but is usually permanently or semi-permanently wet.

N

Natural: Relating to an area existing in or produced by nature, not artificial or imitated, where vegetation is usually dominant, where little human intervention has taken place and which is not intensively utilised by humans.

Natural capital: An economic metaphor for the limited stocks of physical and biological resources found on Earth. Also referring to the capacity of ecosystems to provide ecosystem services.

Nature conservation area: An area that is demarcated and managed according to standard nature conservation principles and practices.

Nature reserve: An area declared as such in terms of relevant legislation with the purpose of protection and managed according to standard nature conservation principles and practices.

O

Open space: An area predominantly free of buildings that provides ecological, socio-economic and place-making functions at all scales of the urban area.

Organisms: Individual life forms that can react to stimuli, reproduce, grow, and maintain themselves – plants, animals, fungi, viruses, bacteria and other forms of life.

P

Peat lands: Wetlands characterised by the accumulation of partially decomposed plant matter.

Predator: An organism that benefits in an interspecific interaction in which it kills and feeds on prey. A predator lives in loose association with its prey.

Protected areas: Areas of land or sea that are formally protected by law and managed primarily for biodiversity conservation. There are numerous categories of protected areas, defined for example by the South Africa National Environmental Management Protected Areas Act (Act 57 of 2003). Four kinds of protected areas are recognised:
- Special nature reserves, nature reserves (including wilderness areas) and protected environments.
- World Heritage sites.
- Specially protected forest areas, forest nature reserves and forest wilderness areas.
- Mountain catchment areas.

Public goods: Goods or services in which the benefit received by any one party does not diminish the availability of the benefits to others, and where access to the goods cannot be restricted.

R

Ramsar Convention: An inter-governmental treaty that provides the framework for international co-operation for the conservation of wetland habitats.

Red Data species: Species that appear on an official list of species, fauna and flora, that require environmental protection, based on definitions of categories such as Endangered, Threatened and Vulnerable, among others.

Resort: A well-developed, multifunctional open space venue that provides controlled access to communities for:
- Community and social interaction.
- Children's recreational play opportunities (playing equipment, informal playing space, swimming pools, water slides).
- Passive leisure opportunities (benches, braai facilities, swimming pools, water slides).
- Overnight accommodation (chalets, camping, caravanning).
- Group function areas.
- Events areas.
- Refreshment facilities.
- Conservation areas and related components.

Resource, non-renewable: A resource that has a finite stock and either cannot be reproduced once it is used or lost, or cannot be reproduced within a time span relevant to present or future generations.

Resilience: A term generally referring to the capacity of a system to absorb expected and unforeseen change, while retaining its character and functionality. See also **Ecosystem resilience**.

Resistance: The capacity of an ecosystem to resist change in the face of disturbance.

Restoration: A process that includes all interventions designed to aid the repair or recovery of a degraded ecosystem, in some cases with a focus on restoring basic ecological functioning, and in others on restoring structure and composition as well.

Rehabilitation (wetland): The reinstatement of the driving ecological functions to a level close to the original system (but seldom fully attaining it) so as to improve the wetland's capacity for providing services to society.

Riparian habitat: (as defined by the South African National Water Act): 'A habitat that includes the physical structure and associated vegetation of the areas associated with a watercourse which are commonly characterised by alluvial soils (deposited by the current river system), and which are inundated or flooded to an extent and with a frequency sufficient to support vegetation of species with a composition and physical structure distinct from those of adjacent land areas.'

Ridges: Topographic features with slopes of a five-degree gradient or more.

River: The geomorphology formed by rainwater run-off and the resultant channels formed and evolved. This contributes to riverbank topography. A river is the result of annual run-off rainwater and has a mean level determined by the climate and the duration of the rainfall period. (Rowntree *et al.* 2000)

Run-off: Total water yield from a catchment, including surface and subsurface flow.

S

Saturated: Relating to soil of which the water table or capillary fringe has reached the soil surface (Soil Survey Staff, 1992), resulting in the spaces between the soil particles being filled with water.

Sequestration (carbon): The process by which plants take in carbon dioxide gas and convert it into solid carbon as part of their structural components, as they grow.

Species: One of the basic units of biological classification, a species is often defined as a group of living things that are capable of interbreeding and producing fertile offspring.

Species richness: The number of species in an area or habitat.

Seep: An area in the landscape where the land surface intersects with the water table so that the subsurface water percolates in a diffuse manner from the soil surface.

Silt: Fine soil material with particles smaller than sand and larger than clay (i.e. 0.02-0.002 mm in diameter).

Site, irreplaceable: A site designated as essential in meeting targets set for the conservation of biodiversity. Options for achieving these targets will be reduced should the site not be protected.

Stakeholder: A person, group or organisation that has vested interests in or is affected by the outcome of a particular activity.

Sustainable development: Development that has integrated social, economic and environmental factors regarding planning, implementation and decision-making, so as to ensure that it serves present and future generations.

Sustainability: Development and maintenance based on the use of resources that can be replaced or renewed and are therefore not depleted. Economic development is sustainable only if it takes into account the limited resources of the biosphere.

T

Threatened ecosystem: An ecosystem that has been classified as critically endangered, endangered or vulnerable based on an analysis of ecosystem threat status. A threatened ecosystem has lost, or is losing, vital aspects of its structure, composition or function.

Threatened species: A species that has been classified as critically endangered, endangered or vulnerable, based on a conservation assessment (Red List), using a standard set of criteria developed by the International Union for Conservation of Nature (IUCN) for determining the livelihood of a species becoming extinct. A threatened species faces a high risk of extinction in the near future.

V

Veld: A South African term referring to open land containing natural vegetation.

Vulnerability: The degree to which a system is susceptible to, and unable to cope with, the adverse effects of climate change. Exposure to contingencies and stress and the difficulty in coping with them.

U

Urban (built up) area: An area that has been completely transformed by human intervention and which is predominantly hard and accommodates intense use.

Watercourse: As defined by the National Water Act, 1998 (Act 36 of 1998):
- 'A river or spring.
- A natural channel in which water flows regularly or intermittently.
- A wetland, lake or dam into which, or from which, water flows.
- Any collection of water which the Minister may, by notice in the Government Gazette, declare to be a watercourse and a reference to a watercourse includes, where relevant, its bed and banks.'

Wetland: As defined by the National Water Act, 1998 (Act No 36 of 1998):
'Land which is transitional between terrestrial and aquatic ecosystems where the water table is usually at or near the surface, or the land is periodically covered by shallow water, that naturally supports vegetation typically adapted to life in saturated soil.'

Wetland health: A measure of the similarity of a wetland to a natural or reference condition.

CHAPTER 1

Perceptions about urban nature conservation

This chapter deals with people's perceptions about urban nature conservation. Occupations listed are from different professions, industries, companies and walks of life. The challenges and the way forward are also addressed.

1.1   PROFESSIONS AND URBAN NATURE CONSERVATION

1.1.1   The town planner

When it comes to city planning, the town planners normally decide on behalf of the local authority what is needed, where to develop and who will benefit, an extensive task engaging various professions. Issues involved are usually roads and residential and business stands. The easy way is to work from a map, to draw lines and do layouts. Planners are under pressure to provide for the hard services – issues that are economically, not ecologically, driven.

Unfortunately, this process often leads to the loss or fragmentation of ecologically sensitive urban nature areas, thus preventing their sustainable functioning.

There is a trend for developers to earmark a piece of land to be developed, the aim usually to develop the maximum surface for financial gain. Pockets of land not suitable for these purposes are then demarcated for park development. The road layout often also provides for the maximum profit for the project, often resulting in a situation where roads and services infrastructure cross ecologically sensitive nature areas. The placement of stands and infrastructures is often not in harmony with adjoining urban nature areas.

The biggest threat to natural areas in the urban environment is the fragmentation of ecologically sensitive areas. The first step in the planning process should be the identification of such areas, and then the placement of the infrastructure in such a way that it would complement the adjacent natural areas. The areas should be demarcated in such a way that they can still be functional and they should be linked

Red-knobbed Coot.

with neighbouring green corridors so that urban wildlife can easily move from one green node to another. The focus should be on the green nodes, green ways, blue nodes and blue ways. (Refer to Chapter 6: Open space: roles and responsibilities.)

A good example of this principle is to border a green area with a road rather than with residential or business stands. Ignore the argument that stands are needed adjacent to a road to reduce the cost of infrastructure development. No money can buy urban green spaces. These soft services are essential to provide the social needs of residents. In this regard, the nature specialist has to come in first (not last as in the past), then the landscape architect to guide the design in such a way that it would enhance urban nature, and then the traffic engineers and the rest of the infrastructure specialists (storm water, water and sanitation, electricity, etc.) may follow.

1.1.2   The landscape architect

Landscape architects are urban green friendly and understand that the environment is very important in the urban design processes. Unfortunately, they do not always focus on or consider the ecologically sensitive processes in the urban context. They are influenced by horticultural designs that are not always nature friendly. Horticultural designs include exotic vegetation, manicured gardens and alien trees on the sidewalks with the aim to beautify the city or town and not necessarily to enhance the urban ecology. This is all about manicured gardens, cutting of grass and green play parks. We do need these greening efforts but it needs to complement the urban nature.

Green lawns can consist of indigenous grass. Street trees can be endemic trees from the region. Gardens can be created to consist of indigenous flowers and plants that will enhance urban wildlife. In South Africa, why are nurseries still selling exotic plants for gardening while this country has the greatest diversity of vegetation available?

1.1.3   Engineers (roads and storm water, water and sanitation, traffic, electricity)

Most engineers will tell you they love nature conservation, they participate in nature activities and that they do not cause any damage to nature areas. Unfortunately, this is not true. They are clever people and well trained in construction. Construction is the biggest threat to urban nature conservation. On the other hand, construction can be carried out in a way that considerably lessens the impact.

Roads normally cross sensitive urban nature areas (because of insensitive layout plans). Storm water is always contaminated by sewerage and diverted to blue ways and nodes (rivers and dams). Sewerage is the biggest threat to urban nature because of its unreliable leakages (see Chapter 9: Wetlands and watercourses within an urban environment). Traffic planning (road planning) normally does not take urban nature impact into consideration. Electricity contributes to visual light pollution, especially adjacent to sensitive urban nature conservation areas.

By nature, an engineer likes challenges and is not afraid to take it on. Engineers and builders will build a reservoir on top of a mountain with a detrimental visual impact on a nature area. They will easily design a bridge to cross a portion of an ecologically sensitive river system. They will construct storm water channels in such a way that a river can become a concrete channel. These achievements must be brought in line to consider the environment.

1.1.4   Horticulture (Parks/urban gardens)

Horticulturists are trained to create gardens. They know how to prune trees, cultivate plants and how to do garden outlays. They can construct sports facilities and sports fields. They can maintain all of these facilities: operate relevant machinery and equipment (grass cutting) and they know how to apply chemicals to combat weeds, insects and diseases attacking their plants.

Unfortunately, the focus falls on beautifying landscapes and creating green areas that look nice but do not necessarily contribute to urban nature conservation. Horticulturists are not trained to be critically aware of ecosystems, food chains, indigenous plant species and endemic plants. They are not responsible for combating alien vegetation and often unwittingly contribute to alien infestations. They are trained in using exotic vegetation to beautify landscapes.

The functions of beautifying urban landscapes are important but can be done with indigenous vegetation. Landscapes can be designed to enhance urban wildlife. The way chemicals are used can be more ecologically friendly.

Horticulture is an accepted practice in the urban environment and can contribute immensely to urban nature conservation. This is part of our open space and a way how green ways and nodes can be linked to each other. The role of horticulturists can be to introduce the residents to urban nature conservation. It is the front line service for urban nature conservation and is needed to establish the right perception with the general public.

1.1.5   Urban agriculture

Urban agriculture is a grey area. It cannot compete against agriculture in the rural areas. The availability and the quality of available land for agriculture, is a limited factor in the urban environment.

Impacts of urban agriculture are the following:
- Water must be available and a substantial amount of usage is needed.
- The type of soil must be of high agricultural value.
- Cultivation taking place can destroy natural vegetation.
- Highly intensive farming practices are a requirement.
- Chemicals used are not environmentally friendly.
- There is always a risk of erosion.
- Urban farming involves high impacts on land earmarked for this purpose.

It is possible to rehabilitate areas where urban farming has taken place but not to their original state. Despite its high impact, it still cannot be compared to the impact that concrete and city development has on urban nature. Urban agriculture can be compared to urban gardening and should not be in competition with urban nature conservation.

1.1.6 Ecologist

An ecologist will always promote the conservation of ecologically sensitive areas. Unfortunately, ecologists are mainly used during specialist studies required by environmental impact assessments (EIA). Ecological inputs are often regarded as not necessary when the focus is on development.

In reality, ecological inputs can enhance development. Examples are the use of nature friendly designs; recycling initiatives, green energy and benefits that can be generated from ecological systems. Ecologists tend to see development as a threat and will not promote construction even when it can benefit both development and urban nature. It is often difficult for an ecologist to sacrifice nature to benefit development for humans. The general perception is that the human benefits of development are always at the expense of nature.

1.2   DEVELOPERS AND URBAN NATURE CONSERVATION

The aim of any developer is to make money and to achieve this, developers always seek cheap prime property. Their target is often soft services like parks and open spaces that belong to the tax payer. They will always be the first to tell you that the piece of land they want to develop is not contributing to the community and holds the potential to add so much to economic development.

One can build houses and supply infrastructure but at some point the residents will ask for parks where they can do outdoor and recreational activities (these can include sports facilities, parks, picnic areas or places where they can relax and enjoy the city nature). If you consult residents, they will rate their preference to these needs as follows:
• Undisturbed nature area
• Green areas with recreational facilities
• A sports facility (mountain bike, sports field, play park, etc.)
• The only requirement for these needs is that the area must be safe, clean and attractive to use.

The developer is seldom interested in these outdoor recreational needs. His/her development will fit in as many structures as possible that will generate money.

Green areas with recreational facilities.

This escalates to projects such as low-cost housing with limited space to open green areas, or commercial development (shops and offices) with no space for urban greening. Urban nature conservation is never on the agenda.

They tend to think that a green space can be created afterwards. The problem is that pristine ecologically sensitive urban nature areas are destroyed to the point where they are lost forever. Pristine urban nature cannot directly supply the developer with money but it can enhance his development as a marketing tool.

Developers and city planners liaise with each other in advance to get the feeling of the economic market. Unfortunately, both parties are ill-informed when it comes to urban nature conservation issues and are too short-sighted to see the indirect benefit it can have for a city or town.

Developers plan a development, then line up contractors for construction but in the meantime also source people to buy or rent these facilities. The buyers and those that rent facilities rely on the promises made by the developer. An example can be that they will create a nature reserve that will enhance the properties for sale. Unfortunately, most marketing ideas do not always materialise.

In the case of a sensitive nature area that was used for a development, the following usually happens: The developer uses the nature area as a marketing tool, then sells off the property and moves on to the next project. The maintenance team that took over the project from the developer are not responsible for the developer's promises. No answers are available to the complaints and problems that emanate out of the project. The promises to benefit the green nature area never materialise and no one is in a situation to reverse the wrongdoings that emanated out of the project.

The aim is to keep development adjacent to urban nature areas (not a restaurant in a nature park). Development should not encroach on urban nature. A plan should be available to extend and not decrease the size of the urban nature area as a result of development.

1.3   THE GENERAL PUBLIC AND URBAN NATURE CONSERVATION

The general public can tell you afterwards what they like but are usually not sure what they want upfront. Urban nature conservation is not their specialty; it does not affect them directly in their day-to-day operations. It benefits them indirectly and they see it as nice to have.

The general public is not usually updated on urban nature conservation. They see it as part of parks. Parks can be anything from sports facilities to urban gardens and picnic braai areas. The general public does not understand urban ecology. They must be exposed to urban nature conservation to see what it really means to them and how they can contribute.

If the general public happens to run into a nature conservator working for a city/town, they will be surprised at what the person is doing there. According to them, nature conservators (game wardens) belong in nature reserves or national parks. Nature conservation is not compatible with a municipality, although they know the local zoo is run by the municipality, and if there is a snake in the garden, they will call the fire department. When there is a monkey in their garden, they will call the Society for the Prevention of Cruelty to Animals (SPCA). Unfortunately, all these people they relate to in connection with these issues are untrained to deal with them.

It is cheaper to maintain urban nature areas than city gardens. Urban nature conservation brings nature back to the city. Not all city dwellers can visit national parks. Nature is on our doorsteps, in our gardens, on open spaces in our townships. Urban nature conservation can introduce residents to the environment they are living in. It can be the place where they play (mountain biking, hiking, game drives, caravanning and camping, picnic and braai, etc.) and spend their outdoor leisure time. It can educate their children on nature and help them live with their local environment in a sustainable way.

During normal working hours, the resident is involved in his workplace. After hours, weekends and holidays the resident needs leisure time and if it is in his

Animals in an urban park.

own environment, it is affordable, easily accessible and a reason to stay at home. It directs the individual to participate in constructive positive leisure time, keep children off the streets, and make time to gather with family and friends, come out in nature and take a break from work-related pressure. The resident will always remember cycling past a group of zebras grazing in the veld. He will remember his child feeding a tame squirrel in the picnic braai area, birdwatching from a bird hide or enjoying lunch at the refreshment facilities. City kids will remember the playground where they played while their parents had a picnic, or the lecture in the snake park, or the owls breeding in their garden.

1.4 BIG COMPANIES AND URBAN NATURE CONSERVATION

Companies are located within cities or towns. Normally their clients and employees are also staying in the same town. The town is the environment in which they conduct their business. This environment should also be important to them; it will have a direct/indirect impact on their business.

Companies are not normally familiar with urban nature conservation issues. Some of them can have an official appointed to address environmental issues; others may appoint someone to consult with or do investigations on their behalf.

Companies are in a much better financial position to contribute to urban nature conservation than individuals or resident groups (see Chapter 15: Friends groups). Most companies have sponsors and marketing portfolios. Any company associated with enhancing environmental issues will gain credit, not only from their clients but also on the marketing platform. Companies can negotiate discounts or credits when they can produce evidence of contributions made to the environment. They can even in some cases qualify for tax reductions.

Companies whose activities have a negative impact on the environment (either by their construction methods or their products) are eager to get involved with sponsorships to the environment. This gives them a more positive image, especially on the marketing side.

Any contribution a company can make to urban nature conservation is a good long-term investment. A company's involvement in this regard will always be positive and it is a nice introductory tool for presentations, applications or future business deals. (Example: If a company can promote this book, their contribution to this subject will already put perceptions related to them on a different level).

1.5 CONSTRAINTS IN GENERAL

Although urban nature conservation is not a new subject, it was ignored for many years. Few landscape architects raised it in the late nineties (Book published on urban nature conservation by Toney Kendle and Stephen Forbes, (published 1997 by E & FN Spon, an imprint of Thomson Professional, 2-6 Boundry Row, London, SE1 8HN, UK). It was always a soft issue that only cost money and could wait. The perception that national parks already address conservation issues and that this function does not belong to city/town development, is a tragic misconception.

Poor exposure to urban nature conservation and no information available on the subject still hamper progress in this regard.

Local authorities do not see urban nature conservation as a high priority and trained staff are unavailable. Academic institutions do not teach subjects that specialise in urban nature conservation. Literature on urban nature conservation is unavailable (which is why this book was initiated).

Mentorship, pilot projects and practical examples are essential to remedy the general lack of awareness. It is not just limited to parks. It is a specialised function that requires field specific knowledge and implementation.

Budget to implement urban nature conservation will always be a constraining factor but it is a long-term investment. It is an important environmental service to the tax payer.

Environmental management services departments should be a standard component within any municipal services structure. Trained staff must be appointed to conduct these services (supply environmental goods and services). Environmental goods are the physical pristine nature areas (urban nature reserves, rivers and ridges). Services comprise the sustainable management of these properties and facilities which include educating and empowering both staff and the public.

1.6   PROGRESS IN GENERAL

The bigger metros do realise that they are responsible for supplying environmental goods and services. There is a trend to protect nature areas within the urban environment.

New legislation came into place, such as requirements for Environmental Impact Assessments (EIA). Public involvement is required for the EIA approvals and this highlights and exposes people to environmental issues that were ignored in the past (see Chapter 12: Environmental Impact Assesments (EIAs)).

Global warming became a big issue and to address this, urban nature conservation will be a contributor in the way cities are planned and managed in the future (ecologically-based adaptation to climate change).

The public in general prefers nature areas above traditional garden parks. They want to utilise it and enjoy trails and recreational activities. They participate in birdwatching and identify different bird species. They are eager to get involved and fight against wrongdoings that concern their local nature reserves.

Cities worldwide have made more progress on urban nature conservation than South Africa. London, England (English nature) is a good example on what can be done. They started off with almost no nature left and through an initiative launched by the mayor of London, they upgraded their urban nature areas very successfully.

The mayor has incorporated the targets for habitat restoration and creation set by the London Biodiversity Partnership into the London Plan. People, Parks & Nature and Improving Londoners' Access to Nature indicate how green spaces can be improved for wildlife and be made better spaces for people.

The regional planning document (London Plan) was first published in its final form on 10 February 2004. The plan is a spatial development strategy for the Greater London area and has six objectives. The 2011 revision objectives include ensuring that the city of London becomes a world leader in improving the environment and mitigating and adapting to climate change.

Locals participated in these processes and today they are leaders in this regard. We can all learn from them, as well as cities in America, Australia, etc.

More info on these initiatives can be assessed through the internet.

1.7   THE WAY FORWARD

Urban nature conservation cannot be ignored any more. It has become as important as global warming. More and more people move to cities and city developments encroach upon nature areas. These encroachments can be managed to accommodate ecologically sensitive urban nature areas. These areas can be utilised in a way that it will benefit the environment people live in.

The focus should be to identify these areas before development takes place. The aim should be to plan development around these nature areas and try to link these nature areas together by means of green ways (mountains and ridges) and blue ways (river systems). The green ways and blue ways should serve as corridors between the green nodes (small local nature reserve, nature area that protects a specific red data species, a nature area protecting a representative habitat) and blue nodes (dams, wetlands).

We should use urban nature to serve in the management of storm water issues. Urban river systems should be natural storm water channels (not concrete channels and piping). Wetlands should be natural flood retention structures as well as filter systems to clean out the city (the kidneys of the city). These urban nature areas must be there to absorb CO_2 and release oxygen back into the air (green lungs of the city). These nature areas will absorb sound pollution, cool down the city by

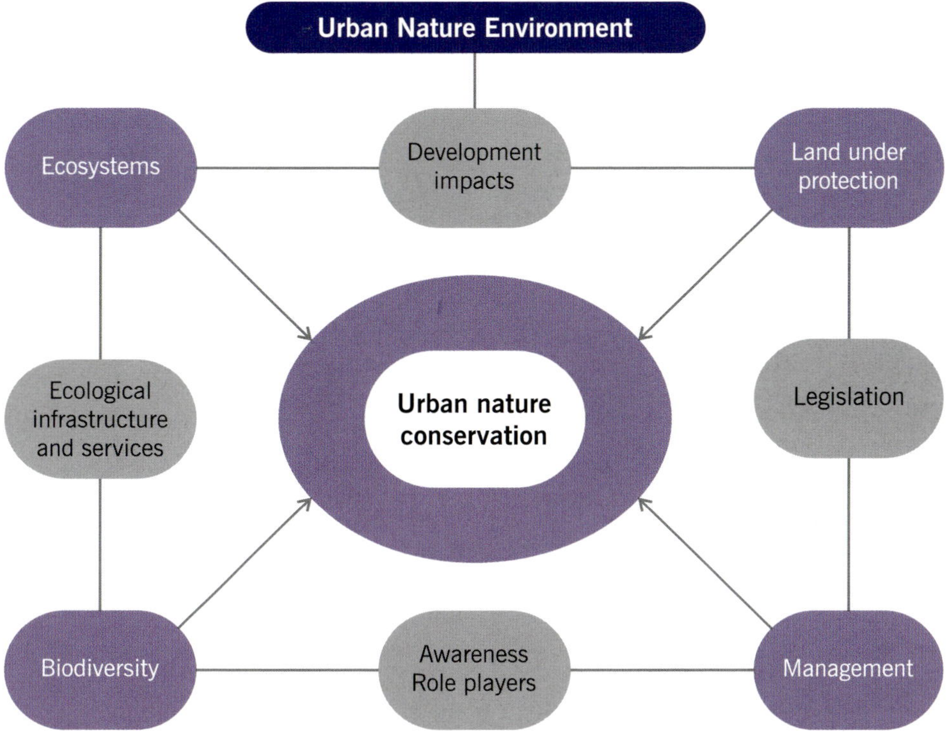

Figure 1.1. Diagram to illustrate how urban nature conservation should function on a local authority level.

supplying shade, conserve moisture and be the reservoirs where urban wildlife can escape to, and survive without threat.

We must try to grade and cultivate the ground surfaces as little as possible. Try to leave the natural trees where they are. Do not replace natural ground covers with non-endemic vegetation (natural vegetation can be maintained similar to cultivated gardens). Do not allow alien vegetation to infest the natural habitat. Start practicing conservation gardening principles and try to keep the original habitat as natural as possible.

Urban nature conservation is the conservation (to protect natural ecosystems) and management (maintain the ecological status of the urban areas) of biodiversity (ecological infrastructure and ecological service) in an urban environment (formalised built-up human settlements).

CHAPTER 2

Functions of urban green areas and how we can add value

(This chapter lists most of the functions of urban green areas. It highlights the principles of the functioning of urban nature and how humans can participate to fit in.)

2.1 FUNCTIONS OF URBAN GREEN AREAS

2.1.1 Purified water

Green areas include river systems, mountains, ridges and wetlands. A city or town has its own water cycle. Built-up areas (concrete buildings, tar roads, hard surfaces) cause air to be heated up, leading to the creation of thermals that cause movement of the air (up, down and horizontal flow). We experience this in the blowing of wind and the formation of thunderstorms.

Rainwater in cities or towns contributes to storm water, which washes off the buildings, roads and other hard surfaces. It cannot penetrate the ground and ends up in all the concrete channels. It takes with it dirt (dust, oil and other fluids) and pollution (tins, paper, plastic). This storm water eventually reaches the closest urban river system available.

If these urban river systems are managed according to proper urban nature conservation principles, the following will happen: the heavy material will sink to the bottom of the river (if there are enough obstacles such as gabion structures). It will be trapped on the spot and the rest of the water will continue to flow to the wetland areas where these natural filter systems will trap the rest of the particles up to a size the naked eye cannot see.

The more wetlands available, the cleaner the water will become. The water that comes from illegal fluent outlets within the storm water system will also be cleaned. These wetlands will conserve moisture and will continue to let water out long after the rain has gone.

We do not have to worry about the trapped material as most of it is visible and can be removed manually. The rest will be absorbed by nature (natural vegetation in the wetland areas).

We wash our clothes, cars and paved areas; urban nature washes itself through the rainwater cycle. Urban nature cleans and purifies our environment and the water within it. If we contaminate our water resources, urban nature can clean it. We need these cleaning actions to prevent diseases and other threatening factors within the urban environment.

2.1.2   Cleans the air

Vegetation produces oxygen and consumes carbon dioxide to grow. Humans and animals need oxygen to breathe and release carbon dioxide in the air. The more vegetation available, the more effectively this balance can be addressed.

Air pollution is a problem in cities and towns. Industries contribute to unwanted gasses. Vehicles and machinery (operating in the city) release unwanted gasses. These gasses must be absorbed or removed for residents to stay in a healthy environment.

Gasses and smoke are released into the air and is not always visible to the naked eye. When inhaled, the negative effects of these gasses are seen when people's health starts deteriorating and lung problems develop.

Fortunately for us, green vegetation can absorb most off these unwanted gasses. Green vegetation can contribute to the cleaning of the air within our urban environment.

2.1.3   Regulate urban climate

Urban nature areas have a positive influence on the urban climate. The urban climate consists of air quality, heat, dust, oxygen and carbon dioxide levels, humidity, wind, temperature, etc.

2.1.4   Temperature

Urban vegetation helps to regulate the city's temperature. The city can heat up to a higher temperature than the adjacent rural areas due to manmade structures and infrastructures (buildings, roads, paved areas, railway lines, iron roofs on buildings and soil areas not covered with vegetation).

Vegetation contributes to shaded areas. Trees are a major contributor to shaded areas. The more shaded areas, the cooler the ground surfaces become and the less heat is produced. Cool ground surfaces cool down airflow above it. The cooler airflow helps lower the general temperature of the surrounding environment and results in a quicker cool down process at night.

Heat consumes water and moisture through evaporation. The ground surfaces dry out and then there is less water available for the plants to grow. Less vegetation results in heat increases.

Trees provide shady areas to cool down temperatures.

All residents love to work and play in a cooler environment. Artificial cooling (air conditioners in cars and buildings) is expensive. Urban nature can contribute to cooling down the urban environment.

2.1.5   Remove dust

Rain is the biggest dust remover in nature. Dust particles are released as sediments in the river systems and are important for the condensation of rain drops in the air.

Dust is bad for humans and animals when inhaled and can result in lung problems.

2.1.6   Humidity

Humidity depends on the amount of moisture available in the air. Plants absorb water through their roots and release moisture into the air through their leaves. When wet areas are heated up, it activates the evaporation process. When wet surfaces dry out, it is because of the heat activating smaller water particles to evaporate into the air.

The evaporation process contributes to the formation of clouds. Clouds in turn produce thunder storms and rain. Moisture contributes to humidity.

2.1.7   Wind brake

Trees can have an influence on wind. It can affect the wind's direction, speed and indirectly the microclimate in the vicinity.

Urban wildlife will make use of trees and vegetation for shelter, shade and influence of the wind on them. The wind is usually an element of the current weather condition. When you can control wind, you can improve your local weather conditions which is necessary in urban environments.

2.1.8   Spiritual enhancement

Urban nature can contribute to spiritual enhancement. It is nice to relax in a nature park compared to a developed area among buildings and hard infrastructure. If you can add urban wild life (animals and birds) it becomes more enjoyable.

Residents in towns need to get out in the open to break away from their homes, offices and work places. They need to relax in a natural environment where they can breathe fresh air, enjoy the sunlight, listen to the birds in the forest, do game viewing, picnic and braai with their family and friends, go on a hiking or mountain bike trail, etc.

A spiritual enhancement close by your home can add value any time you need it. You do not need to plan in advance. You do not need to take leave. You can go with the people who live close to you and it relieves daily stress.

An opportunity to relax next to a river or dam, to do fishing or to camp contributes to the spiritual enhancement regularly needed in our daily life.

2.1.9   Recreation

Recreation consists of resorts and visitor facilities for the city dweller. City planners make provision for housing, streets, electricity and infra-structure but recreation facilities are often neglected. Recreation facilities for sports, picnics and braais with friends, camping, angling, birdwatching, hiking, mountain bike and horse trails, etc. are also needed.

Swimming pools for outdoor leisure are always the focus point in a resort. Children's play equipment and activities that keep them off the streets are essential. Visitor facilities like refreshment outlets, shelters to hire for small functions, etc. are important to the resident staying in a city.

2.1.10   Beauty

Urban nature brings beauty back to the city. We must secure existing urban nature from the start so that we do not need to bring it back afterwards.

Controlled entrance to a resort.

You can create beautiful buildings and infrastructure, but it can never replace or be compared with nature.

The best success is to maintain urban nature in its natural state without cultivating it and then develop a park. This method is more sustainable, consumes less water, requires less maintenance and is better adapted to the endemic environment than an artificial park. It will also attract wildlife and be popular with the residents.

2.2 HOW WE SHOULD CONTRIBUTE

2.2.1 Make sure there is access to nature areas

It is important to determine the clients of these nature areas. Who will visit these nature areas? What are the visitors' needs? If an urban nature area cannot be utilised, there will be no interested in its conservation. It will deteriorate and become a haven for crime activities, dumping of rubble and residents will start to complain about it. Developers will identify it as a cheap piece of land available for development which is better than the threat it poses if not utilised.

Controlled entrance

An example of poor access to a facility.

Access means a visitor can use it to get out in the open, walk the dog, use the hiking trail, picnic, and do birdwatching or any activity that is suitable for that specific urban nature area. The focus should be to enhance urban nature conservation and not to hamper urban nature conservation for the cost of utilisation.

Accessibility also means that the property must be safe to use, fenced off, with a controlled entrance and exit point. Visual supervision, infrastructure-like paths, information boards, and directions must be in place. The infrastructure must be properly maintained.

It is always good to link one or more enhancements to each facility for users to talk about or to refer to other potential customers. Referrals are great for marketing.

2.2.2 Understand how urban nature areas should interlink

I want to refer the reader to Chapter 6: Open space: roles and responsibilities. This is all about green and blue nodes and ways. Natural green spaces encourage plant and animal life in a municipal area. Urban nature is the haven where urban wild life can survive. It is in these green nodes and green ways that they can sustain their ecological processes. They can operate in their food chains and breed successfully.

The green nodes in a city are usually pieces of land that are unsuitable for development and then become urban parks or stays as natural open spaces. If a green node has an ecological value, it is worth transforming it into an urban nature reserve. Green ways are green corridors or belts, and are unsuitable for development. This includes servitudes, power line corridors, road reserves, mountains and ridges. It is very important to link all green ways with green nodes. Whenever there is a fragmentation of these nature areas, it is impossible for urban wildlife to survive. One green node cannot always maintain itself because of its small size. Green ways can link the nodes to help make it more sustainable.

The same principle is applicable for blue nodes (dams, ponds) and blue ways (river systems). If the green and blue nodes and ways can be combined, the success is even better. If role players do not focus on these issues, the city or town's potential to conduct urban nature conservation totally collapses.

2.2.3 Conduct regular nature asset audits

The audits have to address aspects such as the current wildlife present in a specific urban nature area. Which wildlife seems to be missing? Reasons for the shortcomings must be identified and actions to rectify the situation must be implemented.

The population within a municipal environment is dynamic. Needs can change and additional opportunities can materialise. Budget to fund operational and capital plans for the area is a driving element.

When we evaluate urban nature areas, the ecological sensitivity plays a major roll. Conservation actions are important to maintain what is in place. Sometimes it is necessary to rehabilitate or to revamp infrastructure.

The audit must focus on the green and blue nodes and ways and consider the movement of urban wild life (birds, animals, reptiles, insects, etc.). The water courses and ridges should be in a healthy ecological state.

2.2.4   Identify gaps and shortcomings related to urban nature

The above mentioned audit will assist to highlight the gaps and shortcomings. The evaluation template must make provision to score each urban nature area. The different scores can be used to prioritise necessary actions.

I want to refer to Chapter 14: The academic approach to urban nature conservation. It includes Ratcliffe's (1977) criteria for the evaluation of nature sites as follows: (See figure 2.1, page 21 – updated criteria by the author.)

Size: Importance to nature conservation generally increases with size.

Diversity: Variety is better than uniformity; species richness is better than a poor species compliment. Sites with a range of habitats are preferred (but rarity or interest need not coincide with diversity).

Naturalness: Sites which have been least modified by man are most valuable.

Rarity: Sites are more valuable if rare species or communities are present.

Fragility: Fragile communities are more valuable and deserving of protection. They may be vulnerable to internal changes, e.g. low population numbers causes dying out, successional change or vulnerability to external change, e.g. by human action.

Types: One objective is to maintain examples of all habitat types, good examples are as important as rare ones.

Recorded history: Sites which are well researched or documented are more valuable.

The position in an ecological or geographical unit: This relates to landscape ecology, for example, wood which is contiguous with other woods is more valuable than one which is not.

Potential value: Sites with diminished importance, but not irreversible decline, can have a potential value greater than present value.

Intrinsic appeal: This often applies more to species than habitats. Birds and flowers are more conspicuous and more appealing to people.

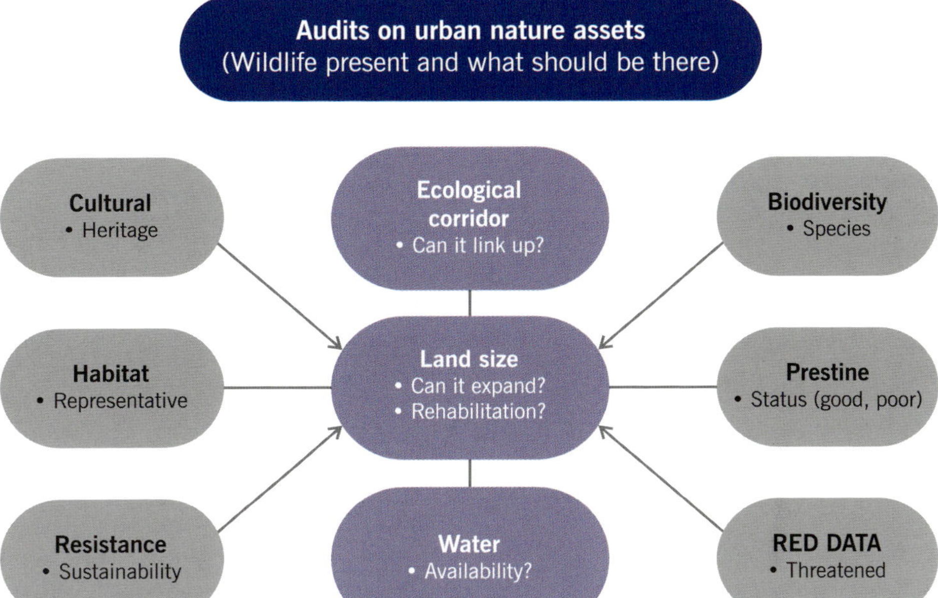

Figure 2.1. Diagram to demonstrate the criteria for evaluation of sites

Rehabilitate: When an urban nature area (that is worth to conserve) is degraded because of erosion, dumping and illegal access, infested with alien vegetation or the veld is in a poor condition rehabilitation is needed.

Extend: When there is potential to add adjacent land to a nature area, or to link it by means of a corridor, etc. Expense should not deter consideration.

Mitigate: This is applicable when things have gone wrong. It can be anything from mismanagement to wrong practices or actions that did not work in the past.

Please also see Chapter 7, section 7.3 (Evaluation of an urban nature area).

2.3   HOW DO I PARTICIPATE IN NATURE-ORIENTATED ACTIVITIES?

2.3.1 Birdwatching

Please review Chapter 4: Wildlife management in a city or town. Take up birding as a hobby. Join a bird club that arranges excursions. Improve your knowledge to identify birds in your local vicinity. It will become a challenge to tick off or to add new sightings to your list and prompt more visits to nature areas.

You can attract birds to your home and local environment. Please read Chapter 3: Residents and urban nature, to see suggested methods. Participate with friends groups to construct new bird hides (see Chapter 15: Friends groups). Visit existing bird hides and bird sanctuaries. These social gatherings and events will enhance your quality of life.

2.3.2 Utilise urban trails

The most popular trails lately are mountain bike trails. It is a high quality sport or leisure activity that provides exercise away from the city traffic.

Many professional people participate in mountain biking, without regarding the expense of their sophisticated bicycles and equipment. This activity has a low impact on nature and it is a great way of utilising urban nature areas.

Hiking trails are another favourite – enjoying nature at a slower pace. It is less expensive than mountain biking and elderly people can also participate.

If you want to be more adventurous, try going on horse trails and 4x4 trails, or go quad biking, canoeing, yacht sailing, abseiling, gliding, etc.

2.3.3 Game viewing

Game viewing is a rewarding experience for the whole family. You can participate in day and night game drives. You can visit the local lion camp. You can go picnic and braai as a combination of activities. The game drive can be self-catering or with a guide. Nature education can be combined with the event.

With game viewing you need binoculars. You need a map usually supplied at the entrance. It is important to be able to identify the different animals to add more value to your outing.

A local game reserve close to a city is a great enhancement to a municipality and adds lots of value to the residents and visitors to that municipality.

2.3.4 Make use of picnic and braai facilities

Every city or town has picnic and braai facilities. What is a better way than to go out to your local nature resort and socialise with friends and family around an open fire to braai and escape from the daily stressful city activities?

You have to supply your own fire wood, meat and drinks. It is informal and everyone can relax. You need your own camping chairs and tables and you can make use of additional outdoor leisure activities (like a swimming pool) to enhance your visit.

A picnic and braai is an affordable option. There is no cleaning up needed comparing it to a home activity. Everyone can socialise on the same terms and conditions.

Hiking trail.

Game drive with a guide.

Picnic area.

Camping area.

2.3.5 Use camping facilities

Camping is the most affordable way in which you go on holiday. It is always nature orientated and it is nature friendly. This is really a true way to socialise with nature. It is informal and a low impact activity on nature.

Equipment is needed; from basic camping equipment up to high sophisticated camping gear.

2.3.6 Get involved in friends groups

Please read Chapter 15: Friends groups, the purpose, how it works and how to establish a friends group.

Mammals: a, Slender Mongoose; b, Bushbaby; c, Brown Hyaena; d, Small-spotted Genet; e, Leopard.

CHAPTER 3

RESIDENTS AND URBAN NATURE

This chapter focuses on local residents and highlights urban nature in their gardens {mammals, birds, reptiles, and insects}. Suggestions follow on how residents can synchronise their lifestyles to help make urban nature more sustainable. It also addresses capacity-building and the importance of spreading the correct message.

3.1 URBAN NATURE IN OUR GARDENS

Urban nature is on our doorstep. Our gardens accommodate not only plants but also birds, mammals, reptiles and insects. Gardens can serve as havens for urban wildlife, a habitat for fauna and flora. Some gardens are still in a natural state and others are artificial. For urban wildlife, fragmentation is always problematic but corridors are the solution.

All homeowners can contribute to urban nature if they are aware of the wildlife present in their garden and surroundings. It is important to work out why these species are still present and how their activities fit into the bigger urban environment. When you start making a list of the species already present in your garden, you will be surprised. When you know what to look for and what can still be added, you are in a position to make a contribution to urban nature conservation.

Habitat (the immediate surroundings or a place to live) is important. Animal species need food and a safe environment where they can live, breed and raise their offspring. Examples of wildlife that can be found in residential areas are the following.

3.1.1 Mammals

Mice/rats

They can come from nearby veld areas, seeking food (as development reduces natural habitat, wildlife will enter residential areas to try and survive). Easy sources of food are seeds from bird cages, dog pellets, food that we throw away, etc. Our gardens should offer enough places to hide and nest-making materials should be available.

Slender Mongoose

These animals are not domestic friendly and can cause damage to pigeons or chicken farmers. They will kill their prey by only eating the head of a bird or their eggs. They consume insects (attracted by lights), lizards, birds and fruit.

Bushbabies

They still appear in many gardens, especially in residential areas within their natural distribution areas. They are nocturnal and feed on insects, tree gum, seeds and fruit available. They move through trees and you will seldom find them on ground level. There are residents that put out fruit for them and watch them with great excitement.

Small-spotted Genet

These nocturnal animals feed on rodents, birds, reptiles and insects (grasshoppers) and like to target chicken farms.

Brown Hyaenas

They are scavengers and roam great distances. In the urban environment, they will go for food in dustbins and any easy prey, even dogs and cats. They are also nocturnal and will eat birds, reptiles and insects. They prefer fresh meat, eggs and cucumbers.

Leopard

Leopards usually tend to roam in mountain areas. Their natural source of food is baboons. They will take domestic animals as an easy prey (this can include dogs). A leopard will have a home range (walking distance area). The Magalies Mountains (Pretoria, South Africa) provide walking ranges for leopards and they have been spotted in and around Pretoria's urban areas..

3.1.2   Birds

Hadidas

Hadidas are loud and regular visitors to our residential areas. They seek wet lawn patches and feed on insects, worms and larvae by using their bills as a pick, digging small holes. This action creates drainage holes for the water and help the lawn areas to trap air and water for better growth.

Black-collared Barbet, Pied Barbet and Crested Barbet

They mainly feed on insects and fruits. You can recognise them by the different sounds they make.

Hadida (*Glosy Ibis*). Photograph: Hein Waschefort.

Birds: a, Crested Barbet; b, African Hoopoe; c, Green Wood-hoopoe; d, Cape White-eye; e, Sunbird; f, Fork-tailed Drongo; g, Western Barn Owl; h, Golden Bishop; i, Southern Red Bishop.

African Hoopoe

They prefer garden lawn areas and feed on insects and ants.

Green Wood-hoopoe

These are very noisy black birds with long tails. They breed and live under house roof areas.

Cape Turtle Dove and Laughing Dove

They are common in our gardens and attracted by seed, such as pigeon feed.

Sunbirds

These birds feed on nectar produced by plants like the indigenous Cape Honeysuckle.

Cape White-eye

They will be found in areas with plants like the highveld cussonia species. These plants host a food chain of plant aphids milked by ants and they are food for birds.

Fork-tailed Drongo

These birds feed on honeybees as well as insects.

House and Cape Sparrows

They nest under roofs. Cape Sparrows are primarily granivorous, and also eat soft plant parts and insects. The Cape Sparrow is common in most of its range and coexists successfully in urban habitats with two of its relatives, the introduced House Sparrow and native Southern Grey-headed Sparrow.

Weavers

Weavers nest in gardens and trees overhanging water bodies. They are very active during the breeding season when they collect nest-making material.

Birds: a, Cape Sparrow female; b, Cape Sparrow male.

Owls

Owls are birds of prey and lots of food like mice and rats are available in residential areas. They hunt during the night and residents will not be aware of their activities. During the day, they spend their time in trees or any other suitable safe place. Breeding space is problematic and some residents take the initiative to build owl boxes (see Chapter 20, Addendum A (owl boxes)).

3.1.3   Reptiles

Lizards

They feed on insects. In residential areas, insects are attracted by light.

Snakes

Snakes are attracted to gardens by mice, frogs, lizards, etc. Snakes are part of the food chain and although most of the residents do not want snakes around their garden, the possibility is always there. It is important to know how to deal with these reptiles. Snakes prefer to avoid humans and will make a sound or mock charge when they feel threatened. They will always try to escape and only attack when they are trapped and feel threatened. When you leave them alone, they will

Reptiles: a, Yellow-throated Plated Lizard; b, Skink; c, Puff Adder; d, Albanian Water Frog.

not be a danger to anyone. In the case of a snake bite, it is important to identify the snake to get the correct anti-venom treatment.

Frogs

They are attracted by the water features in our gardens. They also feed on insects and themselves become prey for snakes. Frog sounds can be rewarding for the city dweller. Many frog species can make sounds by night that can be confused with similar bird sounds.

3.1.4   Insects

Bees

Bees are the major pollinator for plants and feed on the pollen and the nectar of the flowers. The abundance of flowers available in residential gardens can attract bees from the rural areas to towns. Unfortunately, lots of them are killed because of the danger to humans when they defend themselves. Many humans are allergic to bee stings and most people know very little about bees, how they live, operate and contribute to sustainable reproduction in plant life (see Chapter 20, Addendum E).

Earthworms

They form part of the decomposers in your garden. Earthworms are one of our biggest assets. They feed on organic material like leaves and decomposing material. By-products from earthworms are vermicompost and earthworm tea. These substances are the best fertiliser you can ever give to plants (see Chapter 20, Addendum C on how to construct an earthworm bin and how to farm earthworms on a small sustainable scale).

Butterflies

SABCA (South African Butterfly Conservation Assessment), launched in May 2007 and ended in April 2011, was a four-year conservation project aimed at determining the distribution and conservation priorities of all butterfly species in the southern African region, especially those threatened with extinction.

Insects: a, Honeybees; b, Earthworms.

Insects: a, Butterfly; b, Dragonfly.

Dragonflies

These insects roam around open water bodies and are an indication of a healthy environment. Absence of dragonflies at any water body should be a concern. "South Africa has many rare and threatened endemic invertebrates. Among these are certain damselflies and dragonflies that are globally threatened, principally by invasive alien trees; two such species are the Cape Bluet and Ceres Stream Damsel. Both of these species were thought to be extinct: The Ceres Stream Damsel had not been seen since 1920, while the Cape Bluet had not been recorded since 1962. However, in 2004, both species were found inhabiting a small pool of standing water in the Western Cape."

Ants

Ants can be a problem for landowners, especially in homes and their tendency towards sweet and fat meaty areas. Ants have their role to play in the different food chains. Many wildlife feed on different types of ants. Ants also use plant aphids as

Carpenter ants.

milking cows. They look after them, milk them for food and distribute them all over the plant. Imagine the impact you will have on these food chains when you apply chemicals to get rid of aphids. Plants need them and it is part of the balance in nature necessary to maintain food chains.

There are thousands of ant species and most of them can be regarded as beneficial. They help control the number of harmful insects, dispose of carrion and remove all kinds of organic detritus.

However, on their foraging expeditions, ants repeatedly enter human habitations, where they may also build extensive nests, hollowing out walls or floors. Outdoors, they undermine paths and soil with their nests.

There are three main household/indoor ant species in South Africa:
*   *Lepisiota capensis* (Black Sugar Ant)
*   *Linepithema humile* (Argentine Ant)
*   *Pheidole megacephala* (Brown House Ant)

Other species are occasionally encountered indoor and a variety of outdoor carpenter ants generally aren't as destructive as termites, although large colonies are capable of causing structural damage to a house. They damage wood by hollowing it out for nesting. Carpenter ants do not eat wood like their distant cousins, the termites. Instead, they tunnel through it while building and expanding their nests. Their preferred food is honeydew, a sugar secretion of certain plant-feeding insects such as aphids and scale insects. They also feed on other plant secretions and the remains of insects, including members of their own colony. They will readily forage in the kitchen, seeking out sugars as well as fats, grease and meats.

3.2   HOW NATURE WORKS

It is important to know how nature works and the similarities between our artificial methods to try and mimic nature to benefit human needs. I will first use an example to try and illustrate normal nature processes with beneficial outcomes and then I will compare it to how humans do it, in an artificial way.

A lion will stalk its prey and usually trap it in a dense grassy area. This is the type of area where a kill is most successful (this is also the reason why prey animals prefer open areas with short grassland, open vegetation to spot their predators well in advance). These dense, bushy areas are usually underutilised with no active growth and lots of dead material, not a productive habitat for vegetation. During and after the kill, a lot of trampling takes place. All these actions disturb the current vegetation and create an open area. The lions rip open the carcass and start feeding. There are blood and intestinal fluids all over the place (these are brilliant fertilisers for the vegetation present). The rest of the predators and scavengers queue up to feed (vultures, hyenas, jackals, etc.). Suddenly there is heavy wildlife traffic on that specific area that was not there before. The non-active plant materials are opened up and exposed to fresh air. Open spaces are created, fertilisers are suddenly available to the plants in the vicinity. All of these activities can take place in a couple of days. The leftovers from the predator's meal will be utilised by the decomposers. Flies drink the blood from the carcass, then lay eggs and larvae breed out to start the decomposing process of the carcass. The decomposing process will supply fertilisers to the immediate ground surfaces. The predators will leave and the vegetation will respond positively. The new open area will now attract antelope who like to be able to see their predators from far away and plan their escape route easily. Their trampling on the ground will loosen up and soften the immediate ground surface for rainwater penetration. Suddenly, this unproductive area with dense inactive plant material will become productive and a haven to larger populations of antelope. This will result in overgrazing until no food is left and the animals move on to new grazing areas. The veld can rest and recover and the whole process can repeat itself over and over again.

3.3   HOW HUMANS WORK

The current artificial method is as follows: Humans will clear a nature area artificially by clearing the bush and vegetation to plant crops. They will then cultivate the area mechanically with machinery (plough, rip, prepare a seed bed), plant the vegetation and add the necessary artificial fertiliser. Insects are repelled with chemicals. Instead of these traditional and artificial methods, humans can use natural methods to clear vegetation (fire is one way). They can use animals to cultivate the ground (trampling antelopes, pigs digging for plant roots, etc.). The animals' manure are organic fertilisers. They can encourage decomposers like earthworms by leaving dry organic material on the ground surface. This will also protect the ground surface against the sun (drying out action of bare soil surfaces), and against the impact of raindrops hitting open soil surfaces without penetrating the ground. When water starts to run off, it can cause erosion. Dry plant materials on the surface prevent this and create a situation where rain water will penetrate easily. The material will also protect the water from evaporation.

3.4   HOW IT CAN WORK IN YOUR GARDEN

All of this is also applicable to the gardens in our residential areas. If we start gardening nature's way, we will contribute to urban nature conservation. Start by planting indigenous plants (plants growing naturally in our country), or better still, plant endemic plants (plants growing naturally in that specific area). The reason for doing this is because endemic plants will use less water as they are already adapted to the environment. They will be in balance with their related predators. They will never cause problems like alien vegetation (see Chapter 8: Alien invasive plants).

Decide on trees and shrubs that can be a food source to our indigenous birds, which can provide shelter for them to nest in and raise their offspring (indigenous acacia trees are always a good choice in this regard).

Flowers: a, Agapanthus; b, Pink daisy (*Osteospermum* sp.); c, White arum lily (*Zantedeschia aethiopica*); d, Ice-plant (*Lampranthus* sp.); e, Common gazania (*Gazania krebsiana*).

If you want flowers, there is a number of indigenous species available like clivias, arum lilies, torch lilies, cannas, daisies, aloes, etc. Plan your garden to consume less water and be wildlife friendly.

Vegetables can be part of your garden layout. Rows should contrast each other. Place bigger plants like pumpkins, cabbage, potatoes and beans at the rear and smaller plants like carrots, onions, lettuce and beetroot in the front rows. Plant your vegetables according to the amount you need for your family. Harvest time depends on the date planted and can be planned well in advance. Plan the planting time so that you can harvest small amounts throughout the year.

Use organic compost (see Chapter 20, Addendum G, on how to make your own compost bin). Harvest vermicompost and earthworm tea from your earthworm bin (see Chapter 20, Addendum C, on building your own earthworm bin). Organic compost increases the plants' immunity against insects and diseases. No chemical treatment is necessary.

Avoid using chemicals that can kill wildlife in your urban nature garden. Remember that if a problem occurs like excess ants, aphids and mice, etc., the natural food chain has been broken. Identify the shortcomings and encourage or add the necessary predators to restore the balance.

Leave as much dead organic material on the ground and between the plants as possible. This will serve as a blanket and protect the ground against moisture loss. It will help fertilise the soil and water will penetrate easily.

3.5   YOUR LIFESTYLE AND URBAN NATURE

The ability to contribute to urban nature conservation requires that you synchronise your lifestyle with nature in your immediate environment. Create a habit of focusing on green actions that can contribute.

The ABC of green is the following:
- Use less energy because our energy comes from an electricity plant driven by coal. Use renewable sources like solar energy instead.

- Produce less waste. Waste ends up on a landfill site that impacts the urban environment you are living in – create your own recycling system of wet and dry waste. Dry waste includes paper, plastic, metal and glass. Wet waste is organic material like vegetable cut-offs from the kitchen, organic waste with lots of moisture. Wet waste is excellent food for your earthworm bin.

  Reduce food waste and losses. Try to reduce the amount of surplus food. What do people do with leftover food? It does not have to end up in the bin. There are millions of hungry unemployed people worldwide that go without a meal a day. How can we prevent food loss and divert surplus food to the hungry? First, be aware of these situations, make other people aware and plan your cooking in this regard. We can make use of leftovers by using it in menus where it can be reused. Welfare organisations can run food banks (a place to accommodate expired food sources that will not be a health risk).

  A good practise is when you dine out at a restaurant; always ask for a "doggy bag". You may use it for your dog at home but it would be even better to give it to the car attendant or the beggar on the street corner.

- Save on water. Water is scarce and comes from a purification plant that costs money to run. Start to implement a rainwater harvesting method on your property. You can collect rainwater from your roof via a gutter system into a water tank. This water can be used to supply your toilets with flushing water. How many times do you flush the toilet per day? It takes 7 litres at a time and it is a waste to use drinking water for this purpose.

- Avoid the use of chemicals at all cost. Chemicals kill wildlife and disturb the balance in nature as well as in the food chains. Plants utilising organic fertilisers have stronger immune systems that do not require chemical maintenance.

- Supply yourself with your own vegetables by making use of vegetable flower beds instead of decorative plants.

- Do not drive unnecessary distances. Plan your trips for the sake of the toxic emissions produced. Walk or cycle and contribute to the environment and to your health.

3.6   BIRDLIFE IN YOUR GARDEN

The easiest way for any resident to become involved in urban nature conservation is to focus on urban birdlife. As mentioned before, birds are unaffected by demarcating nature areas in a city.

The first step is to learn to identify all the different bird species in our gardens and residential areas. Identification includes what the bird looks like, the sounds it makes, what it feeds on, where it hides and feels safe, where and how it breeds and raises its chicks. You can observe this information as part of your daily routine.

You can purchase a book on birds, attend a course on bird identification, use the internet, download applications to your cell phone, visit bird hides in bird sanctuaries, and join a bird club. You can record the birds on your camera and get help with the identification process. You can do it on your own time and pace. Records of identifications and the numbers of identifications achieved can be very rewarding. These activities will also contribute to your social circles.

As you learn about birds, the information you acquire on what vegetation they utilise, what food they prefer and so forth will indicate which plants you need to add to your garden as well.

You can start a feeding programme for the birds. There are many kinds of bird feeders available (Chapter 20, Addendum B (bird feeders)). Build your own or just feed wherever there is a suitable space. It is important to stick to a routine in the feeding process (specific time of the day at one specific feeding place). The birds will quickly learn when and where. Some bird feeders make provision to feed on an irregular basis. You will be surprised how many visitors of different species will come to the feast. Different species prefer different types of food.

Any water feature is a good place to find birds. This can be a dam, pond or a water feature in your garden. Make a note on the important links in the food chain. If the food chain is not in balance, it will be unsustainable until the missing factors are restored.

Good habitat (the environment the species live in) will include food, water, shelter and safety. If your garden environment can supply this, you will have many permanent wildlife residents on your property. Your house cat can be an enemy. Put a neck collar on the cat with a bell that can make a noise. This will prevent them from killing the birds in your garden. A good pet owner trains his pet to obey. These concerns will normally appear when a chick leaves the nest and the adult bird assists the young one learning to fly.

Birdlife in your garden: a, Heron; b, Speckled Pigeon; c, Create places for birds to perch.

3.7   HOW YOU COMMUNICATE ON URBAN NATURE CONSERVATION

Share the information in this book with friends and family. Tell them what you have learned and experienced by taking part in activities related to urban nature. Share their experiences and help them. Seek answers to questions, read as much on the subject as possible. Do computer research and consult with experts available. You will be surprised how many people are interested. Everyone can benefit, and contributing to nature conservation is also free or very affordable most of the time.

It is the small things in life that count. It is the small five in your garden that will enrich your life, and they are just as important as the big five (elephant, rhino, leopard, buffalo, lion). Not all of us will have the privilege to visit national parks far away from our homes. The city dweller can help bring nature back to the city, to preserve existing nature in the city and to utilise it in a sustainable way.

Tell your friends and family about your local parks or nature reserves, bird sanctuaries, hiking and mountain bike trails, camping and picnic spots. Connect with your local officials that are responsible for urban nature and participate in activities like friends groups (see Chapter 15, on friends groups and how they work).

3.8   HOW DOES THE RESIDENT FIT INTO THE URBAN ENVIRONMENT

One must understand the meaning of all environmental terms used by academic people. Terms like biodiversity, ecological cycles and corridors, ecosystems, habitat, indigenous and endemic, red data species, wetlands, fragmentation, sustainable, rehabilitation, etc. I want to refer to "Glossary of terms" in the beginning of this book for further assistance.

What is "urban nature"? We must understand and be aware of the green and blue ways and nodes in a city. This harbours plant and animal life in a municipal area. Ridges are green ways. Conservation areas (municipal nature reserves, bird sanctuaries) are green nodes. Rivers are blue ways and wetlands, dams' are blue nodes. Please read through Chapter 6: Open spaces: roles and responsibilities.

It is important to familiarise yourself with documents like an ecological management plan (a nature area must have a management plan to be used for management purposes and the community must respect this plan otherwise the nature area will be lost for urban nature conservation). There must be a species action plan as well as a habitat action plan to secure existing animal life in a town (example: a plan for the Cape Clawless Otter in the current dams and water systems or a specific fish species or butterfly). Specific species can only survive in specific habitats. I want to refer to Chapter 7: Understanding biodiversity management in the urban context.

It is also important to know the master terrain development plan for a certain area. What impact will the development in a specific area have on adjacent nature areas? This will address listed activities and environmental impact approvals (see Chapter 12: Environmental Impact Assessments (EIA's)).

Activities to make use of and that are part of your urban nature environment are the following: Bird identification and bird hides in parks and nature areas, urban trails (hiking, horse trails, mountain bike, 4×4), picnic and braai facilities in municipal resorts, camping and caravan sites. All these are discussed in Chapter 13: Sustainable utilisation of urban nature areas.

Participate in the green economy. Make a contribution to fuel consumptions (use economic cars), use solar technology, recycle rainwater and participate in recycling of waste.

See the following Addenda (Chapter 20):
- Addendum A (owl boxes)
- Addendum B (bird feeders)
- Addendum C (vermicomposting with earthworms)
- Addendum D (organic compost)
- Addendum E (honeybees)

Hiking in Moreletakloof.

CHAPTER 4

WILDLIFE MANAGEMENT IN A CITY OR TOWN

(This chapter looks at wildlife management in a city. It focuses on tools and methods to create and maintain suitable habitat for wildlife in an urban environment. Then it touches on the hobby of birdwatching, attracting and feeding birds, and on bird hides. It ends with problems residents sometimes experience with mammals and reptiles in an urban environment).

4.1 BIRDS IN GENERAL[1]

Feral pigeons are common invasive birds in most cities and towns. Their droppings cause physical damage to buildings and paintwork. Their nests are also a health risk as the birds tend to build them close to air vents and air inlets of buildings, causing sinus and allergic conditions in humans. It is very difficult to control these birds because of the campaigns and actions of the Society for the Prevention of Cruelty to Animals (SPCA) and other such groups. The most humane control method is to capture them with traps (fakes) and to put them down by means of Co_2 gas. Shooting the birds in an urban context is unsafe. Mirror prisms placed on rooftops to reflect the sunlight are the most effective deterrents for these birds.

Invader birds must be discouraged in a way that will keep them from affecting the habitat and breeding areas of indigenous species. It is good practice to create bird sanctuaries in as many available habitats as possible in and around a city.

4.1.1 Methods to create bird sanctuaries

The sanctuary property needs customised fences. The habitat must include a water body such as a wetland (with shallow water), with wading areas and deep open water for different waterbird species. Running water is also essential for supplying oxygen to the water body and to accommodate a different habitat utilised by different species. Vegetation of different heights is needed – trees and shrubs as well as grasses of different sizes. The height can be managed during routine cutting,

---

[1] Info on bird identification and descriptions are available in *SAPPI Birds of South Africa*, Briza Publications, Pretoria, First edition 2014.

trimming and maintenance. It is important to create islands for breeding purposes and as hiding places from possible predators.

Birds need various places to perch on, such as rocks, branches and open ground areas. Floating islands can also be used. The vegetation on the shorelines must be removed on some sections (about one third of the surface). This allows birds to access the water body, bake in the sun, rest and feed. Birds also need space to fly in and out of the bird sanctuary and from open water bodies. It is a good practice to introduce basic species which are pinned. If pinned they will stay there and call the other wild species to join them. It is recommended to feed the birds on specific times and on a daily basis, to attract additional and different species to the sanctuary. Large numbers of species can help create a tourist/ visitor venue for birdwatching activities.

4.1.2   Ways to create a bird habitat

Plant vegetation like shrubs and trees and include reed species (*Phragmitus*) for the birds to nest and hide in. They also use the reeds for nesting. These types of vegetation are usually planted in the watercourses where the water enters the bird sanctuary. This serves as a filter system to supply clean water to the sanctuary and to the birds. The habitat should include open and dense areas.

4.1.3   Ways to feed birds in bird sanctuaries

Floating duck pellets are used to feed open water bird species. This is thrown onto the deeper open water surfaces. The pellets float and the birds feed from the water body. It is important to spread the pellets over large feeding areas to prevent competition and dominant behaviour among different species. Other methods are to make use of mixed chicken feed away from the water body to accommodate non-aquatic species like guinea fowl, but beware of attracting too many pigeons. Mixed chicken feed on the shoreline is placed inside buckets or trays filled with water about 10 cm deep, to prevent pigeons from eating it. Water birds do not mind the mixed chicken feed in the water and it supplies feed throughout the day.

4.1.4   Community involvement with bird sanctuaries

The idea when creating a bird sanctuary is that visitors should use it. It is important to construct a hide for visitors to enable them to do birdwatching. In big areas, one can combine a bird hide with a hiking trail. In smaller areas, the bird hide will stand alone. If possible, these activities should be supported by a guide to supply information on the different bird species. The other solution is to construct interpretative facilities where the information is on display. The entrance to the hide must be constructed in a way that birds are not disturbed while visitors enter the hide. The hide must preferably be accessible to all possible visitors – children, adults, disabled persons, etc. Visitors must have enough space to move around inside the hide. The benches must be at the right height with access areas to accommodate a wheelchair. The opening must be suitable for birdviewing. Safety equipment like fire extinguishers, dustbins and ashtrays should be provided.

No smoking signs as well as signs to keep silence can be provided. Information applicable to the sanctuary should be provided. This can include identification posters, contact numbers and visitors' feedback to improve services. Friends groups can be involved in these activities (see Chapter 15: Friends groups).

4.2 BIRDWATCHING, BIRD HIDES AND CONSTRUCTION

4.2.1 Why conserve birds?

Ever increasing numbers of people belong to bird societies. In the UK, more than one million people have joined the RSPB (Bird Life in the UK) – more than the membership of the three largest UK political parties combined, and the number is escalating continuously. In New Zealand, 40 000 people are members of Forest and Bird (Bird Life in New Zealand) and in Malta, the membership of Bird Life Malta stands at more than 3 000, from a total population of 378 000.

4.2.1.1 The birdwatching industry is a growing economic force

Penguin Parade at Phillip Island Nature Park in Victoria is Australia's third largest tourist destination, after the Great Barrier Reef and Ayer's Rock. In 1995, 1 000 local jobs were dependent on the tourist trade to the park which attracted more than half a million visitors who spent an estimated US$63 million.

Every year, 6 000 to 8 000 people visit the Cousin Island Nature Reserve managed by Nature Seychelles. This was once a loss-making coconut plantation, but tourism revenue now sustains this reserve (an internationally important site for seabirds and three globally threatened species) and the local community.

In South Africa, the annual expenditure by birdwatchers is around US$12-27 million, with the Boulders Bay Penguin colony alone worth around US$2.4 million.

In 1991, the birdwatching industry was worth US$5.2 billion in the USA and around 191 000 jobs were dependent upon it. Between the mid-1980s and the mid-1990s, birdwatching in the USA showed a 155% growth in numbers.

Conserving birds clearly has great economic benefits.

4.2.1.2 Birds are indicators of the state of the environment

Studying birds tells us about the habitats on which we all depend. The dramatic decline in Eurasian Skylark numbers in Western Europe is indicative of the relentless intensification of agricultural practices and the unsustainability of the European Union's Common Agricultural Policy.

In Costa Rica, lowland forest birds are extending their ranges up mountain slopes, apparently because the high altitude cloud forests are drying out as a result of global warming.

Common Whitethroat numbers in Europe fell sharply in the late 1960s. The cause was traced to the desertification of their wintering grounds in Sub-Saharan Africa, a problem exacerbated as a result of overgrazing by livestock.

In the 1950s and 1960s, a huge drop in the numbers of Peregrines and other birds of prey in Europe and the USA were linked to the build-up of Dichlorodiphenyltrichloroethane (DDT) in the food chain, traces of which were increasingly found in people. Could population crashes of raptors in Asia and elsewhere be indicative of a similar poisoning of the environment?

In general, places that are rich in bird species are also rich in other forms of biodiversity. Birds are good indicators of these important areas.

4.2.1.3   Conservation Goals

Bird Life (New Zealand) focuses its effort around conservation goals for species, sites, habitats and people. All are vital elements of Bird Life's work.

Species

- **Take action for all globally threatened bird species.**
  Extinction is irreversible. Since globally threatened species are in greatest danger of extinction, they are given highest priority by Bird Life.

- **Conserve, and where possible increase, the populations and natural ranges of declining wild bird species.**
  Declining species will become threatened if conservation action is not taken. Declining bird numbers or distributions reflect overall loss of biological diversity and strongly indicates unsustainable practices.

- **Maintain the populations and ranges of all naturally occurring wild bird species.**
  All bird species are valuable in their own right and act as powerful symbols of the state of our environment.

Sites

- **Take action to conserve, and where appropriate restore, all sites of global, regional and national importance to birds.**
  Sites (Important Bird Areas) are units manageable for bird and biodiversity conservation and restoration. Focussing on areas of global and national importance enables Bird Life to set priorities effectively.

Habitats

- **Take action to maintain, and where appropriate restore, the extent and quality of habitats important for birds.**
  Loss or deterioration of habitats, like forests, wetlands and oceanic islands, has a negative effect on birds, biodiversity and people. Some human practices (for

example agriculture, forestry, fisheries) change habitats and action to conserve birds at the habitat level is therefore most effective.

People

- **Strengthen and grow a network of people who value wild birds, biodiversity and the wider environment.**
  How people think and behave is the most powerful force affecting how we treat the environment; building a network of like-minded people brings direct benefits to birds and the people themselves.

- **Integrate bird conservation needs into wider natural resource management for the benefit of both people and biodiversity.**
  It is important to recognise that people control resources and they should be encouraged to manage these sustainably for their own benefit and for biodiversity.

4.2.1.4   How can I help to promote the cause of bird conservation?

Remember that birds form part of a natural environment and their continued existence depends upon safeguarding their natural home. For instance, certain woodpeckers, once deprived of their special forest habitat, are doomed. They cannot live elsewhere under different conditions. This makes it necessary to set aside and retain samples of the country's main natural communities – forest, marsh, seacoast, etc. – as reserves. It is important that these reserves be large enough to ensure the continued existence of all the community members. A pair of eagles may, for example, require upwards of 16 km^2 of land over which to hunt.

The second point is that modern conservation is not just for animals and plants, but for people as well. Everyone has a stake in the future. Professor E. Mayr said, "If man would save birdlife from himself for himself, then, of course, he must know the ways and needs of birds."

In South Africa, joining bird clubs and the South African Ornithological Society is in itself a contribution towards the conservation movement.

A new site for the vulnerable Grey-necked Picathartes (*Picathartes oreas*) was discovered by a Bird Life survey team in Cameroon.

4.3   ATTRACTING BIRDS

It is not hard to attract birds in most parts of South Africa. For instance, large flocks of doves and sparrows can, without much effort, be enticed to suburban gardens. There are pigeons and starlings in busy city centres and at the coast, seagulls can be bribed and trained by flat-dwellers and office workers to come to their balconies. In the country, the grain farmer easily attracts finches and other seedeaters. The average bird enthusiast, however, wants variety as well as numbers and this takes more effort and ingenuity than just putting out food.

The environment normally determines the variety and numbers of birds. The more diverse the association of habitats are, the wider the composition of the avifauna will be. The landowner must try to provide a variety of both natural and artificial conditions to permanently attract a rich variety of birds. The basics include water, food and shelter, of course.

4.4   BIRD FEEDING

4.4.1   History

James Fisher noted that the first person who recorded feeding wild birds was the sixth century monk, Saint Serf of Fife, who tamed a robin by feeding it. In the harsh winter of 1890–91 in Britain, national newspapers asked people to put out food for birds. In 1910 in the United Kingdom, Punch magazine declared that feeding birds was a "national pastime." Bird feeding has grown into the United States' second most popular hobby after gardening. To celebrate the bird feeding hobby, February was named National Bird-Feeding Month by congressional decree in 1994.

4.4.2   Activity

Bird feeding is typically thought of as an activity for bird enthusiasts. People who feed wild birds often attempt to attract birds to suburban and domestic locations. This requires setting up a feeding station and supplying bird food. The food may include seeds, peanuts, bought food mixes, fat, kitchen scraps and suet. Additionally, a bird bath and grit (sand) that birds store in their crops to help grind food as an aid to digestion, can be provided.

Feeding bread to waterfowl at parks, lakes and rivers is also a popular activity.

4.4.3   Types

Certain foods tend to attract certain birds. Finches and siskin will be attracted by seed and Jays love corn. Hummingbirds love nectar. Mixed seed attracts many birds. Black oil sunflower seed is favoured by many seed-eating species. Different feeders can be purchased for different species (see Chapter 20, Addendum B).

Garden birds can be fed using peanuts, seed, coconut or fat, using a variety of feeders.

After the station is established, it can take some weeks for birds to discover and start using it. This is particularly true if the feeding station is the first one in an area or (in cold areas) if the station is being established in spring when natural sources of food are plentiful. Therefore, beginners should not completely fill a feeder at first. The food will get old and spoilt if it is left uneaten for too long. This is particularly true of unshelled foods, such as thistle seed and suet. Once the birds begin taking food, the feeder should be kept full. Additionally, people feeding birds should ensure that there is a water source nearby. A bird bath can attract as many birds as a feeding station.

4.4.4   Impact

A study conducted in the city of Sheffield, UK, found that the abundance of garden birds increased with levels of bird feeding. This effect was only apparent in those species that regularly take supplementary food, raising the possibility that bird feeding was having a direct effect on bird abundance. In contrast, the density of feeding stations had no effect on the number of different bird species present in a neighborhood.

4.4.5   Economy

Large sums of money are spent by ardent bird feeders, who indulge their wild birds with a variety of bird foods and bird feeders. Over 55 million Americans over the age of 16 feed wild birds and spend more than $3 billion a year on bird food, and $800 million a year on bird feeders, bird baths, bird houses, and other bird feeding accessories. The activity has spawned an industry that sells supplies and equipment for the bird feeding hobby.

In some cities or parts of cities (e.g. Trafalgar Square in London) feeding pigeons is forbidden, either because they compete with vulnerable native species, or because they abound and cause pollution and/or noise.

4.5   MORE ON BIRDWATCHING

Most people rather enjoy counting things. There is a certain satisfaction in recording not merely duck, but the number of ducks on a dam You can identify and record not only the species of birds you see, as well as the number of eggs in a clutch, their length, breadth, and weight. You can observe the number of days it takes an egg to hatch, or the number of times per hour that an adult brings food to its young. Some will identify and listen to the sounds, pitch and rhythms of various bird calls.

4.5.1   Birdwatching or birding

This is the observation and study of birds with the naked eye, with the help of binoculars, or by listening to bird calls. Birding often involves a significant auditory component, as many bird species are more readily detected and identified by ear than by eye. Most birdwatchers pursue this activity mainly for recreational or social reasons, unlike ornithologists, who engage in the study of birds using more formal scientific methods.

4.5.2   Birding, birdwatching and twitching

The term *birdwatching* was first used in 1901; *bird* was introduced as a verb in 1918. The term *birding* was also used for the practice of *fowling* or hunting with firearms as in Shakespeare's *The Merry Wives of Windsor* (1602): "She laments sir... her husband goes this morning a-birding." The terms *birding* and *birdwatching* are used today interchangeably, although many participants prefer *birding*, both because it does not exclude the auditory aspects of enjoying birds, and because it does not have some associated negative connotations.

The term *twitcher*, sometimes misapplied as a synonym for birder, is reserved for those who travel long distances to see a rare bird that would then be *ticked*, or checked off, on a list. The term originated in the 1950s, when it was used to describe the nervous behavior of Howard Medhurst, a British birdwatcher. Prior terms for those who chased rarities were *pot-hunter*, *tally-hunter*, or *tick-hunter*. The main goal of twitching is often to accumulate species on one's lists. Some birders engage in competition to accumulate the longest species list. The act of the pursuit itself is referred to as a *twitch* or a *chase*. A rare bird that stays put long enough for people to see it is *twitchable* or *chaseable*.

Twitching is highly developed in the United Kingdom, the Netherlands, Denmark, Ireland, Finland and Sweden. The size of these countries makes it possible to travel throughout them quickly and relatively easily. The most popular twitches in the UK have drawn large crowds; for example, a group of approximately 5 000 people travelled to Kent, England, to view a Golden-winged Warbler. Twitchers have developed their own vocabulary. For example, a twitcher who fails to see a rare bird has *dipped out*; if other twitchers do see the bird, he may feel *ripped off*. *Suppression* is the act of concealing news of a rare bird from other twitchers.

4.5.3   The history of birdwatching

The early interest in observing birds for their aesthetic rather than utilitarian (mainly food) value is traced to the late-18th century in the works of Gilbert White, Thomas Bewick, George Montagu and John Clare. Although the study of birds and natural history became fashionable in Britain during the Victorian Era, it was mainly collection oriented with eggs and later skins being the artifacts of interest. Wealthy collectors made use of their contacts in the colonies to obtain specimens from around the world. It was only in the late 19th century that the call for bird protection began leading to the rising popularity of observations on living birds. The Audubon Society (an American, non-profit, environmental organisation dedicated to conservation) was started to protect birds from the growing trade in feathers in the United States while the Royal Society for the Protection of Birds began in

Britain. The term "bird watching" appeared for the first time as the title of a book "Bird Watching" by Edmund Selous in 1901. In North America, the identification of birds, once thought possible only by shooting, was made possible by the emergence of optics and field identification guides. The earliest field guide in the US was *Birds through an Opera Glass* (1889) by Florence Bailey. Birding in North America was focused on in the early and mid-20th century in the eastern seaboard region and was influenced by the works of Ludlow Griscom and later Roger Tory Peterson.

The organisation and networking of those interested in birds began through organisations like the Audubon Society that was against the killing of birds and the American Ornithologists' Union (AOU). The rising popularity of vehicles increased the mobility of birdwatchers and this made new locations accessible to those interested in birds. Networks of birdwatchers in the UK began to form in the late 1930s under the British Trust for Ornithology (BTO). The BTO saw the potential to produce scientific results through the networks, unlike the Royal Society for the Preservation of Birds (RSPB) which like the Audubon Society originated from the bird protection movement. Like the AOU in North America, the BOU had a focus mainly in collection-based taxonomy. The BOU changed focus to ecology and behaviour only in the 1940s. The BTO movement towards organised bird watching, was opposed by the RSPB which claimed that the scientification of the pastime was undesirable. This stand was to change only in 1936 when the RSPB was taken over by Tom Harrisson and others. Harrisson was instrumental in the organisation of pioneering surveys of the Great Crested Grebe.

Increased mobility of birdwatchers ensured that books like *Where to watch birds* by John Gooders became bestsellers. By the 1960s, air travel became feasible and long distance holiday destinations opened up and by 1965, Britain's first Birding Tour Company, *Ornitholidays*, was started by Lawrence Holloway. Travelling far away also led to problems in name usage, British birds like "Wheatear", "Heron" and "Swallow" needed adjectives to differentiate them in places where there were several related species. The falling cost of air travel made flying to remote birding destinations a possibility for a large number of people towards the 1980s. The need for global guides to birds became more relevant and one of the biggest projects that began was the "Handbook of the Birds of the World" which started in the 1990s with Josep del Hoyo, a country doctor in Catalonia, Jordi Sargatal and ornithologist Andy Elliott.

Initially, birdwatching was a hobby practiced in developed countries such as the United States of America and the United Kingdom. Nevertheless, since the second half of the 20th century, an increased number of people in developing countries have engaged in this activity. Transnational birding has played an important role in this, as citizens from developing countries that engage in bird watching usually develop this pastime due to influence of foreign cultures that already practice birding.

4.5.4   Growth and economics

In the 20th century, most of the birding activity in North America was on the east coast. The publication of Roger Tory Peterson's field guide in 1934 led to the initial increase in birding. Binoculars became more easily available after World War II. The practice of travelling long distances to see rare bird species was aided by the rising popularity of vehicles.

The 2000-publication of "The Sibley Guide to Birds" sold 500 000 copies by 2002. The number of birdwatchers rose but there appeared to be a drop in birdwatching in the backyard.

About 4% of North Americans were interested in birding. In the 1970s and in the mid-1980s, at least 11% were found to watch birds at least 20 days of the year. An estimate of 61 million birders was made in the late 1980s. The income level of birders has been found to be well above average. According to a U.S. Fish and Wildlife Service study, birdwatchers contributed 36 billion USD to the US economy in 2006, and one fifth (20%) of all Americans are identified as birdwatchers.

North American birders were estimated to have spent as much as USD 32 billion in 2001. The spending is on the rise around the world. Kuşcenneti National Park (KNP) at Lake Manyas, a Ramsar site in Turkey, was estimated to attract birders who spent as much as USD 103 320 074 annually. Guided bird tours have become a major business with at least 127 companies offering tours worldwide. An average trip to a less-developed country costs $4 000 per person and includes about 12 participants for each of 150 trips a year. It has been suggested that this economic potential should be tapped for conservation.

4.5.5   Activities

Most birdwatchers will keep an eye on birds around them at all times but will make specific trips to observe birds fulltime. The most active times of the year for birding in temperate zones are during the spring or fall migrations when the greatest variety of birds may be seen. On these occasions, large numbers of birds travel north or south to wintering or nesting locations. Early mornings are typically better as the birds are more active and vocal, making them easier to spot.

Certain locations such as the local patch of forest, wetland and coast may be favoured according to the location and season. Sea-watching is a type of birdwatching where observers based at a coastal watch point, such as a headland, watch birds flying over the sea. This is one form of pelagic birding, by which pelagic bird species are viewed. Another way birdwatchers view pelagic species is from seagoing vessels.

Weather plays an important role in the occurrence of rare birds. In Britain, suitable wind conditions may lead to drift migration (migrating birds are blown off course by the winds at the time they are in flight) and an influx of birds from the east.

4.5.6   Monitoring

Birdwatchers may take part in censuses of bird populations and migratory patterns which are sometimes specific to individual species. These birdwatchers may also count all birds in a given area, as in the Christmas Bird Count or follow carefully designed study protocols. This kind of citizen science (also known as crowd science, crowd-sourced science, civic science, or networked science – is scientific research conducted, in whole or in part, by amateur or non-professional scientists) can assist in identifying environmental threats to the well-being of birds. It can also help assess outcomes of environmental management initiatives intended to ensure the survival of at risk species or encourage the breeding of species for aesthetic or ecological reasons. This more scientific side of the hobby is an aspect of ornithology, coordinated in the UK by the British Trust for Ornithology. In the United States, the Cornell Lab of Ornithology hosts many citizen-science projects to track the number and distribution of bird species across North America. These surveys help scientists note major changes from year to year which may occur as a result of climate change, diseases, predation, and other factors.

4.5.7   Environmental education

Due to their accessibility and ubiquity, birds are a useful tool for environmental education and awareness on environmental issues. Birds easily transmit values in respect to nature and the fragility of ecosystems.

4.5.8   Competition

Birding as a competitive event is organised in some parts of the world. These are found to be more exciting by some. These competitions encourage individuals or teams to accumulate large numbers of species within a specified time or area with special rules. Some birdwatchers will also compete by attempting to increase their life list, national list, state list, provincial list, county list, or year list. There have,

Moroccan students watching birds at Nador's Lagoon (part of environmental education activities organised by the Spanish Ornithological Society).

Birdwatchers watching Britain's fifth-ever White-tailed Lapwing at Caerlaverock (Scotland, 6 June 2007).

however, been criticisms of such events especially when they are claimed to aid conservation when they may actually mask serious environmental issues.

Competitive birdwatchers events include:
- Big day: teams have 24 hours to identify as many species as possible.

- Big year: like a big day, but contestants are individuals and need to be prepared to invest a great deal of time and money.

- Big Sit or Big Stay: birdwatchers must see birds from a circle of prescribed diameter (e.g.: 17 foot). Once birds are spotted, birdwatchers can leave the circle to confirm the identity, but new birds seen may not be counted.

4.5.9   Equipment and technology

Equipment commonly used for birding includes binoculars, a spotting scope with tripod, a notepad and one or more field guides. Hides or observation towers are often used to conceal the observers from birds, and/or to improve viewing conditions. Over the years, optic manufacturers have learned that birding binoculars sell and virtually all have specific binoculars for just that. Some have even geared their whole brand to birders.

4.5.10   Sound equipment

Recognition of bird calls and noises is an important part of a birder's toolkit. Sound information can assist in the location, watching, identification and sexing of birds. Recent developments in audio technology have seen recording and reproduction

Birders using a tower hide to gain views over foreground vegetation (Bay of Liminka, south of Oulu, Finland).

devices shrink in both size and price, making them accessible to a greater portion of the birding community. The non-linear nature of digital audio technology has also made selecting and accessing the required recordings much more flexible than tape-based models. It is now possible to take a recording of every birdcall you are likely to encounter in a given area out into the field, stored on a device that will slip into your pocket, and to retrieve calls for playback and comparison in any order you choose.

4.5.11   Photography

Photography has always been a part of birding, but in the past, the cost of good cameras and long lenses made this a minority, often semi-professional, interest. The advent of affordable digital cameras, which can be used in conjunction with a spotting scope or binoculars (using the technique of a-focal photography (where the camera with its lens attached is mounted over the eyepiece of another image-forming system such as an optical telescope), have made this a much more widespread aspect of the hobby.

4.5.12   Videography

As with the arrival of affordable digital cameras, the development of more compact and affordable digital video cameras has made them more attractive and accessible to the birding community. Cross-over, non-linear digital models now exist that take

Sound equipment (recording).

Bird photography.

high quality stills at acceptable resolutions, as well as being able to record and play audio and video. The ability to easily capture and reproduce not only the visual characteristics of a bird, but also its patterns of movement and its sound, has wide applications for birders in the field.

4.5.13   Portable media players

This class of product includes devices that can play (some can also record) a range of digital media, typically video, audio and still image files. Many modern digital cameras, mobile phones, and camcorders can be classified as portable media players. With the ability to store and play large quantities of information, pocket-sized devices allow a full birding multimedia library to be taken into the field and mobile internet access makes obtaining and transmitting information possible in near real time.

4.5.14   Remote birdwatching

New technologies are allowing birdwatching activities to take place over the internet, using robotic camera installations and mobile phones set up in remote wildlife areas. Projects such as CONE (a networked Tele-Robotic Observatory Game based in the Welder Wildlife Refuge in South Texas that ran from 12 May 2008 to 9 May 2011) allow users to observe and photograph birds over the web; similarly, robotic cameras set up in largely inhospitable areas are used to attempt the first photographs of the rare Ivory-Billed Woodpecker. These systems represent new technologies in the birdwatcher's toolkit.

4.5.15   Communication

In the early 1950s, the only way of communicating new bird sightings was through the postal system and it was generally too late for the recipients to act on the information. In 1953, James Ferguson-Lees began broadcasting rare bird news on the radio in Eric Simms' *Countryside* programme but this did not catch on. In the 1960s, people began using the telephone and some people became hubs for communication. In the 1970s, some cafes like the one run by Nancy Gull in Cley, Norfolk, became centers for meeting and communication. This was replaced by telephone hotline services like "Birdline" and "Bird Information Service".

With the advent of the world-wide web, birders have been using the internet to convey information; this can be via mailing lists, forums, bulletin-boards, web-based data basis and other media. While most birding lists are geographic in scope, there are special-interest lists that cater to bird-identification, twitchers, seabirds and raptor enthusiasts to name but a few. Messages can range from the serious to trivial, notifying others of rarities, questioning the taxonomy or identification of a species, discussing field guides and other resources, asking for advice and guidance, or organising groups to help save habitats. Occasional postings are mentioned in academic journals and can be a valuable resource for professional and amateur birders alike. One of the oldest, Birdchat (based in the US) probably has the most subscribers, followed by the English-language fork of Eurobirdnet, Birding-Aus from Australia, SABirdnet from South Africa and Orientalbirding.

Yellow-billed Duck.

Several websites allow users to submit lists of birds seen, while others collate and produce seasonal statistics and distribution maps.

4.5.16   Code of conduct

As the number of birdwatchers increases, there is growing concern about the impact of birdwatching on birds and their habitat. Birdwatching etiquette is evolving in response to this concern. Some examples of birdwatching etiquette include promoting the welfare of birds and their environment; avoiding stressing the birds by limiting use of photography, pishing (a pish is an imitated bird call, usually a scold or alarm call, used by birders and ornithologists to attract birds) and playback devices; keeping back from nests and nesting colonies and respecting private property.

4.5.17   Socio-psychology

Ethnologist Nikolaas Tinbergen considers birdwatching to be an expression of the male hunting instinct while Simon Baron-Cohen links it with the male tendency for "systemising". There has been a suggestion that identification of birds may be a form of gaining status. In a study (Sali 2005) of the motivations for birdwatching in New York, it was found that males were interested in sharing knowledge while females found it intellectual and challenging. While the representation of women has always been low, it was pointed out that nearly 90% of all birdwatchers in the United States are Caucasians with only a few African Americans.

Other minority groups have formed organisations to support fellow birders and these include the Gay Birders and the Disabled Birders Association.

The study of birdwatching has been of interest to students of the sociology of science.

4.5.18   Famous birdwatchers

There are about 10 000 species of birds and only a small number of people have seen more than 7 000. Many birdwatchers have spent their entire lives trying to see all the bird species of the world. The first person who started this is said to be Stuart Keith. Some birders have been known to go to great lengths and many have lost their lives in the process. Phoebe Snetsinger spent her family inheritance travelling to various parts of the world while suffering from a malignant melanoma, surviving an attack and rape in New Guinea before dying in a road accident in Madagascar. She saw as many as 8 400 species. The birdwatcher David Hunt who was leading a bird tour in Corbett National Park was killed by a tiger in February, 1985. In 1971, Ted Parker travelled around North America and saw 626 species in a year. This record was beaten by Kenn Kaufman in 1973 who travelled 69 000 miles and saw 671 species and spent less than a thousand dollars. Ted Parker was killed in an air-crash in Ecuador. From 2008, the top life-list has been held by Tom Gullick, an Englishman who lives in Spain and who has logged over 8 800 species. In 2008, two British birders, Alan Davies and Ruth Miller, gave up their jobs, sold their home and put everything they owned into a year-long global bird watching adventure about which they wrote a book called "The Biggest Twitch". They logged 4 431 species on 31 October 2008.

Birdwatching literature, field guides and television programmes have been popularised by birders like Pete Dunne and Bill Oddie.

4.5.19   How can birdwatching fit into an urban environment?

Every municipal urban area has river systems, flood plains and wetland areas that are within the 1 and 50 year flood lines and not suitable for residential or business development. Any development within these areas require Environmental Impact Assessment (EIA) approval with an Environmental Management Plan (EMP) guideline.

River systems in the urban environment are the lowest points and accumulate all drainage disposals of pollution outlets, run-off water and excess storm water. These water systems can be cleaned by the construction of artificial wetlands within the drainage system. These artificial wetlands are the ideal habitat for bird life activities, especially for water bird populations. It is also ideal for building bird hides to accommodate birding activities.

Birdwatching facilities within a urban environment accommodates the need of residents to enjoy their natural environment close to their homes, and contributes to the urban environment by participating, policing and caring for their environment.

City dwellers need to be able to enjoy their environment with minimal effort and contribute to conservation goals.

4.5.20   Analysing habitats for birds

A habitat is a total environment, rocks, soil, plants and animals, especially the first three – differing in one or more ways from other habitats. The sea, for instance, differs from dry land and mountains differ from sand dunes or from wetland areas; and one would expect the birds of each of these to be different, as of course, they are. Finer analysis of bird distribution shows that one can split up such broad environments into smaller units. Thus the bird fauna of the ocean differs from that of the waters inshore.

From the bird point of view, the most important feature of any area is its vegetation or the absence thereof. Steep cliffs and shifting sand dunes have virtually no vegetation and the resident species of birds depend primarily on the vegetation (type, height, density, species, etc.) and in more extreme cases also on the topography and the nature of the substratum.

Habitats relating to fresh water include not only the wetland areas, dams and rivers themselves but also the vegetation on their margins, which usually differs from that on the surrounding countryside.

Most birdwatchers do, in fact, devise some non-systematic habitat classification for themselves, based on the general appearance of the countryside. If you go out with one of them on his home terrain, he will often say "this looks the sort of place to find such-and-such" or "you won't find so-and-so here – not the right kind of place". It is, however, more satisfactory to draw up lists of the birds found in each type of habitat.

4.5.21   More on construction of bird hides

Locality

Where to put the bird hide? It depends on the purpose. Identify places suitable for birdwatching. Is bird life available and will the birds stay when birdwatching activities takes place?

Birds want shelter, food and nesting place to breed. Can your chosen venue supply these requirements? Any water body is always a potential area. Birds prefer shallow water and wading areas. Areas where silt is trapped are always good spots. Mudded areas with small amounts of shallow water will be a successful habitat especially for water birds.

Feeding

The food available will determine the species of birds present. Artificial feeding times can be implemented. Birds want to be fed on specific times and on a regular basis. They will quickly adapt to a specific pattern.

It is always good to have pinned tamed birds permanently at a bird hide venue. The best way is to feed them on a regular basis with more food available than what they need. They communicate with the wild birds passing by who will soon join the pinned ground group for feeding sessions. This will result in large numbers of birds available at the bird hide for bird watchers to monitor.

It is a good practice to place the seeds in plates with shallow water if you want to feed water birds. Pigeons will not be able to steal it and it suits the water birds' habits to feed in shallow water.

Certain species are dominant and will chase other sub-dominant species away. Try to avoid competition in numbers and species and try to increase accessibility as much as possible.

Shelter

Birds need to feel safe, be undisturbed and not threatened. Vegetation is a major role player. Reed beds, thorn trees, accessible water bodies all contribute to these needs. It is important to design the hide in such a way that the birds feel comfortable

Bird hide at Austen Roberts.

Bird hide use material that blend in with the environment.

and safe. The visitor to the hide must access the hide in a camouflaged way. Noise must be prevented as much as possible. Screen off walk and path ways to bird hides as far as possible.

Visitor facilities at bird hides

Parking for vehicles must be available and vehicle noise must not disturb birds at the bird hide. Toilet facilities are usually a requirement and can be part of the parking area. The walkways from the parking area to the bird hide must be designed so that the birds are not affected by people walking to and from the bird hide. In the hide, viewing access must be maximised for the visitor without disturbing the birds. Information displays of bird species, identity, and habitat can be displayed for the visitors but should present samples of birds most likely to be observed at the current facility. Feedback hand-outs, information brochures and possible donation boxes can also be supplied as part of the visitor facilities. Seeds as feeding material can also be sold at an entrance point and income generated from it can also contribute to costs. A formal display area can also supply specific information on the specific bird hide facility.

Materials and layout used in construction of bird hides

The trend is to use natural material that blends with existing environments. Treated wood is always a good choice. Concrete pipe material can be used to concrete wooden poles in permanent water areas. Split and treated poles are durable and standard items for construction. The structure must be safe, comfortable, spacious and easy to maintain.

4.6   MAMMALS

4.6.1   Feral cats

They are a major problem in most cities and towns. It is important that anti-cruelty organisations are involved to help control their numbers by trapping, euthanasia or sterilisation.

4.6.2   Baboons and vervet monkeys

Baboons and monkeys are always a big problem in urban areas, because they are highly intelligent. When they come in contact with humans, they become more tamed. When humans start feeding them, they can then demand food and become aggressive. Bites from these animals are very common. An attack by a baboon can be fatal for an infant or young child.

They must be monitored for aggressive behaviour and removed when they cause problems. The other babboons and/or monkeys will retreat, making management easier.

4.6.3   Rock Hyrax

Rock Hyrax can also become a problem in urban areas. These mammals adapt easily to human activities and garden practises. Urban gardens can provide food for them during winter months when food in their natural environment is not always available. This situation stimulates their breeding numbers. Humans also destroy their natural enemy and this also accelerates their breeding. Their natural enemies are pythons, caracals and birds of prey (Black Eagle).

Hyrax destroy most garden plants by eating them and can cause a health risk by depositing droppings on house roofs, causing bad smells and allergies in humans.

A successful control method is continuous trapping throughout the year. After trapping, they must be relocated to nature areas outside the urban area. In these areas, their natural enemies must be available to control their numbers. The goal of these projects is not to eradicate the species but to substitute the role that their natural enemies play.

4.6.4   Porcupine

Porcupine can become a nocturnal problem animal in urban areas, doing extensive damage to bulb plants in gardens. They can injure dogs and domesticated animals that try to attack them. The best control method is trapping in the areas where they cause damage and relocating them away from city areas (urban nature reserves).

4.6.5   Cane rats

Cane rats can damage lawns at night. They come from wetland areas within the city and be trapped on their foot paths. These animals do not disturb urban human life. They are only nocturnal visitors to residential gardens. They come during winter periods when food (roots of grass) is scarce in the wetland areas and the irrigated lawns in residential areas are still green and attractive. Garden fences can be upgraded by closing gaps and installing electric fences.

4.6.6   Mongoose and genets

They are a common nocturnal predator species in cities and mainly impact waterfowl and poultry runs. The only effective way to address this problem is to trap the ones that cause the damage (by using what they eat as bait) and relocate these individuals more than 50 km away from the problem area.

4.6.7   Caracals and Servals

They target poultry runs, goat and sheep farms and can best be trapped with live bait. Identify their point of entry by looking for their tracks. This helps to plan the capturing exercise.

Baboon in captivity.

Rock Hyrax, Mosselbaai.

Captured Porcupine ready to be released.

Captured, doped baboon.

4.6.8   Leopards

Leopards enter urban areas because of easily available prey, such as dogs or cats. If there is continuous damages in a certain area, tracks can be identified to pin point regular corridors and passages they use. Live bait is essential for trapping and veterinary help will handle relocation.

4.7   REPTILES

4.7.1   Snakes

Snakes are the most common and frequently encountered reptiles in urban areas. It is crucial to differentiate between venomous and non-venomous snakes. Most non-venomous snakes pose no threat to humans and are excellent controllers of pests like mice and rats in urban areas. Venomous snakes however should be captured

Reptiles: a, Monitor Lizard, b, Cobra, c, Crocodile before capturing.

and relocated to a nature area far away from the urban area by a professional snake handler. This is in the best interest of animals and humans.

4.7.2   Monitor lizards

These large lizards damage waterfowl and poultry runs, preying on birds and eggs. A problem lizard can be captured by either trapping it or calling a professional reptile handler. These reptiles do enter roofs of houses, hibernating there for warmth and they make a noise by hunting rats and mice.

4.7.3   Crocodiles

Crocodiles can pose a huge threat to humans in urban areas when they exceed 1.5 meters in length. They are highly intelligent and adapt easily. Whenever a crocodile is reported in an area, it is important to act quickly and place a trap to be removed. Young children and infants playing at the edge of dams and rivers can be at risk. Most of these animals find their way into cities through transportation by humans and are kept as pets while they are still small. They grow rapidly and then become hard to handle by their owners who release them in nearby dams and rivers. Such an animal has already lost its fear for humans.

4.8   GENERAL

Urban nature reserves are islands of nature in built-up areas. These nature reserves have a carrying capacity for animals that are adapted to a specific habitat. Urban nature areas can serve as a sanctuary for problem animals in a city. Problem animals should not be dumped in urban nature areas that are already saturated with the same species.

CHAPTER 5

RED DATA SPECIES

(This chapter deals with information on Red Data Species. Guidance on protected species is provided. Reasons why some species need special protection are given and the dangers for species that are prone to extinction are described.)[1]

The Red List of the International Union for Conservation of Nature (IUCN) is a world standard for evaluating the conservation status of plant and animal species. The IUCN Red List, which determines the risks of extinction of species, plays an important role in guiding conservation activities of governments, non-governmental organisations (NGOs) and scientific institutions, and is recognised worldwide for its objective approach.

The National Environmental Management: Biodiversity Act (NEMBA) (No. 10 of 2004) contains a list of threatened or protected species that are dealt with by South African legislation.

Species on this list are placed in one of four categories:
- **Critically endangered species** – any indigenous species facing an extremely high risk of extinction in the wild in the immediate future.

- **Endangered species** – any indigenous species facing a high risk of extinction in the wild in the near future, although it is not a Critically Endangered species.

- **Vulnerable species** – any indigenous species facing an extremely high risk of extinction in the wild in the medium term future, although it is not a Critically Endangered species or an Endangered species.

- **Protected species** – any species which is of such high conservation value or national importance that it requires national protection.

5.1   WHAT IS A THREATENED SPECIES?

Threatened species are often also referred to as endangered species. These are species that have been classified as at high risk of extinction in the wild. This means that if nothing is done to conserve them and their habitats, chances are very high that they will become extinct.

---

[1] Information in this chapter was extracted from: *A guide to Red Lists and their use in conservation* compiled by the South African National Biodiversity Institute (SANBI)"

Lithops are threatened because of habitat loss.

The Hedgehog is a protected species.

5.2 WHAT IS A PROTECTED SPECIES?

Protected species are species protected by international, national and provincial legislation. Hunting, picking, owning, importing, exporting, transporting, growing, breeding and trading of such species are illegal without valid permits or licences. The names of protected species are listed in international conventions, national acts and provincial ordinances.

Species that are threatened due to other reasons, **such as habitat loss**, require other forms of conservation, and are usually **not included** in the lists of protected species.

Red Lists and Red Data Books are scientific publications that document the conservation status of species. They are based on a system that categorises species according to their risk of extinction.

5.3 WHICH SPECIES ARE MOST PRONE TO EXTINCTION?

5.3.1 Species at higher trophic levels

Predatory species at the top of the food chain occur at much lower densities than their prey and other plants and animals at lower trophic levels. They are often large animals with slow growth and reproduction rates, needing to produce only a few offspring to maintain their populations. This makes them particularly vulnerable to overexploitation and habitat loss.

5.3.2 Localised endemics

This is when periods of environmental change have driven formerly widespread species into small pockets of suitable habitat conditions known as refugia, or where species have evolved in small, isolated areas of suitable habitat, such as islands or lakes. Such species are extremely vulnerable to human-induced habitat loss or degradation, which can quickly wipe out the entire population.

5.3.3 Species with small populations

Small, isolated and unviable groups of species are threatened when their habitats are fragmented as a result of transformation for human use.

5.3.4 Largest members of species guilds

The largest members of a guild have higher metabolic demands, requiring larger areas of intact habitat to survive. They also tend to live longer, take longer to reach reproductive maturity and produce fewer offspring. They therefore tend to occur at lower densities than other guild members. Habitat fragmentation is the most severe threat to such species.

5.3.5   Species with poor dispersal and colonisation ability

Species with highly specific habitat requirements, but a poor ability to disperse to new areas of suitable habitat, are at high risk of extinction, even when their populations are relatively widespread. When their habitats are fragmented, poor dispersers are unable to recolonise areas of suitable habitat where local extinctions have occurred, and individuals become isolated more quickly.

5.3.6   Species with colonial or gregarious breeding habits

Wide-ranging and abundant species that gather in a single place to breed are extremely vulnerable to disturbance or destruction of their breeding sites. Many ocean-roaming seabirds are examples of this category, such as the Spectacled Petrel.

5.3.7   Migratory species

Migratory bird species are not only dependent on the maintenance of their summer breeding and winter foraging habitats, but also on crucial resting points along their migratory routes, where large numbers of birds may gather in small areas. Disturbance and habitat destruction at resting sites can affect large numbers of birds while they are at their most vulnerable, as migration is physiologically highly taxing.

5.3.8   Species dependent on unreliable resources

Species that depend on unreliable resources include desert species that rely on rainfall for critical steps in their life cycles, or nectar-feeding insects dependent on the flowering of particular host plants.

5.3.9   Ecologically naive species

Ecologically naive species have evolved without the threat of competitors or predators (including humans), and have subsequently lost the defensive behaviour patterns of their relatives.

There are thus three categories for threatened species:
- Vulnerable (VU)
- Endangered (EN)
- Critically endangered (CR)

Studies have shown that extinction is most likely to occur within a short time frame when:
- The population size is very small.
- The rate of population decline is high (namely, mortality rate is much higher than birth rate).
- Fluctuations in the population size are larger in relation to the population's growth rate.

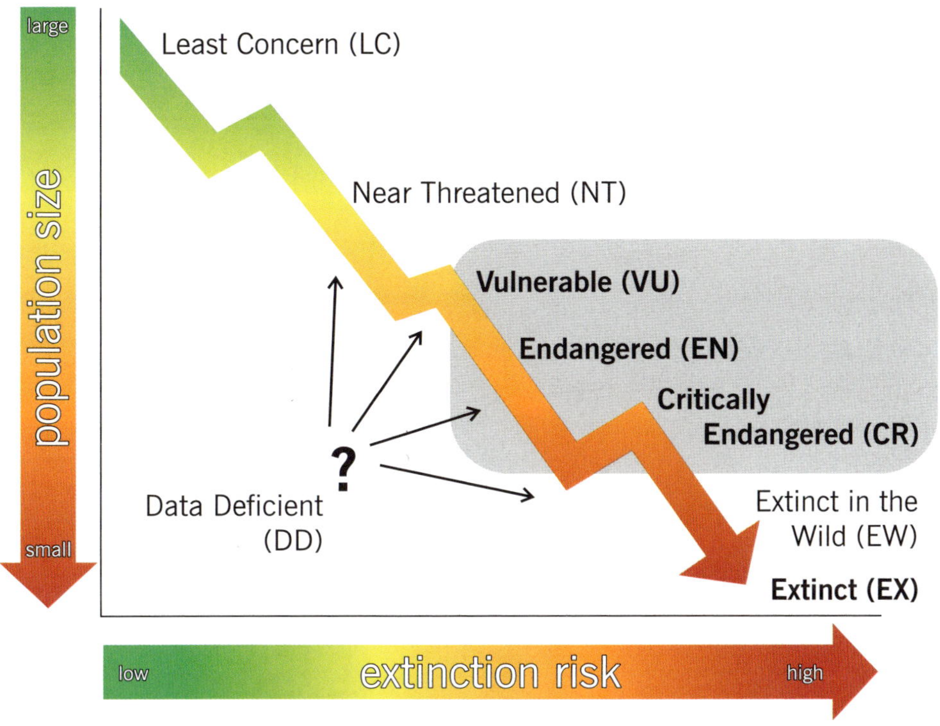

Figure 5.1: The IUCN Red List system categorises species according to their risk of extinction. (*A guide to Red Lists and their use in conservation* compiled by the South African National Biodiversity Institute, SANBI).

5.4　CRITERIA DETERMINING THREATENED SPECIES

Table 5.1: Criteria to determine threatened species

Criteria	Name	Description
A	Population reduction	High rates of population decline
B	Localised endemics	Only occur within a small area
C	Small population	Small population size and decline
D	Critical numbers	Critically small population size
E	Close to distinction	Probability of extinction is high within a short time frame

5.4.1　Criterion A: Population reduction

This identifies species that are at risk of extinction due to high rates of population decline.

THE PASSENGER PIGEON was once the most common bird in North America. It was a migratory species that lived in enormous flocks as large as 1.6 km wide and 500 km long, taking several days to pass. It was estimated that such flocks contained up to a billion birds, which were some of the largest groups formed by any animal, second only to swarms of the desert locust.

On 1 September 1914, Martha, the world's last Passenger Pigeon, died in a zoo in Cincinnati, Ohio. What was probably one of the most abundant birds in the world is extinct today.

What happened? During the early 19th century, Passenger Pigeon meat was commercialised as a cheap source for slaves and the poor, and the birds were hunted on a massive scale. By the 1850s, it was noted that the pigeons were becoming scarcer, but the large-scale slaughter of birds continued and even escalated. One commercial hunter reported shipping three million pigeons to markets in 1878. Between 1800 and 1870, the pigeon population declined slowly, but a catastrophic population crash between 1870 and 1890 resulted in only a few birds remaining by the turn of the century.

Attempts to restore wild populations through captive breeding failed due to the gregarious nature of the birds, which practised communal roosting and breeding in large communal nests housing up to a thousand birds in a single tree. As fewer birds remained, and their social structures had been disrupted, flocks continued to dwindle.

The Passenger Pigeon is a practical example of the principles behind Criterion A, and stands as a lesson to us today that no species is too common to go extinct.

5.4.2   Criterion B: Identify localised endemics

Criteria B present species that are at risk of extinction. This is because they only occur in a small area. This criterion also incorporates other factors contributing to increased extinction risks, such as continuing decline of the habitat or population, extreme fluctuations in population size, and severe fragmentation of the population into small, isolated subpopulations.

THE PEACOCK MORAEA (*Moraea villosa*) formerly participated in great abundance in the mass spring flower displays of the Cape Lowlands.

This attractive flower, which appears from Gordon's Bay to Ceres and Piketberg has lost more than 80% of its habitat to wheat fields and urban expansion.

Only a few populations now remain on small fragments of natural veld surrounded by crop fields, where they are threatened by a lack of fire (plants need fire to stimulate flowering), competition from alien weeds spreading from adjoining fields, loss of pollinators, and pollution by agricultural fertilisers and pesticides.

Moraea villosa.

5.4.3   Criterion C: Small population

This identifies species that are at risk of extinction due to **small population size** and decline. The smaller a species' population, the higher its risk of extinction.

5.4.4   Criterion D: Critical numbers

This primarily identifies species that are at risk of extinction due to **critically small population size**. Criterion D differs in that it identifies species which have already declined to such extremely low population numbers that they are unlikely to persist in the long term.

THE MAURITIUS KESTREL (*Falco punctatus*) declined to only four wild individuals in 1974, primarily due to the destruction of its subtropical forest habitat.

This island endemic was at that stage Critically Endangered according to Criterion D. Other threats that caused this species to decline to critically low numbers were poisoning by organochloride pesticides intended to control malaria-carrying mosquitoes, and predation by introduced black rats, feral cats and small Indian mongoose, which preyed on eggs and chicks.

Intensive conservation interventions, including captive breeding, supplementary feeding, nest-site enhancement, provision of nest boxes, nest guarding, control of predators around nest and release sites, clutch and brood manipulations, treatment of parasite infestations on chicks, and the rescue of eggs and young from falling nests, resulted in a remarkable recovery of the species.

The last captive-bred individuals were introduced in 1994, and since then, the wild population has continued to increase to about 1 000 individuals today.

The Mauritius Kestrel (*Falco punctatus*).

5.4.5   Criterion E: Close to extinction

This is used to classify a species as threatened when a statistical analysis shows that the **probability of extinction is high** within a short time frame.

When *Babiana blanda* was not seen for more than 50 years, it was believed to be extinct. Most of this species' wetland habitat on the lowlands north of Cape Town had been transformed or severely degraded by agricultural and urban expansion, as well as alien invasive plants.

There was little hope of its survival, and it was classified as Critically Endangered (Possibly Extinct). Then in 2006 a number of *Babiana blanda* plants were discovered growing under a dense thicket of alien acacias on a farm north of Cape Town. *Babiana blanda*'s status remains Critically Endangered according to Criteria B and C.

Babiana blanda.

Threatened ecosystems are protected by law, preventing further habitat loss, and promoting effective management in terms of the National Environmental Management Biodiversity Act (NEMBA). The listing of threatened ecosystems is an important legislative tool for the protection of species threatened by habitat loss.

The National Environmental Management Act (NEMA) requires Environmental Impact Assessments (EIAs) to be conducted for proposed developments in order to ensure sustainable development. In terms of the principles of sustainable development, degradation or loss of biodiversity should be avoided if possible, or otherwise minimised or mitigated.

EIAs must therefore report on any threatened species that occur at a proposed development site, as the development is likely to cause a loss of biodiversity, either by increasing the extinction risk, or by directly leading to the actual extinction of the species.

If a site survey finds a threatened species, the EIA report should include clear recommendations on how further decline in the threatened species and its habitat should be prevented, based on an understanding of the Red List status of the species, and the reasons why it is threatened.

The recommendations should provide guidelines to conservation authorities evaluating the EIA report on whether or not the development should be approved, or on specific mitigation conditions under which the development application could be approved.

5.5   INFORMING CONSERVATION PLANNING

Systematic conservation planning is the process of analysing spatial biodiversity data to identify high-priority areas for conservation. The aim of conservation planning is to ensure that viable, representative samples of species, habitats and ecosystem processes are maintained by producing maps to guide land-use planning and decision making at various scales, from municipal to provincial and national level.

The ability to represent and viability are achieved by setting particular quantitative conservation targets for habitat areas or a number of species subpopulations. To set such targets, a good understanding of the biological functioning of species and ecosystems is essential.

Target setting can prevent increasing risks of extinction for species and protect species that are currently at low risk of extinction from becoming threatened.

Target setting for species should therefore focus on those already at risk of extinction as defined by the Red List but also consider other species of conservation concern.

5.6   GUIDING ACTIONS FOR CONSERVATION OF SPECIES

Red List assessments is the first step in identifying species that are in urgent need of conservation and data assembled during assessments can provide guidance on the most appropriate conservation actions.

Red List assessments can also assist in the development of species Biodiversity Management Plans (BMPs). BMPs are not required for all threatened species, but are rather developed for specific ones, particularly those that are important biological resources on which people rely for their livelihoods, or species that can only be conserved through multiple stakeholder co-operations.

The following information is required to determine if a species needs protection:
- Present distribution (where they currently occur).
- Former distribution (where they used to be present).
- Status (rare, peripheral, threatened, endangered and vulnerable).
- Estimated numbers (current population).
- Breeding rate in the wild (record of breeding).
- Reasons for decline (habitat loss, development, pollution, etc.).
- Protective measures (taken or proposed).
- Numbers held in captivity.
- Breeding potential in captivity.
- Current research effort.
- Remarks.

CHAPTER 6

OPEN SPACE ROLES AND RESPONSIBILITIES

(This chapter deals with the roles and responsibilities of local governments towards open spaces and their management. The open space principles and networks are explained. There is a full description of green nodes and green ways, blue nodes and blue ways, brown nodes and brown ways, grey nodes and grey ways, red nodes and red ways.)[1]

6.1   INTRODUCTION

Biodiversity resources are finite. The current way of building cities is destroying our natural resources. Sustainable development is the only alternative to ensure our future existence. Rapid growth is evident almost everywhere in populations, urban sprawl, poverty and dwindling financial resources.

Open space refers to green spaces consisting of any vegetated land, landform, water or geological feature in an urban area as well as civic spaces (or brown space) consisting of squares, market places and other paved or hard landscaped areas with a public function. Some spaces may combine green and civic space elements, but one type or other usually predominates. As such, open spaces are defined along a continuum of soft/green/natural spaces at the one end and hard/brown/urban at the other.

All spaces, regardless of ownership and accessibility (i.e. public and private spaces), contribute to the amenity and character of an area and should be taken into account when assessing existing provisioning and determining future requirements. Although private spaces are not accessible to the general public, they are accessible to designated groups and do form part of the natural system, as ecological processes are not confined to property boundaries.

It is understood within the definition of open space that it includes a variety of spaces from eco-based to activity-based; from personal to public; from those sustained by clear and substantial manipulation, design and intervention to those that reflect little or none.

---

[1] Information from the Tshwane Open Space Framework, executive summary 2006, compiled by the City of Tshwane Environmental Planning Section, Consultation done by Strategic Environmental Focus.

6.2   NEED FOR OPEN SPACE

Open spaces allow room for natural systems, without which human beings cannot survive or function. It purifies water, harbours plant and animal life, cleans the air and regulates the urban climate. This life-giving function of open spaces is the most threatened by urban development.

We need open spaces for their spiritual enhancement, recreation and to conserve our natural environment. It is a blessing to enjoy clean streams, abundant wildlife and witness the unfolding spectacle of nature. Open spaces give coherent structure and beauty to their cities and guides metropolitan growth. Open spaces are important for our individual and collective well-being. Research has shown the importance of open spaces and greenery in the healing process of people and communities.

Open spaces are necessary investments if we are to develop and sustain a healthy community. Open spaces is a legal requirement. A municipality has a major responsibility to preserve the quality of life in a city/town by protecting its ecological processes (environmental goods and services), environmental integrity, recreational opportunities and scenic qualities.

6.3   OPEN SPACE ISSUES

The ecological benefits of open space are two-fold; firstly open space, especially natural open space (ridges, rivers, conservation areas, wetlands and grasslands), increases the potential for biodiversity and secondly, open space ameliorates the impacts of development.

With regard to the **maintenance of biodiversity:** The United Nations' Earth Summit in 1992 concluded that at least 10% of each vegetation type must be conserved. In addition, the resulting United Nations' Convention on Biological Diversity provides a framework for the conservation of the biological diversity of the planet and the sustainable use of biological resources.

It lists three objectives:
- The conservation of biodiversity.
- The sustainable use of biological resources.
- The fair and equitable sharing of benefits arising from the use of genetic resources.

South Africa is a signatory to these agreements, and is therefore committed to ensuring that these objectives are met.

The successful conservation of biodiversity requires the identification of species and rich habitat areas where development and habitat transformation and fragmentation must be discouraged and conservation efforts focused. Such species and rich habitat areas are typically found within pristine or natural open spaces where development intervention has been limited, ensuring that the "health" of all the species have been proportionally maintained. A variety of habitats such as ridges, wetlands and grasslands provides food, shelter, and space for many species to thrive. Grasslands and ridges that supports high percentages of rare species, especially plants, are particularly important, as well as watercourses and wetlands that support a variety of fish, water birds and mammals.

Due to their high spatial heterogeneity, ridges provide vital habitat for many threatened species. Seventy-four (74%) percent of the twenty-two (22) globally threatened plant species occur on the ridges and hills of Gauteng (South Africa), while at least three (3) threatened mammal species, several bird species of conservation concern, three (3) rare reptile species and a Red Data butterfly inhabit ridges.

Even subtle changes in these habitats (like a relatively small reduction in size) can cause a ripple effect throughout the food chain or in adjacent habitats and can starkly illustrate the benefits of open space after it is gone. For example, a mere 12% loss of forest cover in a watershed will begin to show an impact on the invertebrate life of a stream, while a 33% loss of cover will have more major impacts.

The section on wetlands below are relevant to the second ecological benefit – **softening the impact of development.**

6.3.1 Wetlands (see Chapter 9: Wetlands and watercourses)

Wetlands play a specifically important role. They occur where the water table is at or near the surface of the land, or where the land is covered by shallow water and perform the following functions:
* Specific plants and animals habitats maintenance.
* Water storage.
* Storm protection and flood mitigation.
* Shoreline stabilisation and erosion control.
* Groundwater recharge (the movement of water from the wetland down into the underground aquifer).
* Groundwater discharge (the movement of water upward to become surface water in a wetland).
* Water purification through retention of nutrients, sediments, and pollutants.
* Stabilisation of local climate conditions, particularly rainfall and temperature.

Wetlands provide tremendous economic benefits as they:
* Supply water (quantity and quality).
* Maintain fisheries (over two thirds of the world's fish harvest is linked to the health of coastal and inland wetland areas).
* Support agriculture through floodplain water table maintenance and nutrients retention.
* Support timber production.
* Provide energy resources, such as peat and plant matter.

Wetland.

Trees improve air quality.

- Maintain wildlife resources.
- Enable transport.
- Facilitate recreation and enhance tourism opportunities such as bird hides and birding.

6.3.2   Trees and other plants

These play a critical role in improving air quality and ameliorating the increased heat created by urban development. They not only absorb ozone, carbon dioxide, sulphur dioxide, nitrogen dioxide and other noxious air pollutants, but remove dust and particles from the air and release oxygen.

The plants' water transpiration helps control and regulates humidity and temperature. A single tree can remove as much heat from the air as five average-sized air conditioners. Trees and vegetation also break the wind, moderating temperature in winter. The result is a decrease in energy consumption, along with its cost and associated pollution.

6.3.3   Parks

Parks in stream valleys or urban wetlands absorb storm water much more cheaply than in artificial systems. Large open spaces allow rainwater to be absorbed slowly and to percolate into underground aquifers, reducing the danger of flash flooding or erosion due to rapid run-off.

6.3.4   Red Data species (see Chapter 5: Red Data species)

The Red Data categorisation of species is a crucial tool for the prioritisation of conservation efforts and for assessing the significance of environmental impacts in South Africa. Red Data lists give an indication of the conservation status of species and are used directly in conservation planning and implementation. These lists are usually categorised with taxa or groups, i.e. birds, reptiles and plants within Red Data Books.

6.3.5   Ridge systems (see Chapter 10: Mountains and ridges)

The 2001 Gauteng (South Africa) Conservation Ridges Policy has grouped ridges in different classes based on the degree to which they have been transformed. Class 1 ridges are the least transformed and Class 4 the most transformed.

It is significant that at least 40% of Gauteng's threatened plant species are confined solely to the Bronberg ridge and Magaliesberg mountain range.

Development pressure on ridges is increasing because of private ownership, densification and insufficient development guidance in this regard.

Blue Cranes are wetland dependant.

Rigdes: Faerie Glen Nature Reserve.

6.3.6   Watercourses (also see Chapter 9: Watercourses)

This includes catchment areas, storm water run-off systems, flood accommodation structures, wetlands, dams and water storage areas. Collectively they function to process water and regulate run-off with the aim of protecting and regulating the water resource.

Watercourse ecosystems, in association with appropriate buffer strips, are also natural storehouses of biological diversity, providing life support for a wide variety of species.

Watercourse.

6.3.7   Protected areas

This includes nature areas protected by the South African National Environmental Management Protected Areas Act, 2003 (Act 57 of 2003).

6.4   OPEN SPACE PRINCIPLES

6.4.1   Green structuring (Conservation)

Ecologically sensitive open spaces are easily lost and only recovered at high cost and effort, if at all possible. They still sustain life. Urban development can take place virtually anywhere and generally destroys or alters the natural environment. It only makes sense that urban growth should be guided, informed and influenced by ecological factors. This means that ecologically sensitive open spaces (green spaces) should be identified first and used to guide new development into areas where it would be least detrimental and where it could respond to areas with high ecological risks or sensitivity.

Green structuring should however, take into account existing growth nodes and spines and should highlight and ameliorate possible conflict. This is the rationale behind the country's Strategic Environmental Assessment (SEA) process in which the environment informs and directs potential development.

6.4.2   Largest possible green space (Compaction)

In order to protect as much open space as possible for ecological processes, urban development should be concentrated or compacted, as opposed to sprawling. Land for urban development should be regarded as a scarce commodity and be used efficiently.

Concentrating development will not only have the advantage of protecting valuable open space but will also make efficient and economical use of infrastructure and services, minimise the environmental, social and financial cost of new development and reduce commuting distances, which will in turn reduce air pollution from vehicles. In addition, compaction brings people closer to facilities, services and jobs and intensifies economic opportunities.

Urban development should thus be focused, with green corridors introducing nature into the city, giving people easy and convenient access to the countryside, natural areas and continuous public open spaces.

6.4.3   Interconnectedness/an integrated network (Connection)

Functioning ecological processes do not operate within discreet pockets of land, but require linkage and interrelated stretching over the entire city. Open spaces should thus be interlinked to allow ecological processes to operate effectively and to promote the largest possible biodiversity representation of fauna and flora.

6.4.4   Place-making

The natural structure provides the setting for the city and creates opportunities for place-making when combined with urban structure. Elements such as gateways, nodes and landmarks create meaningful places, genius loci, spirit of place especially where there is a confluence of urban and open space structuring elements.

6.5   OPEN SPACE NETWORK

Natural environmental resources are irreplaceable and should thus be one of the major structuring elements guiding the development of a city. Urban growth should not take precedence over open space and continue to destroy ecological sensitivities. It should not ignore open space's equal land use role in building liveable communities, relegating it to mere "leftover space" and "vacant land". The first step in shaping the city is therefore the determination of an open space network, which contains not only ecological processes and systems, but also social value and place-making opportunity.

The open space network is concerned with the spatial structure of "natural" or green areas in the urban landscape and with all planning activities that enable such areas to perform environmental services and contribute to the quality of urban life. The network contains the elements of the open space in itself (vegetation, water, animals, natural materials, etc.) and aims to form various overlaying systems of open spaces. It is thus used to indicate the position of "natural" or green areas in the urban landscape and has spatial, social, place-making and economic value.

There should be an interface between natural and human ecologies. Natural ecology consists of all natural processes and systems whereas the human ecology deals with urban processes and human needs.

6.6   OPEN SPACE CATEGORISATION

Open spaces can be classified in many different ways depending on the parameters that are considered and the aim of the classification.

6.6.1   Scale

Open spaces can range from small (local or neighbourhood spaces such as play parks), medium (regional such as sports fields), to large (metropolitan such as nature reserves).

6.6.2   Form

Linking of open spaces allows for the creation of "ecological corridors" which ensure the passing and the movement of flora and fauna from one system to another, enabling processes and facilitating the "health" and functioning of the system. These "passages" are mainly constituted by vegetation. They can be formed by road underpasses that allow animal movement, vegetation zones dedicated to wildlife, or clear zones along watercourses, where flora and fauna can develop without interferences. Linkages between open spaces also help to define the landscape or city structure, provide links with the natural environment and allow for ease of movement for residents.

Open spaces can be defined as either linear or nodal.

Examples of linear spaces are:
- Natural elements such as ridges or rivers.
- Movement routes such as activity streets and corridors.
- Utility spaces such as railway lines and servitudes.

Examples of nodal open spaces are:
- Natural elements such as nature reserves or bird sanctuaries.
- Planned open spaces such as parks and sport stadiums.
- Economic centres such as business nodes or urban cores.
- Utility spaces such as cemeteries and landfills.

6.6.3   Function

The primary function of open spaces is ecological as this cannot be provided by any other element within the built environment. All open space resources, whether soft or hard, effectively fulfil an ecological function. Open space can, however, also be multifunctional, collectively fulfilling an ecological, socio-economic and place-making function, but will always be dominated by one particular function.

6.6.4   Soft/hard character

Open spaces can be categorised along a continuum between soft/natural/green on the one end of the spectrum and hard/urban/brown on the other. On the "soft" end of the spectrum, open spaces would have an ecological function, e.g. a nature reserve. On the "hard" end of the scale, an open space would be urban in character and fulfil mainly place-making or social-economic functions, e.g. a square.

Although most open spaces will have both hard and soft elements, the character of an open space will be determined by the level of human intervention, the level to which the environment has been transformed, e.g. its dominant visual language and how it is perceived, developed and used by the community. Based on the level of human intervention, open spaces can be classified as:

Natural: An area existing in or produced by nature, not artificial or imitated, where vegetation is usually dominant, where little human intervention has taken place and which is not intensively utilised by humans, e.g. a nature reserve.

Cultivated: An area which is still perceived as predominantly "green" but that is no longer in its natural state and has been developed by human intervention and care for human use, e.g. a park with manicured lawns and shrubs.

Built-up: An area that has been completely transformed by human intervention and which is predominantly hard and accommodates intense use, e.g. a public square.

6.6.5   Locality

Different localities will have an impact on how an open space should be dealt with, managed and developed as well as the challenges faced by an open space, e.g.:

- **Inner city:** Historic cores, offices, businesses and high-rise residential blocks
- **Transition zone:** Mix of different land uses/ settlement types, often the result of quick and uncoordinated development.
- **Urban fringe:** Predominantly agriculture land uses and high ecological sensitivities.
- **Development zone:** Urban pressure zone, often the result of quick and uncoordinated growth and sprawl. High ecological sensitivities may occur here.

6.6.6   Ownership

Ownership can be categorised according to:
- **State-owned open space:** Open space owned, developed and maintained by the state as part of institutional grounds, state headquarters, gardens, memorial complexes, that is either for the use of the general public within pre-determined access times or not accessible at all depending on the relevant state authority.

- **Public open space:** Open space for the use of the general public. Most public open space is provided for during township establishment/development processes, whereafter it is transferred to the local authority, who must develop and maintain it.

- **Private open spaces:** Open space for the exclusive use of the specific community and is typically owned, developed and maintained by a private individual or representative entity such as a Section 21 Company.

Irrespective of its ownership, all open spaces should form a continuous open space network, as ecological processes cannot be limited by property boundaries. The ownership of a property will however determine which role the local government can play in its appropriate management.

Table 6.1: Open space categories *(Tshwane Open Space Framework. Executive summary 2006)*

Function	Form	
	Nodal	**Linear**
Ecological	**Green node** (e.g. protected area, conservation area, GDACE irreplaceable site, GDACE important site, high ecological sensitivity hills)	**Green way** (e.g. Ridge System)
	Blue node (e.g. dam, wetland, peat land, an area defined by the presence of a permanent water body or water saturated soils, housing aquatic fauna and flora. Not an area for the outright purpose of storm water management)	**Blue way** (e.g. watercourse of any order, defined by a natural contour low point. Not a watercourse for the outright purpose of storm water management). Inclusive of both the riverine and riparian zones within the 1:50 year flood line.
Socio-economic	**Brown node** (e.g. capital, urban and metropolitan core, multipurpose sports facility, sports stadium, recreational park, resort)	**Brown way** (e.g. corridor, linkage, activity street, collector street)
	Grey node (e.g. landfill site, cemetery, mine, quarry, parking lot)	**Grey way** (e.g. servitude, railway line)
Place-making	**Red node** (e.g. gateway landmark, culture historical feature/destination, square)	**Red way** (e.g. ceremonial street, boulevard)

6.7 GREEN NODES

Description: Green nodes are areas within which ecological systems, processes and values are concentrated. They include important habitats for fauna and flora and areas representative of local biomes, vegetation types and high ecological sensitivity such as protected areas, irreplaceable and important sites.

Value: Green nodes are the most important elements in the provisioning of environmental goods and services, the protection of biodiversity, endangered species and ecological systems, as well as eco-based activity. Green nodes must be protected for conservation purposes.

Scale: Green nodes are of metropolitan significance and influence.

Character: Green nodes can occur in a pristine or natural state, but are generally characterised as natural. Every attempt must be made to retain green nodes in as pristine a state as possible. As little as possible human intervention must be allowed. Human intervention must be sensitively located with a minimum footprint (cluster and space principle). A network of low impact movement between human interventions can be allowed. Activities must focus on ecological research education, conservation of biodiversity, eco-tourism, trails and guided walks.

Only endemic vegetation must be allowed. It can be complimented with a network of trails. Strict control of development and invader species must be practiced. Rehabilitation of disturbed areas must be sought at all times.

Green node: Groenkloof Nature Reserve.

6.7.1 Protected area

- Protected areas are strategically important ecological structuring elements within the open space network and must be conserved.

- Earmarked protected areas need to be formally declared as protected areas according to relevant legislation.

- The management of protected areas must aim to maximise ecological functioning and environmental goods and service rendering and must facilitate the improved utilisation and exposure of such open space resources.

- The policy on Red Data species must be used as a decision-making and decision support tool in the evaluation of development applications. Developments must have support by outcomes of an Environmental Impact Assessment (EIA).

- The policy on ridges must be used as a decision-making and decision support tool in the evaluation of development application. Developments must have support by outcomes of an EIA.

- Alternative service delivery partnerships within protected areas should only be considered after and in accordance with the outcome of a Strategic Environmental Assessment (SEA) and/Environmental Management Framework (EMF).

- Integrated environmental management plans must be drafted for each protected area, managed and maintained in line with such plans.

6.7.2 Irreplaceable, important and high ecological sensitivity site

- These are strategically important ecological structuring elements in an open space network.

- Development interventions on these sites depend on open space sensitivities identified through an EIA process.

- Biodiversity conservation must be identified and where not in public ownership, alternative service delivery mechanisms and partnerships must be facilitated with private owners to ensure the protection of such areas.

- The policy on Red Data species must be used as a decision-making and decision support tool in the evaluation of development applications. Developments must be supported by outcomes of an EIA.

6.8 GREEN WAYS

Description: Green ways consists of ridge systems. Such ridges are defined as areas steeper than 5 degrees in which ecological systems processes and values are concentrated. Green ways also represent important habitats for fauna and flora, areas representative of local biomes, vegetation types and high ecological sensitivity as well as areas of linkage and connectivity.

Value: Green ways are the most important elements in the provisioning of environmental goods and services, the protection of biodiversity, endangered species and ecological systems, as well as eco-based activity.

Class 1 and 2 ridges are predominantly ecologically pristine and must be conserved. Class 3 and 4 ridges have been predominantly transformed by human intervention, but remain valuable and need to be retained and rehabilitated where possible as ecological and spatial linkages.

Scale: Green ways are of metropolitan significance and influence.

Character: Green ways (Class 1 and 2 ridges) mostly occur in a pristine or natural state but are generally characterised as natural. Every attempt must be made to retain green ways in as pristine a state as possible. As little as possible human intervention must be allowed: Human intervention must be sensitively located with a minimum footprint. A network of low impact movement between human interventions can be allowed. Activities must focus on ecological research, education, conservation of biodiversity, eco-tourism, trails and guided walks.

Green ways (class 3 and 4 ridges) are natural in character, but have been impacted on by built-up elements.

Ridge system, Moreletakloof.

Only endemic vegetation must be allowed. It can be complemented with a network of trails. Strict control of development and invader species must be practiced. Rehabilitation of disturbed areas must be sought at all times.

6.8.1 Ridges

- Must be conserved as far as possible.

- There should be a policy in place on how to manage ridges.

- The ridges policy must be used as a decision-making and decision support tool in the evaluation of development applications on ridges.

- No development can be supported on ridges if not compliant with relevant ridges policy. Any development needs to comply with the outcomes of an EIA.

- The exercising of existing rights on private properties that is situated within a defined ridge must be guided by site specific sensitivity analysis. It should comply with the outcomes of an EIA.

- Municipality must ensure the formal protection of publicly owned ridge systems through the implementation of all necessary legal processes and procedures.

- Ridges must as far as is possible, be obtained as zoned public open space during the development application process. Where not possible, the privately owned ridge`s conservation and management must be facilitated through an alternative service delivery mechanism or partnership.

- Conservation lines on privately owned ridges must be determined and established in accordance with the ridges policy.

6.9 BLUE NODES

Description: Blue nodes include dams, wetlands, peat lands as well as any area defined by the presence of a permanent water body or water saturated soils, housing aquatic fauna and flora. Blue nodes should not be confused with areas for the outright purpose of storm water management.

Value: Blue nodes are the most important elements in the provisioning of environmental goods and services, the protection of biodiversity, endangered species and ecological systems, as well as eco-based activity. Therefore, blue nodes must be conserved.

Their value furthermore lies in the ability to maintain natural hydrological and ecological cycles, such as conserving valuable aquatic systems, purifying water, recharging water tables, preventing flooding and providing drinking and irrigation water. Blue nodes have a secondary socio-economic function.

Scale: Blue nodes are of metropolitan significance and influence.

Wetland.

Character: Blue nodes are mainly natural in character and must be retained in as pristine a state as possible. As little as possible human intervention must be allowed: Human intervention must be localised with a minimum footprint with focal point development at confirmed least detrimental areas. A network of low impact movement between the focal point developments can be allowed. Activities must focus on ecological research and education and preservation of biodiversity. Where used for recreational purposes, this must be limited to specific areas and must not compromise ecological processes.

Only endemic vegetation must be allowed. It can be complimented with a network of walkways and cycle paths. Strict control of development and invader species should be practiced. Rehabilitation must be sought at all times.

6.9.1   Wetland

- Wetlands are strategically important ecological structuring elements within the open space network and must be conserved.

- The primary purpose of wetlands is that of ecological functioning and the rendering of environmental goods and services. Where other service infrastructure requirements such as storm water management and sewer management need to be accommodated within and around wetlands, such requirement must acknowledge and ensure the continued effective and efficient ecological functioning and environmental goods and service rendering of the resource, without compromising its integrity.

Bronkhorstspruit Dam.

- Storm water management and design solutions which could impact on wetlands must be based on ecologically sound principles (balanced pre- and post-development flows, water retention, detention, infiltration, quality, recycling, etc.) and not only with functional safety aspects in mind.

Transformed and degraded wetlands must be actively rehabilitated and such rehabilitation must be based on site-specific, ecologically sound principles.

6.9.2   Dam

- Dams are strategically important ecological structuring elements within the open space network and must be conserved.
- The infill of the overflow design flood line/level of a dam will not be allowed due to the cumulative negative impact on such dam's riparian systems.
- Any development adjacent to a dam must reserve the overflow design flood line/level area as zoned public open space.

6.10   BLUE WAYS

Description: Blue ways include all watercourses (rivers and brook areas) in the city irrespective of their character and order. Such areas are defined by natural contour low points and the 1:50 year flood line or 32 meters from the centreline of the Blue way, whichever is the greatest. It accommodates permanent and perennial water flow and does not include channels and channels constructed purely for storm water purposes.

Value: Blue ways are the most important elements in the provisioning of environmental goods and services, the protection of biodiversity, endangered species and ecological systems, as well as eco-based activity, therefore blue ways must be conserved.

Scale: Blue ways are of metropolitan significance and influence.

Character:
- **Natural:** Blue ways consist of ecologically pristine areas with the riverine and riparian zones as ecological focal point. The river/brook must be maintained in its natural setting with a natural flood line. Human intervention must be localised with a minimum footprint. Activities must focus on ecological research, education, conservation of biodiversity and passive recreation. Continuity of movement along rivers such as hiking trails and cycling routes must be facilitated. Strict control of development and invader species have to be practiced and only endemic landscaping allowed.

- **Cultivated:** Blue ways are characterised by manicured riparian zones as the basis for passive and active recreational activities. Trees must define the edges of the green structure and buildings should weakly define the bigger space. The use of indigenous grass must be promoted at all times.

- **Urban:** Blue ways have historically been totally transformed. It consists of a linear space with strong edge definition. Here, buildings must focus on the blue way with activities and openings linking onto and interacting with the open space. The interface with other land uses must be a balance between hard and soft to improve ecological functioning.

Rehabilitation of disturbed areas within all blue way character types must be sought at all times.

6.10.1   Watercourse

- All watercourses (natural, cultivated and built-up) are strategically important ecological structuring elements within the open space network and must be conserved.

- The primary purpose of watercourses is that of ecological functioning and the rendering of environmental goods and services. Where other service infrastructure requirements such as storm water management and sewer management need to be accommodated within watercourses, such requirements must acknowledge and ensure the continued effective and efficient ecological functioning and environmental goods and service rendering of the resource, without compromising its integrity.

- Storm water management and design solutions must be based on ecologically sound principles (water retention, detention, infiltration, quality, recycling, etc.) and not only with functional safety aspects in mind. Permission for the discharge of storm water within watercourses must be subjected to proof of adherence to such principles.

- The management of watercourses must aim to maximise ecological functioning and environmental goods and service rendering and therefore the rehabilitation of watercourses must be actively pursued.

- Where rehabilitation of watercourses to their natural state is not feasible, a linear ecological system must be established through open space acquisitioning and appropriate, public development interventions along the watercourse.

- The canalisation, transformation (through artificial linings) and exotic cultivation of watercourses can no longer be allowed.

- Urban agriculture within watercourses should not be supported within the defined 1:100 year flood line area.

- The amendment of the 1:50 year flood line by infilling, will not be supported due to the resulting cumulative negative impacts on riverine and riparian systems.

- No development will be allowed within the 1:50 year flood line.

River.

- Watercourses must be managed as integrated components and may not be segmented or fragmented ecologically, physically and visually as this will compromise ecological functioning, storm water risk management and disaster management. Fragmentation can only be considered where already compromised at existing road crossings.

- All new infrastructure within, over or alongside watercourses must aim to minimise the ecological, physical and visual fragmentation of the watercourse.

- Any development adjacent to a watercourse (natural, cultivated or built-up) will be required to reserve the 1:50 year flood line area or an area that extends 32 m from either side of the centre line of a watercourse (whichever is the greatest) as zoned "Public Open Space" and transfer such land to the municipality.

- Should a private party wish to participate in the management of zoned "Public Open Space" watercourses, an alternative service delivery mechanism or partnership can be entered into.

6.11   BROWN NODES

Description: Brown nodes include predominantly informal and formalised recreational Open Spaces (such as resorts, recreational parks, and sport facilities) as well as socio economic centres (such as urban cores).

Value: The value of brown nodes lies in their socio-economic function in terms of recreation, socialising and community interaction as well as their potential for economic development.

Scale: Brown nodes significance and influence relate to all scales – metropolitan, regional and local.

Character:
- **Natural:** Brown nodes are still predominantly in a natural state, displaying little human intervention and manipulation. Any development intervention must aim to retain and incorporate natural elements on-site. Preference must be given to endemic landscaping and horticultural manicuring must be minimal. Should ecological features occur on the open space, development interventions must occur outside designated sensitivities.

- **Cultivated:** Brown nodes contain manicured vegetation: irrigated lawns, tree, shrubs, flowers and sports fields. Any development intervention must aim to satisfy a wide variety of activities and needs and must display high standards of horticultural practice. Preference must always be given to indigenous landscaping.

- **Urban:** Brown nodes are mainly hard-surfaced open space. Buildings must focus/face on the brown node with activities and openings linking onto the space. The open space must be well detailed with urban design elements such as street furniture, setbacks, decorative trees, and provide robust and multi-functional elements.

Caravan camping.

Fountains Resort swimming pool.

6.11.1 Core

- Urban and metropolitan cores must be structured and developed around well-planned and designed public spaces that are integrated within the open space network.

Where green networks and blue networks form part of a core, such networks must be integrated within the core and be supported by compatible land uses and activities.

Sport facility: Loftus Versfeld.

6.11.2 Recreational park

- The development of multifunctional regional recreational Brown Nodes must be actively pursued by means of collective internal financing initiatives in order to address the identified under provisioning of such open spaces throughout the city.

Recreational Parks must be secured during the development cycle as public space, accessible to the majority of the city's residents.

6.11.3 Sport facility

Sport facilities must be secured during the development cycle as public space, accessible to the majority of the city's residents.

6.12 BROWN WAYS

Description: Brown ways include different types of "movement" space, the most important being corridors, linkages, activity streets, collector roads, their full road reserves and adjacent open space elements.

Value: The value of brown ways lies in their contribution towards experiencing and moving through the city (from both a vehicular and pedestrian perspective) as well as providing opportunity for commercial activity and socio-economic interaction.

Scale: Brown ways' significance and influence relate to all scales – metropolitan, regional and local.

Character:
- **Cultivated:** Brown ways are characterised by human intervention in terms of formal and informal landscaping elements. Tree planting is the main spatial definition element and must be facilitated at all times. Pedestrian movement is critical and must be encouraged through the provisioning of well-developed walkways and site furniture (litterbins, etc.)

- **Built-up:** Brown ways are characterised and lined by intense activity generating and typically non-residential land uses, formalised road reserves, street furniture and formal landscaping. Trees define edges of the space together with buildings.

6.12.1   Brown way policy

- The planting of trees within brown ways is a service of equal importance to other engineering services within the road reserve and must be actively pursued.

- Existing trees along brown ways must be protected and new corresponding trees must be planted where gaps have occurred.

- Development adjacent to brown ways will be required to upgrade and maintain such open space, in terms of landscaping, road reserve trees and pedestrian walk ways, as an integral component to the development.

Road reserves (street trees).

6.13   GREY NODES

Description: Grey nodes include open space with services and urban utilities such as water reservoirs, quarries, landfill sites and cemeteries.

Value: The value of grey nodes lies in their socio-economic functioning; the rendering of and support to primary service delivery, as well as their potential to supplement ecological (as linkages) and recreational functioning (once closed and developed as such).

Scale: Grey nodes' significance and influence relate to all scales – metropolitan, regional and local.

Character: The character of grey nodes depends on their function and context but inevitably reflect human intervention:

- **Cultivated:** Grey nodes, such as cemeteries, reflect open space with manicured vegetation, irrigated lawns and trees. Any development intervention must favour the use of indigenous vegetation and the incorporation of natural features.

- **Built-up** Grey nodes, such as landfills. Quarries and reservoirs reflect significant, but localised human intervention, sometimes amounting to total transformation. The potential with quarries and landfills exist in their rehabilitation and utilisation as recreational open space or to restore ecological and spatial linkages. This must be facilitated at all times.

Cemetary.

6.13.1   Grey nodes

- Grey nodes occur as utility open space (such as quarries, landfill sites and mines) and must be considered as possible future usable open space resources.

- The proposed planning and development of all new grey nodes (landfill sites and cemeteries especially) must take into consideration the potential open space function of these utilities within the city network and only be implemented upon recommendation of an EIA.

Parking lots are considered important grey nodes on local open space plans that must be planned, developed and maintained as quality urban open spaces in terms of the open space development strategy.

6.14   GREY WAYS

Description: Grey ways include open space with service and urban utilities such as railway lines and servitudes.

Value: The value of grey ways lies in their socio-economic functioning: the rendering of and support to primary service delivery, as well as their potential to supplement ecological (as linkages) and recreational functioning (once closed and redeveloped).

Scale: Grey ways' significance and influence relate to all scales – metropolitan, regional and local.

Railway line.

Character: The character of grey ways depends on their function and context, but is typically natural or cultivated.

6.14.1   Servitude and railway line

- Grey ways are important ecological linkages and movement corridors within a city open space network improving accessibility to and continuity of the open space network.

- Servitudes must as far as is possible, be managed in their natural state to improve the open space type's potential ecological functioning.

- Public access to servitudes must be pursued wherever possible, but must be cognisant of proper planning and design standards as well as public safety aspects.

- The proposed planning and development of new servitudes and railway lines must take into consideration and actively pursue the potential open space function it can perform within the city network.

6.15   RED WAYS

Description: Red ways include ceremonial routes and boulevards that link symbolic elements (red nodes) or brown nodes.

Value: The value of red ways lies in their contribution towards experiencing the city, place-making and supporting the image of a city.

Scale: Red ways are of metropolitan significance and influence.

Character:
- **Built-up:** Red ways are lined by intense activity generating land uses surrounding the space. They contain highly formalised road reserves, street furniture and formal planting. Double rows of significant trees define the edges of red ways together with buildings.

6.15.1   Ceremonial street/boulevard

- Red ways must take on the form of well-designed, landscaped, tree, pedestrianised and major place-making destination people spaces.

- Linear open spaces (parks and road reserves) along red ways on metropolitan and regional open space plans are integral components to the red ways and cannot be alienated.

- The planting of trees within red ways is regarded as a service of equal importance to other engineering services and must be actively pursued.

Boulevard.

- The choice of trees within red ways should be indigenous and preferably endemic to the city environment. It should enhance and strengthen the place-making and identity of the endemic environment as first priority.

- Existing trees along red ways must be protected and new trees in line with the endemic environment must be planted where gaps have occurred.

- The commissioning and installation of public art within red ways must be actively pursued.

6.16   RED NODES

Description: Red nodes consist of the most important "place-making moments" in the city structure. They are well defined in terms of geographical setting, spatial features, and historical relevance and include landmarks, gateways, squares and culture historical elements or places.

Value: The value of red nodes lies in their place-making function and in creating a high quality urban environment that supports the image of a city or town.

Scale: Red nodes significance and influence relate to all scales – metropolitan, regional and local.

Character: The character of red nodes is dictated by their context, their symbolic meaning or design intent but can vary from natural to urban character.
- **Natural:** Red nodes display little/limited human intervention and are charac-terised by dramatic natural features and settings such as hills, ridges, etc. Such

features must be protected and retained in as pristine a state as possible to maintain the node's visual and spatial integrity and relevant "sense of place".

- **Cultivated** Red nodes are formalised and altered features are of a very high development quality. It can contain ecological and recreational features, but must be managed as "destination" spaces.

- **Urban:** A totally transformed space within a well-defined and predominantly hard urban environment. Landscaping features are more ornamental and the focus is on urban design features, integrated within the surrounding context.

6.16.1   Culture historical site or destination

- Culture historical sites are irreplaceable socio-economic reflections of "historical events" and must be protected at all times and integrated within the open space network.

- Culture historical sites must be actively managed and conserved within open space resources.

6.16.2   Square

- The development of existing and new squares within the city's cores must be actively promoted.

Church Sqaure, Pretoria, South Africa.

- Squares must take on the form of well-designed, landscaped, tree, pedestrianised, and significant place-making destinations. The focus should be on creating people spaces.

The commissioning and installation of public art within red nodes must be actively pursued.

6.16.3   Gateway

- Existing gateways to the city must be protected from inappropriate development and land uses such as motor showrooms, cell phone masts, outdoor advertising structures, retail and commercial development.

- Gateways must be developed on important entrance routes to the city/town in order to announce the visitor's/tourist's arrival and to improve the legibility of the city/town.

6.17   OPEN SPACE POLICIES

This provide a basis for consistent and integrated decision-making by authorities affecting open space resources and guides all scales of land use and infrastructure management aspects on metropolitan, regional and local scale:

6.17.1   Open space general

- Open space planning must be included in the Integrated Development Process (IDP) and must inform the budgeting process.

- Open space planning must be used as a supplementary decision-making tool with regard to development applications (all daily land use management decisions).

6.17.2   Open space value

- Open space must be viewed as a land use and service of equal importance to any other land use and service. It should not be viewed as vacant, undeveloped land, which is available for development.

- Open space, due to its ecological (environmental goods and services), socio-economic and place-making functioning, is irreplaceable. The value of open space therefore should not only reflect market value, but should also ultimately be an expression of the benefit to present and future communities and not just those who buy and sell property.

- Open space adds ecological, social, economic and place-making value to any development and the integration and appropriate response of development to open space must at all times be facilitated.

- All natural resources within a municipality's open space network should be actively protected and conserved.

6.17.3   Open space conservation

- Ecological structuring elements (green ways, green nodes, blue ways, and blue nodes) within the open space network must be conserved, maintained to nature conservation standards and not to horticultural standards,

- Degraded and disturbed ecological structuring elements (green ways, green nodes, blue ways, and blue nodes) must be rehabilitated to ensure the optimum rendering of environmental goods and services.

- All declared weeds and invasive plants must be removed from ecological structuring elements.

- All known Red Data populations must be conserved in-situ and protected in accordance with legislation.

6.17.4   Open space in public trust

- Open spaces must be retained, protected and secured as public land with community access thereto as far as is possible.

- Open space should be an asset to the community and must be managed (planned, developed, maintained) as such.

- Ecological structuring elements (green ways, green nodes, blue ways, and blue nodes) must be secured during the development cycle as public land as far as is possible. This is critical to ensure the realisation of the rendering of environmental goods and services, the integrated and holistic functioning of the underlying systems and ensuring singular accountability and responsibility in the management of such resources.

- In cases where ecological structuring elements (green ways, green nodes, blue ways, and blue nodes) remain in private ownership and cannot be secured by a municipality, the municipality must actively engage with such owners by means of alternative service delivery mechanisms and partnerships to ensure the realisation of rendering of environmental goods and services, the integrated and holistic functioning of the underlying systems and to ensure singular accountability and responsibility in the management of such resources.

6.17.5   Open space alienation

- No municipality-owned land forming part of open space plans, (especially green ways, green nodes, blue ways, blue nodes as well as all land immediately adjacent to the aforementioned) may be subdivided or sold off.

- Alternative service delivery mechanisms and partnerships can be entered into on the above municipality-owned land for purposes of enhancing the overall network, improving environmental goods and service rendering and encouraging the improved utilisation of the open space resource without compromising the resource's carrying capacity and integrity. Such alternative service delivery mechanism or partnership must be informed by Strategic Environmental Assessments (SEA) and Environmental Management Frameworks (EMF).

- Under no circumstances must a municipality-owned open space, forming part of an open space plan, be compromised or sold to solve social problems (crime, loitering, etc.) Design and management solutions should be sought at all times as highlighted within the safety strategy.

- Under no circumstances must a municipality-owned open space, forming part of an open space plan, be compromised or sold on account of its disturbed state as such a resource can be rehabilitated with success to effectively render environmental goods and services.

- In the evaluation of a municipality-owned open space, forming part of an open space plan, consideration must be given not only to market value, but also to its social and ecological (environmental goods and service rendering) value before a final decision can be made on the quantitative value of the resource.

6.17.6   Open space funding

- Any income generated by the municipality through open space contributions, alienation and alternative service delivery partnerships, must be used for the benefit (purchase, development and maintenance) of the open space plan. This can be achieved by means of fair/trade exchange of open space goods and/ or services as well as a dedicated budget allocation for the purchase of open space. Such dedicated budget allocation can be set off against open space income generated per financial year.

- Funding and alternative service delivery options must be facilitated to ensure the realisation of the open space plan.

6.17.7   Open space land use management

- Sufficient open space must be provided for within new developments to ensure the realisation of the open space plan and the ecological, socio-economic and place-making functioning of open space resources. (2.4 ha/1 000 population for socio-economic open space is a good standard.)

- Where an application site contains a green way or blue way and such a site is planned for development, the development application must include such open space resource as an integral part of the development proposal's boundaries. As an example: a watercourse that forms part of agricultural land, which is the subject of a township establishment process, may not be excluded from such township boundaries.

- Cash contributions will not be accepted in lieu of open space provisioning unless otherwise indicated by a local open space plan.

- Land provided in terms of open space provisioning will be evaluated not only according to quantitative guidelines, but also according to the qualitative guidelines as set out in the open space development strategy.

- Any development within or adjacent to the open space network, must be compatible to the function and aesthetics of the open space in terms of land use, scale, massing, spatial interaction, appearance and landscaping. Such development must actively contribute to the protection and enhancement of the network without harming the quality of the open space in any way. In this regard, filling stations, motor show rooms, cellular phone masts and outdoor advertising structures are not considered compatible land uses and developments to open space (excluding sports stadiums and brown ways).

- Development within the open space network must be true to the intrinsic character and "make-up" of the city's representative ecological systems. This means that landscaping and materials should be based on local products and endemic species.

- The illegal occupation and use of land forming part of the open space plan must be curtailed at all times.

6.17.8   Open space resource management

- Open space planning and design must pay particular attention to the implementation of strategic and catalyst projects identified in the metropolitan, regional and local open space plans.

- Open space capital development projects must respond to priorities set by the city; must be prioritised with due consideration of the open space development strategy; must be primarily informed by planning consideration and must be well representative of the metropolitan, regional and local scales.

- Open space maintenance must clearly differentiate between conservation practices (for purposes of ecological functioning, environmental goods and service rendering) and horticultural practices (socio-economic and place-making functioning) to ensure an appropriate response to the functional requirements of open space.

6.18   OPEN SPACE MANAGEMENT AND RESPONSIBLE AGENTS

The term "management" related to open spaces includes planning, development implementation and operational maintenance aspects that can be defined as follows:

Table 6.2: Open space roles and responsibilities (Tshwane Open Space Framework. Executive Summary 2006)

<table>
<tr><td rowspan="8">OPEN SPACE AGENT</td><td>Planning</td><td>Development implementation</td><td>Operational maintenance</td></tr>
<tr><td colspan="3">Ecological open space (green nodes, green ways, blue nodes, blue ways)</td></tr>
<tr><td>Environmental planning; metropolitan planning; regional spatial planning</td><td>Nature conservation and resorts</td><td>Nature conservation and resorts</td></tr>
<tr><td colspan="3">Socio-economic open space (brown nodes, brown ways)</td></tr>
<tr><td>Environmental planning; metropolitan planning; regional spatial planning; streetscape management; roads and storm water</td><td>Streetscape management; parks and horticultural services; cemetery services; waste management; sport and recreation; roads and storm water; water and sanitation; electricity</td><td>Parks and horticultural services; cemetery services; waste management; roads and storm water</td></tr>
<tr><td colspan="3">Place-making open space (red nodes, red ways)</td></tr>
<tr><td>Environmental planning; metropolitan planning; regional spatial planning; streetscape management; roads and storm water</td><td>Streetscape management; parks and horticultural services</td><td>Parks and horticultural services</td></tr>
</table>

6.19   ALTERNATIVE SERVICE DELIVERY STRATEGY

Role players: The successful development of the open space network depends on a variety of role players, each of which can make a contribution to the development of open spaces.

6.19.1   Public

- Provincial, national and local government
- Parastatals
- Semi-public institutions
- Public

6.19.2   Private

- Business
- NGOs
- CBOs

6.19.3   Other

International role players

The strategy contains various options in terms of alternative service delivery **partnerships** and **mechanisms.**

Partnerships include:
- Lease agreements
- Co-operative agreements
- Conservation easements
- Land trusts
- Conservancies and private nature reserves
- Business improvement districts (BIDs), park enhancement districts (PEDs), and special park districts (SPDs)
- Transfer or purchase of development rights

Mechanisms include:

- Fair/trade exchange: The re-investment of income derived during the alienation of open space into remaining open space resources
- Open space service level agreements: The negotiation of a service level agreement with a developer through the basis that the developer provides an appropriately-sized portion of land as open space contribution
- Expropriation of land
- Promulgation of protected areas
    1. Protected natural environment (PNE)
    2. Special nature reserve (SNR)
    3. Limited development areas (LDA)
    4. Nature reserves
    5. National heritage site
    6. Designated management area
- Incorporated association not for gain (Section 21 company)
- Sectional titles
- Share Block

CHAPTER 7

UNDERSTANDING BIODIVERSITY MANAGEMENT IN THE URBAN CONTEXT

(This chapter deals with ecosystem services. It describes various threats to the environment such as fragmentation and habitat loss, and then it shows how an evaluation of an urban nature area can be conducted. It also describes a template for an ecological management plan. The last part of the chapter deals with biodiversity and ecosystem restoration for sustainable development. Examples of habitat and species action plans are explained.)

7.1 ECOSYSTEM SERVICES

Functioning ecosystems are the foundation of human well-being and most economic activities, because almost every resource utilised on a day-to-day basis by humankind relies directly or indirectly on nature. The benefits that humans derive from nature are known as **ecosystem services.** These can be divided into four categories: **provisioning services, regulating services, habitat or supporting services,** and **cultural services** (Millennium Ecosystem assessment 2005; TEEB Foundations 2010).

Table 7.1: Ecosystem services (Millennium Ecosystem assessment 2005; TEEB Foundations 2010)

Ecosystem categories and types relevant to cities

Service	Icon	Description	Example
Provisioning services (energy outputs)			
Food		Manage agro ecosystems to provide food for human consumption	Havana, Cuba (1996), food was produced within urban gardens
Raw materials		Provide materials for construction, fuel, wood, bio-fuels and plant oils	Rubber, latex, rattan and plant oils
Fresh water		Play a role in providing drinking water (ensure flow, storage, purification)	South African mountain fynbos ecosystem

Table 7.1: Ecosystem services (Millennium Ecosystem assessment 2005; TEEB Foundations 2010) (cont.)

Medicinal resources		Provide plants used as traditional medicines	80% of world's people dependent on traditional herbal medicine

Regulating services (air quality, food and disease control)

Climate and air quality regulating		Plants lower the temperature, influences rainfall and regulate air quality	Cascine Park forest removes pollutants in Florence, Italy
Carbon sequestration and storage		Ecosystems store greenhouse gas (remove and store CO_2)	Urban tree sequestrate carbon
Moderation of extreme events		Act as buffer against disasters (damage from extreme weather events, floods, storms, tsunamis, avalanches and landslides)	Marshes and wetlands around Californian Napa City, USA, control flooding
Waste water treatment		Wetlands filter effluents and control disease-causing microbes	Wetlands used for wastewater treatment in Louisiana, USA
Erosion prevention and maintain soil fertility		Vegetation cover prevents soil erosion, contributes to soil fertility and nutrients for plant growth	Save cost to repair damage caused by erosion
Pollination		Pollinators survive in wetlands (insects, birds and bats)	Food corps depend upon pollination
Biological control		Predator activities in ecosystems regulate pests and diseases (birds, bats, frogs and fungi)	Water hyacinth was brought under control in southern Benin using natural enemies

Habitat or Supporting services (provide and maintain diversity of plants and animals)

Habitats for species		Ecosystems provide food, water and shelter	Habitat loss is the biggest threat to Red Data species
Maintain genetic diversity		Genetic diversity. Habitats accommodate a high number of species (biodiversity hotspots)	Need this genetic diversity to breed crops, animals for human consumption.

Table 7.1: Ecosystem services (Millennium Ecosystem assessment 2005; TEEB Foundations 2010) (cont.)

Cultural services (benefits to people – aesthetic, spiritual and psychological)

Recreation, mental and physical health		Walking in green spaces help to exercise and to relax (mental and physical health)	Recreation and amenity
Tourism		Ecosystems create tourism nodes that can stimulate the economy.	Visits to Coral reefs in Hawaii contributed to significant income generation.
Aesthetic, inspiration, art and design		Natural landscapes are a source of inspiration and art, culture and science	Prehistoric rock art present evidence on how nature inspired art and culture
Spiritual (sense of place)		Forests, caves or mountains can have a religious meaning (sense of belonging)	The Maronite church of Lebanon protects a hill in their possession because of the Maronite culture, theology and religion.

7.2 THE BIG FIVE HUMAN THREATS TO THE ENVIRONMENT

- Habitat loss and fragmentation.
- Unsustainable harvest.
- Pollution.
- Climate change.
- Introduction of exotic invasive species.

These threats combined or individually are rapidly not only destroying and degrading our ecosystems; they are also depleting and ruining the very services on which we base our health and prosperity.

7.2.1 Habitat loss and fragmentation

In an urban environment, habitat loss is unavoidable. It is very important to determine ecologically sensitive areas (river catchment areas, ridges, wetlands, Red Data species habitats, etc.) upfront before development takes place. It is also important to preserve these sites in pristine conditions and prevent rehabilitation actions needed because of degrading.

Transformation of pristine habitat in an urban environment is also very difficult to prevent. Development cultivation results in habitat transformation. Exotic gardens in the urban environment also impact directly on pristine urban nature areas. This is why we need to promote indigenous/endemic gardens. We must remember that biodiversity is dependent on the preservation of pristine habitat.

Fragmentations have a direct impact on pristine habitat that impacts on wildlife movement and sustainability in urban nature areas. Fragmentations break up ecosystems, it hampers the processes animals, plants and micro-organism need for survival. Examples of fragmentations are roads through a wetland system, development within a water catchment area, bridges crossing over river systems, roads going through a mountain area, etc.

7.2.2   Unsustainable harvesting

This is when a resource is harvested more than it can produce and therefore cannot sustain itself. A simple example is the harvesting of fire wood until there are no trees left to be harvested (a common practise in Africa). A wetland can be harvested for compost but be unable to replace the amount of production that took place over many years of existence.

Harvesting should take place in such a way that it does not destruct the habitat. When there is habitat loss, biodiversity disappears. The disappearance of biodiversity is an indication of ecosystem destruction. Ecosystems sustain not only wildlife but humans as well.

Benefits that people obtain from ecosystems are provisioning services (e.g. food, water, timber); regulating services (e.g. regulation of climate, floods, disease, waste and water quality); cultural services (e.g. recreational, aesthetic and spiritual) and supporting services (e.g. soil formation, photosynthesis and nutrient cycling).

Ecosystems ensure pollination, so crucial for agricultural production and it includes supply of water not only for irrigation and household use, but also for cooling in industrial processes, dilution of toxic substances. It is also critical to health, through water supply and quality and through natural filtering of wastewater.

In the urban environment the ways that residents' harvest biodiversity are:

- Through visitors making use of urban nature areas (cultural services – recreational, aesthetic and spiritual). Each nature area will therefore have a carrying capacity for visitor numbers and activities to be able to sustain it. Examples are the number of vehicles allowed into an urban nature reserve, the number of boats allowed on dams, number of visitors to a picnic site, etc.

- Through making use of ecosystem supporting services (residents make use of photosynthesis coming from vegetation, soil that was formed by ecosystems over many years and nutrient cycling).

- By using regulating services from ecosystems (use a healthy climate regulated by ecosystems, produce floods because of built up areas but accommodated by ecosystems, contribute to diseases that ecosystems absorb, produce waste that ecosystems have to absorb, use quality water produced by wetland filter systems).

- By making use of ecosystem provisional services (food, water and timber ecosystems provide).

7.2.3   Pollution (including nutrient enrichment)

There are different forms of pollution. Air pollution is not always visible with the naked eye. It is generated by artificial gasses from engines in vehicles, manufacturing, enterprises, and gasses as by-products from burning coal or manufacturing of any other products. Air pollution can also be from excessive dust or other particles artificially produced that becomes airborne.

Waste is another form of pollution. Waste is divided into dry and wet waste. Dry waste consists of plastic, paper, glass and metal. These kinds of waste can easily be recycled, wet waste is normally organic and consists of leftovers from restaurants that includes all processed food or cut-offs from food ingredients (peels from vegetables and all organic material that follows the decomposition route). Fortunately organic waste can be turned into compost (see Chapter 20, Addendum C on vermi-compost with earthworms)

Normally nature areas cannot absorb these products that are generated by pollution. It is visually unattractive. The decomposition generates a smell. It contributes to unhealthy conditions. It can make nature areas toxic to urban wild life and humans.

With these unhealthy conditions in place, biodiversity (the number and variety of plants, birds and animals) is under threat. If there is a decline in biodiversity it is an indicator of poor ecological conditions. Poor urban ecology leads to unhealthy conditions for humans to live in.

Waste is a by-product of human living conditions and must be managed to maintain a healthy urban environment. Healthy urban environments that look nice, smell good and are attractive contribute to positive social living conditions.

In the urban environment, pollution is very visible when waste collection does not take place. This waste is washed down by rain water to the urban river systems where it gathers in obstructive areas to rot and stink. The next step is the development of unhealthy toxic conditions and the threat to urban wildlife. Urban wildlife disappears because their natural habitats are destroyed. This leads to a decline in urban biodiversity.

Nutrient enrichment is a big contributor to urban pollution. It is mainly sewer fluids that land up in the storm water systems and then enrich the urban rivers, wetlands and urban nature areas with toxic nutrients. Nutrient enrichment normally escalates into anaerobic conditions. A lot of oxygen is absorbed and make urban wildlife conditions unsuitable. This leads to the disappearance of urban wildlife and a direct threat to urban biodiversity.

Sewerage management is crucial for residents as well as urban wildlife. It often happens that sewer pipelines develop leakages, sewer infrastructure gets blocked or sewerage mixes with storm water collection. This contaminates the open water areas and the ground. Untreated sewerage is a direct threat to humans and urban wildlife. This contributes to a decline in urban biodiversity.

The discharge of urine and faeces (either by humans or animals) is a natural process and is supposed to add fertiliser to the recycling process, but it must be controlled and properly managed. A big concentration of these nutrients can have a detrimental effect on humans and urban wildlife.

7.2.4   Climate change

Wildlife is adapted to a specific climate. This forms the habitat wherein they live, feed and breed. Any change to habitat can cause them to move to more suitable habitats or try to survive or die. An urban environment causes a change in habitat for wildlife and therefore will have a direct impact on biodiversity.

Urban areas create their own microhabitat. It transforms the natural habitat that used to be there for something new. If city and town development can preserve nature areas between the new developments, it will serve as a haven for urban wildlife to escape to. If these areas are big enough to be sustainable, wildlife will remain there. This means that urban wildlife can adapt to urban nature if there is space allocated for them.

Unfortunately, urban development not only influences microhabitat but also the bigger surrounding areas that are important for biodiversity sustainability. Therefore city and town management should include the management of these impacts (pollution, air quality, fragmentation, storm water, sewerage, etc.).

A city has its own ecology and cycles that must interact in a sustainable way. What comes into the city must go out. The carrying capacity of a city or town must be balanced in the development and the infrastructure. The required amount of water must be available or imported and after consumption, the waste water must be accommodated. The water imported either by pipelines or rains must be recycled and unused water let out of the municipal area into rural areas. The sewerage produced by residents must be recycled or let out into sufficiently clean river systems. Paper plastic, metal, fluent, organic material imported and used must be recycled or disposed of in a sustainable manner.

This means that the activities within a city or town will directly impact the surrounding climate (in terms of climate change) as well as rural land. Both the micro and macro habitats must be monitored to determine climate change. Sometimes habitat is created artificially by manicured gardens especially for birdlife. This is the reason why you can identify birds within a city area that are not common to those areas and far away from their natural habitat. Conversely, developments may also not accommodate a climate (habitat) for previous existing species which will become extinct if they have nowhere else to go.

7.2.5   Introduction of exotic invasive species

Introduction is the bringing in of species from their natural and historical distribution area to a new area where they have never occurred before.

Exotic means the species are not from their country of origin.

Indigenous means the species represents their country of origin.

Endemic means the species only occurs in their original habitat and it has adapted for survival.

Invasive means the species originated from the **introduction** of an **exotic** species that has adapted to its new environment with so much success that it starts to invade the **indigenous/endemic** species in this new environment.

Species is a term that includes all fauna and flora representing individuals that can be individually identified on a scientific criteria.

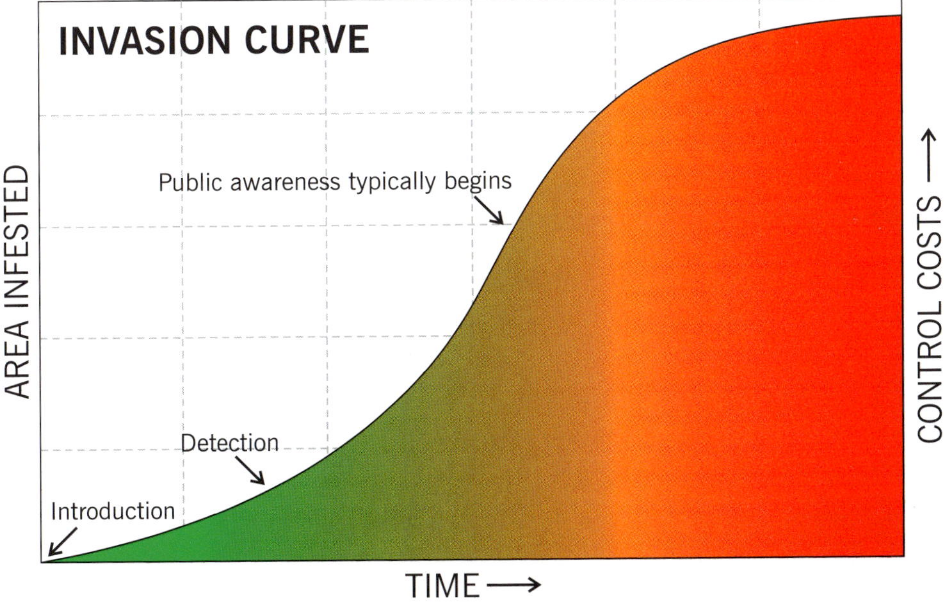

Figure 7.1: Costs related to alien invasive control.

Why is the introduction of exotic invasive species a human threat to the environment?

Humans' actions in this regard cause the threat. Exotic invasive species win the competition (for water and nutrients) with endemic species because their natural predators are not present. These predators were left behind in the exotic species' country of origin during the introduction process. Predators control population numbers and help keep an ecosystem in balance. Without predators, the exotic species start to invade (take over/encroach) the habitat they are present in, upsetting the balance of the ecosystem. This results in habitat destruction and lost biodiversity.

Examples of exotic invasive species in South Africa include the encroachment of wattle trees from Australia, the invasion of the Indian minas (birds) from India and the invasion of Jacaranda trees from South America.

7.3   EVALUATION OF AN URBAN NATURE AREA

Urban nature areas include all existing nature areas left over after development took place, including nature reserves, water courses (river systems), ridges and mountain areas as well as wetlands.

These areas were traditionally allocated to parks and marked for park development. Unfortunately, park development includes cultivation (An area that is still perceived as predominantly green but that is no longer in its natural state and has been developed by human intervention and care for human use).

All urban open space should first be prioritised for conservation purposes and if it is unsuitable, it can be allocated for horticultural park development or a combination of conservation and cultivation.

The nature conservation status of a property in a built-up area must be evaluated and managed in a way that contributes to urban biodiversity management.

The criteria for the evaluation process are discussed below (see Chapter 20, Addendum F (template for an ecological management plan)).

7.3.1   Biological status

Is water available on this property?

Water is always a big contributor to sustain urban wildlife. Permanent water bodies add to the biodiversity potential and create more variety in habitat. For example, a nature area with a small dam, wetland or river system will accommodate grassland birds and water birds. These types of habitat supply the wildlife with water needs and make it more sustainable.

Infrastructure that promotes the use of an urban nature area that includes water bodies is more attractive and sustainable. A bird hide can be added, hiking trails can be constructed, lookout points can be established, etc.

It is important to plan for the use of urban nature areas because it provides a reason for protection and maintenance.

Does this habitat make a contribution to the representation of habitat for urban nature conservation?

All original different habitats within the urban environment should be conserved, including threatened ecosystems, vegetation types, vegetation condition and fragmentation.

For example the following Low and Rebelo (1996) vegetation types present in Tshwane (Pretoria, South Africa), can be summarised as follows:

Mixed bushveld: This vegetation varies from a short, dense bushveld to an open tree savannah. The structure of this vegetation type is primarily determined by fire and grazing. It is represented in a number of smaller provincial nature reserves.

Clay thorn bushveld: This vegetation is dominated by various *Acacia* species (thorn trees) and includes dense swards of a variety of grass species. The distribution is determined by extremely clayey soils. It is poorly conserved.

Rocky highveld grassland: The habitat for this vegetation is rocky mountains, hills and ridges especially along the crests of hills and ridges. It is characterised by a large diversity of grass and forb species with frost playing an important role in the distribution of woody vegetation, trees and shrubs. It is highly threatened within Gauteng due to pressure of urban development, mining, industrialisation and to some degree agriculture and is poorly conserved.

Moist, cool grassy highveldveld: This grassland is widespread and covers the central eastern part of the highveld in the Free State. Only a small portion of this vegetation type occurs within the City of Tshwane on the southeastern boundary. In its pristine condition, the red grass *Themeda triandra* dominates and is poorly conserved.

Are there Red Data species involved?

This is a list of fauna and flora that require environmental protection, based on the International Union for Conservation of Nature (IUCN) definitions of endangered, threatened or vulnerable species.

I want to make use of info extracted from the Tshwane Open Space Framework (TOSF) Executive Summary 2006, related to the importance of Red Data species for the City of Tshwane (Pretoria, South Africa).

Within the City of Tshwane's nature conservation areas, a total of 23 of the larger mammal species are found. These include the white rhino, hippo, buffalo, giraffe and cheetah and others. About 470 bird species can be found, including some of the rarer species such as the Crowned Crane (Mahem), Blue Crane, Fish Eagle and Black Eagle.

A crucial tool for the prioritisation of conservation efforts and for assessing the significance of environmental impacts in South Africa is the Red Data categorisation of species. Red Data lists give an indication of the conservation status of species and are used directly in conservation planning and implementation. These lists are usually categorised with taxa or groups, i.e. birds, reptiles and plants, within Red Data books.

Red Data species and areas of ecological importance have been captured within the Gauteng Open Space Plan, 2003 and more specifically within a component known as the Conservation Plan or C-Plan. C-Plan differentiates between protected areas, irreplaceable sites and important sites.

Protected areas are areas provided for within the South African National Environmental Management Protected Areas Act, Act 57 of 2003:
* Special nature reserve, nature reserves (including wilderness areas) and protected environments.
* World Heritage sites.
* Specially protected forest areas, forest nature reserves and forest wilderness areas.
* Mountain catchment areas.

An irreplaceable site is a site designated as essential in meeting targets set for the conservation of biodiversity. Options for achieving these targets will be reduced should the site not be protected.

Important sites are marked for the conservation of biodiversity, the significance of which is subject to ground trothing. This site is important but not essential and can be replaced by a similar site, but a trade-off in the efficiency of the conservation plan may be the result.

A resource can be non-renewable. This is a resource that has a finite stock and either cannot be reproduced once it is used or lost, or cannot be reproduced within a time span relevant to present or future generations.

The Gauteng State of the Environment Report, 2004 noted that 7.8% of Tshwane is considered irreplaceable and 15% is considered important for conservation purposes.

The dominant Red Data species in the City of Tshwane region are predominantly associated with ridges, grasslands and wetlands. The Juliana's Golden Mole is one of the most important Red Data mammals within the City of Tshwane and occur primarily around the Bronberg ridge. It rates amongst the 10 most critically endangered mammals in South Africa, with the highest risk of extinction.

Other significant recorded Red Data Species in Tshwane include the Grass Owl, Melodious Lark, Blue Crane, Secretary Bird, South African Hedgehog, Giant Bullfrog and Rock Scorpion.

What is the coverage (size in hectares) of this potential conservation area?

Property size (larger properties can encompass a greater suite of ecological processes). The aim should be to include as much as possible. The area should not be demarcated or fragmented. This is needed to enable free movement of wildlife. The question should be if wildlife can survive in this area? What level of sustainability can be achieved?

Will it make any contribution to urban nature conservation/local biodiversity?

What value can be added, direct or indirect? Will it be utilised by residents and what value will that add? Is there an education potential? How will it enhance the urban biodiversity?

What is the status of species diversity?

A species count is necessary. This is needed for fauna as well as flora. This criterion examines the conservation importance of a site based on the species that occur. One must take in consideration the species that should be present according to the species natural distribution records. This means the specific habitat will be the indicator of what species should be present. The more species available to present the specific habitat the higher point out of 5 this item will score.

What is the invasive alien species status of the site?

Alien invasive plants are a big problem in the urban environment. The reason is that manicured gardens adjacent to urban nature areas are planted with exotic species that can spread to these urban nature areas. Most of the time invasion of alien species will only occur when these urban nature areas are disturbed from its ecological status. The higher the degree of invasive species the lower the score will be out of 5.

What is the rehabilitation status of the site?

The aim is to determine the disturbance status of the site. How is the ecological status of the land under evaluation? Is there erosion? Is it overutilised? Is the ground coverage sufficient? Is the site still in a pristine condition or does it need rehabilitation?

7.3.2   Availability of the land

What is the local authority-owned status of the land?

Does the land belong to the local authority or to a private person? When it belongs to the city council it will score a high point. It can be that only part of the property

Secretary Bird.

Red Data species: a, Rock Scorpion; b, Giant Bullfrog.

belongs to the local authority and the rest is private. If this is the case, the council needs to purchase the property to make it viable and then it will score a lower point.

What will the expenditure costs be if the council needs to obtain the land?

This means does the council have the capacity to purchase the land? If not, it is not a viable option and it will score a lower point.

7.3.3   Development status

What will the impact be of the current development (excavations, roads, buildings, power lines, housing and landfill) on the conservation status of this site?

It is important to assess the impact of all development inside and adjacent to an urban nature area. This can include power lines, pipelines, and canalisation of a river, road crossings, roads and surrounding developments. The aim is to determine how much these developments degrade the ecological status of the urban nature area.

7.3.4   Utilisation potential of this site for urban conservation

What will the potential be for outdoor recreational activities that will enhance urban nature conservation?

Consider the outdoor leisure activities that can be implemented. We look at picnic braai facilities, trails (hike, mountain bike, horse, and dogs), shelters for functions, caravan and camping, overnight accommodation, etc.

What is the environmental education potential for this site?

What is important here is to determine the viability for educational visitors to come and visit the site. Are there schools in the vicinity? Is the infrastructure available to accommodate visitors and infrastructure such as a bird hide? It is important to address signage and information boards and the possibility of an education centre.

Will it make a contribution to feeding and breeding habitat for endemic species?

We need to determine if the habitat is in place for endemic species. This will enhance biodiversity.

Is this site in line with the conservation plan?

Can the site accommodate any shortcomings in the plan?

Will residents get involved with activities on this site? Can a friends group or stakeholder make a contribution?

If urban nature areas are not used, it will be harder to protect and sustain them. Will residents take ownership or get involved?

7.4   ECOLOGICAL MANAGEMENT PLAN

An ecological management plan is an academic document that is compiled by a specialist with training in ecological management. This should be a document with inputs from a specialist group and needs to guide the manager of a nature area on how to manage this area according to the findings and recommendations in the management plan.

This document will ensure that all previous actions are recorded. The information is passed on to the new manager in future and will empower the next generations responsible for the management of the nature area.

The basic structures and guidelines will always stay more or less in place, but the detailed information and findings will be recorded and altered if necessary. This is a live dynamic document that must be updated regularly and monitored to make sure managers on nature areas stay on track.

The template for an ecological management plan can be found in Addendum G. South African environmental legislation requires an ecological management plan for each nature area that wants to be proclaimed as a nature reserve. A nature reserve is required to have an ecological management plan which encompasses biological diversity aspects, socio-economic development, cultural-historical and development aspects.

The ecological management plan should strive to achieve the following objectives:
- To ensure that the nature reserve or nature area is proclaimed as a nature reserve subject to legislation.
- To list the unique biological, socio-economic, cultural-historical and development characteristics of the area.

- To provide an accurate inventory of natural resources within the area.
- To provide an inventory of management and visitor related infrastructure and services.
- To list norms and standards with regards to the management of this protected area.
- To prescribe management actions which complies with the prescribed norms and standards.
- To set performance indicators by which compliance can be gauged for adaptive management purposes.

Each section of the ecological management plan should contain the following aspects:
- Ecological filing system references.
- The vital attributes or special features being dealt with under each section.
- Historical information with regard to previous management strategies.
- Management principles, norms and standards.
- Current areas of concern regarding non-compliance with legislation.
- An action plan to deal with and rectify legislative deficits.

Please browse through Chapter 20, Addendum G (template for an ecological management plan) which is a self-explaining document. This serves as a sample document of what is required for the Gauteng Province.

7.5 A RAPID RESPONSE ASSESSMENT [1]
(United Nations Environment Programme, GRID Arendal.)

Effective conservation is the cheapest and most optimal option for securing services, costing only from tens to a few hundred USD per hectare. However, protected areas cover only 13%, 6% and <1% of the planets land, coastal, and ocean area, respectively, and many are not under effective management. Of the remaining 80–90% of the planet, almost one-third of the world's ecosystems are already directly converted for human activities such as for agriculture and cities, and another one-third have been degraded to some extent. With such levels of degradation it is apparent that major improvements and efforts are needed to restore and manage ecosystems also outside protected areas at a much greater scale than today.

7.5.1 Recommendations

7.5.1.1 Prioritise conservation issues

Protect biodiversity and ecosystem service hotspots, even when partially degraded, to halt further degradation and allow for commencing restoration planning.

---

[1] Nellemann, C., E. Corcoran (eds). 2010. Dead Planet, Living Planet – Biodiversity and Ecosystem Restoration for Sustainable Development. ISBN: 978-82-7701-083-0 Printed by Birkeland Trykkeri AS, Norway

Conservation, within the context of spatial planning, provides by far the most cost-efficient way to secure ecosystem services. This is particularly critical for areas with a high degree of land pressures and development.

7.5.1.2   Do long-term planning

Ensure that investments in restoration are combined with long-term ecosystem management in both restored and surrounding areas to ensure gradual recovery. Overseas development agencies, international finance agencies and other funders including regional development banks and bilateral agencies should factor ecosystem restoration into development support; job generation and poverty alleviation funding.

7.5.1.3   Allocate funding

A project that causes damages to an ecosystem should set aside funds to restore a similar degraded ecosystem elsewhere in the country or community. Payments for ecosystem services should include a proportion of the payment for the restoration and rehabilitation of damaged and degraded ecosystems. One percent of GDP should be considered a target for investments in conservation and restoration.

7.5.1.4   Multidisciplinary approach

Apply a multidisciplinary approach across stakeholders in order to make restoration investments successful. Wise investments reduce future costs and future public expenses, but the driving force behind the initial degradation are addressed to secure progressive recovery. This will prompt local stakeholders to become involved and benefit from the restoration process.

7.5.1.5   Take changes into account

Ensure that restoration projects take into account the changing world: Ecosystem restoration should be implemented in consideration of scenarios for change in a continually changing world, including climate change and land pressures. Changes in surrounding areas or in the prevailing environmental conditions will influence both the rate of recovery and ultimate restoration success.

7.5.1.6   Address the range of scales

Restoration needs to address a range of scales from intense hotspot restoration to large-scale restoration to meet regional changes in land degradation. Degrees of biodiversity restored are often linked to quality of services obtained and is intrinsically linked to successful outcome.

7.5.1.7   Ensure that ecosystem **restoration** is implemented

This should be guided by experiences learned to date, to ensure that this tool is used appropriately and without unexpected consequences, such as the unintended introduction of invasive species and pests and sudden abandonment of restoration targets in the process.

7.5.1.8   Create a policy

Apply ecosystem restoration as an active policy option for addressing challenges of health, water supply and quality and waste water management by improving watersheds and wetlands, enhancing natural filtration.

7.5.1.9   Address disaster prevention

Apply ecosystem restoration as an active policy option for disaster prevention and mitigation from floods, tsunamis, storms or drought. Coral reefs, mangroves, wetlands, catchment forests and vegetation, marshes and natural riparian vegetation provide some of the most efficient flood and storm mitigation systems available. Restoration of these ecosystems should be a primary incentive in flood risk and disaster mitigation planning.

7.5.1.0   Ensure adaptation

Enhance further use of ecosystem restoration as a means for carbon sequestration, adaptation to and mitigation of climate change. The restoration targets for sequestration includes forests, wetlands, marine ecosystems such as mangroves, sea grasses and salt marshes, and other land use practices.

7.5.1.11. Ensure food security

Improve food security through ecosystem restoration. Given the significance of food production and its relations to biodiversity and ecosystems loss, expanded recommendations are presented:
* Improve natural weed pest and decease control.
* Restore soil fertility.
* Ecological cultivating methods.
* Improve irrigation systems.
* Improve water supply and quality.

Ecosystem services

An ecosystem is the dynamic complex of plant, animal and micro-organism communities and the non-living environment interacting as a functional unit. It assumes that people are an integral part of ecosystems (MA, 2005).

Almost one third of the world's ecosystems has been transformed or destroyed, and another third heavily fragmented and disturbed, and the last third already suffering from invasive species and pollution (UNEP, 2001; www.globio.info). Over 60% of the ecosystems services are considered degraded (Millennium Ecosystem Assessment – MA, 2005).

7.6   ECOSYSTEM RESTORATION

Ecosystems are removed or degraded through acute events, or more often as a result of chronic contamination, degradation from development and other human activities. This eventually results in costs and problems such as lowered productivity, food insecurity and health problems, thus threatening sustainable development.

7.6.1   What is ecosystem restoration?

Restoration can be defined as re-establishing the presumed structure, productivity and species diversity that was originally present at a site that has been degraded, damaged or destroyed. In time, the ecological processes and functions of the restored habitat will closely match those of the original habitat (Society for Ecological Restorations - SER, 2004; Food and Agricultural Organisation – FAO, 2005).

The objective of rehabilitation is to re-establish the productivity and some, but not necessarily all, of the plant and animal species thought to be originally present at a site. (For ecological or economic reasons, the new habitat might also include species not originally present at the site). In time, the protective function and many of the ecological services of the original habitat may be re-established (Food and Agricultural Organisation – FAO 2005).

Recovery of a habitat is linked to the ecological succession of a site – the site returning naturally to the state it had been before it had been degraded or destroyed without any intervention from humans (Centre for International Forestry Research – CIFOR websites).

7.6.2   Ecosystem restoration for biodiversity conservation

The conservation of biodiversity is recognised as important due to the role biodiversity plays in underpinning many of the ecosystem services which humans depend upon for their well-being (MA 2005). Furthermore, it is well documented globally that habitat loss is a direct driver of specie loss, and one mechanism to bring species diversity back to a site is through restoration of the ecosystem or habitat (SER 2010). And while it has been documented that restoration does not necessarily achieve the same value of biodiversity or ecosystem services found in intact ecosystems (Benayas *et al* 2009), there are many good examples of where informed ecological restoration programmes have been able to deliver biodiversity, including the recovery of threatened species and ecosystems (Lindenmayer *et al.* In press).

The services humankind receives from complex ecosystems include regulation of water supplies and water quality, maintenance of soil fertility, carbon sequestration, climate change mitigation and enhanced food security, to mention a few.

Mountain regions all over the planet are crucial water towers. Meandering rivers and wetlands serve not only to slow the speed of water, but also to allow gradual sedimentation of organic matter sediments, and create spawning habitats for fish, amphibians and reptiles, insects and birdlife. Wetlands have been estimated to provide ecosystem services to the value of around 5 000–20 000 USD/ha/year

(Costanza *et al.*, 1997; Zhao *et al.*, 2005; both in 2010 USD) or globally over 6 615 trillion USD per year.

Restoration is financially viable (TEEB, 2009): Cities like Rio de Janeiro, Johannesburg, Tokyo, Melbourne, New York and Jakarta all rely on protected areas to provide residents with drinking water. They are not alone – a third of the world's hundred largest cities draw a substantial proportion of their drinking water from forest protected areas (Dudley and Stolton 2003). Forests, wetlands and protected areas with dedicated management actions often provide clean water at a much lower cost than man-made substitutes like the water treatment plants in Venezuela.

Restoration of wetlands to help filter certain types of waste water can be a highly viable solution to waste water management challenges (Ko *et al.*, 2004). Securing safe water and reducing the unregulated discharge of waste water are among the most important factors influencing world health. The WHO estimates that worldwide some 2.2 million people die each year from diarrhoeal disease, 3.7 % of all deaths and at any one time over half of the world's hospitals beds are filled with people suffering from water related diseases (UNDP 2006). Of the 10.4 million deaths of children under five, 17 % are attributed to diarrhoeal disease, i.e. an estimated 1.8 million under-fives die annually as a result of diarrhoeal diseases (UNEP, 2010). Unmanaged waste water is a vector of disease, causing child mortality and reduced labour productivity, but receives a disproportionately low and often poorly targeted share of development aid and investment in developing countries.

Wetlands, river deltas, lakes and marshes play a crucial role not only in sedimentation of pollutants and organic matter, cultures and harvest of fish and provision of nesting or feeding habitat for birdlife all across the planet, they also serve as important filters for pollutants. Intensive management to increase agricultural production – through irrigation and the application of fertilisers and pesticides – can further reduce the water quality available for consumption. Such intensification has had major direct impacts on biodiversity, such as on farmland birds and aquatic species, but also on algae blooms and water quality, and in return, on people's health.

7.6.3   Ecosystem restoration for climate change mitigation

Much recent attention has been given to the potential of ecosystems, especially forests, to take up (sequester) additional carbon and hence mitigate climate change. Unfortunately, this process is disrupted when natural ecosystems are converted for agricultural use. This releases much of the carbon stored in plants and soil, and also alters the physical and biological effects of the landscape on the climate (Bala *et al.*, 2007).

Some of these effects warm the climate, whilst others cool it. The high albedo (reflectivity) of grassland and deserts plays a role in atmospheric cooling (Hansen *et al.*, 1998; Thompson, 1998). High rates of evapotranspiration (release of water into the atmosphere) from tropical forest reduce surface air temperature and increase rainfall (Bonan, 2008). The structure of vegetation also influences the regional climate.

The marine environment also has a key role in climate regulation. The oceans store and conduct heat, while ocean chemistry is important in regulating carbon uptake (IPCC, 2007; Reid *et al.*, 2009).

Restoration of terrestrial and marine ecosystems therefore protects and enhances the climate regulating services of ecosystems as well as the carbon stocks that aid climate change mitigation.

Encourage any process, activity or mechanism that removes a greenhouse gas, an aerosol or a precursor of a greenhouse gas or aerosol from the atmosphere (IPCC 2007c).

Ecosystems are currently carbon sinks (they store more carbon than they lose). The IPCC Fourth Assessment Report (AR4) suggests that the size of the terrestrial sink is approximately 0.5–1.5 GtC per year while the marine sink is approximately 1.8–2.6 GtC per year (IPCC, 2007). However, land use change and degradation damages the terrestrial sink as well as generating carbon emissions (Ong, 1993; Anser *et al.*, 2005; Eliasch, 2008; Lal, 2008).

Ecosystem restoration can therefore play a role in mitigating climate change, mainly through increasing carbon sequestration and storage.

Wetlands and peat lands are rich in carbon. Peat lands, although forming only 3% of the world's land surface, contain 30% of all global soil carbon (Parish *et al.*, 2008). Large areas of wetland and peat land have been drained or disturbed, releasing CO_2 into the atmosphere. Restoration could reverse this process and prove to be a low-cost greenhouse gas mitigation strategy (IPCC, 2007), though restoration of much degraded areas can be a slow process (Lal, 2008). Restoration of wetlands can therefore increase carbon storage as well as maintaining other climate regulation services.

How to mitigate climate change: The role of natural ecosystems

Brown carbon: Carbon generated from industrial emissions of greenhouse gasses that affect the climate.

Green carbon: Carbon stored in terrestrial ecosystems, e.g. plant biomass, soils, wetlands and pasture.

Blue carbon: Carbon bound in the world's oceans. An estimated 55% of all carbon in living organisms is stored in mangroves, marshes, sea grasses, coral reefs and macro-algae.

Black carbon: Formed through incomplete combustion of fuels and may be significantly reduced if clean burning technologies are employed.

7.7 ACTION PLANS

Action plans are needed to ensure that biodiversity's shortcomings are addressed and to monitor progress in this regard. This is also necessary to commit to a target and to ensure that action will take place. With an action plan in place there will be a record available of what has been done and what still needs to be done. Suggested action plans are discussed below.

7.7.1 Habitat action plan

As mentioned previously, habitat destruction is a major threat to biodiversity. The following is a template to be used to conduct a habitat action plan:

HABITAT ACTION PLAN *(forest, grassland, savannah, bush veld, wetland, flood plain marsh area, peat land, river system, dam, pond, ridge, mountain)*

Current status and condition

1. Biological status
   - Soils.
   - Topographic features.
   - Geology.
   - Typical management principals.
   - Definition of habitat.
   - Climates.
   - Coverage.
   - Estimate remaining habitat.
   - Flora.
   - Fauna.
   - Number of scarce or declining species for which it provides a feeding and breeding habitat.
   - Contribution it makes to local biodiversity.

2. Links with other action plans
   - Priority species.
   - Special operations.
   - Projects.
   - Research.

Current factors affecting the habitat

- Reduced quality and quantity of habitat.
- Increased risk of species extinctions.
- Horticultural and agricultural intensification by use of fertilisers, herbicides and pesticides, re-seeding or commercialisation of open spaces.

- Pollution and waste (residential and industrial).
- Overgrazing, trampling, supplementary feeding and long-term nutrient enrichment.
- Development activities such as mineral and rock extraction, road building, power lines, housing, and landfill.
- Localised forestations with hardwoods and softwoods.
- Recreational pressure bringing about floristic changes associated with soil compaction at some key sites.
- Invasion by non-native plants.
- Atmospheric pollution and climate change.

Current action

1. Legal status
   - Special protection regulations applicable.
   - Priority type.
   - Protection criteria for species for which it provides a feeding and breeding habitat.

2. Management, research and guidance
- Landowners and agreements.
- Incentives to encourage management principals.
- Management plans, policies and guidelines.
- The responsible persons taking account of nature conservation.
- Contributions by NGOs.
- Research projects.

Action plan objectives and targets

- Implementation plan to stop habitat removal.
- Guideline to improve quality and quantity of habitat.
- Project to remove invasive alien species.
- Strategy to prevent climate change.
- Rehabilitation management of habitat.
- Secure favourable condition.
- Attempt to re-establish habitat.

Proposed actions with lead agencies

1. Policy and legislation
- Implement conservation requirements applicable on development schemes.
- Develop and implement strategies to restore habitat, taking into account negative effects of isolation, fragmentation.
- Support initiative habitat conservation in integrated planning processes.
- Consider mechanisms to extend existing habitat.

2. Site safeguard and management
   - Monitor coverage and notify further sites as necessary to fill significant gaps.
   - Prepare and implement management plans (target date).

- Management agreements with non-municipal landowners (site management plans with clear targets and associated priority species).
- Encourage the development of new management techniques where required.
- Contribute to the implementation of relevant species action plans for rare and declining species associated with applicable habitat.

3. Advisory
- Encourage best practise principles.
- Produce guidelines for appropriate methods and approaches to establish applicable habitat.
- Encourage the use and establishment of private and public demonstrations.

4. Networking, benchmarking
- Exposure to demonstrations and visits, other organisations and people that are involved in management of similar habitats.
- Make use of information technology to access applicable data (internet).

5. Research and monitoring
- Online information.
- Undertake vegetation surveys and assessments.
- Formulate rehabilitation targets.
- Review research needs into the conservation and restoration management of the habitat.
- Encourage and support conservation studies on scarce animal and plant taxa associated with the habitat.
- Evaluate the need for impact assessment of development on the habitat.
- Develop and implement appropriate surveillance and monitoring programmes to assess progress toward action plan targets.
- Marketing to promote conservation of the habitat.

6. Communications and publicity
- Seek opportunities to present habitat conservation in the press and popular media.
- Encourage appropriate public access for observation and enjoyment of the habitat.

Costing

Source of funding	Current financial year	Next 5 years

Key references

- Publications.
- Research documentation.

- Action plans.
- Surveys.
- Management plans.
- Reports.

Lead partner(s)

- (Friend groups, main role players).

Local implimentation

- List all local biodiversity action plans (LBAPs) that are applicable to this habitat.

Publication details

- List all applicable publications done for this specific habitat within the municipal area (speeches, presentations, booklets, brochures) and where to get it.

7.7.2   Species action plan

A species action plan is needed to have a strategy in place on how you aim to manage a species for a specific habitat, combinations of habitats, region or urban nature areas within a local authority. The following is a template to be used to conduct a species action plan:

SPECIES ACTION PLAN *(example the Otter Lutra lutra)*

Current status and condition

- Current distribution (locations and numbers).
- Threatened status.

Current factors affecting the species

- Pollution.
- Insufficient prey.
- Habitat.
- Incidental mortality.

Current action

- Framework for species conservation.
- Surveys been conducted (amount and intervals).
- Research (what has been done and what needs to be done).

- Conservation management procedures (example: provide logs in river catchments for the otter).
- Management of the habitat suitable for this species.
- Management guidelines of best practise principals.
- Any project current running to enhance the species.

Action plan objectives and targets

- Maintain existing populations.
- Expand existing populations.
- Relocate species to habitat previously occupied by species.

Proposed actions with lead agencies

1. Policy and legislation
   - Agreements on species conservation.
   - Incentive scheme for species.
   - Current legislation on species.
   - Identify and resolve problems with existing legislation.

2. Site safeguard and management
   - Habitat action plans for species.
   - Relocate species under guidelines set out in conservation framework.
   - Attempt to limit accidental killing or injury of species, particularly on key habitat issues.

3. Advisory
   - Ensure the provision of information on species requirements and conservation to key populations.
   - Advice to landowners, role players and interested parties.

4. Future research and monitoring
   - Collect information on species.
   - Analyse problems.
   - Investigate the effects of disturbance of populations.
   - Develop and implement methods to estimate species numbers and permit population modelling.
   - Monitor populations and distribution of species.
   - Implement and update database for species.
   - Develop a methodology for identifying suitable habitat and produce guidelines for the protection and creation of habitat.

5. Communications and publicity
   - Use this species to publicise the importance of habitats to biodiversity.

6. Links with other action plans
   - List links if available.

Lead partner(s)

- Friend groups, main role players.

Local implimentation

- List all local biodiversity action plans (LBAPs) that are applicable to this species.

Publication details

- List all applicable publications done for this specific species within the municipal area (speeches, presentations, booklets, brochures) and where to get it.

CHAPTER 8

ALIEN INVASIVE PLANTS

(This chapter supplies information on alien invasive plants, invader species and control methods to use. Different categories of alien plants are explained and why their threats are so important.)

8.1   INTRODUCTION

As mentioned in Chapter 7, alien invasive species are the fifth biggest threat to our environment. This chapter focuses on plant species and most of the wrongdoings emanating from the urban environment where alien plants were introduced, often accidentally and not on purpose.

Invasive plants usually originate from a foreign country and were usually introduced with good intentions. Unfortunately, many alien plants have the ability to distribute themselves among indigenous vegetation to such an extent that they take over all growth. Such plants can be trees, shrubs, weeds or aquatic plants. They are called invaders because of their ability to crowd out indigenous vegetation in a very aggressive manner. Once invasion has taken place, the affected land is not easily rehabilitated. The only solution is to identify alien invasive species, know how to control the problems they cause and which alternative plants to use.

I want to use South Africa as an example.

Invaders in South Africa originate from the following countries:
11 species from Australia.
7   species from South America.
4   species from Central America.
3   species from southern Europe.
1   species from North America.

69% of invaders in South Africa originate from Australia and South America because of the similarity of ecological habitat with South Africa.

8.2   WHY PEOPLE IMPORTED THESE PLANTS

Early pioneers often wanted plants they were used to and brought plant material from their home countries with them. They tried to simulate their home environments by planting familiar trees and shrubs in their new country. There was of course, a lack in knowledge about the indigenous vegetation and its possible usage.

It is a pity to mention that most of these actions were conducted by botanical gardens as well as plant specialists. Most of this vegetation was promoted by missionaries. Botanical gardens cultivated exotic species to be used on floating sand, sand that was blown away by wind and also plants that were used in the tannery industries (wattle species).

The distribution of exotic seeds and plants to the public was an important practise from the state forestry in the 1880s. This spread large amounts of potential invaders all over the country and today, most of them are regarded as aggressive invaders. These plants were chosen because of their ability to grow fast and their successful adaptation to the new climate.

8.3 WHY INVADER PLANTS ARE SO SUCCESSFUL

All plants depend on water, sun, light and minerals (elements for survival). Each habitat (the environment they live in) has a different combination of these elements to which plants adapt. There is a constant competition between plants for these elements to survive. Plants that have the ability to compete successfully and adapt well to changing environments can invade existing vegetation.

Encroach is when a plant species starts to grow in a population where it never grew before.

Invasion is when a plant species starts taking over a population where it never grew before.

Competition is where elements for survival are not enough to sustain all the vegetation and plants start to compete against each other for these elements.

The ability to compete with other plants depends on negative biological factors (insect damages and diseases), natural resources (water, sun, light and minerals), and the success rate to utilise these resources.

Competition between plants of the same species is intensive because their competition is at the same time, in the same ground levels and air levels for the same resources. Competition between plants of different species is more complex. In undisturbed veld, different plant species utilise the resources at different times, in different ground levels and air levels.

When you introduce invaders into a complex plant population, it will disturb the balance and can lead to a situation where the invader takes over the plant population. This eventually results in the replacement of indigenous plant populations and plant diversity is reduced to a homogeneous plant population of invaders.

Invaders from indigenous plants are different and are normally the result of poor management practices (agriculture). When indigenous species take over a plant population, it is normally because of a disturbance of the natural vegetation due to mismanagement. These types of invaders (indigenous species) will not happen in undisturbed veld conditions. Invaders from other countries will take over disturbed as well as undisturbed veld conditions.

The most important reason for the success of invaders is because they have adapted to their new environment without the strains of their natural enemies that were left behind in their country of origin. Invaders therefore live in a healthier condition compared to the indigenous plants they compete with. They can grow more aggressively and reproduce better while the indigenous species have to fight diseases, insects, grazing and other predators.

8.4   CONTROL OF INVADER PLANT SPECIES

The legislation stresses that, when land users control plants that occur in areas where they are not allowed, appropriate control methods should be used for the species concerned as well as the ecosystem in which they occur. One or a combination of the following control methods may be used: uprooting, felling, cutting, burning, treatment with registered herbicides, biological control or any other recognised and appropriate method. Repetitive follow-up actions are mandatory until the required control has been achieved.

The aim of control is to reach a point where, ideally, the plants concerned no longer occur in that particular area or, at least, where the plants can no longer grow, produce viable seeds or spores, coppice, sprout or produce root suckers, reproduce vegetative, propagate themselves in any other way, or spread into other areas. If this is not possible, the plants must be contained and their multiplication limited as far as possible.

When controlling weeds and invaders, damage to the environment has to be limited to the minimum. Sometimes rehabilitation methods could be necessary to protect the soil and enhance the recovery of natural vegetation.

Control can be done mechanically, chemically or biologically. The method preference depends on many factors like the size of the plant, the age, the ability to reproduce, the type of environment, the season and also the availability of labour and capacity to implement.

8.4.1   Chemical control

Although chemicals are available to treat almost any invader, their use is not always possible. The ideal method is to do selective plant control. This is when a chemical will only affect the target species and no other adjacent species

In South Africa, the use of chemicals is controlled by law. Each chemical must be tested and will then be registered for that specific species before it will be recommended.

8.4.2 Mechanical control

The removal of invaders by mechanical efforts, for example, axes, cutting, burning, ground clearance by machinery, etc. Plants that have been chopped down require special attention because of their regrowth potential (roots, seeds, etc.). Mechanical methods can include the following:
*   Pulling out by hand.
*   Digging out with shovels.

Control of invasive species: a, chemical control; b, Stem treatment; c, mechanical control.

- Removing the bark of a tree (at the bottom above the ground to prevent the transportation of water and nutrients).
- Cutting of trees as close as possible to the ground.
- Cutting of trees below ground level.
- Cutting of trees and doing stump chemical treatment and burning.

8.4.3   Biological control

Biological control is the use of host-specific natural enemies (such as insects and disease occurring micro-organisms) to reduce the invasiveness of alien plants. It may only be initiated by and carried out under the supervision of an academic or research institute or organisation established by legislation, which practises and researches biological control of weeds and invader plants.

Scientists first test these natural enemies from the plant's country of origin under quarantine conditions to ensure that they will not damage crops and indigenous plants in South Africa before they are released.

8.4.4   Important information regarding control of alien invasive plant species

In South Africa, the import of new plant species are controlled by law since 1947. It is illegal to import any plant species from another country without an import permit.

Biological control.

Unfortunately, plant collectors, gardeners, and other people still smuggle alien species into the country.

8.5   HOW TO HELP CONTROL INVADER PLANT SPECIES

- Know how to identify alien invasive plant species.
- Familiarise yourself with the legislation and ensure that others know what the implications are of harbouring declared weeds and invader plants.
- If you manage your own land, keep it clear of invasive alien plants. Do not plant exotic vegetation. Try to plant indigenous and better endemic species in your garden.
- Tell family and friends about the problems and threats posed by invasive alien plants.
- Do not buy invasive alien plants from nurseries. Boycott and report those that stock them. Help nurseries to promote indigenous and endemic vegetation.
- Consult a professional for advice on clearing methods for alien invasive species.
- Do not bring foreign plants or animals into our country and do not send or take our plants and animals to other countries.
- Respect quarantine requirements where applicable.

8.6   SOUTH AFRICA'S LEGISLATION ON ALIEN INVASIVE PLANTS
(Conservation of Agricultural Resources Act 43 of 1983 – CARA).

The legislation makes provision for **four** groups. The first three groups consist of undesirable alien plants:
- 122 species of declared weeds under Category 1.
- 76 species of plant invaders under Category 2.
- 39 species of dangerous plants under Category 3.

Indicators of bush encroachment, which are indigenous plants that require sound management practices to prevent them from becoming problematic , are listed in the fourth group.

8.6.1   Category 1 plants, or declared weeds

These are prohibited plants that will no longer be tolerated on land or on water surfaces, neither in rural or urban areas. These plants may no longer be planted or propagated, and all trade in their seeds, cuttings or other propagative material is prohibited. They may not be transported or allowed to disperse. Plant species were included in this list because their harmfulness outweighs any useful properties they might have. Some of their harmful qualities might be that they pose a serious health risk to humans or livestock, cause serious financial losses to land users, are able to invade undisturbed environments and transform or degrade natural plant communities, use more water than the plant communities they replace or are particularly difficult to control.

Most of the plants in this category produce copious seed quantities which are dispersed by wind or birds, or have highly efficient means of vegetative reproduction. Some of these plants were introduced inadvertently, have no obvious function to fulfil in South Africa and are generally regarded as undesirable and some of them are **popular garden or landscaping plants**.

Examples:
- Trees or shrubs (several Australian species like wattle, lantana, cat`s claw creeper, ornamental granadilla-species, yellow bells, etc.)
- Succulents (queen of the night, various cactus species, etc.)
- Herbaceous plants (moth catcher, Mexican poppy species, pom-pom weed, dodder species, wild tomato, etc.)
- Grasses or reeds (Spanish reed, feathertop, etc.)
- Aquatic plants (red water fern, water hyacinth, water lettuce, etc.)

Cat`s Claw (*Macfadyena unguis-cati*).

Gaint reed (*Arundo donax*).

Queen of the Night (*Cereus jamacarca*).

Pom-pom weed (*Campuloclinium macrocephalum*).

Yellow Bells (*Tecoma stans*).

Bugweed (*Solanum mauritianum*).

Lantana (*Lantana camara*).

Yellow Oleander (*Thevetia peruviana*).

Oleander (*Nerium oleander*) (Selonsroos).

Aquatic invasive species: a, Water fern (*Azolla*); b, Water Hyacinth (*Eichhornia crassipes*).

8.6.2 Category 2 plant invaders (commercial value)

These are plants with proven potential to become invasive, but which nevertheless have certain beneficial properties that warrants their continued presence under certain circumstances. Provision is made for Category 2 plants to be retained in special areas demarcated for that purpose, but those occurring outside demarcated areas have to be controlled.

The growing of Category 2 plants in a demarcated area qualifies as a water use, and is subject to the requirements of Section 21 of the National Water Act. According to this act, the land user need to obtain a water use license if the demarcated area is 1 hectare or larger and used for commercial purposes. The plants in a demarcated area have to primarily serve a commercial or utility purpose, such as a woodlot, shelter belt, building material, animal fodder, and soil stabilisation, medicinal or consumption. These conditions under which they are cultivated have to be controlled. All reasonable steps have to be taken to curtail the spreading of seeds or vegetative reproducing material outside the demarcated area. All specimens outside the demarcated area have to be controlled.

Seed or other propagative material of Category 2 plants may only be sold to and acquired by land users of areas demarcated for the growing of that species, or for the establishment of a bio-controlled reserve. Category 2 plants may not occur within 30 m from the 1:50 year flood line of watercourses or wetlands unless authorisation has been obtained in terms of the South Africa National Water Act.

Examples:
- Wattle species, several pine species, white and grey poplars, commercial guava, castor oil plant, weeping and crack willows, etc.

Black Wattle (*Acacia mearnsii*).

Category 2 plant invaders: a, Cluster pine (*Pinus pinaster*); b, Grey Poplar (*Populus canescens*).

8.6.3   Category 3 plant invaders (ornamental value)

These plants are undesirable because they have a proven potential for becoming invasive, but most of them are nevertheless popular ornamentals or shade trees that will take a long time to replace.

Category 3 plants will not be allowed to occur anywhere unless they were already in existence when the legislation came into effect. The conditions that a land user with such plants must adhere to are that they do not grow within 30 m from the 1:50 year flood line of watercourses or wetlands and that all reasonable steps are taken to keep the plant from spreading.

Propagative material of these plants, such as seeds or cuttings, may no longer be planted, propagated, imported, bought, sold or traded in any way. It will, however, be legal to trade in the wood of Category 3 plants, or in other products that do not have the potential to grow or multiply.

Examples:
- Pepper Tree, Jacaranda, Chinese and Pink Tamarisk, etc.

Jacaranda (*Jacaranda mimosifolia*).

Seringa (*Melia azedarach*).

8.7   BUSH ENCROACHMENT

Bush encroachment is a term used for "stands of plants where individual plants are closer to each other than three times the mean crown diameter". Plants in this group are not alien plants, but indigenous plants that tend to become abnormally abundant when the area is degraded because of mismanagement, e.g. overgrazing

Bush encroachment.

or uncontrolled fires. In such circumstances, the land users must remove the cause of deterioration and combat the encroachment of indicator species. Among the prescribed measures are the uprooting, felling or cutting of plants, the controlled application of registered herbicides, livestock reduction and the correct utilisation and protection of veld.

CHAPTER 9

WETLANDS AND WATERCOURSES IN AN URBAN ENVIRONMENT (BLUE NODES AND BLUE WAYS)[1]

(This chapter highlights wetlands and watercourses. The first part explains the hydrology, soils and vegetation of wetlands in the urban environment. The second part raises all issues related to watercourses and the management of watercourses and their associated riparian zones. The chapter ends with a section on zones.)[1]

9.1　　WETLANDS

The differences between wetlands and riparian zones are the following: Riparian zones can be distinguished from adjacent terrestrial areas by observing the presence or absence of a few key indicators. Although very wet riparian areas may display some wetland indicators, in the generally semi-arid climate of southern Africa, riparian zones are usually not saturated long enough for wetland indicators to develop. While wetland vegetation and soils adapt to, and indeed are determined by, prolonged or even permanent periods of saturation, riparian zones are adapted to the physical disturbances due to frequent overbank flooding from the associated river or stream channel.

It is therefore clear that wetlands reflect the very low-energy forms of drainage lines and that riparian areas, on the other hand, are representative of the fast-flowing, higher-energy forms of drainage lines or rivers.

The word "wetland" is a family name given to a variety of ecosystems, ranging from springs, seeps and mires in the upper catchment, to marshes, pans and floodplains and finally coastal lakes, mangrove swamps and estuaries at the bottom of the catchment. These ecosystems all share a common primary driving force: water. Its prolonged presence in wetlands is a fundamental determinant of soil characteristics and the associated plant and animal species composition. Any part of the landscape where water accumulates for long enough and often enough to influence the soils, plants and animals occurring in that area, is therefore regarded as a wetland.

---

[1] Most of the information on wetlands refers to: COLLINS, N.B. 2005. Wetlands: The basics and more. Free State Department of Tourism, Environmental and Economic Affairs – South Arica.

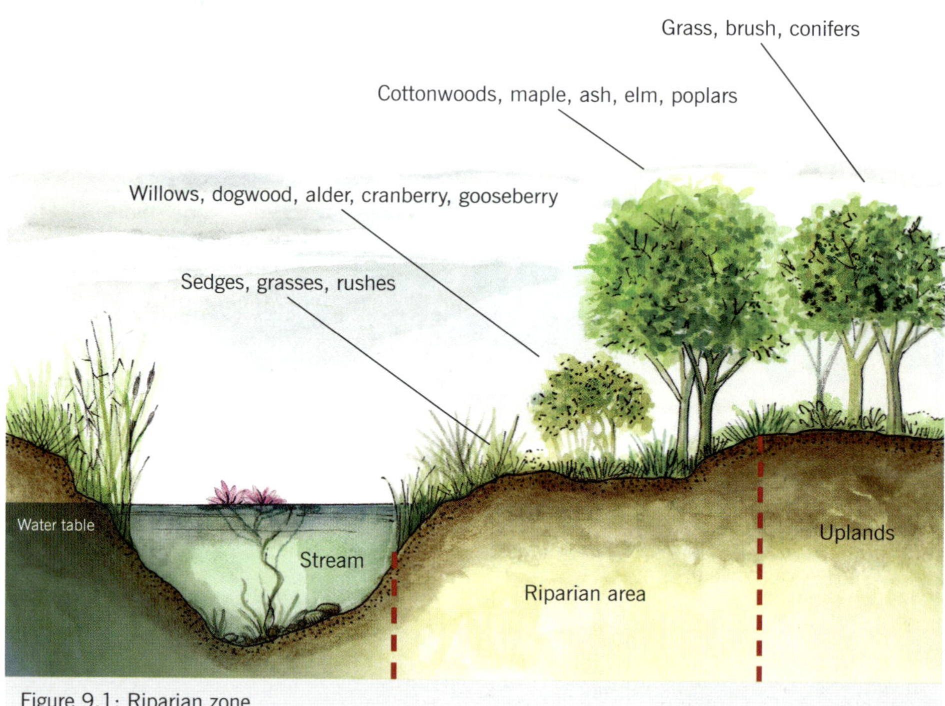

Figure 9.1: Riparian zone.

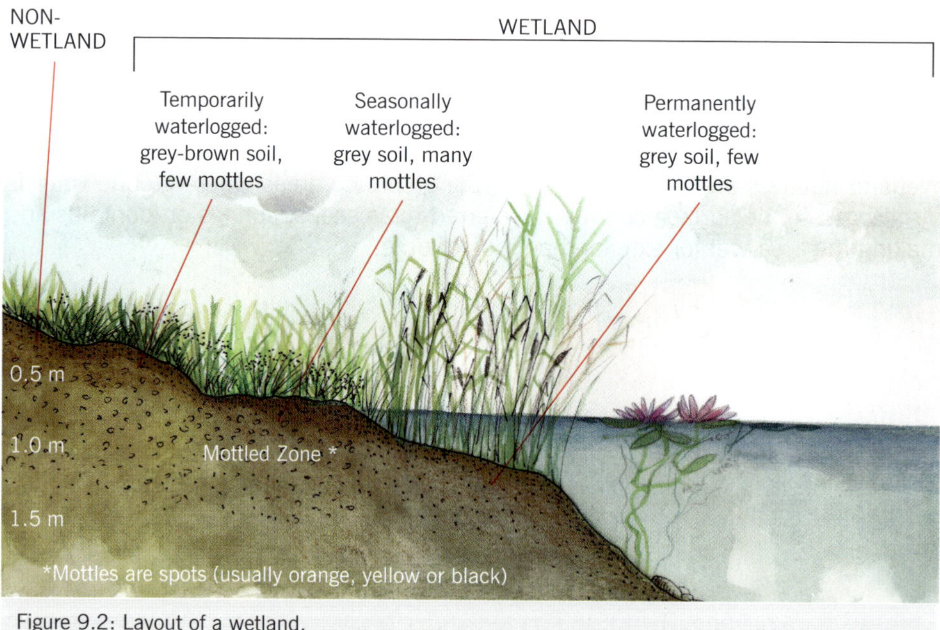

Figure 9.2: Layout of a wetland.

Figure 9.3: Wetland summery.

There is a variety of wetland types. This includes different kinds of habitats where the land is wet for some period of time each year, but not necessarily permanently. The plants in these areas (hydrophytes) are adapted to wet conditions and affects the soil and slowing down the movement of water. It also produces organic matter that accumulates in the soil.

Wetland habitats are associated with ground surface areas where groundwater is discharged to the surface commonly referred to as seeps, springs or fountains and making the area wet for extended periods of time.

A wetland is defined by the South African Water Act as "land which is transitional between terrestrial and aquatic systems where the water table is usually at or near the surface, or the land is periodically covered with shallow water, and which in normal circumstances supports or would support vegetation typically adapted to life in saturated soil."

Land becomes a wetland when saturation takes place long enough to allow the development of hydric soils which can support hydrophyte vegetation.

Hydrology implies that the land is covered by water. Saturated soil is soils containing water for long periods. Hydric soil means that the soil has been depleted of oxygen

Bulrushes.

Bulrushes.

through a reduction process. Reduction is a chemical process of translocation and oxidation of Fe and Mn oxides.

Essential characters of a wetland are:
* Wetland hydrology.
* Hydric soils (the soil becomes anaerobic).
* Hydrophyte vegetation.

Species known to be hydrophytes are e.g. the common reed (*Phragmites australis*) and bulrush (*Typha capensis*).

Requirements for anaerobic soil conditions to form (Richardson and Vepraskas, 2001):
* The soil must contain organic tissue that can be oxidised or decomposed (source of electrons, e-).
* The soil must be saturated or inundated to exclude atmospheric oxygen (O_2).
* An active microbial population that is oxidising (decomposing) the organic tissue.
* The water should be stagnant or moving slowly.

9.1.1   Wetland hydrology

"Wetland hydrology" generally refers to the hydrological characteristics responsible for the existence and ecology of the wetland, which includes the source of the water (precipitation, surface water inflow and groundwater inflow), the way in which the water moves through the wetland (surface flow and subsurface flow) and also the way in which the water exits the wetland (evaporation, surface water outflow and groundwater outflow).

Precipitation: This means rain, sleet or snow falling directly onto the wetland as well as intercepted mist and condensation.

Evapotranspiration: This is water moving from the soil, open water or plant surfaces in the wetland to the atmosphere. It includes transpiration.

Run-off: This is water moving down slope across the land surface, in streams or through shallow layers of the soil into the wetland.

Lateral inflow: This is water moving laterally through the soil from a ditch, river or lake into the wetland. The wetland water table level is lower than that in the issuing water body.

Drainage: This is water moving laterally over land or through the soil from the wetland to a ditch, river or lake. This may be natural or enhanced by artificial drains. The wetland water table level is higher than that in the receiving water body.

Over-bank flow: This is water moving from a ditch, river or lake onto the wetland's surface. The water level in the issuing body is higher than the ground level of the wetland. This can be time dependant, e.g. only during high run-off events (floods).

Outflow: This is water moving from a wetland down slope. This does not include water flowing back to a river after overbank flooding when the river level has dropped.

Pumping: This is water moved between a wetland and a river, lake or ditch by a mechanical pump. Water may be pumped into or out of the wetland. This water transfer mechanism is of particular importance to depression type wetlands (pans) affected by mine discharges.

Spring: This is water issuing from an aquifer onto the surface of a wetland. Often this is associated with the location of an aquiclude beneath the aquifer.

Groundwater discharge: This is water moving vertically upwards into a wetland from an underlying aquifer. The piezometric head/water level of the aquifer is higher than the water level in the wetland. There may or may not be a lower permeability layer between the wetland and the aquifer that could limit water flow.

Groundwater recharge: This is water moving vertically downwards from a wetland to an underlying aquifer. The piezometric head/water level of the aquifer is lower than the water level in the wetland. There may or may not be a lower permeability layer between the wetland and the aquifer that could limit water flow.

Groundwater seepage: This is water moving laterally into a wetland from an adjacent aquifer. There may or may not be a lower permeability layer between the wetland and the aquifer that could limit water flow.

9.1.2   Types of wetlands

Slope wetlands

- Surface water feed (Input from precipitation, surface run-off and possible spring flow. Output by evaporation and surface outflow.)

- Surface and ground water feed (Input from groundwater seepage, precipitation and surface run-off. Groundwater input may be restricted by lower permeability layer. Output by evaporation and surface outflow.)

- Groundwater feed (Input dominated by groundwater seepage, supplemented by precipitation and surface run-off. Output by evaporation and surface outflow.)

Valley bottom wetlands

- Surface water feed (Input dominated by overbank flow and lateral flow, supplemented by precipitation and surface run-off. Output by drainage, surface outflow and evaporation. Inflows and outflows are controlled largely by water level in the river or lake.)

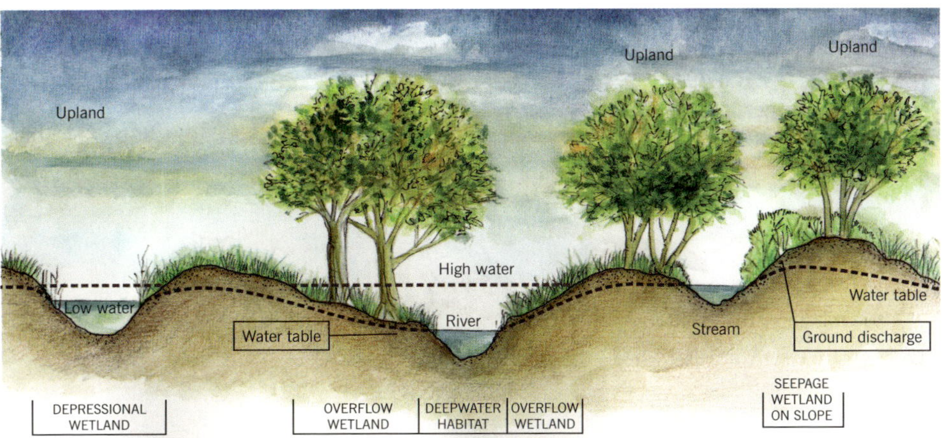

Figure 9.4: Different wetland types.

- Surface and groundwater feed (Input from overbank flow and groundwater discharge, supplemented by run-off and precipitation. Groundwater flow may be restricted by intervening low permeability layer. Output by drainage, surface outflow, evaporation and groundwater recharge.)

- Groundwater feed (Input dominated by over-bank flow and groundwater discharge, when groundwater table is high, supplemented by run-off and precipitation. Output by groundwater recharges when water table is low, drainage, surface outflow and evaporation.)

Depression wetlands

- Surface water feed (Input dominated by precipitation, surface run-off and possible spring flow. Output by evaporation only).

- Surface and groundwater feed (Input from groundwater discharge, when groundwater table is high, precipitation, surface run-off and possibly spring flow. Groundwater input may be restricted by lower permeability layer. Output by evaporation and groundwater recharge when groundwater table low).

- Groundwater feed (Input dominated by groundwater discharge when groundwater table is high, supplemented by precipitation, surface run-off and spring flow. Output by evaporation and groundwater recharges when groundwater table low.)

9.1.3   The water budget

The balance between the inputs and outputs of water in a wetland is called a water budget (or water balance). Quantification of the water budget of a wetland provides information on its hydrological functioning, including flood control and ground water recharge. When the water budget is used as the basis for a hydrological model, the impacts of various developments, such as the building of dams, can be predicted (Acreman, 2000).

Over the long term in a sustainable wetland system, water inputs equal outputs. Over shorter time intervals, however, wetlands may temporarily store and release water. Therefore, the water budget equation also has a storage term (U.S. Army Corps of Engineers, 2004).

The wetland hydro period

The hydro period of a wetland is the result of its water balance, i.e. the changes in water inputs and outputs of the wetland (Cronk & Siobhan Fennessy, 2001). The term hydro period therefore describes the different variations in water input and output that forms a wetland and eventually characterises its ecology.

The hydro period of a wetland significantly affects a number of wetland characteristics, including the vegetative composition and diversity, primary productivity, organic matter accumulation, nutrient cycling and nutrient inflows. Hydro period may be one of the wetland characteristics that are most sensitive to anthropogenic impacts. Wetland ecosystem response to changes in the hydro period may be manifested in major habitat changes (through shifts in vegetation community abundance, diversity, and invasive/opportunistic species occurrence), as well as altered flood storage capacity and altered chemical properties.

What is a hydrophyte?

According to Tiner (1999) a hydrophyte is defined as "an individual plant adapted for life in water or periodically flooded and/or saturated soils (hydric soils) and growing in wetlands and deep-water habitats; it may represent the entire population of a species or only a subset of individuals so adapted".

9.1.4   Wetland plant communities

One of the simplest wetland classification systems, based on a particular set of plant and animal associates that recur, recognises the following types of wetlands (Keddy, 2002):

- **Aquatic**: This refers to a wetland community dominated by truly aquatic plants, growing in and covered by at least 25 cm of water.

- **Marsh**: A frequently or continually inundated wetland characterised by emergent herbaceous vegetation adapted to saturated soil conditions. In European terminology marshes have a mineral soil substrate and do not accumulate peat (Mitch and Gosselink, 2000). Marshes can be subdivided into deep and shallow marshes.

- **Deep marshes**: Deep marsh plant communities have standing water depths of between 15 cm and 1 000 cm or more, during the growing season. Herbaceous emergent, floating-leaved, and submergent vegetation compose this community, with a strong dominance of cattails, bullrush and reeds.

Wetland plant communities.

- **Shallow marshes**: Shallow marsh plant communities have soils that are saturated, inundated, by standing water up to 15 cm deep through most of the growing season. Herbaceous emergent vegetation, such as grasses and sedges, characterise this community.

- **Mire:** A term mainly used in Europe to include any peat-forming wetland (bog, or fen).

- **Bog**: A peat-accumulating wetland that has no significant water inflows or outflows and supports acidophylic mosses, particularly Sphagnum (Mitch and Gosselink, 2000) (usually acidic; pH <7).

- **Fen**: A peat-accumulating wetland that receives some water from surrounding mineral soil and usually supports marsh-like vegetation (Mitch and Gosselink, 2000) (usually alkaline; pH >7).

- **Swamp**: A wetland dominated by trees and shrubs (Mitch and Gosselink, 2000).

- **Wet meadow**: A grassland with waterlogged soil near the surface but without standing water for most of the year (Mitch and Gosselink, 2000).

9.1.5   Why are wetlands important? (Kotzé and Breen, 1994)

Wetlands are important because of the functions and values that they provide which benefit mankind. Until very recently the benefits of wetlands to society were often not recognised, and many wetlands have been destroyed, or poorly managed.

*Wetland **benefits**/goods and services (Kotze et al., 2005).*

Indirect benefits:
- Hydrological (water purification, sustained stream flow, flood reduction, ground-water recharge/discharge, erosion control).
- Biodiversity conservation – integrity and irreplaceability.
- Chemical cycling.

Direct benefits:
- Water supply.
- Provision of harvestable resources.
- Socio-cultural significance.
- Tourism and recreation.
- Education and research.

9.1.5.1   Indirect benefits from wetlands

Flood plains benefits (Wetlands)
- Attenuation and sediment trapping.

- Nitrate and toxicant removal.

- The shallow waters promote sunlight penetration, contributing to the photo-degradation of certain toxicants.

- The accumulation of organic matter and fine sediments in the wetland soils results in the wetland slowing down movement of water. This increases the storage capacity of water, and prolongs the contribution of water to a stream system in the adjacent environment.

- Perform a number of water quality enhancement functions, for example, removing excess nutrients and inorganic pollutants produced by agriculture, industry and domestic waste (Rogers, Rogers and Buzer, 1985 in Kotzé *et al.*, 2005; Green, 1995 in Kotzé *et al.*, 2005; Ewel, 1997 in Kotzé *et al.*, 2005; Postel and Carpenter, 1997 in Kotzé *et al.*, 2005).

- Slow down the velocity of flowing water (because of: (1) the characteristically gentle slopes of wetlands, and (2) the resistance offered by the dense wetland vegetation).

- By slowing down the movement of water and detaining it for a while, wetlands act like sponges, reducing floods and also prolonging stream flow during low flow periods.

- Wetlands are natural filters, helping to purify water by trapping pollutants [i.e. sediments, excess nutrients (especially nitrogen and phosphorus) heavy metals, disease-causing bacteria and viruses, and synthesised organic pollutants such as pesticides]. The water leaving a wetland is therefore often cleaner than the water that entered it.

- Wetlands may have an important influence on the recharge or discharge of groundwater.

*Wetlands are able to **purify water** effectively because:*
- They slow down the flow of water causing sediment carried in the water to be deposited. This also results in the trapping of other pollutants (e.g. phosphorus) which are attached to soil particles.

- Surface water is spread out over a wide area, facilitating exchanges between soil and water.

- There are many different chemical processes taking place in wetlands that remove pollutants from the water.

- Some pollutants such as nitrates (NO_3) are taken up by the rapidly growing wetland plants.

- The abundant organic matter in wetland soils provides suitable surfaces for trapping certain pollutants such as heavy metals.

- Wetlands micro-organisms help decompose man-made organic pollutants, such as pesticides.

Flood reduction

Because of the ability of wetlands to slow down the velocity of flowing water, as well to absorb some of the water within the system, the peaks of floods are often reduced. This implies that instead of all the water flowing down the river in one big flood event, some of the water is held back to be released later, so that the same volume of water flows down the river over a longer period of time. This decreases the peak of the flood, thereby preventing or attenuating potential flooding events.

Sustained stream flow

By acting as sponges, the water that is captured during the rainy season is slowly released during the dry season; this causes rivers and streams to have sustainable flows long after the rain has stopped.

Erosion control by wetland vegetation

Wetland vegetation is generally good at controlling erosion by: (1) reducing wave and current energy; (2) binding and stabilising the soil; and (3) recovering rapidly from flood damage.

Biodiversity

Wetlands are usually places where there is much plant growth because of the abundance of water and nutrients in the soil; the plants, in turn, provide food and shelter for animals. There are many different plants and animals that depend on wetlands for survival. Several of these species, such as the White-winged Flufftail (*Sarothura ayresi*) and Wattled Crane (*Bugeranus carunculatus*) are threatened.

Chemical cycling

In wetlands, the decomposition of organic matter is slowed down by the anaerobic conditions present in wetlands. This results in wetlands trapping carbon as soil

Biodiversity: a, White-wing Flufftail; b, Eurasian Bittern (Photo: David Martin); c, Wattled Crane.

organic matter, instead of releasing it into the atmosphere as carbon dioxide. Presently too much carbon dioxide is being released into the atmosphere when fossil fuels (i.e. coal and oil) are used to produce energy, resulting in the global climate being disrupted. Coal is, in fact, formed from plant material accumulated under wetland conditions in swamps that existed millions of years ago. Thus, instead of destroying wetlands and releasing carbon dioxide into the atmosphere, we should be conserving wetlands and thereby help reduce carbon dioxide levels in the atmosphere.

9.1.5.2　　Direct benefits

Wetlands are used for livestock grazing, fibre for construction and handcraft production, fisheries, hunting waterfowl and other wildlife as well as valuable land for cultivation.

Wetlands are often drained so that plants not adapted to the waterlogged conditions can be grown. This has important environmental impacts, requiring that the cultivation of wetlands be well-controlled.

Some wetlands are used for timber production, but because of the impact that trees have on wetland benefits, strict controls are required.

Wetlands store water and provide sites for the supply of water for domestic and livestock use, as well as for irrigation. The storage capacities of wetlands

Ground Orchid, Western Cape.

Marsh Lilies.

are sometimes increased through damming; however, this often has significant negative effects.

Economically efficient waste water treatment

The fact that wetlands have the ability to clean polluted water has been mentioned. Natural wetlands provide this service to society "free of charge" and are therefore sometimes purposefully used to treat polluted water, while many artificial wetland areas are being created for waste water treatment. Several factors must be considered to assess how effectively a wetland will purify the water:

- The pollutant, the wetland soil, flow patterns, the size of the wetland, and the climate affecting the wetland, all of which determines the capacity of the wetland for purifying the waste water. For example, more pollutants are likely to be trapped in a wetland where the flow is spread out across all of it, than in one where a channel concentrates flow in only part of the wetland. If the pollutants are heavy metals, then a wetland with soils rich in organic matter is likely to be more efficient at trapping heavy metals than one with soils poor in organic matter.

- The amount of pollutant relative to the capacity of the wetland. The capacity of the wetland is obviously limited and if the amount of pollutant greatly exceeds this capacity, the wetland will not effectively purify the water. The impacts of pollutants on the wetland must also be considered.

Aesthetics and the appreciation of nature

Although wetlands which fringe estuaries, rivers and streams are adjacent to open water, the open water is usually limited. They are thus generally not good sites for water sports. However, wetlands are good places to see birds, specifically wetland birds. Wetlands also add to the diversity and beauty of the landscape; they have a diverse range of colours and textures and some very attractive flowers, such as marsh lilies (*Crinum* spp.) and ground orchids.

9.1.6 Wetland degradation and wetland loss

The manner in which we use wetlands and the scale on which we do so, determines the extent of our impact. Uses which provide good economic returns are not necessarily sustainable. Land-use activities (e.g. growing crops or damming water) often affect how a wetland functions, and what benefits it provides to society. In many cases, the effects are negative, such as when a wetland is disturbed in order to plant crops, the wetland's function of trapping sediment and holding the soil is reduced. This reduces the benefits that society receives from the wetland in purifying water and controlling erosion.

Impacts on wetlands result from both "on-site" activities at the wetland site (e.g. drainage, disturbance through cultivation, infilling, and flooding by dams) and from "off-site" activities in the wetland's surrounding catchment (e.g. afforestation, mining and crop production).

9.1.6.1 On-site impacts (Kotzé and Breen, 1994)

- Changes to the flow pattern within the wetland through drainage channels, which causes flow to become more channelled and less diffused, thereby reducing the wetness of the area.

- Disturbances of the soil, making it more susceptible to erosion.

- Changes in the surface roughness and vegetation cover (when these are reduced the ability of the wetland to slow down water flow reduces erosion and purified water is reduced).

- Replacement of the natural vegetation by introduced plants, which generally reduces the value of the wetland for wetland dependent species.

Drainage and the production of crops and planted pastures

When wetlands are converted to croplands, most of their indirect benefits are lost, especially if they are drained. Drained wetlands are less effective at regulating stream flow and purifying water, because the drainage channels speed up the movement of water through the wetland. Drainage increases the danger of erosion by concentrating water flow and thus increasing the erosive power of the water. Also, the hydrological changes resulting from drainage have negative effects on the soil (e.g. reduced soil organic matter and moisture levels and, sometimes, increased risk of underground fires, and increased acidity due to the oxidation of sulphides to produce sulphuric acid).

The soil is disturbed when crops are planted, and crops do not bind or cover the soil as well as the natural wetland vegetation. Thus, erosion is controlled less effectively, which may be a very serious problem in areas with high erosion hazards. Adding fertiliser and pesticides (which may leach into the river system) further reduces the effectiveness of the wetland in purifying water. The impact of cultivation can be reduced if practices characteristic of low input/traditional cultivation are followed.

Traditional cultivation practices are more sensitive to the functioning of the wetlands and include the following:

- Planting crops (e.g. madumbes) which are tolerant of water logging, minimising the need to drain.

- Tillage and harvesting by hand, resulting in less soil compaction and potential disturbance than with mechanical tillage and harvesting.

- Not using pesticides and artificial fertilisers, which reduce the impact on water quality.

- Not planting extensive areas, leaving indigenous vegetation between cultivated patches.

In South Africa, wetlands are protected by, amongst others, the Conservation of Agricultural Resources Act 43 of 1983 (CARA) (administered by the Directorate: Resource Conservation) that prevents land users from cultivating or draining wetlands.

Timber production

Timber plantations have a high impact on the water storage function of wetlands because a lot of water is lost by the trees through transpiration. Some trees (e.g. *Eucalyptus* spp.) use more water than other trees (e.g. poplars, which lose their leaves in winter). Trees also have a strong negative effect on the habitat values of wetlands. With increased shading beneath the trees, the vigour of indigenous plants which are not adapted to these conditions is reduced and they are often out-competed by alien invasive plants. In South Africa, there is a law (Section 75 of the Forestry Act No. 122 of 1986) which prevents the planting of wetlands with timber.

Grazing of undeveloped wetlands by domestic stock

Grazing may have both positive and negative effects on the indirect benefits of wetlands. In wetlands which have some areas grazed short and other areas left tall, the diversity of habitats is increased; however, those which are completely grazed have decreased habitat diversity.

Heavy grazing may cause valuable grazing species to be replaced by less productive and/or palatable species. Some wetlands erode easily when disturbed by trampling and grazing. The most easily eroded are those wetlands with unstable soil and where water flowing diffusely across the wetland, concentrates into a channel. In these situations, erosion can cause the channel to cut into the wetland and dry it out, destroying most of its functions and values. Thus, grazing pressure should not be too high and cattle need to be kept away from these areas of flow concentration.

Burning

Wetlands are burned for many reasons: to improve the grazing value for livestock by removing old dead material and increase productivity; to improve the habitats value for wetland dependent species; to assist in alien plant control; and to reduce the risk of run-away fires.

Wetland fires usually burn above-ground plant parts and most plants recover rapidly from this. Some fires also burn soil and plant parts below the ground, which usually destroys the plants. This generally detracts from the values of the wetland (e.g. by increasing the risk of erosion).

However, by burning away the upper soil layers, open water areas may be created, which may enhance the diversity of the wetland.

While burning has short term impacts such as killing some animals which are not able to escape, it also has many positive effects (e.g. controlling alien plants and increasing the productivity of the indigenous plants, which may increase the breeding success of certain wetland dependent animals). Whether or not the overall effect will be positive or negative depends on many factors including: timing, frequency and extent of the fire, and the type of fire (determined by conditions at the time of the fire, such as humidity and air temperature). Late winter burning is least likely to impact on breeding animals, as very few species are likely to be breeding at this time, while early winter or summer burns are more likely to affect breeding animals.

It appears that in the high rainfall areas of South Africa, a fire every second year is unlikely to have a negative effect on known wetland dependent species. However, when a wetland area is burnt, it is important that unburnt areas are present nearby where animals can seek cover while the burnt area is re-growing.

Back fires (burning against the wind) tend to have a greater impact on the growing points of plants than head fires (burning with the wind). Burning when humidity is high and air temperature low generally has a lower impact than burning when humidity is low and air temperature high.

It is generally not recommended to burn a wetland on purpose (high risk practise). If a wetland has dried out (because of channelisation) and it starts burning, the fire will go down into the dry peat areas (organic material) and will burn like a cigarette until all the organic material is gone. In such cases, it is very difficult to stop the burning process or to try and control it. The burning of dry peat will cause the destruction and loss of the wetland. The only way to rehabilitate such wetlands is to stop the channelisation that took place, spread the water flow over the whole wetland area and give it time to re-instate its functioning. This can be a long process and may take many years to achieve.

Damming

Many wetlands in South Africa have been flooded by dams, as wetlands are often found in places which are ideal dam sites. Dams do fulfil certain wetland functions (e.g. sediment trapping and water storage) but they do not perform all of the other wetland functions as well. The habitat required by specialised wetland dependent species is frequently lost when a wetland is dammed. The vegetation which develops around the shoreline is limited in many dams by sudden fluctuations in the water level and the steep sides of the dam.

When a series of dams occurs along a stream, the cumulative effect that the dams have in reducing the stream flow may be considerable, particularly where water is pumped out of the dams.

Purification of wastewater

Using a wetland to purify wastewater will affect the functioning of the wetland and may cause a loss of some of its other benefits, particularly if the pollutant loadings are close to, or greater than, the capacity of the wetland for purification. For example, under increased nutrient inputs, the Bulrush *(Typha capensis),* a very common wetland species that competes well under nutrient-rich conditions, may out-compete and eliminate less common wetland species – this would reduce the diversity of the wetland. Standards have been set by the South Africa Department of Water Affairs and Forestry for the discharge of wastewater into streams and these should not be exceeded.

9.1.6.2   Off-site impacts (Kotzé and Breen, 1994)

Most of the water in a wetland originates from the catchment surrounding the wetland. Therefore wetlands are strongly influenced by activities in the surrounding catchment, even when they are distant from the wetland. When assessing the impacts of off-site land uses on wetlands, one must consider how the land uses change the hydro period of the wetland and how this, in turn, affects the functioning and benefits of the wetland.

Irrigation and afforestation is two of the surrounding areas of a wetland that needs attention. As a general rule, trees use more water than natural grassland. Gum trees use the most water (sometimes increasing water loss by more than twice that of natural grassland), followed by wattle and pine trees. Sugarcane also increases water loss. The extra water used by trees, sugarcane or any other crop that has a high transpiration rate means that this no longer reaches the wetland.

There are several land uses that may affect the quality of run-off water that reaches a wetland area, including:
* Mining.
* Intensive animal production.
* Sewerage works.
* Industries.
* Crop production.
* Poorly managed grazing lands.
* Human settlements with inadequate sanitation.

Run-offs from mines typically have high pollutant levels. For example, iron sulphate-bearing rocks dug up to mine coal are exposed to oxygen and water, which produces sulphuric acid and under these acidic conditions, metals such as manganese and zinc become more soluble and may reach toxic concentrations. Wastewaters from many industries also have high levels of a wide range of pollutants. Wastewaters from intensive animal production operations and sewerage works typically have high levels of nutrients and disease-causing bacteria and viruses.

By law, water from point sources has to meet certain water quality standards set by the South Africa Department of Water Affairs and Forestry. However, in many cases, even though wastewaters receive some treatment before being allowed to continue down the catchment, the water quality standards are not met.

Human settlements without adequate sanitation usually produce pollutants consisting of nutrients and disease-causing bacteria and viruses. These pollutants can either get washed into the wetland by surface run-off, or seep into the groundwater, which ultimately ends up in the wetland.

Roads are often constructed through wetlands, thereby dividing them and changing their nature. In addition, the run-off from roads may create unexpected water movement or erosion some distance from the roads, thereby leading to unanticipated impacts on wetlands.

In the urban environment the impact of run-off water from storm water increases at the same rate as development increases. This is because more hard surfaces are established by the construction of roads, buildings, parking areas pavements, etc. With more hard surfaces, less water infiltrates into the ground. This increases erosion and underground water levels drop. Normally this excess run-off water lands up in the nearby urban streams, rivers or storm water channels. High water levels and the risk of floods increase in the urban environment. Storm water engineers want these levels to decrease as quickly as possible so they channelise water courses. It will solve immediate flooding threats in the short term, but over time it hinders water conservation, the banking of underground water for future usage and the purification of the run-off water. Uncontrolled storm water always has a negative impact downstream in the rural areas adjacent to the cities or towns.

A wetland (either if it is natural or artificially created) can serve as a flood attenuation structure in the storm water system. Firstly, it will not create an obstruction (the wetland vegetation bends down to ground level during a flood situation and forms the ideal surface for masses off water to run over it). After the flood, the vegetation bends upward and continues to grow. Secondly, the wetland slows down the speed of the water flow and spreads the water over a greater surface area. When this happens, water can penetrate the ground surfaces. Thirdly, the sediment and heavy particles in the storm water can drop down to the surface where the reed bed can absorb heavy metals, etc. Lastly, with the water captured in the wetland, the purifying process begins to clean the water. This water is then released slowly long after the flood situation occurred and it is purified for downstream usage.

It is important to determine the flood lines during town planning processes and to make enough provision for wetlands as well as creating artificial wetlands. These blue nodes are the kidneys of the city or town and are essential to clean the town from pollution and possible diseases. Open, wet, saturated green areas in the city should be kept as such and not dried up for the purpose of development (planting blue gum trees to get rid of excessive water levels, etc.). This normally happens if a wetland is artificially drained and losing many of its benefits to society. Natural flood lines expand as development increases because of increased run-off water. Under no circumstances must any development be allowed below the determined 1:50 year or even 1:100 year flood lines (under urban development conditions).

9.1.7   Conclusion

We have seen that functioning wetlands may have many benefits to society. Some of these benefits, particularly the indirect benefits, are not obvious and can be easily overlooked. This is partly why many of the wetlands in South Africa have been destroyed through development and degradation. If wetland activities are not positively influenced, the results could be very serious. In a water-poor country such as South Africa, continued destruction of wetlands will result in:

- Lower agricultural productivity.
- Less potable water.
- Less reliable water supplies.
- Increased downstream flooding.
- Increasingly threatened plant and animal resources.

9.1.7.1   Recommended wetland inputs to ensure effective policies

- To prohibit any activities that will detract from the ability of a wetland to perform or deliver upon its inherent functions and values. In instances where such impacts cannot be avoided, the functions and values to be lost must be mitigated for, through off-site mitigation. This goal also implies preventing further degradation of wetlands.

- Priority catchments must be identified and the extent of wetland loss within these must be determined. Strategies to prevent further function loss through wetland loss and degradation must be sought and implemented.

- Government and non-government organisations must be made aware of the functions and values of wetlands and how different land uses and disturbances negatively impact upon these. Such departments must be made aware of the constraints and the opportunities that wetlands could impose and how these should be dealt with.

- An inventory of wetlands must be compiled. The spatial information must be supplemented by the appropriate attribute data, to allow for the compilation of a list of wetlands of importance. Such wetlands should be assigned the appropriate classification (e.g. Ramsar status) and measures to secure these wetlands must be put into place.

- Collaborate with relevant stakeholders to identify different land uses and activities that are compatible with wetland conservation. Encourage and support the implementation of such practices.

Wetlands are superb habitats for birds, especially water birds. It also accommodates smaller mammals and creates grazing for bigger antelope like buffalo, eland, hippo, etc. The saturated water levels enable wetlands to stay green throughout the natural dry winter periods and therefore serve as a food bank during these periods. It is during these times that the wetlands are harvested, channels are opened up and excessive vegetation is removed.

Birds use wetlands for shelter, to feed on and to breed in. In the urban environment, a wetland not only cleans run-off water but can be the ultimate spot for outdoor leisure activities like bird watching. A bird hide overlooking a wetland give visitors access to the biodiversity it contributes to.

Wetlands can be compared to underground dams where the open water levels are so shallow that vegetation can grow in it. This way of banking water is a very effective natural system and can easily sustain itself.

All of us need help to establish nature reserves in wetlands and to promote training in the fields of wetland research, management and warding.

9.2   WATERCOURSES

Watercourse ecosystems all share a common primary driving force: Water. They process water and regulate run-off with the aim of protecting and regulating the water resource.

Wetlands within the watercourse systems act as giant sponges, to hold back water during floods and release it during dry periods. Wetlands furthermore regulate water flow during floods, reduce flood damage, help prevent soil erosion, recharge groundwater sources and remove pollutants from water.

Besides performing these vital functions at very little financial cost, watercourse ecosystems, are also natural storehouses of biological diversity, providing life support for a wide variety of species, some of which are totally reliant on wetlands for their survival. Many of these species are used for food, craft manufacture, medicines, building material and fuel, both for subsistence and commercially.

Within watercourses, a river or stream typology consists of several distinct zones. These zones – riverine, riparian and terrestrial – have specific individual characteristics and functions, but collectively function as an integrated system where the slightest change in the environment will have an impact on the watercourse's ability to provide its environmental goods and services. The appropriate management and conservation of these zones are therefore important. Riverine includes the actual water body (vegetation growing in the water, floating vegetation and living organisms

Healthy river

Canopy –
Shade from trees help keep water cool.

Complexity –
Fallen trees attract insects and create waysides for fish.

Shrubs, trees –
Plants along river banks holds of silt and pollutants.

Damaged river

No trees –
sun can heat up the water.

No shrubs –
Allows more polluted runoff to enter the river, adding fertilizer, pesticides, oil and silt.

Pipes –
Pollutants from treated sewage to industrial stormwater, go directly into the water.

Pumps –
Farms that tap river water lower stream levels, increasing water temperatures.

Figure 9.5: The difference between a healty river and a damaged river.

in the water body). Riparian includes the shoreline adjacent to the waterbed (sedges, grasses, herbs and bulbs, woody shrubs and trees). Terrestrial zones include all vegetation adjacent to the riparian shoreline, a distance away from the waterbed (1:50 + 1:100 year's flood line).

Together with the ridge ecosystems, the watercourse ecosystems are the two most important structural elements within a city or town. The watercourse systems can stretch over major distances and form important ecological linkages throughout the urban environment.

In an urban environment, not all of the watercourse systems are pristine in terms of their vegetation and physical form. However, they still provide vital environmental goods and services in providing habitats, acting as filtering systems and improving water quality.

Increased development pressure, especially on the terrestrial and riparian zones of rivers and streams, engineering focused on storm water management, poor sewerage management and a general disregard for the ecological functioning of water courses, have led to the degradation of a significant amount of watercourse systems.

All watercourses are part of the blue ways.

Description

Blue ways include all watercourses (rivers and brooks) in the city, irrespective of their character and order. Such areas are defined by natural contour low points and the 1:50 year flood line or 32 m from the centreline of the blue way, whichever is the greatest. It accommodates permanent and perennial water flow and does not include channels and canals constructed purely for storm water purposes.

Value

Blue ways are the most important elements in the provisioning of environmental goods and services, the protection of biodiversity, endangered species and ecological systems, as well as eco-based activity. Therefore blue ways must be conserved.

The value of blue ways is their ability to maintain natural hydrological and ecological cycles, such as conserving valuable aquatic systems, purifying water, recharging water tables and prevent flooding. They also provide drinking and irrigation water needs of the city. Blue ways have a secondary socio-economic function and contribute to aesthetic values.

Character

Natural blue ways consist of ecologically pristine areas with the riverine and riparian zones as ecological focal points. The river/bank must be maintained in its natural setting with a natural flood line. Human intervention must be localised with a minimum footprint. Activities must focus on ecological research, education, conservation of biodiversity and passive recreation. Continuity of movement along rivers such as hiking trails, cycling routes, bird watching, etc. must be facilitated.

Strict control of development and invader species must be practiced and only endemic landscaping allowed.

Cultivated blue ways are characterised by manicured riparian zones as the basis for passive and active recreational activities. Trees must define the edges of the green structure and buildings should weakly define the bigger space. The use of indigenous grass must be promoted at all times.

Urban blue ways have historically been totally transformed. It consists of a linear space with strong edge definition. Here, buildings must focus on the blue way with activities and openings linking onto and interacting with the open space. The interface with other land uses must be a balance between hard and soft to improve ecological functioning.

Rehabilitation of disturbed areas within all blue way character types must be sought at all times.

9.2.1   Actions related to watercourses should be the following

- All watercourses (natural, cultivated and built-up) are strategically important ecological structuring elements within a city or town open space network and should be conserved.

- The primary purpose of watercourses is that of ecological functioning and the rendering of environmental goods and services. Storm water management and sewer management within watercourses must acknowledge and ensure the continued efficient ecological functioning and environmental goods and service rendering of the resource, without compromising its integrity.

- Storm water management and design solutions must be based on ecologically sound principles (water retention, detention, infiltration, quality, re-cycling, etc.) and not only with functional safety aspects in mind. Permission for the discharge of storm water within watercourses must be subjected to proof of adherence to such principles.

- The management of watercourses must aim to maximise ecological functioning and environmental goods and services rendering and therefore the rehabilitation of watercourses must be actively pursued.

- Where rehabilitation of watercourses to their natural state is not feasible, a linear ecological system should be established through open space acquisitioning and appropriate, public development interventions along the watercourse.

- The canalisation, transformation (through artificial linings) and exotic cultivation of watercourses can no longer be allowed.

- Urban agriculture within watercourses should not be supported within the defined 1:100 year flood line area.

- The amendment of the 1:50 year flood line by infilling, should not be supported due to the resulting cumulative negative impacts on riverine and riparian systems.

- No development should be allowed within the 1:50 year flood line.

- Watercourses must be managed as integrated components and may not be segmented or fragmented ecologically, physically and visually as this will compromise ecological functioning, storm water risk management and disaster management. Fragmentation can only be considered where already compromised at existing road crossings.

- All new infrastructure within, over or alongside watercourses must aim to minimise the ecological, physical and visual fragmentation of the watercourse.

- Where an application site contains a watercourse and such a site is planned for development, the application should include such watercourses as an integral part of the development proposal boundaries.

- Any development adjacent to a watercourse (natural, cultivated or built up) will be required to reserve the 1:50 year flood line area or an area that extends 32 m from either side of the centre line of a watercourse (whichever is the greatest) as zoned public open space and transfer such land to the municipality.

- Should a private party wish to participate in the management of zoned public open space watercourses, an alternative service delivery mechanism or partnership can be arranged.

9.2.2   Riparian zones

Riparian zones are described as "the physical structure and associated vegetation of the areas associated with a watercourse which are commonly characterised by alluvial soils, and which are inundated or flooded to an extent and with a frequency sufficient to support vegetation of species with a composition and physical structure distinct from those of adjacent areas."

Riparian means the bank of a watercourse and adjacent land. Where the boundary of the riparian area is undetermined, the riparian area is 32 m or the 1:100 year flood line, whichever is furthest from the water edge.

Riparian zones can be distinguished from adjacent terrestrial areas through their association with the physical structure (banks) of the river or stream, as well as the distinctive structural and compositional vegetation zones between the riparian and upland terrestrial areas.

Unlike wetland areas, riparian zones are usually not saturated long enough for redoxymorphic features to develop. Riparian zones instead develop in response to (and are adapted to) the physical disturbances caused by frequent overbank flooding from the associated river or stream channel.

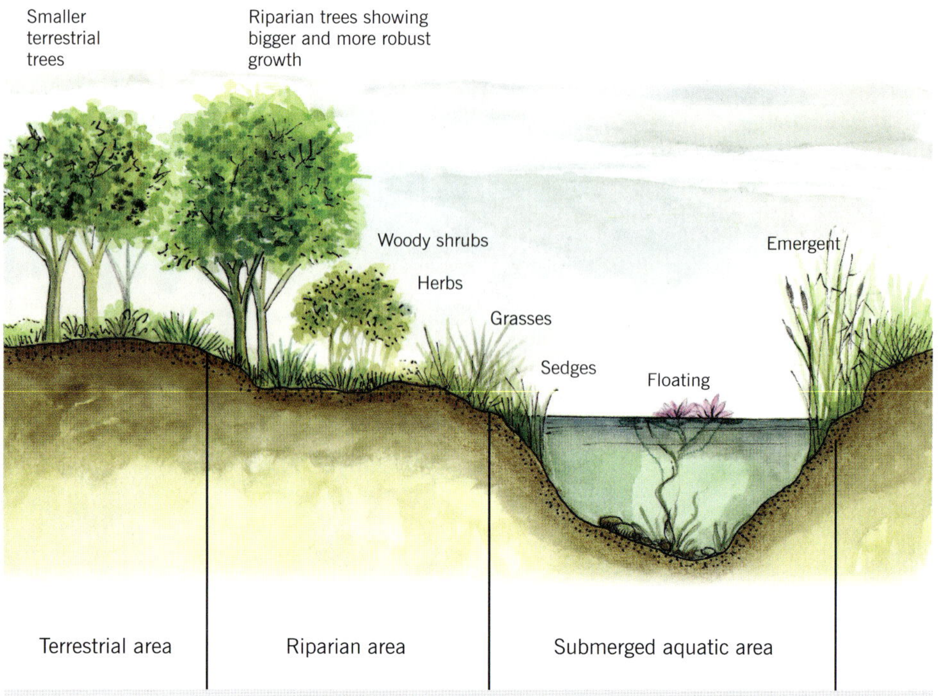

Figure 9.6: Riparian area (Dept Water, Agriculture and Forestry).

The riparian zone is usually small in headwater streams, becoming larger in mid-sized streams where it is likely to form a distinct band of vegetation whose width is determined by long-term (>50 years) channel dynamics and the size of the larger, very infrequent flood discharges. Riparian zones of large streams may form physically complex floodplains with long periods of seasonal flooding, lateral channel migration, oxbow lakes in cut-off channels and an associated diverse vegetative community. In the case of wide floodplains, some wetland elements may also be present (such as oxbow lakes and backwater swamps).

Riparian areas may thus range from a few metres wide adjacent to small stream channels to more than a kilometre wide in floodplains. Both perennial and non-perennial streams support riparian vegetation. Riparian areas represent the interface between aquatic and upland ecosystems so the vegetation in the riparian area may have characteristics of both aquatic and upland habitats. Many of the plants in the riparian area require plenty of water and are adapted to shallow water table conditions. Due to water availability and rich alluvial soils, riparian areas are usually very productive. Tree growth rate is high and the vegetation under the trees is usually lush in comparison to the upland terrestrial vegetation.

Riparian areas perform a variety of valuable functions such as protection and enhancement of water resources and provision of habitat for plant and animal species.

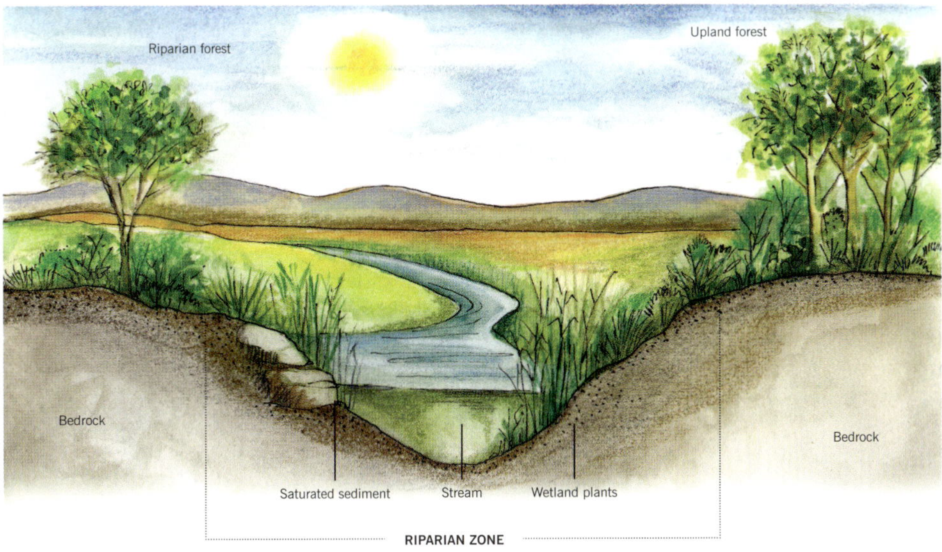

Figure 9.7: Riparian corridor.

Riparian areas can variously:
- Store water and help reduce flood peaks.
- Stabilise stream banks.
- Improve water quality by trapping sediment and nutrients.
- Maintain natural water temperature through shading for aquatic species.
- Provide shelter, food and migration corridors for movement of both aquatic and terrestrial species.
- Act as a buffer between aquatic ecosystems and adjacent upslope land uses.
- Can be used as recreational sites.
- Provide material for building, muti, crafts and curios.

In summary, riverine areas provide the following functions:
- Flood attenuation.
- Sediment trapping.
- Habitat provision.
- Carbon storage.
- Water quality improvement.
- Aesthetic/recreational use.
- Subsistence/cultural use.

9.2.3 Flood attenuation

FISCRWG (1998) explain that the floodplain provides temporary storage space for floodwaters and sediment produced by the catchment. This flood storage capability is called flood attenuation. This attribute serves to add to the lag time of a flood –

the time between the middle of the rainfall event and the run-off peak. If a stream's capacity for moving water and sediment is diminished, or if the sediment loads produced from the catchment become too great for the stream to transport, flooding will occur more frequently and the valley floor will begin to fill (sedimentation and deposition). A reduction in the ability of the stream to attenuate floods will increase the time between the middle of the storm event and the peak run-off. This indicates an increase in velocity of the water in the stream which has more energy and more erosive power and reduces deposition of silt and sediment trapping.

In summary, flood attenuation protects landscapes from flood damage, moderates the velocity of flood waters, reduces high flows and floods and decreases downstream flooding through flood water storage and/or uptake (Forman 1995 in FISRWG 1998: P2-86).

9.2.4   Sediment trapping

"During flooding and regular flow the stream acts as a sediment trap. Sediments include nutrients, contaminants, silt, nitrogen and phosphorus. Dissolved substances such as nitrogen, phosphorus and other nutrients, entering a vegetated stream corridor are restricted from entering the channel by friction, root absorption, clay, and soil organic matters" (FISCRWG, 1998:P2-86).

The Working Group (1998) recognise that suspended sediment plays an important role in water quality, both in the water column and at the sediment-water interface, but fine sediment can also severely alter aquatic communities. Sediment may clog and abrade fish gills, suffocate eggs and aquatic insect larvae on the bottom and fill in the pore space between bottom cobbles where fish lay their eggs. Similarly, sediment interferes with recreational activities and aesthetic enjoyment of water bodies by reducing water clarity and filling in water bodies with deposition. In addition, nutrients and toxic chemicals may attach to the sediment particles on land and wash into surface waters via run-off, where these pollutants may settle with the sediment or dissolve into the water. For example, in Johannesburg, the Klip River wetlands have trapped tonnes of heavy metal toxins from the mine dump run-off. However, the rapidly eroding wetlands are threatening the release of these pollutants back into the Klip River and ultimately the Vaal River – the source of drinking water for Johannesburg.

In summary, sediment trapping provides for the storing and recycling of organic matter and nutrients (Barling and Moore, 1994 in Soman 2007:3) and the removal of nutrients such as nitrogen, phosphorous and sediment from surface and subsurface flow (Lowrance et al., 1985, Hill 1996, USDA-WRCS 1999, in Soman 2007, p3).

9.2.5   Habitat provision

Human-induced impacts on rivers regularly affect the habitat provision, water quality and flood attenuation functions provided by riverine corridors. "In the context of Eco

Classification, habitat is defined as any combination of velocity, depth, substrate (bedrock, cobbles, vegetation, sand, gravel, mud), physicochemical characteristics (such as chemical composition, turbidity, oxygen concentration, temperature) and biological features (food source and predators) that will provide the organism with its requirements for each specific life stage at a particular time and locality. These habitats can be grouped into specific invertebrate biotopes such as Stones-in-current, Stones-out-of-current, Aquatic vegetation (in or out of current), Fringing vegetation (in or out of current)" (WRC, 2008b).

The important role that riparian forests play in stream ecology is often diminished in urban watersheds since tree cover is partially or totally removed along the stream as a consequence of development. Even when stream buffers are reserved, encroachment often reduces their effective width and indigenous species are replaced by alien and invasive trees, shrubs and ground covers. The loss of tree cover and exposure of impervious surfaces, ponds, and poor riparian cover in urban watersheds can increase the average summer stream temperatures by 4°C. Since temperature plays a central role in the rate and timing of living (biotic) and non-living (abiotic) reactions in the stream, such increases have an adverse impact on streams.

Further impacts to habitat integrity include:
- Fragmentation of the lateral and longitudinal connectivity of the channel and upland terrestrial area. This connectivity is an essential link in migration and dispersal of riparian and aquatic organisms and enhances the recovery process following disturbances (Søndergaard and Jeppesen, 2007).

- Connectivity also refers to the continuity of ecological processes such as nutrient, sediment, phytoplankton and zooplankton movement from a floodplain into the river during a flood event (Bain and Stevenson, 1999). The longitudinal movement of sediment and nutrients is also included in this concept.

- Impoundments may change the downstream temperature regime and influence migration cues.

- Reduced access to refuge from where biotic re-colonisation may take place following periods of disturbance (Novotny, *et al.*, 2005).

- Hydrological modifications may limit passage during periods when migration occurs or limit and even prohibit escape routes for biota during stressful periods (e.g. low flows, or artificially high flows). Laterally, even within the stream channel, access to certain habitats required for completion of certain phases of the life-cycle such as side channels and backwaters may be broken.

- Biologically impassable structures, such as dams, culverts, road crossings, bridges, etc., may alter downstream temperature regimes and may also function as sediment and nutrient traps and modify ecological processes and eventually biological assemblages (Søndergaard and Jeppesen, 2007).

- Urban areas, mines and industries may all be pollution sources that limit or prohibit fish passage through a zone where they formerly moved freely. Thermal plumes from industrial activities may also result in fragmentation (Novotny, *et al.*, 2005).

* Artificially modified river sections (concrete-lined channels, culverts) with very high (supercritical) flow may have velocities too high for fish to traverse or may lack suitable resting places (Novotny, *et al.*, 2005). In addition, such structures may limit lateral access to floodplains.

Interpretation of the severity of impacts is based on the natural characteristics of the river. The premise is that the severity of impacts on the habitat integrity of a river will vary according to the natural characteristics of the river. In other words particular river types will be more sensitive to certain impacts than other types, for example, impacts or tolerance of sandy rivers will differ to those of rocky rivers.

9.2.6   Carbon storage

"As a heat-trapping gas, carbon dioxide is a key component of nature's thermostat. If the carbon cycle removes too much CO_2 from the atmosphere, the earth will cool; if the cycle generates too much, the earth will get warmer" (Miller, 1998, p.113). The earth has developed a natural process for regulating the CO_2 levels in the atmosphere, this is based on carbon storage. Carbon storage takes many forms, including in sedimentary rocks such as limestone, plants such as rainforests, and the ocean floor. However, human interventions such as mining, burning of forests and fossil fuels, noxious industry, etc., disturb these natural processes and release greater volumes of CO_2 into the atmosphere; this phenomenon is called global warming.

"Carbon is stored in woody vegetation. Highly productive wetlands (including active floodplains of rivers) store large amounts of carbon. Under certain conditions, some deposits of dead plant matter and bacteria accumulate faster than they are decomposed in wetlands and other ecosystems. These deposits are locked away in underground sediments. Over millions of years such buried organic matter is compressed between layers of sediment, where it forms carbon-containing fossil fuels such as coal and oil. While stored, this carbon is not released into the atmosphere as CO_2, unless geomorphological processes expose them to air, e.g. excavation and erosion. Similarly, where carbon is dissolved in water, as the water warms, e.g. by more exposure to sunlight, more dissolved CO_2 returns to the atmosphere" (Miller, 1998 p.113)" In South Africa, carbon stored as peat and coal are actively mined, usually with dire consequences for the adjacent watercourses and ecosystems.

9.2.7   Water quality

The riverine zone and its components provide an important service of improving water quality by filtering and trapping pollutants. Pollutants can be reduced through sediment trapping, prolonged exposure to sunlight, carbon trapping, etc. Improved water quality benefits human usage.

9.2.8 Subsistence and cultural

Riverine zones provide resources such as food, fuel wood, reeds for weaving, medicinal plants, etc., that are used by humans for subsistence and cultural purposes. Where riverine zones are degraded, their production of these resources either reduce or cease.

9.2.9 Aesthetic and recreational

Riverine zones provide aesthetic quality and scientific and educational opportunities (USDA-NRCS 1999 in Soman, 2007 p.3). It visually diversifies a rural or suburban landscape, enhancing landscapes aesthetically and expanding recreational opportunities (Dosskey *et al.*, 1997, Postal and Carpenter, 1997, Field *et al.*, 2006 in Soman, 2007 p.3). Unfortunately a decrease in ecological functions usually results in an inverse improvement in aesthetic and recreational use of watercourses, e.g. the clearing of riparian vegetation provides access for fishing and similarly the construction of impoundments results in the provision for sailing, canoeing, fishing and swimming, etc.

9.2.10 Summary

Not all riparian areas would be able to perform these functions to the same extent. Whilst some may be very good for flood attenuation, others may play more important bank stabilisation roles. The protection of the riverine function requires a suitable buffer to be maintained between land use activities in the terrestrial areas and the possible impacts within the aquatic river channel itself. Maintaining riparian zones – including their naturally dense vegetation – also allows for riverine functions to be maintained.

It is important that a riverine area's capacity to provide the functions is not reduced. Many of these areas are best managed as natural areas, rather than being converted to other land uses.

9.2.10.1 Actions to include in a management plan for a catchment area or river system

- **Assessment:** Completed status quo documents must be compiled. This should include the current status (1:50 and 1:100 year flood lines, ground formations, biomes, habitat, vegetation, alien infestation, erosion, water quality, fauna and flora that should be present, flood control, potential usage to encourage sustainability, etc.)

- **Identify problems:** Address issues such as environmental law enforcement, pollutions, invasive species, squatters, security, lack of funding, development impact, lack of continuous monitoring, etc.

- **Prioritise action:** Problems can be prioritised according to short term and long term solutions. Take funds and manpower available as criteria. Draft a master plan and budget accordingly.

- **Action plans:** Implement action plans to address each problem. Put maintenance in place.

- **Monitoring:** Continuous monitoring and actions ensure that everything stays on track.

9.2.10.2   The proposed way forward

Rivers in a city can be classified in 4 different classes according to their transformation status (Class one = 0-5% transformed, Class two = 5-35% transformed, Class three = 35-65% transformed, Class 4 = 65-100% transformed).

All catchment areas must be identified. The main rivers in each catchment must be listed with all the sub- and sub-sub river systems feeding the main stream. Use the existing river names already allocated to them. Determine the distance and the open space size in which it is allocated.

Each named river must be accessed, problems identified and actions plans compiled. All class one rivers need to be prioritised. Cost allocations must be done to request funding on a budget. Responsible nature conservation staff members must be allocated to these systems and take accountability for the monitoring and action plan implementations.

All role players (roads and storm water, water and sanitation, etc.) must be involved or updated on issues found in the assessment and action plans. Local awareness of all residents and local councillors must be addressed. Environmental programmes focusing on adjacent schools must be executed (clean-up campaigns, etc.).

9.3   BUFFER ZONES

Buffer zones are areas of vegetation upslope of riparian/wetland boundaries, which are requested to protect the river/wetland from effects of adjacent development and/ or land use change. These buffer zones may variously protect the receiving wetland/ stream from concentrated peak run-off volumes, provide feeding/breeding areas for wetland/river fauna and may enhance the corridor function of drainage lines.

9.3.1   General

- No current national guidelines, or legislated requirement regarding buffer zones exist in South Africa.
- Normally guided by local/provincial recommendations.
- An agreed minimum buffer distance of 20 m is required next to watercourses in afforested areas.
- Specific (defensible) objectives should be identified.

Remaining natural and even artificially altered wetlands and rivers need to be protected from the impacts of urban life if they are to continue to provide habitats

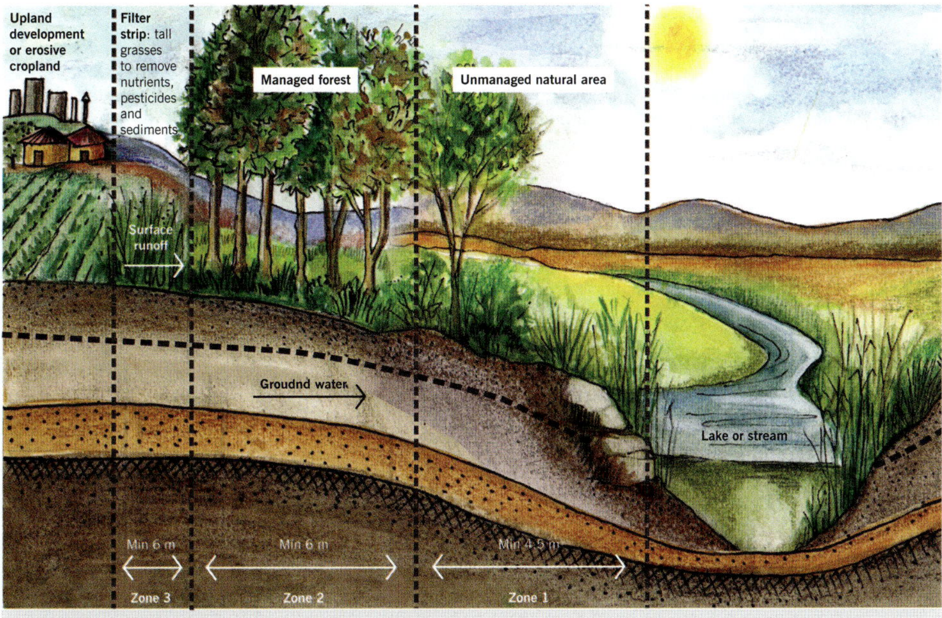

Figure 9.8: Different zones impacting on water courses.

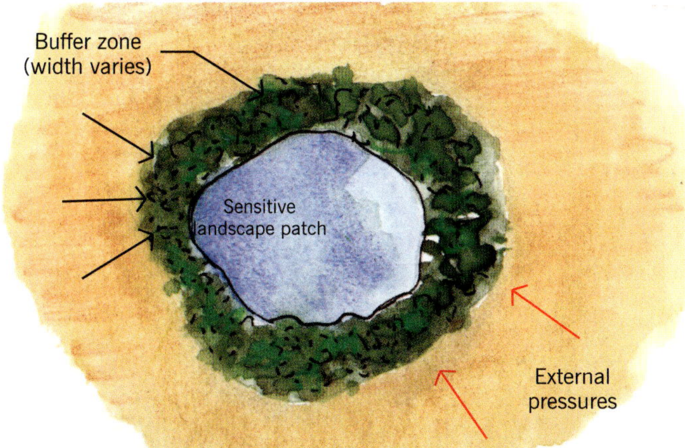

Key considerations

- Base buffer width on specific ecological functions.
- Modify buffer width according to landscape context and external pressures.
- Manage activities within buffer to benefit goals in the landscape patch.

Figure 9.9: Buffer zones.

and important services for human communities. Providing them with ecological buffers is one of the most important ways of protecting these ecosystems.

9.3.2   What is an ecological buffer?

An ecological buffer area (also called a development setback area) is a vegetated strip of land adjacent to a watercourse, wetland or marsh that is required for the protection and enhancement of these ecosystems.

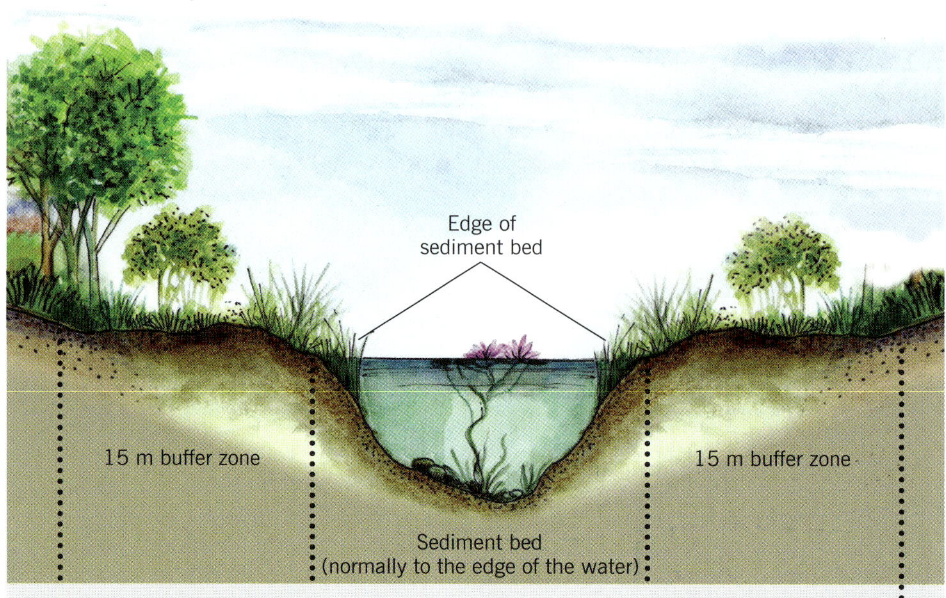

Figure 9.10: Measure buffer zones.

Groot Brak River, Eastern Cape, South Africa.

9.3.3   Buffer functions

The primary purpose of a buffer is to provide enough space between aquatic ecosystems and urban activities, infrastructure (such as roads, pylons, pipelines) or other developments to dissipate the following negative effects on the ecosystems:
- Noise and disturbance associated with human movement and vehicles.
- Rapid, concentrated and frequently polluted run-off from hardened surfaces.
- Spread of alien plants, such as kikuyu grass.

Well-vegetated buffers assist with stream-bank stabilisation and protection from erosion, and also provide habitat and safe continuous corridors for animal movement.

9.3.4   How big should a buffer be?

All aquatic ecosystems are required to have a buffer. Buffer widths vary between 10 m for small streams or concrete canals, up to 40 m for rivers and 70 m for wetlands.

The actual width of the buffer required to protect a particular wetland, marsh or river depends on the type of ecosystem, its sensitivity and ecological importance and the kinds of impacts that are likely to affect it.

9.3.5   From where is the buffer measured?

The buffer is measured from the top of a river bank or the outer edge of a wetland. This edge must be determined by a specialist, using nationally accepted guidelines/ methodologies.

9.3.6   Buffer do's and dont's

The main purpose of a buffer area is to protect the aquatic system. Any activity or development within the buffer that affects its ability to carry out this function, or that adds impact, should not be permitted. Thus, buffers should not be hardened with paths, patios or parking areas, fertilised, planted with alien plants (including kikuyu grass) or drained. At the same time, buffer areas can lend themselves to a range of other, compatible functions. For example, they can provide:
- Areas for controlled walking of dogs.
- Recreational areas for fishing, picnicking, walking or cycling.
- Opportunities for birdwatching and sites for environmental education.
- Dry-season play areas or informal sports fields.
- Space for the improvement of storm water run-off quality, using swales, treatment wetlands and other, similar sustainable urban drainage system measures.

Rock Elephant Shrew.

CHAPTER 10

MOUNTAINS AND RIDGES

(This chapter describes mountains and ridges in the urban environment. There are guidelines on ways to control development in and around mountainous areas. Ridges as biodiversity hotspots are also explained, also the importance of ridges for Red Data species and their contribution to ecological urban infrastructure.)

10.1　MOUNTAINS [1]

10.1.1　Introduction

Background

Mountains are complex features to define. From a visual perspective some mountains rise above the surrounding landscape and can consist of rocky or vegetated land features, others can be free-standing or part of a range. Mountains vary in height, steepness of slopes and relief and can be located at different altitude levels. This broad overview has been specifically chosen to incorporate a wide range of environmental features, from hills such as the Tygerberg Hills and Botlary Hills, to remote mountains such as the Cedarberg Mountains. Most mountains are in private ownership, often resulting in a range of development pressures, which can range from mines to farms and game farms, resorts, 4x4 trails, and industrial activities.

Some reasons for the protection of mountains are:
- Mountains form catchment areas for valuable surface water resources (especially relevant for South Africa).
- Mountain biotas are vulnerable to air, soil and water pollution.
- Mountains are a last refuge for many rare plants and animals eliminated from the often more transformed lowlands.
- Mountains have high scenic value and attract tourists and recreational users.
- Mountains provide some of the last wilderness areas on earth sought by an important and productive sector of the global community for spiritual renewal, mental equilibrium and confidence building.
- Mountains provide an opportunity to have a primitive, "return to nature" type of experience.

---

[1] Information captured from the guidelines for appropriate development in and around mountain areas in the Western Cape, RSA – Prepared by: IAIA/PAWC work group for sensitive areas: Mountain environments, 25 November, 1999)

- Mountain environments contain wetlands and vegetated slopes that ensure perennial water supply. Mountain environments are dynamic and susceptible to erosion, silting dams and slowing plant growth.

Some of the characteristics that promote development opportunities in mountain areas are:
- Mountains provide views that are aesthetically pleasing to inhabitants of mountainous areas.
- Some mountain areas are rich in minerals.
- Some mountain slopes are suitable for forestry and agricultural practices, particularly flower harvesting and livestock farming.
- Mountains provide opportunities for resort and holiday related developments.
- Mountains provide suitable locations for infrastructural developments such as dams, cable cars and communication towers on summits.

The primary objectives for guiding development in mountain areas are to promote ecological sustainable development by minimising detrimental impacts and optimising positive impacts. More specifically:

Mountains provide views.

1. To prevent where feasible, any:
    - Reduction in visual integrity, wilderness qualities, sense of place or cultural value;
    - Net loss of biodiversity or damage to natural processes/ systems;
    - Reduction in water yield or quality, and erosion;
    - Loss of viable conservation areas containing scarce and unique resources;
    - Increase in physical danger – fire hazard or slumping (landslides/rockfalls);
    - Fragmentation/disturbances of natural environment.

2. To rehabilitate damaged areas where feasible through:
    - Optimisation of recovery of habitat, or other beneficial land use.
    - Restoration to an ecologically stable system.
    - Removal of pollutant sources and/or visually displeasing features.

3. To promote sustainable non-consumptive use of natural resources in suitable areas.

10.1.2   Draft guidelines to control development in and around mountain areas

10.1.2.1   Proposed mountain zoning

For the purpose of this guideline a mountain is described as a physical landscape feature, elevated above the surrounding topography, where key issues of concern

Devilspeak Mountain, Cape Town, South Africa.

are biodiversity protection, aesthetics and safety from fires, erosion and slumping. A mountain may contain one or more of the following zones:
- A natural/wilderness zone.
- A rural and agricultural zone.
- An urban-edge zone.

These zones constitute the transition that can be found when one moves from the developed lowlands up to an often undeveloped natural environment on the higher slopes. To help suitable/appropriate developments and activities in mountain areas, three zones are established to separate the degrees and types of development that are suitable, and the extent of controls necessary.

10.1.2.2   Fundamental principles

- This refers to any change in land use or activity that could have an impact on the environment. Such activities could include those associated with agriculture, forestry, residential housing, resort developments, roads, tracks, etc.

- Any development must be in accordance with an acceptable development line, i.e. on or below the general contour to which any development has taken place on landscape level. (This is distinguished from the building line that usually refers to the line up to where infrastructure has been constructed). The development line represents that line along the slope of a mountain that delineates the upper reaches of general existing development along the slopes. Specific developments (e.g. an agricultural field, a house or road) that are situated higher than the general altitude of surrounding development should be regarded as non-conforming development. A realistic development line should not be compromised by including such extreme existing non-conforming developments.

10.1.2.3   Determining the different zones

- The urban-edge zone is characterised by a predominantly developed nature, ranging from a residential character in urban areas to intensive agricultural fields in a rural environment. In general the rural and agricultural zone forms the transition between developed and non-developed areas.

- The boundary between the rural agricultural zone and the urban edge zone should constitute the transition between a developed and a semi-developed environment.

- The natural/wilderness zone constitutes the predominantly undeveloped natural vegetation areas in mountains.

- The development line separates the natural/wilderness zone from the rural and agricultural zone below it.

10.1.2.4   Overarching management objectives

Management objectives for natural/ wilderness zones are:
- To give protection to wild mountain areas before unused pristine land is exploited for short-term gain.

- To conserve water sources for the sustained production of unpolluted, unsilted water.
- To conserve biodiversity and genetic resources.
- To rehabilitate degraded areas where feasible.
- To undertake scientific research to attain understanding of natural processes and to test management techniques for conservation and sustainable utilisation of natural resources.
- To minimise adverse impacts of activities and developments on natural processes/systems.
- To promote sustainable recreational use, eco-friendly tourism and to increase public awareness about mountain environments.

Management objectives for rural and agricultural zones are:
- To minimise the bio-physical and visual impacts of agriculture and associated activities on the adjacent natural zone.
- To minimise impacts on adjacent zones, through the management, regulation and control of the nature and scale of development.
- To minimise adverse impacts of activities and developments on natural processes/systems.
- To promote ecologically friendly tourism and to increase public environmental awareness.

Management objectives for urban-edge zones are:
- To minimise impacts on adjacent zones, through the management, regulation and control of the nature of development.

10.1.2.5   Natural/wilderness zone

Grading: Undeveloped

Description: This refers to a predominantly natural and unmodified mountain or canyon area, retaining its primeval character, containing samples or major ecosystems of ecological diversity and genetic resources. A natural zone can contain a national monument, national park, and World Heritage Site, biosphere reserve or conservancy.

Example: Mountain land in reasonably pristine conditions and intact natural resources, largely unmodified. This includes mountain land being minimally exploited by landowners, e.g. for flower picking.

Access: Existing footpaths or gravel or paved roads or 4x4 tracks.

10.1.2.6   Rural and agricultural zones

Grading: Semi-modified/developed

Description: Land beyond the urban edge, used for rural or agricultural purposes (including forestry) and associated services and infrastructure. This includes fallow land and land zoned for rural/agricultural use, but not actively utilised as such. Appropriate mining and industrial activities could take place in this zone.

Example: Any rural or less developed agricultural uses – cultivated land, pastures, etc., e.g. viticulture on the slopes, stock (grazing) farming and could contain farm buildings, sheds, dams, quarries, etc.

Access: Access via public or private gravel and paved roads, rail or air.

10.1.2.7   Urban-edge zones

Grading: Fully transformed/modified

Description: Modified landscapes consisting primarily of urban development and associated infrastructure. This can include informal settlements, land within the urban edge that is zoned for urban uses (e.g. sub divisional areas), currently not utilised as such.

Mining and industrial activities could take place in this zone.

Example: Numerous, ranging from city-edge development on the slopes of the peninsula mountain chain, to smaller isolated developments/hamlets, and fully/ intensively developed agricultural areas, to intensive agricultural areas.

Access: Mostly paved roads and a well-developed infrastructure. Access is via public or private road, rail or air.

Undisturbed mountain areas.

10.1.2.8   Proposed procedures to be followed for applications in mountain areas

Any person, who proposes development in mountain areas, should follow the following procedure:

- Determine the zone and its boundaries (if applicable) within which the proposed development will be situated.

- If the proposed development is situated in the rural/agricultural zone, the development and building lines must be determined (and motivated). The area above the development line should then be regarded as part of the natural zone, and development should be situated below this line. In the case of built infrastructure, new developments should be situated below the building line.

- It must be determined if the proposed development theoretically suits the zone and

- If so, whether credible professionals verified the proposal. The following aspects must be taken into account:
  - That the potential effect on biological functioning, local communities and recreational users would not exceed limits of acceptable change (to be determined for specific areas with stakeholder input).
  - If the limits are exceeded, that there are detailed descriptions of what mitigation steps are to be taken (targets), when, how, and by whom.
  - The developer can prove beyond reasonable doubt to have the capacity to implement the environmental management programme during construction and operational phases.
  - The proposed development theoretical suitability for the zone.

This proposed procedure must not be regarded as a replacement of the Environmental Impact Assessment (EIA) requirements. This procedure is to ensure that suitable development takes place in mountain areas.

10.1.2.9   Overarching guidelines for development

- Comply with all relevant legislation, structure plans and policies.

- Ensure the continued functioning of the ecosystems, and maintain species diversity through habitat protection.

- Preserve landform features, particular skyline, view sites and important site lines.

- Ensure the siting of facilities is related to environmental resilience and visual screening capabilities of the landscape.

- In the absence of clear or definitive data or until the boundaries of specific mountain zones has been formalised, to make informed decisions, adopt a precautionary approach, or in the case of recommendations, follow a best practice philosophy.

- Scale, density and nature of activities or developments should be harmonious and in keeping with the sense of place and character of the areas.

More specific guidelines for appropriate development proposals in and around mountain areas.

Table 10.1: More specific guidelines for appropriate development proposals in and around mountain areas. *(Guidelines for appropriate development in and around mountain areas in the Western Cape, RSA – Prepared by IAIA/PAWC work group for sensitive areas: Mountain environments, 25 Nov. 1999)*

Proposed change in activity or land use	Natural/wilderness zones	Transitional/rural and agricultural zones
Minimum requirements (as in ALL areas sensitive to disturbance)	A comprehensive environmental process as stipulated in the EIA requirements must be followed for all activities listed in the requirements. Where applicable requirements of other legislation must also be adhered to.	A comprehensive environmental process as stipulated in the EIA requirements must be followed for all activities listed in the requirements. Where applicable requirements of other legislation must also be adhered to.
Subdivision and rezoning	Not to be considered unless it is part of a suitable development proposal with important benefits to society (and particularly local communities) that outweighs the need to conserve wilderness integrity, i.e. no subdivision, rezoning or any development in special or pristine mountain wilderness areas for a profit motive only.	Not to be considered unless it is part of a suitable development proposal.
Facilities linked to recreational, educational and experiential activities	Potential activities permitted: hiking, mountain biking, horse-riding, sport-climbing, traditional climbing, bouldering, environmental education, guided and unguided wilderness excursions.	Potential activities permitted: hiking, mountain biking, horse-riding, sport-climbing, traditional climbing, bouldering, paragliding, orientation, abseiling, environmental education, 4x4 trails. Demonstrate how numbers & routes will be controlled, and waste products disposed of.

Facilities linked to recreational, educational and experiential activities (cont.)		Sensitive features, physical and other environmental constraints must be identified and taken into account.
Residential	Only existing development rights should be allowed appropriate to its context within natural areas. Examples: hiking cabins or facilities linked to appropriate low impact outdoor recreational opportunities. Placement of residential units must be done with adequate environmental motivation and evaluation.	Suitable development nodes on lower slopes should be considered below the development and/or building line. The proposed development must also fit in with the character of the area. Sensitive features, physical and other environmental constraints must be identified and taken into account.
Resorts and commercial developments	Developments and increased activities are discouraged in natural zones.	Suitable development nodes on lower slopes should be considered below the development and/or building line. The proposed development must also fit in with the character of the area. Sensitive features, physical and other environmental constraints must be identified and taken into account. Not to be considered unless backed-up by a well-motivated development proposal to the relevant environmental authorities.
Agricultural	Limited to wild flower harvesting, game etc., i.e. sustainable use of natural resources.	Agricultural activities must be situated below the development line. Sensitive features, physical and other environmental constraints must be identified and taken into account.

Industrial	None.	Only to be considered in urban areas and if it is in line with integrated development framework of structure plan for the area. Sensitive features, physical and other environmental constraints must be identified and taken into account.
Water supply	Only new dams of regional importance for water supply should be considered. Structures associated with water supplies such as weirs and pipelines must also follow EIA and DWAF regulations.	New facilities and infrastructure must be situated below the development line. Follow DWAF requirements.
Afforestation	No new afforestation.	New afforestation must be situated below the development line. Follow DWAF guidelines.
Mining	No new mines.	New mines should be situated below the development line. Follow Department of Mineral and Energy Affairs guidelines.
Landfill sites	No new sites.	New landfill sites should be situated below the development line. Follow DWAF guidelines.
Fire breaks	In consultation with relevant conservation authority.	In consultation with relevant conservation authority.
Masts & power lines and telecommunication structures	Only on existing developed sites. No new masts taller that ?m (if visually acceptable) should be considered. No new roads and power lines must be considered.	New facilities should be situated below the development line.

Bulk services	No bulk services.	Must be situated below the development line and in keeping with the existing character and future planning vision of the area. Only to be considered in urban areas and if it is in line with the integrated development framework of structure plan for the area. Sensitive features, physical and other environmental constraints must be identified and taken into account.
Landing strips and helipads	No new facilities. Over-flying and landing is discouraged in natural zones.	Must be situated below the development line.
Roads	No new roads or tracks. Roads and tracks are only permitted when linked to appropriate development rights, or to improve an existing route for rehabilitation purposes.	Must be situated below the development line. Roads associated with appropriate development and infrastructure is permitted.
Advertising (billboards, lighting) and signage	No advertising and minimal cryptic signage.	Not encouraged, but where necessary only in consultation with local or regional authorities.

10.2   RIDGES [1]

10.2.1   Introduction

The biodiversity and socio-cultural value of ridges and their essential role in ecosystem processes is absolutely imperative to adopt a no-go development policy for the ridges. The conservation status of ridges is important to try and stop the severity of ridge loss due to urbanisation.

The quartzite ridges of Gauteng, together with the Drakensberg Escarpment are important natural assets in the entire region of the northern provinces of South Africa. They are characterised by a unique plant species composition that is found nowhere else in South Africa or the world (Bredenkamp and Brown, 1998).

Due to similar biodiversity, ecological and aesthetic values, the term ridge refers loosely to hills, koppies, mountains, kloofs, gorges, etc. The essential characteristic defining these topographic features is the slope of the site, whereby any topographic feature in the landscape that is characterised by slopes of 5° is defined as a ridge.

10.2.2   The value of ridges

10.2.2.1   Ridges as biodiversity hotspots and future refuges

Varied topography is recognised as one of the most powerful influences contributing to the high biodiversity of southern Africa. The interplay between topography and climate over a long period of time has led to the evolution of a rich biodiversity (Samways & Hatton, 2000). Landscapes composed of spatially heterogeneous abiotic conditions provide a greater diversity of potential niches for plants and animals than do homogeneous landscapes. The richness and diversity of flora has been found to be significantly higher in sites with high geomorphological heterogeneity and it can reasonably be assumed that associated faunal communities will also be significantly more diverse in spatially heterogeneous environments (Burnett *et al.*, 1998).

Ridges are characterised by high spatial heterogeneity due to the range of differing aspects (north, south, east, west and variations thereof), slopes and altitudes all resulting in differing soil (e.g. depth, moisture, temperature, drainage, nutrient content), light and hydrological conditions. The temperature and humidity regimes of microsites vary on both a seasonal and daily basis (Samways & Hatton, 2000). Moist cool aspects are more conducive to leaching of nutrients than warmer drier slopes (Lowrey & Wright, 1987). Variation in aspect, soil drainage (Burnett *et al.*, 1998) and elevation/altitude (Primack, 1995) has been found to be especially important predictors of biodiversity. It follows that ridges will be characterised by a particularly high biodiversity, as such their protection will contribute significantly to the conservation of biodiversity in Gauteng.

The diversity of plant communities on ridges can easily be observed, with grassland communities associated with the crests of hills and the southern slopes while woody species grow on warmer northern aspects (Lowrey & Wright, 1987) as well as on protected areas on southern slopes and on rocky outcrops (Grobler, 2000). Biotic communities differ between the tops and bottoms of koppies (Samways & Hatton, 2000). Associated faunal communities are similarly diverse. For example, a wide variety of bird groups utilise ridges, koppies and hills for feeding, roosting and breeding. These groups include some owls, falcons, nightjars, swifts, swallows, martins, larks, chats, thrushes, cisticolas, pipits, shrikes, starlings, sunbirds, firefinches, waxbills, buntings, canaries, eagles and vultures. Ridges provide important habitat for sensitive species such as bats (roosting sites) and the Rock Elephant Shrew. Ridges

---

[1] (Information obtained from a Policy document issued by SA Department of Agriculture, Conservation, Environment and Land Affaires - Michèle Pfab, scientific services and contributions from Marianne Forsyth (invertebrates), Dean Peinke (mammals), Craig Whittington-Jones (birds, reptiles, amphibians) 19 April, 2001).

Ridge urban area.

and kloofs also form caves, an important habitat for highly specialised animals, e.g. bats. Variable microclimate conditions has resulted in a vast array of invertebrate communities associated with the high plant diversity characterising ridges. Hills and koppies generally have more insects (both in terms of individuals and species) than the immediate surroundings (Samways & Hatton, 2000).

Some taxonomic groups, e.g. the poorly known and undercollected bryophytes, are found predominantly on ridges, hills, koppies and in kloofs. For example, the Magaliesberg is a recognised centre of most species diversity (Van Rooy, 2000).

As such, the conservation of ridges will provide habitat for significantly high numbers of species allowing for their continued survival in rapidly urbanizing areas, a desirable long-term conservation goal. Ridges are particularly suitable for providing a future refuge for biodiversity in an urbanised landscape as they function as islands even within a natural landscape due to their structural and environmental isolation from the landscape (Samways & Hatton, 2000). Furthermore, according to climate change modelling, level topography will be particularly sensitive to future climate change and major extinction in these areas can be expected (Rutherford *et al.*, 2001). As such, in a landscape affected by climate change, chances of species survival will be higher on ridges.

10.2.2.2   Ridges as habitat for Red Data/Threatened species

Many Red Data/threatened species of plants and animals inhabit ridges (Policy DACEL document on Ridges, April 2001). Due to their threatened status, Red Data species require priority conservation efforts in order to ensure their future survival. As such, the conservation of ridges will contribute significantly to the future persistence of these species.

Plants

The ridges form vital habitat for many threatened or Red Data plant species. 65% of Red Data plant species has been recorded growing on ridges in the Gauteng Province (South Africa), while 42% of Red Data plant species are confined solely to this habitat type. Furthermore, it should be emphasised that 71% of Gauteng's endemic plant species, i.e. plant species that occur nowhere else in the world, has been recorded on ridges, while 41% of the Gauteng plant endemics are confined solely to the ridge habitat. Many of the latter plant species are critically endangered or endangered, the highest categories of threat to which species can be assigned. These Gauteng endemics are predominantly threatened by habitat transformation and fragmentation and the accompanying resulting decline in habitat quality, all brought on by urbanisation of "prime real estate properties" that the ridge environment offers. Similarly, high percentages of Red Data plant species grouped within the second highest priority grouping (designated as A2 species) grow on ridges, while 63% are confined to ridges. It follows that protection of the ridges of Gauteng from development pressures will significantly contribute to the conservation

Threatened species: a, Juliana's Golden Mole (photograph: Craig Jackson); b, Melodious Lark (*Mirafra cheniana*).

of 65% of Red Data plant species and 71% of Gauteng plant endemics. Similarly, 50% of all near threatened plant species (those species that are close to qualifying as vulnerable) will be protected through the protection of ridge environments.

Mammals

At least three threatened mammal species occur within the ridge environment including Juliana's Golden mole (*Amblysomus julianae*), which is perhaps the most threatened small mammal in Africa.

Birds

Several bird species occurring in Gauteng that are on the South African or international Red Data lists, or are considered to be of conservation concern are dependent on ridges, koppies and hills (Barnes, 2000; Ginn *et al.*, 1989; Maclean, 1993; Tarboton, 1997) including Cape Vultures *(Gyps coprotheres)*, the Peregrine Falcon *(Falco peregrinus)*, the Lanner Falcon *(Falco biarmicus)*, the Cape Eagle Owl *(Bubo capensis)*, the Melodious Lark *(Mirafra cheniana)*, the Short-toed Rock Thrush *(Monticola brevipes)* and the Ground Woodpecker *(Geocolaptes olivaceus)*.

Reptiles

Three rare reptile species that occur in Gauteng utilise rocky habitats such as those provided by ridges (Jacobsen, 1988; Broadley, 1990; Branch, 1992).

Amphibians

The Northern Pygmy Toad *(Bufo fenoulheti)* and the Common River Frog *(Rana angolensis)* are found in kloofs (Frogs of Gauteng & North West Provinces, CD produced by Wildlife & Environment Society of South Africa). Numbers of the latter species are declining in Gauteng (Cook, 2000).

Invertebrates

Many Red Data butterflies (especially those belonging to the *lycaenid* group) occur on the southern slopes of ridges, e.g. the Heidelberg Copper Butterfly *(Chrysoritis aureus)* is restricted to the rocky southern slopes of the Alice Glockner Nature Reserve. *Metisella meninx* is a vulnerable butterfly species that occurs at altitudes above 1 600 m and as such these butterflies are often present on ridge systems. A rare species of scorpion is apparently confined to the Witwatersrand ridges and Magaliesberg range (Astri Leroy, Spider Club, pers. comm.). A rare spider also seems to be confined to ridges and is an obligate rock-living spider (Astri Leroy, Spider Club, pers. comm.).

10.2.2.3   The importance of ridges for invertebrates

Invertebrates are reliant on hilltops as thermal refuges from winter cold air drainage (Samways, 1994).

Some invertebrate species utilise ridges for survival. For example, the developmental phenology and timing of adult emergence of some butterfly species may rely directly on a ridge environment, with the distribution of larvae changing between years by shifting from cool slopes to warmer slopes as the population size increases (Samways, 1994). Because of the variety of micro-topographies on hills, insects can thermo-regulate by moving in and out of the shade of rocks. They can also seek shelter from predators and fire (Samways & Hatton, 2000).

Ridges are particularly important for many insects to carry out behavioural activities. Many southern African butterflies engage in "hilltopping", principally as a mate-meeting mechanism (Samways, 1994). Males of these species establish territories on high points in the landscape, from which intruders are chased and within which courting and mating with females occurs (Williams, 1994). Fruit chafers have also been seen hilltopping, where females tend to wander around on the ground at the hilltop and the males fly in a circling fashion until they locate the females via pheromones. Hypothesised reasons for this behaviour include access to host plants, increased mating potential via a common activity that promotes rendezvous and avoiding predators through concentration of activities (Chuck Bellamy, Transvaal museum, pers. comm.). Similarly, hilltops often support clouds of flies and hymenopterans (Samways & Hatton, 2000).

The honeybee also seems to exhibit hilltopping behaviour, since drone congregation areas (where drones mate with the queens) are normally close to hills and ridges (Mike Allsopp, Agricultural Research Council, Plant Protection Institute, pers. comm.). This is a particularly important value of ridges to emphasise considering the current major pollination crisis. Disruption of pollination systems, and declines of certain types of pollinators, including the honeybee, has been reported on every continent except Antarctica. The crisis, which will have a major impact on both natural and agricultural systems, has been caused by habitat fragmentation and other changes in land use, agriculture and grazing, pesticide and herbicide use, and the introduction of non-native species (Kearns *et al.*, 1998).

Dragonflies take up feeding beats along ridges and small hills for capturing prey. Some other species of dragonfly make use of the thermal characteristics of the sheltered and rocky landscape to gain warmth for prolonged foraging (Samways, 1994).

If ridges are allowed to become developed, it will have serious implications for the future survival of many invertebrate species, many of which provide essential pollinator services.

10.2.2.4   Ridges as important wildlife corridors

Natural corridors, which are present in unfragmented landscapes, such as rivers, riparian zones and topographic features, should be retained following fragmentation (Loney & Hobbs, 1991). Such corridors may remain relatively self-sustaining after fragmentation as they continue to be essentially isolated in a larger matrix, unlike remnant corridors that require substantial management to counteract the external effects of the surrounding matrix. Remnant corridors only become corridors when the surrounding landscape is fragmented and until that time had been part of the overall matrix (Loney & Hobbs, 1991).

The protection of ridges in their natural condition will greatly improve the biogeographical capability of the urban open space network (Poynton & Roberts, 1985) as ridges can be viewed as natural existing corridors that can functionally interconnect isolated natural areas (Adams & Dove, 1989) and require minimal or no management (Loney & Hobbs, 1991). Protecting naturally existing corridors promotes ecological processes and benefits regional and local biological diversity. In contrast, the creation of linear patches intended to function as corridors (i.e. remnant corridors such as servitudes) may cause the local extinction of species and thus erode biological diversity (Rosenberg *et al.*, 1997).

The ridge systems represent vital natural corridors as they function both as wildlife habitat, providing resources needed for survival, reproduction and movement and as biological corridors, providing for movement between habitat patches. Both functions are potentially critical to conservation of biological diversity as the landscape becomes increasingly fragmented into smaller, more isolated patches (Rosenberg *et al.*, 1997).

10.2.3   The role of ridges in ecosystem processes

Ridges may have a direct effect on temperature/radiation, surface airflow/wind (Samways, 1994), humidity and soil types. Ridges also influence fire in the landscape, offering protection (Lowrey & Wright, 1987) for those species that can be described as "fire-avoiders".

As a consequence of the influence of topography on rainfall, many streams originate on ridges (Prof Kevin Rogers, Centre for Water in the Environment, University of the Witwatersrand, pers. comm.) and control water inputs into wetlands (Samways, 1994).

The protection of the ridges in a natural state will thus ensure the normal functioning of ecosystem processes. In contrast, development of a ridge will alter these major landscape processes. For example, water run-off into streams and wetlands will increase.

10.2.4   The socio-cultural value of ridges

Ridges provide aesthetically pleasing environments for the surrounding inhabitants and attract tourists and recreational users. Ridges can also be viewed as a source of spiritual renewal, mental equilibrium and confidence building (Eber, 2000). In general, natural areas in the urban environment can provide opportunities for human recreation, relaxation and education. Many surveys of urban areas have indicated that urban residents attach high value to wildlife around the home (Adams & Dove, 1989).

In South Africa the Gauteng Department of Agriculture and Rural Development GDARD compiled a policy (2001) to protect ridges from further development. According to this policy, ridges are classified into classes according to current transformed status as follows:
- Class 1: Ridges 0–5% transformed.
- Class 2: Ridges 5–35% transformed.

- Class 3: Ridges 35–65% transformed.
- Class 4: Ridges 65–100% transformed.

Within the policy, Class 1 and Class 2 ridges are highly sensitive due to limited disturbances and therefore are considered "no-go" areas in terms of future development.

CHAPTER 11

THE INDUSTRIAL AND TECHNOLOGICAL IMPACT ON URBAN NATURE

(This chapter focuses on the impact of industries and technological development on urban nature areas. It then deals with storm water pollution issues and ways to address these challenges.)

11.1 IMPACTS ON URBAN NATURE

Industry and technology contribute to development. Any development will have an impact on nature. Development encroaches into nature areas because of human survival. Money is the driving element and dictates relevant market forces to generate more money to ensure better human survival.

In nature, any change, improvement or degradation of natural resources is driven by survival of a species in that specific environment. All these species (birds, other animals, plants) are part of a food chain. Disturbance of the balance can cause damage (examples: overgrazing, erosion, drought, etc.). Survival is the driving force and dictates the change in the environment to ensure a better life for birds, other animals and plants.

Humans are at the top of all animal life. A human being is not only a top predator, but his/her actions can affect the entire environment with the potential for a catastrophic impact on nature.

It is possible to limit these negative effects in such a way that human activities are synchronised with nature and benefit from it in the long run. We have to understand the way nature works and try to adapt our activities to be more nature-friendly.

11.1.1 Background

Our predecessors or ancestors utilised top-quality natural resources for a living (survival) and for making more money for the sake of a better life. They built their houses on prime agricultural land, in places with sufficient water resources. These resources were also utilised by wildlife before humans arrived. Because humans are the top predators in the food chain, wildlife will slowly decline and disappear. Humans have won the competition for natural resources. The reality is that humans will need these resources for the rest of their life. If they do not practise sustainable usage, it will have a negative impact on everybody. Somehow we have to return to nature what we have taken.

What happened in the past does not give us reasons to continue with practices we should not have implemented in the first place. There is space for urban nature in our towns and cities. We need urban nature from a social as well as a health point of view. To be able to create this we need to understand how we can contribute to urban nature conservation.

It is much easier to protect a pristine urban nature area than to try and rectify damages already done. Rehabilitation is expensive and can never reinstate the original environment. This does not mean that the wrongs cannot be addressed. The concept should be to bring nature back to the city. Start off with habitat protection/ rehabilitation/creation, and urban wildlife will come back and adapt to the urban circumstances humans are involved in.

11.1.2   The impact of development on urban nature areas

It is clever, intelligent, highly educated people that cause the most severe negative impacts to nature. Engineers building roads through mountains, construct sewer lines on river beds, building bridges for river crossings, etc. High technology masts and power lines designed by engineers not only have a visual impact but affect fly paths for birds. Industrial noise and pollution not only degrade the urban environment but also causes a health risk to every one living in the city. The mining industries really spoiled the urban environment and contaminated underground water resources.

It was in Seattle (America) that the city management of that town identified the following problems within their city; the town at that point in time was dull, dirty and dangerous. Dull, meaning not attractive for residence to stay in. Dirty because of pollution. Dangerous because of crime committed.

They then started planning how to change this unwanted situation. They started off by creating parks and beautiful nature areas within the town. They spent time looking after the recreational needs of their residents. They created facilities to address the residents' outdoor leisure needs (environment).

They focused on clean-up actions. They addressed the litter issues and encouraged a culture to contribute in actions to keep the town clean. They made an effort to address petty crime. They focused on the broken window syndrome (when a window is broken in a building you repair it immediately, or more windows will be broken).

The results were rewarding. Slowly, the town became a nice place to stay in. Big companies decided to establish their businesses there (Boeing, Microsoft, etc.). The economy of the town expanded.

It is important to acknowledge that the industry has to consider their immediate environment as one of their biggest assets. The industry and technology has to evaluate their actions with the aim to be environmentally friendly. Companies must be accountable for the products they sell, even beyond their life expectancy. When a certain manufacturer produces cars, he must take responsibility for his product towards the environment till the end of the products' life cycle. When a company digs gravel for roads, the same company is responsible for the rehabilitation of the site they used to sell their product.

It is necessary to make provision for these accountabilities during the planning phase and budget process. Plan and budget for rehabilitation and recycling. Plan and budget so that the resource materials (to manufacture a product) are environmentally friendly. Companies must determine the impact of their products/actions on the immediate environment and have to put in an effort to try and minimise all these negative outcomes.

Nature is a product that can sell itself. Most people like nature and can associate with it. There is a natural trend for humans to be positive about nature issues, but they need to be addressed on a long-term basis. There is no short-term solution when the environment is affected.

The solution is to focus on renewable resources (solar energy, recycling, organic material that will not impact negatively on the environment). Then we need to engage incentives (profit or indirect benefits) to the solution of products that have a negative impact (put a money value to plastic bags to prevent it from being litter contributors). It is, for example, better to use glass that can be recycled or reused instead of plastic bottles or containers that are not environmentally friendly. Jobs can be created during the recycling processes.

Development brings in roads, buildings, waste materials, noise, gasses, smoke, hard surfaces, run-off water, degrading in natural vegetation, fragmentation of ecological sensitive areas, disruption in food chains, etc. The great impact is habitat loss. With lost habitat for animals, wildlife disappears. These impacts (ugly buildings, little vegetation, and no animal life) make our surroundings look dull. The waste materials, gasses and smoke pollute our environment. An environment like this accommodates dangerous activities, and eventually people move away and the economy will grind to a halt.

We do need technology, industries and development to survive as human beings, but we need to be in balance with our environment we are living in. Roads can fragment nature areas in such a way that ecological processes stop. Urban wildlife needs corridors within the urban environment to move between fragmented urban nature areas. Birds do not have a problem with this because they can fly across the barriers. This is applicable to most insects but the small mammals and reptiles need to cross roads and get killed in the process. Corridors can be openings underneath bridges, rivers and servitudes.

Waste can be collected by litter traps in river systems and gabion structures (wired baskets filled with rocks) serve to break water flow, catch up silt and forms filter systems. If the waste is organic it will be absorbed through the decomposing system.

Noise can be reduced by urban vegetation. Street trees and enough green areas between buildings will absorb a lot of noise. Water also contributes to hide urban noise. On coastal areas, the sea plays a major role in softening urban noise (one of the reasons why people love coastal towns – they hear the sea all the time). In city gardens/nature areas and river systems, artificial waterfalls can be created. It will absorb urban sounds but also add oxygen to the flowing urban water systems and enhance the quality of urban open water, with better habitat for urban wildlife.

Gasses can also be absorbed by urban vegetation. Street trees and urban vegetation consume carbon dioxide and release oxygen back into the atmosphere.

It is important to try and soften hard surfaces, like parking areas and other paved areas. They can be designed to reduce the visual impact with greening (trees and vegetation beds). Hard surfaces create run-off water. This water should actually penetrate the ground and add moisture to the underground surfaces. It is thus important to divert and collect these run-offs and channel them into nearby urban wetlands.

11.1.3   How technology and development can benefit urban nature

When industries tell their clients the benefits they can create for urban wildlife, clients will be more attracted to their products because of their contribution. It always works; you can try it but make sure you did your homework to determine what the contribution is.

It is important to understand client's needs. An underlying need that will not necessarily relate to your product is to stay, live, shop and work in a clean beautiful environment. Unfortunately, this need is not always a top priority when funds are allocated for projects.

A business or company is in a better position (capacity and financial) to plan and budget for environmental benefits than an individual. What is the relationship with my client, the product I sell and the environment? Where will my product end up? What waste will my product produce? Can I recycle my product? How can it be done? How will it affect/benefit the environment? Is the benefit a donation, action, message, sponsor, awareness, etc. What do I promote to enhance our environment?

Companies should see a contribution to the environment as an investment with indirect benefits. This should also be part of the company's management system

The following example illustrates the concept of development impact. A bridge must be built as a river crossing in a town. It can be planned to cross the river at a

Water inlet structure on upstream side of bridge.

Overflow weir collects incomming water and creates a waterfall to trap oxygen.

point where it will have the least impact (narrow part, not through a wetland area, where you do not alter the natural flow, etc.). The bridge should cross the river at a 90 degree angle (shortest effected area). Design a water inlet structure on the upstream side of the bridge.

The structure must serve as an overflow weir to let the incoming water make a waterfall effect (to trap enough oxygen downstream for animal life).

The inlet structure must serve like a miniature dam wall to create a wetland on the water entry side. This wetland will slow down the speed of the water (reduce erosion effect) and allow for sediment to gravitate to the bottom (accumulate silt). The silt will contribute to a reed bed that can escalate into a small peat-land site, which will purify the water as a filter system. The dam will accommodate a small portion of open water but most of the moisture will be under ground level. This will feed the underground water table and contribute to water conservation.

The spinoffs of this structure will be aquatic wildlife (insects, frogs, small fish and lots of food for bird life). The reed bed will create nesting sites for the birds, cane rats using the plant materials, snakes after the cane rats and frogs, birds feeding on fish and frogs, crabs feeding in the open water become prey for the Cape Clawless Otters in the river system.

Humans in a city environment can observe this as a leisure activity. A parking area with a bird hide can be constructed. Nearby residents will enjoy the sounds created by the birds and frogs and so on. Imagine the boost to cities on urban wild life if all the river crossings by roads in towns have these structures in place.

Miniature dam with supporting wetland.

This planning should start with the urban nature conservator to map out all ecological sensitive areas (rivers, wetlands, ridges, etc.). Then do the map layout and determine how it will affect the nature areas. Remember, when you start off it is pristine and you only have one chance to make the best of it. When it is disturbed, it is difficult to rehabilitate. Buildings and roads can be changed afterwards; nature cannot easily be altered and can be lost after development.

The industry should not wait for government or the municipality to implement proposals like this. Funding is always a constraining factor and the cheapest way will be a structure through the shortest route (sometimes a wetland), destroying a pristine ecological sensitive urban nature area.

Companies sponsor sport teams to brand their names for their potential clients. They want their clients to see they contribute to the client's favourite rugby team, etc. Why can't companies not sponsor and brand their potential client's environment? A company need customers, customers prefer where they want to stay (their environment will play a major role). What does the immediate environment of a company look like? Big companies contribute to unacceptable waste outlets. They contribute to high pollution levels, dump waste at unacceptable levels and ignore the environment where they try to conduct their business.

11.1.4   Why humans must conduct nature friendly development

Results from human errors impact directly on us. Without knowing we make our living environment bad for ourselves. Because it is a slow process we are not aware

Reed bed forms wetland on water entry side of bridge.

of the results. By the time we become aware of it, it is already too late. Everyone is so busy making a living (to try and survive) that we miss the boat in the long run.

I want to use an example of greening with a negative outcome. My example is modern day nurseries where residents buy plants for their gardens. The majority of plants in a nursery are alien/exotic/non endemic species. Although it is green and you contribute to the right action namely to plant a tree and make your environment green, the impact on the endemic (local) environment is negative.

These plants are not synchronised with the endemic environment. This means that their natural consumers (birds, insects) are not available (plants from foreign countries) and they win the competition in the food chain. They utilise more water and nutrients. They grow stronger and overtake endemic vegetation. It looks nice, it does not sound nice and the impact is negative towards indigenous/ endemic vegetation. It causes an impact on insects and birdlife and the only people that benefit is the nurseries and the uninformed individuals.

A green golf course with exotic grass and trees is a green desert. It consumes a lot of water, changes the natural environment and only contributes to recreation. The other way around is a golf course with endemic vegetation and animals, low on maintenance (cut endemic grass and only maintain greens) with the same recreational outcome.

Beautiful Jacaranda trees with beautiful flowers became a declared alien that invested our natural environment (please read Chapter 8, on alien plant control). A tree like Van Wykshout can look similar to Jacaranda trees to the laymen, but it is indigenous and will contribute to urban wildlife for instance in the Pretoria South African region.

Green developments (landscaping) should have positive impacts on hard core development in urban nature areas (not mountains cut away to sell stone for roads, wetlands filled with rubble to form terraces, peat lands dried and compacted to build houses).

Developments create jobs. Jobs mean money and possible fortunes to be made. Wealth expectancies motivate people to move to cities and towns and more and more people do this to try and survive. If there is no balance (sustainable usage) nature spirals into unbalanced conditions with effects like global warming, pollution, unhealthy environment and crime.

We have to plan in advance. We need to inform people and to educate the community. We all need to understand and contribute to planning for a better environment; it is not cheap and not easy, this is hard work and should be part of everyday life.

More examples of industrial and technological impacts on nature that we have to live with are addressed in the rest of this chapter, focusing on storm water pollution.

11.2   STORM WATER POLLUTION

Rain water in the urban environment captures polluted material and contaminates water resources in the urban environment. We need to put a system of storm water management in place that effectively manages and mitigates all storm water impacts on water resources. Pollution affecting the watercourses originates from development and industries.

11.2.1   Literature review

To fully understand the storm water pollution problem, it is helpful to step back and review the water cycle, also known as the hydrologic cycle. The water cycle is simply the constant movement of water from the sky to the ground and back again. The main components of the water cycle are precipitation, infiltration, evapotranspiration (evaporation and transpiration, the process by which plants release water they have absorbed into the atmosphere), surface and channel storage, and groundwater storage. As part of that cycle, when rainwater falls on the ground, or when snow or hail on the ground melts, that water may take several paths.

The storm water pollution problem has two main components: the increased volume and velocity of surface run-off and the concentration of pollutants in the run-off. Both components are directly related to development in urban and urbanising areas. Together, these components cause changes in hydrology and water quality that results in a variety of problems including habitat loss, increased flooding, decreased aquatic biological diversity, and increased sedimentation and erosion. Run-off pollution occurs every time water picks up contaminants from a wide variety of sources as it flows across rooftops, roads, parking lots, construction sites, golf courses, lawns, and other surfaces. The oily sheen on rainwater in roadside culverts is but one common example of urban run-off pollution. Studies have shown that storm water alone can be almost as contaminated as sewerage/storm water mixtures.

While the magnitude of these effects varies across catchments depending on the precipitation patterns, soil types and other factors, the underlying principles remain the same. In a typical undeveloped area, for example, with natural ground cover such as undisturbed veld, a large fraction (perhaps 50%) of the water infiltrates the soil. Much of this water may remain near the surface from which it often resurfaces into lakes or streams. Other infiltrated water descends to a deeper level, perhaps recharging an underground aquifer used for drinking water. A significant share (40%) of the water returns to the atmosphere through evapotranspiration. Only a small amount of the water – the remaining 10% – remains on the surface of undeveloped land to run off into streams and other water bodies.

Urbanisation can dramatically alter this water cycle, increasing run-off and reducing infiltration, at times to almost zero. This can completely alter the physical and chemical character of the receiving water body.

The causes of storm water pollution

Impacts from an increase in impervious surfaces

Increased imperviousness (volume, peak flow, duration, stream temperature, base flow, and sediment loadings) leads to flooding, habitat loss (e.g. inadequate substrate, loss of riparian areas, etc.), erosion, channel widening and streambed alteration (Source: Urbanization of Streams: Studies of Hydrologic Impacts, EPA 841-R-97-009, 1997).

11.2.2 Increased volume and velocity: the impervious cover factor

Types of impervious cover

Human-made impervious cover comes in three varieties: rooftop imperviousness from buildings and other structures; transport imperviousness from roadways, parking lots and other transportation-related facilities; and impaired pervious surfaces, also known as urban soils, which are natural surfaces that become compacted or otherwise altered and less pervious through human action.

Figure 11.1: Stormwater run-off carries pollutants into our waterways.

Cumulative figures show that worldwide, at least one third of all developed urban land is devoted to roads, parking lots, and other motor vehicle infrastructure. Rainfall on transportation surfaces drains directly to a stream or storm water collection system that discharges into a water body usually without treatment. The creation of additional impervious cover also reduces vegetation, which magnifies the effect of the reduced infiltration. Trees, shrubs, grass and wetlands, like most soil, intercept and store significant amounts of precipitation. Vegetation is also important in reducing the erosional forces of rain and run-off.

Research has shown that when impervious cover reaches between 10% and 20% of the area of a watershed, ecological stress becomes clearly apparent. After this point, stream stability is reduced, habitat is lost, water quality becomes degraded, and biological diversity decreases.

Increased volume of run-off

The effect of impervious surfaces on the volume of storm water run-off can be dramatic. For example, a 25 mm rainstorm on a 0,4 hectare natural veld would typically produce 0,17 cubic metre of run-off, enough to fill a standard size office to a depth of about 600 mm. The same storm over a 0,4 hectare paved parking lot would produce 2,7 cubic metre of run-off, nearly 16 times more than the natural veld, and enough to fill three standard size offices completely.

Mangrove stream pollution.

Greater stream and run-off velocity during storm events

Impervious surfaces increases the speed of run-off as it drains off the land. Unlike grassy meadows, hard, impervious cover, such as parking lots and rooftops, offers little resistance to water flowing downhill, allowing it to travel faster across these surfaces. In addition, the faster rate of run-off delivers more water in a shorter time to receiving waters than would occur under natural conditions. The increased velocity and delivery rate greatly magnifies the erosive power of water as it flows across the land surface and once it enters a stream.

Increased peak discharges

Increased imperviousness not only changes the volume of storm water flows, but also the distribution of flows over time. When land is undeveloped, the initial storm water flow following a rain event is relatively small, since the land absorbs and infiltrates much of the water. However, impervious cover forces rainwater to run off the land immediately, causing a sharp peak in run-off immediately following the rain event. Impervious covers can double, triple, quadruple or even quintuple peak discharge. Streams receiving these increased urban peak flows are described as "flashy," meaning that they are prone to sporadic and unstable discharges including flash floods or sudden high pulses of storm flows. An increase in peak flow can have significant impacts on the human and natural environment. Greater peak flows lead to increased flooding, channel erosion and widening, sediment deposition, bank cutting, and general habitat loss.

Reduced stream base flow

Impervious cover reduces infiltration and forces storm water to run off the land immediately, so it also typically reduces the amount of groundwater available to recharge streams when there is no rain. Hydrologists often refer to groundwater zones under urban areas as "starved" since they are not replenished. This groundwater-charged stream flow, known as base flow can fall to 10% of the regional average when the level of imperviousness in the stream watershed reaches 65%. Prolonged low flow can have a significant impact on aquatic life and in some cases a greater impact than extreme peak flows.

Decreased natural storm water purification functions

Municipal storm water departments often replace the beds of creeks, streams, and other drainage ways with concrete open channels, or completely replace those drainage ways with subsurface concrete storm drain lines. These changes degrade or eliminate habitat and dramatically alter hydrology. Canalising disconnects a river from its floodplain and reduces its ability to modify floods naturally. Similarly, this and other development fills, converts, or otherwise eliminates swamps, marshes and other wetlands. Eliminating these natural drainage ways reduces flow storage and detention and soil moisture maintenance and can increase overall flooding and erosion. In addition, natural streambeds and floodplains provide a hydrologic link between groundwater and surface water and can naturally clean waters. By capturing and slowing storm water, these areas trap sediment, trace metals, and soluble forms of nutrients. Studies have shown that wetlands can retain up to 100 percent of the metals present in water. Wetlands reduce nitrogen discharges, both through the process of bacterial denitrification and through plant uptake, but less effectively reduce phosphorous when soils are saturated.

However, use of wetlands, streams, and other natural systems is not desirable unless storm water is delivered at a rate at which pollutants can be assimilated. Natural wetlands, while playing an important role in managing the quality and quantity of run-off, should not be viewed as a sink for polluted run-off. While wetlands help remove pollutants from run-off, some pollutants can accumulate in wetlands or be converted to more potent forms, thereby degrading the natural ecosystem functions and values of these systems and impact the organisms living there. Therefore, use of these systems for storm water management should be carefully considered, realising that these systems need quality water delivered at an appropriate rate to function properly.

11.2.3   Increased deposition of pollutants

The second aspect of urbanisation that contributes to urban storm water pollution is the increased discharge of pollutants. As human activity increases in a given area, the amount of waste material deposited on the land and in drainage systems increases. While many activities can be a source of contaminants, certain activities are particularly significant contributors. Industrial sites, for example, can be major sources of metals and organic chemicals.

Vehicle use

Driving a car or truck contributes a number of different types of pollutants to urban run-off. Pollutants are derived from automotive fluids, deterioration of parts, and vehicle exhausts. Once these pollutants are deposited onto road and parking surfaces, they are available for transport in run-off to receive water during storm events. Brake pad wear contributed 50% of the total load, and 25% came from atmospheric deposition, the eventual settling of metals from tailpipe emissions onto the ground. Tyre wear is a substantial source of cadmium and zinc; concentrations at outfalls often exceed acute toxicity levels. Engine coolants and antifreeze containing ethylene glycol and propylene glycol can be toxic and contribute high BOD to receiving waters.

Home landscaping and public grounds maintenance

Landscaping practices are another potential source of pollutants in urban run-off. Landscaping practices includes fertilisers used at home and on golf courses, cemeteries, and public parks that can add nutrients to run-off. Monitoring has shown a direct link between the chemicals found in lawn care products and urban water quality. Similarly, harmful pesticides found in storm water, such as chloropyrifos, 2,4-D, and diazinon come from golf courses, municipal parks, highway medians and roadsides, and residential lawns and gardens.

Construction sites

Construction activity is the largest direct source of human-made sediment loads. Since erosion rates are much higher for construction sites relative to other land uses, the total yield of sediment and nutrients is higher. Studies indicate that poorly managed construction sites can release 7 to 1 000 tons of sediment per acre during a year, compared to 1 ton or less from undeveloped land. Construction activity can also result in soil compaction and increased run-off.

Illicit industrial connections to storm sewers

Businesses that illicitly connect pipes containing wastewater from industrial processes to the storm sewerage system rather than to the municipal sewers can add metals, solvents or other contaminants to storm water.

Informal settlements

Pollution from diffuse sources such as informal settlements is very difficult to control. Inadequate sanitation facilities adds large bacterial loads to water bodies with consequent health risks, as well as to contribute to the total nutrient load of surface waters. (DWAF: 2002)

Littering

Not only does storm water frequently receive no treatment, it also often does not even have the benefit of simple filtering or screening for visible objects. As a result,

Polluted stream.

paper cups, cigarette butts, virtually anything made of styrofoam, newspaper, and other materials that people toss on the ground are carried into storm sewer systems and eventually into lakes, streams and oceans.

This list, exhaustive as it is, is incomplete. Galvanized roofs, unpaved roads, the dust that collects on paved streets and countless other aspects of daily life in urban areas contribute to polluted run-off. The first step in storm water management is not to memorise any particular list, but rather to recognise the breadth of opportunities for pollution prevention and the need to think holistically about the entire chain of human activities that affect run-off quantity and quality.

Categories of principal contaminants in storm water (Source: Urbanization of Streams: Studies of Hydrologic Impacts, EPA, 1997)
- Metals = zinc, cadmium, copper, chromium, arsenic, lead.
- Organic chemicals = pesticides, oil, grease.
- Pathogens = viruses, bacteria, protozoa.
- Nutrients = nitrogen, phosphorus.
- Biochemical oxygen demand (BOD) = grass clippings, fallen leaves, hydrocarbons, human, and animal waste.
- Sediment = sand, soil, and silt.
- Salts = sodium chloride, calcium chloride.

While the rain cannot be controlled, its storm water impacts can be managed to a large degree. Management, planning, development design, or material substitution or reduction that incorporates storm water pollution prevention before an activity takes place, are almost always the most effective and cost-effective means to reducing storm water pollution. However, in already highly urbanised areas, such measures may not be possible. In such cases, several communities have found treatment of run-off with structural measures to be an effective alternative.

Preserving and utilising natural features and processes has many benefits. Many communities and developers found management measures that rely on natural processes to be highly effective and efficient. Undeveloped landscapes absorb large quantities of rainfall; vegetation helps to filter out pollutants from storm water. These communities have benefited from implementing environmentally friendly alternative site design or "green infrastructure" by saving money and optimising open spaces. Buffer zones, conservation-designed development, sensitive area protection, or encouragement of infill development all enhances natural processes and are amongst the most effective storm water programmes.

11.2.4   Strategies

11.2.4.1   Addressing storm water in new development and redevelopment

By far the most important category of storm water strategies focuses on land use and development. It encompasses a wide range of measures, from regional planning to the use of site-specific structural and non-structural measures. These measures, with the exception of incentives for infill and redevelopment, apply more in developing and suburban areas than in ultra-urban areas that are already built up. In areas where there is less opportunity for regional or site planning or conservation-oriented design because they are already built up and largely covered by impervious surfaces, municipalities will need to rely more on the other elements of a storm water programme or on storm water treatment measures.

As one of the principal causes of urban storm water pollution is the creation of impervious surfaces, **one of the best strategies a municipality can employ is to minimise the aggregate amount of new impervious surfaces**, since where impervious surface increases, treatment or control of run-off is needed. Case studies demonstrated that minimising impervious surfaces, within desired growth targets, can be a highly effective and beneficial strategy.

While development that reduces impervious cover by concentrating houses on smaller lots increases density and therefore the percentage of impervious cover on the developed portion of the site, it reduces the overall impervious cover, largely by reducing roads. Furthermore, by concentrating the impervious cover, it becomes technically easier and more cost-effective to implement structural run-off controls.

11.2.4.2   Growth management

Concentrating development in certain areas within an entire metropolitan area or region has the same benefits as concentrating development on a particular site. Less imperviousness is created for a given number of residences or businesses, creating fewer disturbances to the water cycle. Locally, however, the concentration of imperviousness will result in greater storm water run-off and more polluted flows. Therefore, heavily urbanised areas will often require structural management measures.

11.2.4.3   Transportation-orientated design

Many case studies demonstrate that alternatives to automobile transportation are feasible and realistic, and can be a key factor in reducing storm water pollution. Regional planning provides a context for the development of bicycle routes and paths, and mass transit in the form of bus and rail systems or carpooling. Development concentrated within one part of a region makes all of these alternatives more useful for residents and makes public transportation more financially viable for the municipalities or regions that operate them. Even if development is not concentrated in one area, multiple nodes of concentrated development along public transportation corridors, known as transit-oriented development, can have the same effect. By concentrating development near transportation and commercial services, vehicle kilometers travelled are reduced as is the associated infrastructure. As previously discussed, **fewer roads and vehicle kilometers travelled minimises two principal components of storm water run-off – impervious cover and pollutant discharge.**

11.2.4.4   Watershed planning

Watershed planning has provided several municipalities the opportunity to consider all the resources in the watershed as a single, interrelated system. As the name implies, watershed boundaries, not political boundaries, are the basic unit of management, often requiring a municipality to work with other local governments or regional organisations. (A watershed is the land area, or catchment, that contributes water to a specific water body.)

Effective watershed planning focuses on the relationship between land use and water quality. Watershed planning begins with an evaluation of the current and desired condition for each of the relevant water bodies in the watershed, as well as a comprehensive mapping of current land use practices in the watershed. Armed with these data, planners determine what land uses are consistent with the desired conditions in the water bodies. Watershed residents and other stakeholders are usually involved in the process. The municipalities then put in place a watershed plan along with land-use ordinances that designate new development and land use changes to appropriate levels, types and locations.

11.2.5   Buffers and open space preservation

Many municipalities employ stream and wetland buffer requirements, open space preservation, and other laws or programmes as a cost-effective means for reducing storm water run-off and achieving other public goals. These programmes are often the specific means of implementing larger growth management goals and are often linked with incentives to aid development in other areas. In addition to zoning-type ordinances, municipalities can also use economic incentives to reduce impervious cover or implement storm water control through storm water utilities where the fee is based on amount of impervious cover, inspection and permit fees linked to compliance, or dedicated contributions from land developers.

Many local governments have had great success, apparently often more than they expected, with a buffer system of protected natural areas around water bodies, sensitive areas, or steep slopes. Forested buffers are an essential part of natural stream, lake, and wetland protection. They often provide highly desired community amenities as well. Not only do buffers allow the water resources to function more naturally, they also help reduce a site's overall imperviousness. An average buffer width of 30 m can reduce imperviousness by up to 5% of a watershed. Stream buffers often include the 100-year flood plain allowing the river system to naturally handle peak discharges, thereby avoiding expensive flood control structures. This aspect alone has saved millions. Furthermore, buffers act as filters, producing effective pollutant removal particularly for sediment, trace metals, and hydrocarbons. The more extensive and natural the buffer systems are, the more effective the benefits and results. Open space often serves many community needs and can both reduce the storm water problem and be part of the solution.

Brownfield development and infill redevelopment

Policies to encourage redevelopment of existing facilities and new infill development in already developed areas can also help prevent storm water pollution. Reuse and renovations of existing commercial buildings or industrial sites provides the opportunity for economic development with little or no addition of impervious cover – and in some cases a reduction in such cover. Redevelopment and new infill development allows businesses and citizens to take advantage of existing municipal infrastructure. Such infill development also reduces pressure to develop currently natural areas, the greenfields and can revive urban neighbourhoods. A key to all these area-wide measures is enforcement.

11.2.6   Site design measures

Minimising imperviousness, which is prevention focused, is more cost-effective than treating storm water run-off and much more cost-effective than restoring water bodies after they have been polluted or damaged.

Regulators may make storm water-conscious site design more difficult due to the street, setback, density, or other site development requirements and it is therefore important for local governments to allow flexibility.

Conservation design

Conservation-design development concentrates on homes on a limited percentage of the land comprising a residential subdivision, while leaving the rest of the land as open space. Several of the case studies showed that conservation design also reduces the amount of impervious road surfaces created, since the homes are not spread as far apart, and preserves a much greater percentage of undeveloped land. Narrower roads, shorter setbacks from residential streets that allow shorter driveways, or shared driveways also reduce impervious cover when designing residential developments.

The concept of conservation development designs have recently been expanded by ecologists to integrate native landscapes as functional elements of a development to provide water quality management, wildlife benefits, biodiversity protection, and human enjoyment. This is very different from the approach of simply not developing certain areas. For example, some developments using all the land as part of a storm water treatment train have a committed restoration and management programme for all portions of the property in order to maintain ecological integrity and water management functions.

On commercial and municipal sites, developers have frequently minimised imperviousness by implementing alternative parking arrangements. For example, businesses with parking demands at different times, such as a medical practice and a restaurant, have successfully shared the same parking area. Other parking alternatives consist of planning lot capacity for average rather than peak parking demands, placing parking areas beneath commercial buildings, and constructing multi-storey parking garages.

Another tool to reduce overall imperviousness is gaining more popularity. Porous pavements allow water to pass through it into the soil while retaining enough strength to support vehicular traffic. (It has largely been used in areas of light to

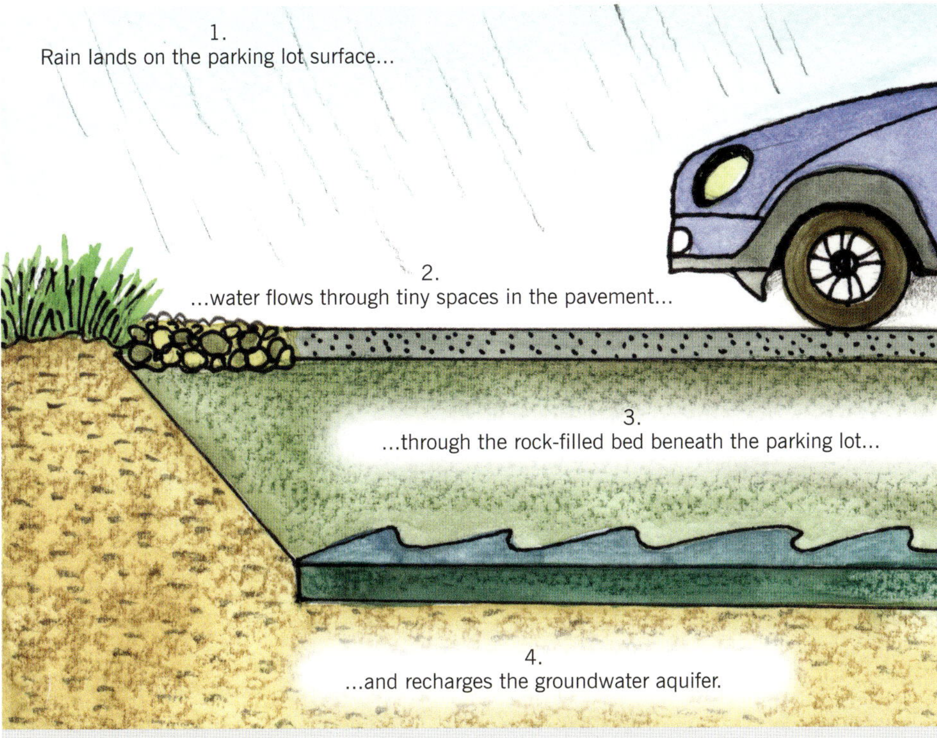

Figure 11.2: Conceptual diagram showing how porous pavement functions.

Restore stream to natural state.

moderate, not heavy, traffic.) Porous asphalt and concrete differ from regular asphalt and concrete because fine materials are not added to fill in the gaps between the coarser aggregate in the pavement material, so that a myriad of small holes allow water to infiltrate. Grass paving systems use plastic or concrete grids buried at soil level to add strength to normal turf. While not suitable for daily use, grass paving may be appropriate for parking areas used intermittently. Some experience suggests, however, that pervious pavements can require more maintenance.

Preservation of sensitive areas has helped address run-off on a site-specific basis as well as on an area-wide basis, as discussed above. On their own and not due to area-wide requirements, numerous extremely successful developments have kept imperviousness to a minimum and protected sensitive areas by specifying buffer zones around water bodies and by not developing areas where steep slopes, forests, or wetlands are present.

11.2.7   Site-specific/structural run-off control and treatment, best management practices

The management measures discussed above aim to preserve natural infiltration and pollutant-removal capabilities and reduce generation of storm water pollutants. This is clearly the most effective and cost-effective method of storm water pollution prevention. Depending on the circumstances, however, these types of measures may not be adequate to deal with storm water problems caused by new development or redevelopment, and are usually insufficient in areas already fully developed. Where new development is concentrated on in one area, for example, the storm water from that highly developed area needs more intensive management. In places where infilling is occurring or where land is less available or more expensive, there is often less interest in area-wide measures.

In such cases, municipalities then turn to site-specific run-off control and treatment. Typically, these best management practices (BMPs) are structures engineered to remove contaminants from run-off and to control its flow. These structural BMPs are best suited to and may be the only option available for areas of dense impervious cover. In highly urbanised areas where space is limited, retrofitting an existing storm water control structure to be a treatment structure is also effective.

For some types of treatment, structural BMPs may involve significant construction, usually at a comparatively high cost, and require continued operation and maintenance. Critical to the effectiveness of structural BMPs are proper design and installation that considers site-specific conditions. Furthermore, structural methods only partially mitigate the impacts of urbanisation. Non-structural BMPs, on the other hand, are prevention-focused and therefore often achieve greater environmental benefits. They are also very cost-effective; an ounce of prevention is worth a pound of cure. Structural storm water "cures" can also have unfortunate side-effects; for example, wet ponds and detention basins cause an increase in water temperature, which impacts on aquatic organisms.

The bottom-line appears to be that while prevention-focused, non-structural BMPs such as planning and design offer many advantages, in the densely populated sections, some structural BMPs are often needed.

Four categories of structural management measures are found: detention practices, bio-filtration practices, infiltration practices, and filtration practices. Some of the greatest successes have come from using more than one of these four functions in series, sometimes referred to as a "storm water treatment train". Other successes have been achieved by retrofitting detention and retention systems to add storm water treatment components to existing conveyance or storage facilities.

11.2.7.1   Detention practices

Detention practices temporarily store run-off, and then discharges it through a pipe or other outlet structure into streams or other water bodies. Use of wet and dry detention ponds are the most common of such practices. Dry ponds release all of their water within a specified time period (generally up to 48 hours), while wet ponds keep some water at all times and retain excess water for a longer period than dry ponds. When designed to be such, wet ponds can be an aesthetic or recreational amenity. The fundamental purpose of detention ponds is to reduce peak flows. They can also improve water quality by holding water for a long enough period to allow some sediment and other contaminants to settle out before the water drains. Wet ponds, by virtue of the longer detention times and frequent presence of aquatic plants and other life, can provide additional water quality treatment through bio-filtration and chemical processes.

11.2.7.2   Bio-filtration and bio-retention practices

These practices filter storm water to reduce contaminant loadings using plants as an additional filter medium. Plants absorb nutrients and metals to a certain extent and facilitate microbial breakdown, but most of the pollutant removal from these

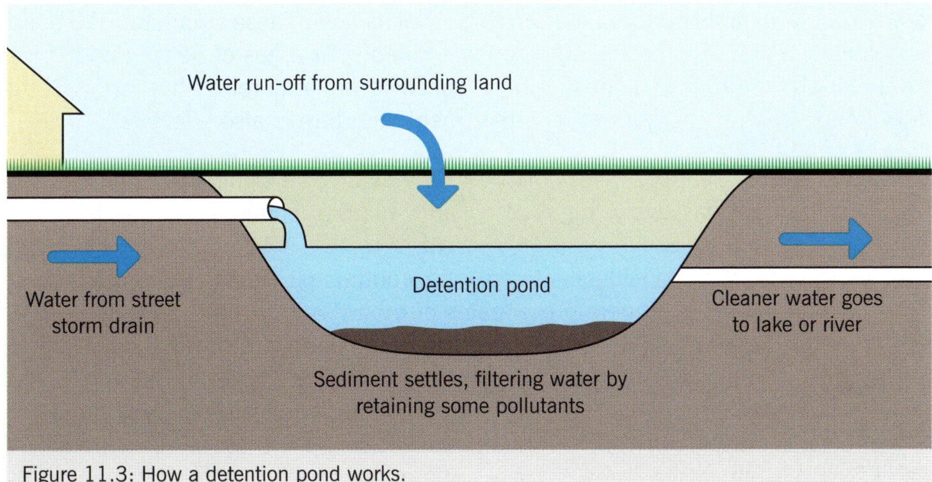

Figure 11.3: How a detention pond works.

Rain garden.

practices occurs when the presence of the plants physically blocks the storm water flow, slowing the flow and allowing contaminants to settle out. Bio-retention areas, also known as rain gardens, capture run-off and allow it to slowly infiltrate into the ground. Infiltration enhances pollutant removal and allows the water to be cooled. As with other structural BMPs, occasional maintenance to remove the accumulated pollutants from the storm water is required.

Constructed wetlands are artificial versions of natural wetlands, using shallow bodies of standing water filled with reeds and other wetland vegetation to filter the water. Engineered filter strips are slightly sloped, flat land planted with grasses, trees or other vegetation which remove storm water pollutants as the storm water moves gently across the strip in an even, sheet-like flow. Swales are wide ditches with moderate sloped banks and bottoms covered with filtering turf; in many cases swale also permit infiltration as well and cleans the water. Bio-retention areas are constructed forested or vegetated beds, usually composed of gravel, soil, trees and shrubs, a sand layer, and a grassed swale.

11.2.7.3   Infiltration practices

Infiltration practices temporarily store run-off in basins from which the water percolates slowly into the soil below. Like detention practices, they reduce peak flows. However, infiltration practices also recreate, to a greater or lesser extent, the natural pattern of water infiltration into the ground that existed before increased imperviousness covered the land. When designed and installed correctly and maintained regularly, infiltration practices are amongst the most effective structural

BMPs, and often addresses most of the storm water impacts previously discussed. Studies have shown that infiltration of this can get 98% of storm water into the earth, cool storm water to 55° F, remove up to 83% of nitrogen, and remove up to 98% of copper. The principal reason why infiltration is often a preferred method is that run-off is cooled as it flows through the ground, thereby reducing the detrimental thermal affects that run-off has on aquatic ecosystems.

Retention basins look like dry detention ponds, but have no outlet, forcing water to infiltrate through the bottom of the basin. Infiltration trenches are generally filled with rocks and gravel to surface level, creating a reservoir that holds water until it passes into the surrounding soil. Dry wells are deeper, narrower versions of infiltration trenches. Some of the most successful are wide-spread use of French drains, small infiltration trenches placed at the bottom of the discharge pipe from roof gutters that allow water to infiltrate on site rather than passing into the storm sewer system.

11.2.7.4   Filtration practices

Filtration practices address water quality problems rather than water quantity. Some consist of a chamber containing a filter medium buried at ground level through which storm water flows, while some are filter inserts for catch basins in the storm sewer system. As storm water flows it passes through the filter medium, that removes particles and other contaminants. The filtering materials most frequently used are sand, peat, or compost, and sometimes synthetic filter media.

It is important to note, however, that these measures are not magic bullets and must be carefully evaluated and monitored in order to ensure effectiveness. For example, some studies have shown that pollutants can accumulate in wetlands, and in some cases may approach levels of concern, yet little is known about the long-term effects of contaminants on these systems. Studies have also shown that wetlands may transform some pollutants such as mercury into more problematic forms. Catch basin inserts and filtration devices can lose effectiveness over time due to clogging or structural failure, or may not work well under certain conditions. To remain effective, these systems must be carefully selected, monitored and maintained. Infiltration basins are not appropriate in certain areas, depending on soil and water table. Areas near vulnerable ground water resources such as drinking water recharge areas or in areas with a high likelihood of contaminated run-off such as industrial sites or major roads and highways should be avoided. Detention ponds allow warm storm water to enter directly into receiving waters.

Storm water collected in ponds may heat to 95° F or more on a hot summer's day. Since aquatic ecosystems are sensitive to changes in water temperature, these warm waters can cause a loss of fish and other aquatic organisms. For these and other similar reasons, experts recommend that a combination of BMPs be used to broaden treatment, improve effectiveness and avoid undesirable side effects. Furthermore, the case studies and research for this report demonstrate that the most successful programmes choose storm water BMPs based on site use and characteristics as well as the targeted pollutants and established removal goals.

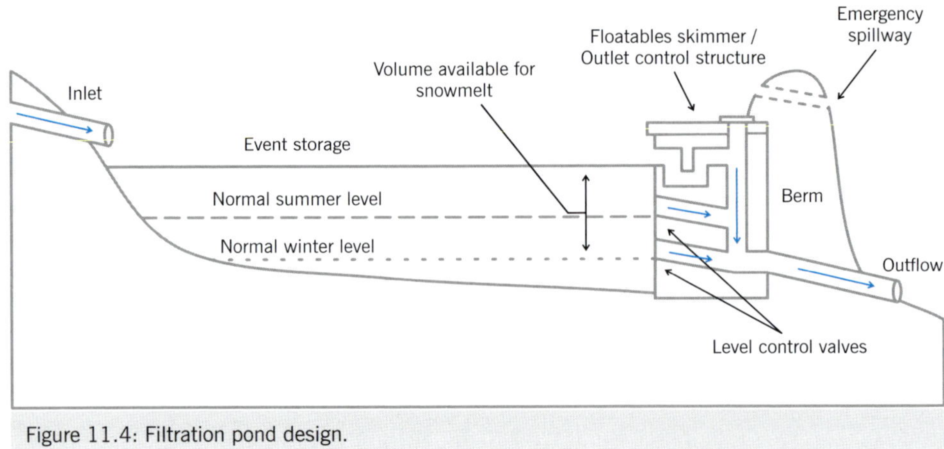

Figure 11.4: Filtration pond design.

Post-construction storm water management is the most significant element of a storm water plan. This category of measures – planning, site design, constructed facilities – attempts to reduce the overall impact of storm water from developed, or developing areas. While this represents the most far-reaching storm water measures, the most successful strategies documented links post construction storm water management to the other measures discussed below: public education, construction site controls, elimination of illegal discharges and illicit connections, and improved municipal practices.

11.2.7.5 Promoting public education and participation

Experience demonstrates that local governments need, and can get, the support of the broader population in addressing storm water pollution. Individuals play a key role in reducing storm water impacts both in their own day-to-day activities and in showing support for municipal programmes and ordinances. Case studies have suggested that the effectiveness of BMPs in other categories is often tied to the effectiveness of the public education programme.

Public education programmes documented in the case studies has been successful in addressing a wide range of activities. For example, programmes encourage citizens and businesses to reduce the chemical pesticides and fertilisers used on their lawns and gardens, or switch to natural pesticides and fertilisers. Programmes also have allowed or assisted citizens to monitor water quality in local water bodies or inventory and sample storm water outfalls. Restoration projects – repairing damaged water bodies by cleaning up debris dumped in streams or wetlands or by helping out with stream bank stabilisation – both achieve immediate environmental results and have proven to be among the most successful public education programmes. Municipal education programmes appear most successful if carefully targeted. School children, homeowners, business operators, outdoor recreation enthusiasts all have different interests. The most effective material distinguishes among different audiences and provides information interesting to them. In particular, public education targeted at local businesses can offer ways to contribute to citizen efforts or can focus on a pollution problem that is particular to a specific sector. Education efforts focused on petrol stations, car washes, or lawn care companies have made important progress.

Another form of public participation is participation in the political process. Municipalities reap multiple rewards encouraging citizens to participate in public hearings concerning storm water management ordinances and programmes, growth management regimes, approval for highway or residential development projects, public transit planning and budgeting, and other government activities affecting storm water pollution.

Providing decision makers with sound and accurate information is partly education, partly municipal operations, and partly planning. By focusing on familiar issues and local examples, these programmes help place broad, complex issues into context. Ideally all municipal officials should think about the storm water implications of their decisions.

11.2.7.6   Controlling construction site run-off

Effective local construction site storm water management strategies aim both to reduce run-off volume to levels that will not cause erosion and to capture as much of the sediment and other pollutants that do wash off. While existing programmes rely on a fairly wide variety of erosion and sediment control practices virtually all successful strategies require proper planning and phasing of construction activities to avoid disturbing more land than necessary during construction.

The most effective local programmes rest on four cornerstones that lay in pairs: enforcement and education; erosion prevention and sediment control. However, the first and overarching necessity is a clear set of requirements. The research for this indicates that vague guidelines or performance standards achieve vague results. Clarity and as much detail as possible is directly linked to the degree of implementation and ultimate success.

It appears that, even more than with respect to other industries, education and enforcement can achieve measurable storm water pollution reduction. Effective education programmes surveyed include a few essential elements: close cooperation with both local developers and citizen groups; a variety of outreach and communication modes, including brochures, training workshops, and on-site assistance; clarity in communicating both regulations, and technical methods. Compiling a set of clear, performance, BMP, and design-based standards in one easy-to-read manual or booklet appears helpful. Many effective construction-site education programmes also employ contractor certification to help ensure a baseline of knowledge for the development community. Whatever the education programme, however, they have not proven successful without the accompanying "teeth" of enforcement.

Effective enforcement programmes are found to require staffing adequate to the intensity and total acreage of development activity, stable funding, frequent inspections, clear enforcement authority, and partnerships with citizens. In addition, success is often greatly enhanced where top local elected and appointed officials make it clear they will not tolerate anyone not meeting environmental requirements.

Local governments' partnerships with citizens have added successful strategies in a number of ways. Partnerships training citizens in construction requirements offer additional eyes and ears watching sites for compliance. Partnerships with developers that provide some successful incentives such as positive publicity for good actors also appear popular and effective in studies.

The second pair of cornerstones of effective construction storm water strategies is erosion prevention and sediment control measures. Common erosion prevention techniques use site planning and construction phasing to minimise the unregulated areas exposed at any one time and shelter graded or denuded soil from rain and snowmelt. Sediment controls attempt to capture sediment after it has eroded off a hillside or graded area, using collection devices such **as sediment basins or inlet filters**, or controls such as silt fences at the perimeter or throughout larger sites.

Erosion prevention practices are an element of the more successful strategies because they can keep from mobilising the more harmful fine-grained particles that sediment controls cannot capture. In addition, erosion prevention techniques often require less maintenance since they are "planning-based" and non-structural.

It is also important for contractors to protect sensitive areas such as steep slopes, sensitive soils, wetlands, and other water resources. Effective programmes prohibit construction activities near sensitive areas or require measures to protect those

Gabion structure, Colbyn wetland, Pretoria.

features using vegetated buffers, silt fences, and dikes. A final element of successful construction storm water strategies addresses chemicals and other hazardous substances from storm water. Proper operation, maintenance, and storage of heavy equipment and materials prevent oil, petrol, diesel, paints, solvents and the like from leaking or spilling onto the ground.

11.2.7.7 Detecting and eliminating improper or illegal connections and discharges

Identifying and eliminating illicit connections and discharges is a remarkable simple and cost-effective way to eliminate some of the worst pollution from storm water and to improve water quality. Two factors are critical to the success of this element of storm water programmes: tracking or finding illicit connections and discharges, and enforcement. Since connections to storm sewers are usually underground, discouraging illicit connections is not always easy. Routine inspections or system surveys help prevent this problem.

Individuals or businesses may dump waste oil, excess pesticides and other chemicals, into storm drains as a cheap way to dispose of unwanted materials. In other cases, businesses or individuals connect waste water lines from toilets, sinks, floor drains and industrial processes to the storm sewer systems rather than to the sanitary sewer system.

In addition to these intentional illegal discharges, negligence adds to storm water pollution. When people store materials outside, or spill or dump oil or chemicals on the ground, storm water picks up the substances and transports them to receiving waters. Septic systems overflow and leave sewerage on the ground. Municipal sewer lines leak and discharge pathogens and nutrients from residential waste water and chemicals from industrial waste water into nearby storm water lines. Many non-industrial and often unregulated, improper discharges also degrade water quality, including household and charity car washing; mobile pressure washing of buildings, parking lots, and industrial equipment; draining swimming pools; and irrigating lawns and gardens.

Enforcement and education are closely linked. Enforcement engenders less opposition when people know what they are supposed to do and why. Conversely, enforcement appears to be a great motivation to pay attention to education efforts. One city official found that, "The more educated people become, the stricter we're able to be in our enforcement of the rules." Phrased differently, as a local activist said, "The best education programme is a good enforcement programme." As noted before, storm water management efforts build synergistically off each other; the most successful municipal strategies cover all programme elements effectively.

11.2.7.8 Implementing pollution prevention for municipal operations

A wide range of municipal operations can affect storm water quantity and quality. Some local governments have been able to manage their municipal operations to make a significant positive contribution to reducing storm water pollution.

Stormwater fed rain garden.

Successful municipal storm water operations strategies address areas of municipal activity (in addition to planning and regulatory/enforcement efforts discussed above) in a variety of ways.

First, a number of municipal services that primarily provide for other purposes can curb storm water pollution. Street sweeping, collection of leaves and other yard waste, collection and recycling of used oil or other substances, and general trash control all keep contaminants out of urban run-off. Improvement or expansion of such programmes significantly assists storm water pollution prevention and because people want these programmes, builds support for the broader issue of storm water management.

Second, municipalities engage in a number of activities that directly causes storm water pollution. They operate and maintain vehicle fleets of municipal buses, police cars, and waste collection trucks. These vehicles emit nitrogen and particulates which eventually end up on the ground and then in the storm water. These vehicles also deposit oil, grease, and metals onto roads and parking lots. Municipalities apply pesticides and fertilisers to municipal parks and cemeteries.

Municipalities can include storm water control requirements in all contracts for construction work and other contracts where such provisions are relevant. Most simply (and a very common action), timely maintenance of vehicles reduces the amount of oil, grease and metals left on roads and parking lots. More dramatically, municipal fleets can be converted to low-emission or zero-emission vehicles powered by natural gas, electricity, or other energy sources to reduce emissions and thus deposition of nitrogen and particulates. A number of municipalities reduce or even eliminate the use of artificial pesticides and fertilisers by employing sound landscaping practices such as planting native species and using integrated pest management.

Third, municipalities often manage some type of storm sewerage or storm drain system; how they do so can make the difference between simply moving the water to another place and successfully addressing storm water pollution. For example, if catch basins are not properly cleaned, the material that collects in them – sediment, trash and other storm water contaminants – can be re-suspended in storm water during a storm and eventually flow into a stream or water body. Local governments have found effective designing devices to reduce velocity using vegetated swales to facilitate infiltration and purify storm water run-off, or using preserved natural areas to store or convey storm water.

Fourth, training and education efforts that targets municipal officials and agency personnel have also proven to be important. Park and utility workers educated in integrated pest management, fertiliser use, and composting; fleet workers educated in fluid disposal; construction workers educated in erosion controls – all these have made noticeable differences in the storm water impacts of municipal operations. In municipalities constrained by human resources, programmes that provide training or certification for non-government personnel, such as citizen construction site or storm drain and outfall inspections has proven effective. Furthermore, the case studies demonstrate that well-trained and informed staff improve interactions with the community, raising community awareness, improving credibility and setting positive examples for the community.

CHAPTER 12

ENVIRONMENTAL IMPACT ASSESMENTS (EIAs)

(This chapter explains the procedure and implementation of environmental impact assessments (EIAs). It highlights the way how biodiversity is affected by development. There is a section on grasslands, wetlands and coasts, with an explanation of the EIA processes for each of these habitats.)[1]

12.1   PURPOSE OF THE EIA PROCESS

The environmental impact assessment process:

- Requires a developer/applicant to subject a listed activity to both a basic assessment of scoping and an EIA process, depending on the nature of the listed activity.

- Requires a developer/applicant to take a hard look at the activity he/she intends to undertake and to consider the environmental impacts of the proposed activity or development and to consider alternatives and mitigation measures that will reduce negative environmental impacts.

- Provides the public with a meaningful opportunity to understand and comment on the proposed activity.

- Provides the government's decision makers with important information to assist them in deciding whether to approve or refuse an application for environmental authorisation to proceed with the activity.

- Gives interested and affected parties the legal right to participate in the EIA process. This toolkit is aimed at assisting interested and affected parties in understanding the EIA process and participating in meaningful ways.

The main stakeholders/parties involved in the environmental impact assessment process are: the applicant/developer (the party requesting the authorisation); the environmental assessment practitioner (the party managing the process on behalf of the applicant); the competent authority (based on the outcome of the EIA process will either grant or refuse the requested environmental authorisation); and you, the interested and affected parties.

---

[1] The information in this chapter was extracted from the document compiled by the Endangered Wildlife Trust – EWT). This information is based on the regulations enacted under the South African National Environmental Management Act (No.107 of 1998).

Exemption: A person may only be exempted from a provision in the environmental impact assessment regulations, requiring or regulating a public participation process, if the rights or interests of other parties are not likely to be adversely affected by the exemption.

Basic assessment: A basic assessment is applied to activities that is considered less likely to have significant environmental impacts and therefore, unlikely to require a full-blown and detailed environmental impact assessment. A basic assessment report is a more concise analysis of the environmental impact of the proposed activity than a scoping and EIA report. However, basic assessment still requires public notice and participation, consideration of the potential environmental impacts of the activity, assessment of possible mitigation measures and an assessment of whether there are any significant issues or impacts that might require further investigation.

Scoping: Scoping and EIA is the thorough environmental assessment required for activities contained in listing 2. The activities listed in listing 2 are activities that due to their nature and/or extent are likely to have significant impacts that cannot be easily predicted. Listing 2 activities are therefore higher risk activities that potentially cause higher levels of pollution, waste and environmental degradation.

The scoping report (including plan of study for EIA) requires a description of the proposed activity and any feasible and reasonable alternatives, a description of the property and the environment that may be affected and the manner in which the biological, social, economic and cultural aspects of the environment may be impacted by the proposed activity; description of environmental issues and potential impacts, including cumulative impacts that have been identified, and details of the public participation process undertaken. In addition, the scoping report must contain a roadmap for the environmental impact assessment, referred to as the "plan of study for the EIA", specifying the methodology to be used to assess the potential impacts, and the specialists or specialist reports that is required.

Environmental authorisation: Environmental authorisation usually called a record of decision. It is the written statement from the competent authority permitting or refusing the proposed activity. The authorisation may contain specific conditions which must be complied with. The applicant must have an environmental authorisation granting permission before commencement of a listed activity.

12.2   BIODIVERSITY AND THE EIA PROCESS

12.2.1   What is biodiversity?

Biodiversity is all the living creatures, plants and animals, on and in the earth, water and air in a particular place. Biodiversity also describes the interaction between these living creatures and the area (ecosystem) in which they live.

12.2.2   Why is biodiversity important?

Biodiversity supports human life and livelihoods in that it provides a number of ecosystem services:

- A source of food, medicine, fuel, grazing for livestock, and building materials.

- A contribution to food supply, for example the pollination of commercially viable crops, such as citrus, grapes and apples; the continued productivity of soils, and the control of pests and diseases.

- Aids in the regulation or control of natural processes that support human life, for example, soil formation, reduction of carbon that contributes to global warming (the potential increase in the temperature of the earth's atmosphere caused by pollution), recycling of nutrients, and the supply and purification of water.

- It helps to regulate floods and protects against storm surges.

- Provides space for leisure and tourism.

- Social, health and spiritual benefits for humans, and a contribution to their quality of life.

12.2.3   How is biodiversity affected by development?

- Habitat loss and degradation, for example, the destruction of wetlands, grasslands and indigenous forests for housing estates or low cost housing.

- Habitat fragmentation – ecosystems and the species therein, need a certain amount of interconnectivity for processes to continue. If a specific natural area is broken up into smaller pieces, eventually species disappear and certain functions are lost. For example, a large intact wetland can fulfil its functions far better than a wetland that is divided into two pieces.

- Loss of species, for example, the plants and animals endemic to a particular habitat will not be able to survive if that habitat is destroyed or altered by development.

- Natural environmental processes, such as continued river flow, water purification, and erosion control are affected. This can lead to an accumulated effect on both habitat and species, or this can continue to affect habitats and therefore species in the long-term until they die out.

- Direct impacts, for example, birds colliding with power lines, electrocutions.

- Alien invasive organisms that can transform natural habitats.

- Pollution effects on ecosystems and thus species.

12.2.4   How to consider biodiversity in the Environmental Impact Assessment (EIA) process

What should happen during the EIA process is that the impacts on biodiversity is investigated by specialists – people with the correct qualifications in botany, ecology, entomology, etc. usually at a postgraduate level. Specialists who can focus broadly on the impacts across the ecosystem should be brought in early. These specialists will not focus merely on fish for example, but more generally on the entire freshwater ecosystem, or not merely on mammals but on the entire terrestrial ecosystem. Later, once the general impacts are identified, specialists on fish, botany (plants), mammals, birds, geology, etc., could be involved where relevant. The specialist could be an ecologist from the local conservation agency or a consultant. These specialist studies are usually conducted in the following fields of biodiversity (depending on the type of development):

- Botany or terrestrial ecology (which could include a wetland, grassland, fynbos, forest or other habitat component).
- Freshwater ecology (which could include wetland, riverine, grassland or other habitat component).
- Marine or estuarine ecology (coastal, sea or estuarine habitats).
- Geology (soil erosion, suitability for development).
- Mammals.
- Birds.
- Amphibians.
- Reptiles.
- Invertebrates (animals without a backbone).

The specialist has to look at how ecosystems and species could be affected by development and how best the development can be designed, located and managed to avoid negative impacts, or results in benefits to biodiversity.

It is not only essential to assess the impacts on the affected site, but also to consider the impacts beyond the site (in a regional and catchments context). In addition, it is important to think of both direct (e.g. clearing of vegetation) as well as indirect impacts (e.g. downstream impacts of on-site changes in water flow) and cumulative (additive) impacts.

Generally, the impacts are assessed by the specialists according to the following criteria:
- Extent of the impact

    Site specific – Extending only as far as the activity, or limited to the site and its immediate surroundings.

    Regional – A development can often have a regional impact on biodiversity. If a feeding site for birds or mammals is destroyed, the population might leave the area or go extinct if they don't find other suitable areas. The same applies for national and international impacts if one considers the cumulative impacts. Studies have shown that housing developments can lead to losses of up to 90% of the species in an area whereas stock farming on natural veld ensures that up to 80% of the species remain.

    National – Will have an impact on a national scale – particularly if an ecosystem or species of national significance is affected.

International – Will have an impact across international borders or will impact on an ecosystem or species of international significance.

- Duration of impact

Short term – 0-5 years

Medium term – 5-15 years

Long term – (16-30 years) Impact will cease after the operational or working life of the activity, either due to natural process or by human intervention.

Permanent – Impact will be where mitigation or moderation by natural process or by human intervention will not occur in such a way or in such a time span that the impact can be considered transient or temporary.

Discontinuous or intermittent – Impact may only occur during specific climatic conditions or during a particular time of year.

- Intensity

Low impact – Affects the environment in such a way that natural, cultural and soil functions and processes are not affected.

Medium – Affected environment is altered by natural, cultural and soil functions and processes continue although in a modified way.

High – Natural, cultural or social functions or processes are altered to the extent that they will temporarily or permanently cease.

- Probability of occurrence

Improbable – Low likelihood

Probable – Distinct possibility

Highly probable – Most likely

Definite – Impact will occur regardless of any prevention measures

- Determination of significance

No significance (The impacts do not influence the proposed development and/ or environment in any way)

Low significance – The impacts will have a minor influence on the proposed development and/or environment. These impacts require some attention to modification of the project design where possible, or alternative mitigation (a choice of other methods to alleviate the impacts).

Medium significance – The impacts will have a moderate influence on the proposed development and/or environment. The impact can be ameliorated (lessened or improved) by a modification in the project design or implementation of effective mitigation measures. Should have an influence on decision, unless it is mitigated.

High significance – The impacts will have a major influence on the proposed development and/or environment. The impacts could have the "no-go" implication on portions of the development regardless of any mitigation measures that could be implemented. Influence decision, regardless of any possible mitigation.

- Confidence (low, medium, high)

12.3 GRASSLANDS AND THE EIA PROCESS

12.3.1 What are grasslands?

- South Africa is divided into 9 biomes (large ecological community having plants and animals which have adapted to the conditions in which they live) that share certain ecological and climatic characteristics. The grasslands form the biggest of these biomes, covering about a third of the country.

- The grassland biome does not contain only grass species. In fact, only one in six plant species in the grassland biome is a grass. The remainder are bulbous plants that include arum lilies, orchids, red-hot pokers, aloes, watsonias, gladioli and ground orchids.

- Other species, habitats and ecosystems forming an important part of the grassland biome are riverine and wetland systems.

Grassland.

12.3.2   Why are grasslands important?

- Grasslands play a vital role in ecosystem processes. Grasslands are the great collectors of rain water in South Africa. They reduce run-off and thus erosion, hold the water as groundwater or in wetlands and release it slowly throughout the year. This sponge effect ensures that rivers run throughout the year, even in the dry season.

- Ensuring a steady supply of water is critical to human survival and to economic development.

- The supply of water from the grassland catchments around Wakkerstroom in south-eastern Mpumalanga, for example, is crucial to the functioning of the highveld power stations and SASOL's Secunda petrol-from-coal plant.

- In many of the deep rural areas within the grassland biome, poor people depend largely on ecosystem resources for their livelihoods. Grasslands, for example, provide free grazing for sheep and other livestock.

- Many grassland plants are used as traditional and main line medicines. For example, the leaves of arum lilies are used to treat headaches, as a poultice (to heal wounds and inflammations) or even to treat miscarriages; the sap of some euphorbias is used to cure toothache, to treat leprosy, or to remove warts. Where a bulb is used for medicinal purposes, the plant is usually destroyed, which means that many of these plants are highly threatened in the wild.

- Grasslands support a wide diversity of plant, animal, and bird species.

- Four of the twelve bird species commonly found in grasslands – Rudd's and Botha's Larks, Southern Bald Ibis and Yellow-breasted Pipit – are considered to be globally threatened. Another five – Blue Korhaan, Mountain Pipit, Orange-breasted Rockjumper, Buff-streaked Chat and Drakensberg Siskin – are considered to be near threatened. In addition Rudd's Lark is the only bird species classified as critically threatened in South Africa, making it the country's most threatened bird. 31 of the 102 threatened butterflies in South Africa occur in the grassland biome.

- 13 of the 93 species of threatened reptiles and amphibians in South Africa occur in the grassland biome. 11 of these are endemic to (particular to that location) the biome, e.g. Yellow-bellied House Snake, Sungazer Lizard, Drakensberg River Frog.

- Mammals typically found in the more humid grasslands are Black Wildebeest, Blesbok, Oribi and Grey Rhebuck. 15 of the 34 mammals endemic to South Africa can be found in the grassland biome. Four of these – Black Wildebeest, Rough-haired Golden Mole, Natal Red Rock Rabbit and Sloggett's Rat – are endemic to the grassland biome.

12.3.3   Where is the grasslands biome?

In South Africa, the grasslands biome covers an area ranging from the interior of the Eastern Cape and KwaZulu-Natal provinces over the escarpment and into the central plateau. The bulk of the grasslands occur in six provinces. The majority

Biodiversity: a, Blesbok typically in humid grasslands; b, Drakensberg River Frog (photograph: Tyrone Ping); c, Pipit; d, Sun Gazer Lizard; e, Yellow-bellied House Snake.

of people in South Africa live in the grasslands because it contains the economic heartland of the country. It is also the largest urban complex, it harbours large coal deposits and gold fields and it is agriculturally productive land.

12.3.4   What are the major threats to grasslands?

- Expansion of agriculture and timber plantations especially into high priority or sensitive areas.

- Urban and industrial expansion – Gauteng is in the grasslands.

- Mining – more than 2 000 km^2 of grassland is taken up by South Africa's major gold and coal deposits. Mining impacts and their extent is minimal but absolute as it completely destroys the grassland.

- Poor land use management practices that result in degradation of the veld.

- Invasive alien plants.

- Pollution – many highly polluting industries are located within the grassland biome, e.g. coal-fired power stations; pulp and paper mills; steel, gold, chrome and other metal-processing industries. This air pollution impacts not only on the grasslands but also has an effect much further afield as it is carried by the wind. While pollution has other environmental impacts, it is not usually something we consider as a key impactor on grassland biodiversity.

12.3.5   How to consider grasslands in the EIA process

The presence of grasslands and their associated plants and animals should be identified early in the basic assessment or scoping and EIA process.

It is necessary for the developer/specialist to evaluate the following criteria:
- Which birds, plants, mammals, butterflies live in the grasslands?

- Are any of these creatures threatened?

- What will be the impact of the proposed activity on the grasslands and the species that live there?

- Will the proposed activity have an impact on the grasslands even if it is not in the grasslands?

- Look at cumulative impacts. For example, one housing development might not destroy much of the grassland but it is important to evaluate all housing for the greater environmental impacts.

- Remember that once disturbed by ploughing, mining, timber plantations or housing estates, most of our grasslands cannot be rehabilitated.

Find out:
- Whether the appointed specialist has the necessary qualifications to enable him to do a grassland plant and animal survey?

- How threatened is the specific grassland type? Some grassland types have as little as 3% remaining intact.

12.4   WETLANDS AND THE EIA PROCESS[2]

12.4.1   What is a wetland?

- Wetlands are water-saturated ecosystems or habitats for specific plants and animals. The presence or absence of water determines their formation, processes and characteristics.

- Wetlands are characterised by specific vegetation, particular soils and the presence of water at least for a period of time in the year. A wetland may have all of these characteristics or only one or two of them.

- Floodplains, marshes, bogs, deltas, swamps, peat lands, estuaries, river catchments and lakes are all wetland types.

- Wetlands occur in areas ranging from higher altitude mountain ranges (seeps), through to mid-catchment areas (marshes), through to estuaries at the coast.

- Some wetlands are constantly wet but others become temporarily dry.

The type of wetland present depends on the soils, the rainfall, climate and the topography.

Read Chapter 9 on Wetlands for more information.

12.4.2   Why are wetlands important?

- Water purification – wetlands are natural filters that trap pollutants.

- Reducing flooding – the vegetation in wetlands slows water down and helps reduce flooding.

- A wetland functions as a sponge and releases water throughout the year and recharges ground water supplies – stream flow regulation.

- The vegetation in wetlands reduces soil erosion.

- Biological diversity – wetlands provide habitat for a wide variety of species.

- Wetlands are some of the most biologically productive ecosystems in the world by allowing recycling of nutrients.

- Benefits for people – wetlands supports a variety of fish and birds which can be a source of food; they also provide different types of reeds for building materials and handicrafts from which people can fulfil their basic needs and make a living.

- Agricultural use – livestock grazing.

- Recreational use – birdwatching, aesthetics.

---

[2] The information contained in this section was obtained from the following document: "Summary, National Grassland Biodiversity Programme, May 2005".

12.4.3   How are wetlands affected by developments?

Developments can affect the way a wetland functions. The type of development and the scale of the development will have an impact on the wetland, whether it is within the wetland or in the catchment area surrounding it. All the wetland functions mentioned above will be impacted on and could either be reduced or lost.

12.4.4   How are wetlands harmed by development?

- By the use of too much fertiliser. Fertiliser run-offs from land cause algal blooms or rapid growth of algae in the water. Too much algae depletes all the oxygen in the water thereby killing the plants, fish and animals that live there.

- The incorrect application of non-selective pesticides or herbicides that run into the wetlands degrades natural animal and plant populations and impacts on water quality.

- Direct destruction. Wetlands are often drained and permanently altered in order to accommodate building or the planting of crops.

- Direct degradation of wetland systems – damming for water storage, irrigation or recreation, draining through ridge and furrow technique for agricultural purposes.

- By direct disturbance – constant human activity in or close to the wetland.

Birds in a wetland area.

- In a water-poor country such as South Africa, continued destruction of wetlands will result in:
    - Lower agricultural productivity.
    - Less pure water.
    - Less reliable water supplies.
    - Increased downstream flooding.
    - Increasingly threatened plant and animal resources.

12.4.5   How to consider wetlands in the EIA process?

A wetland is classified as the most threatened ecosystem in the world.

In the EIA process, the following should be done:
- The wetland should be delineated or sketched in an outline.

- The biodiversity within the wetland should be assessed to determine its value.

- The impact of the development on the wetland (whether within the wetland or its catchment) – and its functions – should be assessed, and mitigation measures (actions to moderate) put in place to reduce these impacts.

- The cumulative impact on the broader catchment or the effects on the entire wetland environment should be taken into account.

- Wetlands must always be buffered with an appropriate area from any type of development which may impact on the wetland ecosystem.

12.5   CONSIDERING COASTAL AREAS IN THE EIA PROCESS

South Africa's diverse coastal and marine environments are a valuable resource, providing recreation and pleasure for residents and tourists alike. In addition, these resources are of great biological and economic value to the country.

12.5.1   What are coasts?

- The coast is a unique part of South Africa's environment; it is a meeting place of land and sea.

- Coasts are extremely dynamic and complex areas. They include many different creatures and ecosystems, ranging from microscopic organisms to insects, shellfish, fish, plants, animals and birds. Many of the interactions between natural processes and human activities in coastal areas are not always well understood.

- The South African coast extends for about 3 000 km from the border with Namibia to Mozambique. It links the east and west coasts of Africa and connects the Africa continent to the Indian, Atlantic and Southern oceans.

- There is no single definition of the coastal zone. As a practical matter, local, municipal, provincial, and national governments all may use different definitions of a coastal zone. In addition, different pieces of legislation and international treaties may define a coastal zone differently.

- The coast is generally accepted to be the area of land that directly influences the sea or is influenced by the sea. The coast can be defined as an area with a landward and a seaward boundary that includes:

  - Coastal waters, which extend from the low water mark into the sea, up to the point where these waters are no longer influenced by land and land-associated activities.

  - The coastline or sea shore, which is the area between the low and high water marks.

  - Coastlands, which are inland areas above the high water mark that influence or are influenced in some way by their proximity to coastal waters (these areas may stretch many kilometres inland).

- The coastal areas of South Africa hosts a range of diverse ecosystems including water catchment areas, rocky shores, sandy beaches, coastal forests, mangrove habitats, coastal dunes, wetlands, estuaries and lagoons, mud flats, kelp forests, and coral reefs. The environmental impacts of development on each of these coastal environments will vary.

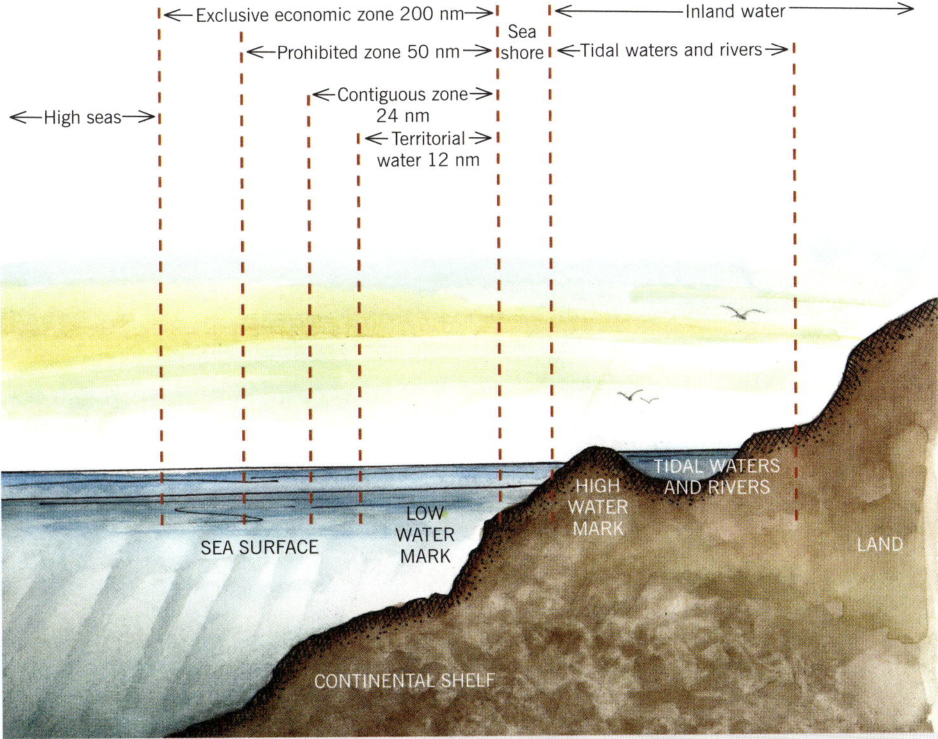

Figure 12.1: Components of a coastal shoreline (Summary, National Grassland Biodiversity Program).

- A variety of landward and seaward boundaries have been used to define the coast for different activities in South Africa (Figure 12.1 on page 255). Provincial and local government will define specific coastal boundaries on an issue-by-issue basis, depending on their areas of jurisdiction and management goals.

12.5.2   Why are coasts important?

Coastal ecosystems provide a range of direct and indirect benefits to us:
- Direct benefits include subsistence food production and commercial food production (fishing and agriculture), raw materials (mining), transportation, recreation, tourism, and aesthetic value (seafront property turnover).

- Indirect benefits or ecosystem services that are used but not paid for include, erosion control, soil formation, water regulation and supply, nutrient cycling, biological control, habitats, pollination, climate regulation, genetic resource, gas regulation, existence value. The coast and its adjacent areas on- and offshore are an important part of a local ecosystem as the mixture of fresh water and salt water in estuaries provides many nutrients for marine life. Salt marshes and beaches also support a diversity of plants, animals, and insects crucial to the food chain.

- The estimated value of the direct benefits obtained from coastal goods and services is about 35% of our annual gross domestic product. Indirect benefits are estimated at an additional 28% of the GDP.

- Over 33% of South Africa's population lives in coastal areas. Economic growth is fastest in South Africa's four major coastal cities – Cape Town, Port Elizabeth, East London and Durban.

Coastal areas host a variety of human activities, many of which can be conflicting. Careful and innovative planning and management of the coastal areas is therefore essential.

12.5.3   Activities supported in coastal areas

Extractive industries
- Mining (diamond and titanium)
- Dredging

Farming
- Agricultural crops
- Grazing
- Intensive animal production

Fisheries
- Commercial fishing
- Recreational fishing
- Subsistence fishing

- Bait collecting
- Aquaculture/mariculture

Forestry
- Wood for building industries
- Wood for energy
- Wood products

Manufacturing
- Industrial goods
- Goods for domestic consumption or export
- Chemicals, including medicinal drugs, paints, plastics, etc.

Oil, gas and offshore engineering
- Oil and gas exploration/exploitation
- Petroleum production

Tourism and recreation
- Resort and tourism facilities development
- Boating (sail boats, power boats, jet skis, paddle boats)
- Surfing
- Swimming, snorkelling and scuba diving
- Hiking/camping
- Bird watching
- Whale/shark diving

Social need to enjoy nature (Mountain bike).

Caravan camping.

- Golfing
- Parasailing

Services
- Production of electricity, gas, water and wind
- Processing and disposing of wastes (liquid and solid)
- Social services (education, health)

Transport and its related infrastructure
- Roads
- Railways
- Shipping
- Ports
- Airports

Development
- Residential development
- Commercial developments

12.5.4   How are coasts affected by developments?

- Developments can affect the way a coast functions. The type of development and the scale of the development will have an impact on the coastal area. All the benefits related to the functions mentioned above will be impacted on and could either be reduced or lost.

- Although coastal ecosystems are resilient, they are finite and vulnerable to over-exploitation, pollution from both marine and land-based sources and damage from improper and unplanned land use and development.

- Inappropriate decisions can result in degraded coastal resources and lost development opportunities. For instance, a bridge built across an estuary can disrupt the natural functioning of the ecosystem. Degraded coastal ecosystems that are no longer functioning properly can result in the exposure of human life and property to high risk, for example, through flooding or storm damage.

12.5.5 How to consider coasts in the EIA process?

- South Africa's coastal areas are diverse in terms of physical, social, economic, political and institutional characteristics. Different management responses are therefore required at provincial, regional and local levels according to the context.

- The impacts of developments or activities in the coastal area should typically be investigated in a holistic, integrated and coordinated way by specialists. A coordinated approach to coastal management acknowledges that the coast is a system and that different human uses of coastal resources are interdependent.

- A multiplicity of policy and legislation is applicable in the coastal area including the Constitution Act (108 of 1996); the White Paper on Sustainable Coastal Development (2000), the Marine Living Resources Act (18 of 1998), the Environment Conservation Act (73 of 1989), the National Environmental Management Act (107 of 1998) and the development Facilitation Act (67 of 1995), the Sea Shore Act (21 of 1935), and the Maritime Zones Act (15 of 1994).

- In addition a range of other national legislation, provincial laws and ordinances as well as local authority by-laws are relevant to the coast, for example, legislation relating to local government restructuring, development planning, heritage, disaster management, natural resource management, water, biodiversity, mining, transport, energy and pollution control.

- The Department of Environmental Affairs and Tourism (DEAT) has introduced regulations to control potentially harmful activities to the coastal environment, such as earthworks, dune stabilisation and dredging, within demarcated sensitive coastal areas (SCAs).

- Local authorities administer the regulations if private landowners are applying for permits, but local authorities themselves have to apply to the relevant provincial department for a permit if they wish to undertake activities covered by SCA regulations.

Boardwalk, Wonderboom, Pretoria.

CHAPTER 13

SUSTAINABLE UTILISATION OF URBAN NATURE AREAS (FOCUS ON VISITORS) [1]

(This chapter explains the impact of utilisation on urban nature areas. It deals with sustainable utilisation of urban nature areas. Visitor carrying capacity is highlighted, as well as ways to determine visitor numbers. The last part of the chapter focuses on recreational facilities within urban nature areas, various visitor activities and how these should be synchronised with the urban environment.)

13.1 SUSTAINABLE USE OF NATURE AND ECOSYSTEMS

Our forests, minerals, oil, land and water are not limitless and neither is the capacity of our world to absorb pollution. The financial rewards obtained from exploiting natural resources are of no use to a species driven to extinction as a result of such exploitation. If we leave a ravaged planet to our descendants, all the money in the world would be of little value to them. So, those responsible for drafting policies and laws must ensure that legislation indeed prevents overuse of natural resources, overburdening of natural systems and unfair distribution of pollution. The principle – indeed, duty – of sustainable use limits the ability of politicians and businesses to do whatever they want in their country or on their property, without regard for the impact on others, the planet and future generations.

13.1.1 Natural resource management

Natural resource management refers to the management of natural resources such as land, water, soil, plants and animals, with a particular focus on the way management affects the quality of life for both present and future generations (stewardship).

Natural resource management deals with managing the way in which people and natural landscapes interact. It brings together land use planning, water management, biodiversity conservation, and the future sustainability of industries like agriculture,

---

[1] Defining, measuring and evaluating carrying capacity – members of the Environmental Planning Laboratory of the University of the Aegean, Greece, Athens, December 2001.

mining, tourism, fisheries and forestry. It recognises that people and their livelihoods rely on the health and productivity of our landscapes, and their actions as stewards of the land play a critical role in maintaining this health and productivity.

Natural resource management is also congruent with the concept of sustainable development, a scientific principle that forms a basis for sustainable global land management and environmental governance to conserve and preserve natural resources.

Natural resource management specifically focuses on a scientific and technical understanding of resources and ecology and the life-supporting capacity of those resources. Environmental management is also similar to natural resource management.

13.1.2   Environmental governance

Environmental governance is a concept in political ecology or environmental policy related to defining the elements needed to achieve sustainability. All human activities – political, social and economic – should be understood and managed as subsets of the environment and ecosystems. Governance includes not only government, but also business and civil society and emphasises whole system management. To capture this diverse range of dynamic forces, environmental governance often necessitates finding alternative systems of governing, for example watershed-based management.

Natural resources and the environment should be seen as a global public good, belonging to the specific category of goods that are divided up when shared. The global nature of these goods stems from the presence of each of the constituent elements that form an integrated system. This means that everyone can benefit from the atmosphere, climate and biodiversity, to name a few, while the entire planet suffers the dramatic consequences of global warming, reduced ozone layer and the disappearance of species. This planetary dimension requires a collective management approach.

A public good is non-rivalrous – a natural resource acquired by one person can still be acquired by someone else – and non-excludable – it is impossible to prevent someone consuming the good. Nevertheless, public goods are recognised as beneficial and therefore have value. The notion of a good global public thus emerges, with a slight distinction: it covers vital necessities that must not be under the control of one person or state.

The non-rivalrous character of the good therefore calls for a management approach that is neither competitive nor plundering of free market characteristics which would lead to its extinction. It also entails attributing an economic value to the resource, since the lack of such value would lead to the same result. Water is possibly the best example of this type of good.

However, environmental governance as it currently stands is far from meeting one or more of these imperatives. The need to deal with the complex character of environmental issues calls for the adoption of coherent multilateral management by a great variety of stakeholders. However, the global community has proved incapable of meeting this challenge and environmental governance is currently victim to a great many afflictions. Thus, "despite a great awareness of environmental questions from developed and developing countries, there is environmental degradation and the appearance of new environmental problems. This situation is caused by the parlous state of global environmental governance, wherein current global environmental governance is unable to address environmental issues due to many factors. These include fragmented governance within the United Nations, lack of involvement from financial institutions, proliferation of environmental agreements often in conflict with trade measures; all these various problems disturbs the proper functioning of global environmental governance. Moreover, divisions amongst northern countries and the persistent gap between developed and developing countries also have to be taken into account to comprehend the institutional failures of the current global environmental governance."

13.2   CARRYING CAPACITY

In the urban environment, carrying capacity is a very important measurement to implement. On a cattle farm the farmer needs to determine the carrying capacity of the numbers of livestock (cattle) the farm can carry sustainably and this will determine if the farmer can make a living out of this carrying capacity. When the carrying capacity is sustainable, the farm can be regarded as an economic unit.

This concept is valid for all other enterprises that depend on natural resources. Carrying capacity is applicable with mining activities, water harvesting, firewood collection, absorption of pollution products, number of visitors to a nature area or a tourist facility, etc.

We need to determine the amount of parks and nature areas a city needs or has available in relation to the number of residents and activities taking place. A city or town will have various types of carrying capacity (for the amount of water available, the amount of electricity, availability of work, the natural resources available to serve in their social needs, amount of outdoor leisure for residents, etc.). Market needs will always determine carrying capacity, but where it is applicable to urban nature areas, the damages will occur long before the market needs can be evaluated.

Criteria to consider when we try to determine carrying capacity on urban nature areas:
- Ecological impact.
- Type of activity.
- Limited experience to apply carrying capacity.
- Physical-ecological.
- Socio-demographic.
- Political-economic.

Tourism creates pressures on the natural and cultural environment, affecting resources, social structures, cultural patterns, economic activities and land uses in local communities. These concerns increase and dominate public policy agendas as modern societies give increasing consideration to issues such as environmental conservation, quality of life and sustainable development.

Locality: This is the basis on which to structure tourism development. What local resources are available? How vulnerable are the natural ecosystems involved? What is the size of the population that we target? What economic structure is in place? Are culture and local heritage involved?

Type: What is the motive for visiting the facility? What mode of transport will visitors need? How long will they stay? What are the visitors' expectations, attitudes and behaviours?

The tourism interface: Impact of visitors on the environment and the degradation of the environment on tourism.

Protected areas: Tourism in protected areas is associated with appreciating and observing nature, scientific endeavour and education. This type of tourism is associated with minimal development of infrastructure and small scale interventions in areas of normally strong control and restrictive management. Carrying capacity issues concern the number of tourists, visitor flows and spatial patterns of concentration/dispersion vis-à-vis the protection of nature and the functioning of ecosystems but also the quality of the visitors' experience.

"Carrying capacity is not a scientific concept of formula in obtaining a number, beyond which development should cease. The eventual limits must be considered as guidance. They should be carefully assessed and monitored, complimented with other standards, etc. Carrying capacity is not fixed. It develops with time and the growth of tourism and can be affected by management techniques and controls" (Saveriades, 2000).

The process to determine tourist carrying capacity consists of two parts (Shelby and Heberlein, 1986; Jordaan, 2005).

Part A = descriptive with particular importance to
* Constraints: Limiting factors that cannot be easily managed.
* Bottlenecks: number of visitors at a particular place.
* Impacts: intensity and type of use.

Part B = evaluative part. Describes how an area should be managed and the level of acceptable impacts. The identification of the following is particularly important:
* Goals/objectives: Define the type of experience or other outcomes that a recreation setting should provide.
* Evaluative criteria: Specify acceptable levels of change (impacts).

Components that impacts on tourism in an area that can be analysed in terms of three major axes: physical environment (natural and man-made including infrastructure), social (population and social structure and dynamics) and economic (including institutional and organisational). These can also provide the basis for analysing and assessing tourist carrying capacity.

Physical-ecological component: This comprises all fixed and flexible components of the natural and built-cultural environment, as well as infrastructure. They cannot be manipulated by human action. They should be carefully observed and respected as such. Flexible components (infrastructure) are the following: water supply, sewerage, electricity, transport, social amenities. Their values cannot be used as a basis for determining carrying capacity.
- Congestion or density in key areas/spatial units (parks).
- Acceptable loss of natural resources without degradation of ecosystem functions or biodiversity or loss of species.
- Acceptable levels of pollution on the basis of tolerance of the local ecosystems
- Intensity of transport, facilities, services and infrastructure.
- Demand on water supply, electricity, waste, sewerage and telecommunications.
- Availability of health, safety, accommodation and community services.

Socio-demographic component: Social and demographic issues, such as available manpower or trained personnel and the tourist experience. The capacity threshold for these components is difficult to evaluate.

Social carrying capacity includes the levels of tolerance of the host, as well as the quality of the visitor's experience. This can be expressed in terms of:
- Number of visitors and activities which can be absorbed without affecting the sense of identity, life style and social patterns and activities of the host facility.
- Tourism which does not alter local culture (belief systems, customs and traditions).
- Tourism that will impact negatively on amenities.
- Number of visitors and compatibility of types of activities in an area without decline of visitor's experience.

Political-economic component: These components include impacts on local economic structures and activities and divergence in values, attitudes within the local community vis-à-vis tourism. These components may be expressed in terms of:
- Level of specialisation.
- Loss of labour in other sectors due to tourism attraction.
- Revenue from tourism.
- Level of tourism employment.

13.2.1   How to measure tourist carrying capacity

13.2.1.1   Setting levels of acceptable tourism

- Numbers of tourists per unit of time or density.

13.2.1.2   Analysis of key features

- Natural resources.
- Species under protection.
- Cultural and social patterns.
- Traditions.

13.2.1.3   Determine the tourism development

- Limits applicable.
- Constraints applicable.
- Bottlenecks predicted.

Measuring the following:

- Define the boundaries.
- Do data collection (hydrology, coastal dynamics, vegetation patterns and cover, wildlife species distribution, land use patterns, transport network, water supply and sewerage disposal). Determine those aspects which might affect the use of resources and conflicts.
- Determine durations.
- Are development and activities environmentally friendly?
- Identification of problems and threats.
- Determine pressure on resources.
- Calculating costs.
- Identification of bottlenecks.
- Identification of constraints.
- Consider alternatives.
- Determine employment opportunities.
- Identification of local population preferences. Residents are an important part of the tourism system around a destination.
- Assessment of the level of tourist satisfaction.
- Consider presence of traditional activities.
- Determine average income.
- Determine the capacity to manage problems.
- Consider plans for land use and regulations.
- Determine the total number of visitors that can be allowed to a city without hindering the other functions that the city performs.

13.2.2   Analysis of tourism development

- Tourist supply and demand.
- Type of tourism development.
- Level of tourism development (are overnight facilities necessary).
- Future red/ potential tourist demand.
- Identify tourism attractions (beaches, natural areas, wild life) and classify (is it seasonal, festival, etc.).
- Analysis (duration of stay, activities and events).

- Identify character of visitors (age, sex, income, race, expectations, ethnic origins).
- Identify tourist behaviour.
- Define profile of the area.

13.2.3   Application of tourism carrying capacity

Issues to be considered: Carrying capacity is a powerful concept for policy making, although from a scientific perspective it is met with considerable controversy due to the analytical difficulties in arriving at a "calculated" capacity (threshold or limit). This difficulty stems from the multiple dimensions of the concept and the inherent constraints in estimating limits in natural and human ecosystems. Getz (1987) identified six different approaches of interpretations or methods of determining carrying capacity: tangible resource limits, tolerance by the host population, satisfaction of visitors, excessive rate of growth of change, capacity based on the evaluation of costs and benefits and the role of capacity in a systems approach. In recent literature, the interest on carrying capacity has shifted from an objectively assessed threshold to policy useful and desired conditions providing more advantages to planning and decision making. Alternative concepts have also been suggested in the spirit of management-by-objective approaches such as visitor impact management, limits of acceptable change, visitor experience, resource protection frameworks, instead of tourism carrying capacity (Jordaan, 2005).

There is a growing concern for developing and using tools that could facilitate planners and decision makers in their efforts to control tourism development. However, there is limited, almost non-existent, experience not only in implementing tourism carrying capacity but also in measuring it. Within this context, the following should be taken into account:

Spatial considerations: Carrying capacity is easily defined in limited, well-defined areas. In addition, tourism carrying capacity could vary among the different parts of an area (e.g. centre of the town vs. surrounding areas, or in various sub-areas within ecologically sensitive areas, etc.). In some cases, entire regions can be considered, for example in the case of islands or river valleys, etc. Through planning tools such as zoning, and management techniques such as visitor flow management, the impacts of tourism (and therefore the capacity of an area to sustain itself) can be mitigated.

The role of actors
- To control access to a destination in order to protect it. Development of institutional measures/mechanisms is essential. An effective legal framework could help to reduce/mitigate the negative impacts of tourism.
- An agreement on the goals for tourism development with key stakeholders is necessary.
- Cultural elements must be considered.

Integrating tourism carrying capacity in planning process and institutional context means planning for sustainable development.
- Evaluation and monitoring help assess and implement carrying capacity.

Constraints in implementing tourism carrying capacity
- Determine the role players (state, private sector, concessions). Pressure on ecologically sensitive areas increases, since recreational activities may grow and expand to increase profits.

- Action is generally encouraged at local and national level. Managing pressures at local level often requires policies at a higher level.

- Integrated planning is not always in place. Fragmentation of responsibilities occurs.

- Sophisticated systems to measure carrying capacity do not always prove useful. This can discourage managers and policy makers. There are limited efforts and resources available to implement tourism carrying capacity. Promotion of more pilot projects is needed.

Institutional tools to implement tourism carrying capacity
- Habitat directive and the Red Data species are valuable instruments for nature protection and for defining control levels for ecologically sensitive sites so as to limit tourist development.

- Compensation principles can be considered by assigning nature a price in order to protect it.

- Using environmental impact assessments should be applied to proposed development projects and programmes. Alternative sites for development should be considered.

- Tourism carrying capacity should be addressed during the SEA (strategic environmental assessment) since this reflects anticipating development on the basis of the compatibility of the site.

13.2.4   Management tools for implementing tourism carrying capacity

Regulatory

- *Zoning* that is applied mainly in protected areas. A typical division in zones is the following;
    1. Zone A – Most valuable and vulnerable. Entry only to authorised scientific teams.
    2. Zone B – Highly sensitive. Escorted visits in small groups.
    3. Zone C – Considerable natural interest. Some traditional and tourism activities, limited car access.
    4. Zone D – Mild development and buffer: Tourism and visitor facilities, car access and parking, compatible activities.

- *Limits to free access.* To prevent access on the basis of various practical factors.

- *Limits to specific activities.* All kinds of tourist activities have to be evaluated in order to prevent impacts on the environment. Some activities may be forbidden in some French National Parks because it disturbs fowls.

- *Eco-labels.* Eco-labels in visitor facilities will make visitors aware of impacts.
- *Concentration and tourist flows.* The idea is to avoid visitor concentration to be able to manage tourist flows. Try to address this in the design and layout plans.
- *Land use.* Guides by accessing carrying capacity or the use of institutional mechanisms for ecologically sensitive areas. Development and visitor flows need to be taken in consideration.

Economic

- *Pricing.* This is always the most appropriate tool to use in order to limit/control tourism development/growth.
- *Taxes.* Implement to prevent environmental destruction or discourage tourists as well as possible developers.
- *Cost-benefits analysis.* Costs are always higher in the earlier phases of tourist development.
- *Incentive schemes.* Should be applied in both public and private sectors in order to spread tourism demand over time and space and optimise the use of accommodation.

Organisational

- *Reservation and booking systems.* Visitors pay up front for all needs during their visit and can be controlled to be compatible with the facilities available.
- *Information management.* Crucial information like congestions, peaks and traffic can result in preventing excessive demand from visitors.
- *Education.* Educate the local community to understand and support tourism carrying capacity.
- *Training.* Train local planners and managers in the use of various techniques, etc.
- *Market control.* Undertake promotions for periods in which there is available carrying capacity.

13.2.5   Indicators

The sensitivity of the sites is important. Use indicators like endemic and threatened species, carrying capacity limits to identify criteria for determining the amount of visitors and type of activities compatible to visitor facilities.

Three types of indicators are suggested (for coastal areas, islands, protected areas, rural areas, mountain resorts and urban nature areas).
- Physical-ecological indicators.
- Socio-demographic indicators.
- Political-economic indicators.

Physical-ecological indicators

- Natural environment and biodiversity.
- Air quality.

- Noise pollution.
- Energy.
- Water.
- Waste.
- Cultural heritage.
- Tourist infrastructure.
- Land.
- Landscape.
- Transport and mobility.

Socio-demographic indicators

- Demography.
- Tourist flows.
- Employment.
- Social behaviour.
- Health and safety.
- Psychological issues.

Political-economic indicators

- Tourism earnings and investments.
- Employment.
- Public expenditure and revenue.
- Policy for tourism development.

Driving forces that impact on the indicators are:

- Pressures and stresses.
- The state of the natural environment and the resources.
- Impacts and consequences.
- The effectiveness of management efforts and implementation actions (responses).

Indicators are furthermore divided into three major categories:
- Sustainability indicators.
- Sustainable tourism indicators.
- Tourism carrying capacity indicators.

Sustainable tourism indicators: Aims to describe the general relationship between tourism and the environment, the impact of visitors on the environment and the responses required for promoting and safeguarding a more sustainable development of tourism and recreational activities.

Sustainability indicators: Useful and can provide an overall indication of the state of the system in terms of sustainability.

Tourism carrying capacity indicators: Aims to describe the pressures that are exerted, the state of the system and the impacts from tourism development. However, in this case only the key factors, problems, etc. are considered.

13.3 VISITORS TO URBAN NATURE AREAS AND VISITOR ACTIVITIES

13.3.1 General

There is a social need for residents to enjoy nature, relax and get out of their residential or working environment. The need is even greater when the weather is suitable for outdoor activities.

13.3.2 Selection criteria for developing visitor facilities in an urban environment [2]

Infrastructure and support services

The proximity of a site to existing infrastructure (water reticulation, sewer, power) and to existing public transport routes and nodes are critical.

Ownership of land

A potential site should preferably be owned by a municipality or authority responsible for recreation services.

Social consideration

Due to the large volumes of visitors a recreational area attracts in terms of vehicular traffic and large crowds of people, it would have an unacceptable impact on residents, should the site be located too close to or within a residential area. Community facilities such as schools, crèches, playschools, churches and places of worship can be disturbing when playing loud music. In light of this, it is important to consider the following:

- The largest possible open areas should be served.

- The site should not be located near facilities which are vulnerable to vandalism.

- The facility should not be located close to areas sensitive to loud noise such as hospitals, retirement and frail care facilities, crèches, playschools, schools, churches, places of worship.

Ecological Considerations

The natural environment can add value to a recreational area. Features such as rivers, dams and ridges can increase the diversity and richness of the activities available at a recreational area.

---

2 The following data was extracted out of a "Site selection criteria used by Strategic environmental focus for a report to identify a recreation resort for the City of Tshwane, August 2004 – SEF REF No. 1314"

However, at the same time, without careful planning these natural resources can be degraded to the point where their ecological integrity and their value to the recreational area are lost. In light of this it is important to consider the following:

- Take advantage of present natural assets such as water bodies, rivers, ridges and areas of natural vegetation.

- Avoid sites located within areas of special ecological sensitivity or where Red Data species occur.

Planning consideration

Certain land uses and combinations of land can act as magnets resulting in a concentration of people. This is typical of economic development nodes, urban cores and transport transfer nodes. One must consider the following as important:

- The site should be located within or immediately adjacent to the urban edge.

- The site should take into account surrounding land use and aim for areas of mixed land use, take into consideration urban cores and take advantage of existing activity centres.

- A site in excess of five (5) hectares should be identified, but properties in excess of one hundred (100) hectares would be required to include meaningful natural assets.

- The site could include disused buildings.

13.3.3   Ridges

Ridges are natural assets that can add significant value to a recreational area. Their elevated nature ensures unbeatable visibility and legibility in a typically flat topography. They are in most cases covered in natural vegetation comprised of a diversity of trees, shrubs, grasses and frogs that provide a habitat for small animals, birds and insects. The opportunity exists for environmental education and nature trails. According to ridge policies, certain classes of ridges cannot be developed upon but it will benefit a recreational area if it can be linked to it for sustainable utilisation.

13.3.4   Water bodies

Water bodies such as dams and pans add an important dimension to the range of water related activities that can be provided. The utilisation should also be sustainable and not degrade a pristine natural environment.

13.3.5   Conservation worthy areas

While the location of a recreational area close to conservation worthy area would increase the opportunities for environmental awareness and education, these areas should be avoided for development due to their ecological sensitivity.

13.3.6   Various scales of recreational facilities

Play park: A well-developed and aesthetically pleasing open space within a residential context that provides free access to and opportunity for:

- Community and social interaction.
- Children's recreational play areas (play equipment, informal play space).
- Passive recreational opportunities (benches, lawn areas).

Local resort: A well-developed and aesthetically pleasing localised open space venue within the larger suburban context that provides controlled access to and opportunity for:
- Community and social interaction.
- Children's recreational play opportunities (play equipment, informal play space, swimming pool(s), water slides).
- Passive leisure opportunities (benches, braai facilities).
- Small scale group functions (shelters).
- Small scale refreshment facilities (kiosk).
- Conservation components (ridge area, bird sanctuary).

Regional resort: A well-developed and aesthetically pleasing regional open space venue within the metro municipal context that provides regional communities, wider city residents and tourists controlled access to:
- Children's recreational play opportunities (play equipment, informal play space, swimming pool(s), water slides).
- Passive leisure opportunities (benches, braai facilities).
- Overnight accommodation (chalets, camping, caravanning).
- Large scale cultural, music and other associated events/festivals.
- Conservation areas (linked to a full scale urban nature reserve or nature area).

13.3.7   Recreational activities

A list of recreational activities can be grouped together into the following categories:
- Water related activities.
- Passive recreation.
- Accommodation.
- Nature/environmental related activities.
- Informal play activities/ active recreation.
- Events/social interaction.
- Paid for facilities/concessions.
- Management.
- Miscellaneous.

13.3.7.1   Water-related activities

- Swimming pools (paddling/wading pools, swimming pools).
- Water slides and tubes.
- Boating (paddle, sail, canoes, kayaking).

13.3.7.2   Passive recreation

- Picnic areas.
- Braai areas.
- Strolling paths.
- Children's play parks.
- Sand pit and jungle gym.
- Feature gardens.
- Orientation nodes, possibly including:
  1. Artistic features.
  2. Fountains.
  3. Seating.
  4. Orientation and interpretative signage.

13.3.7.3   Accommodation

- Guest lodges and conference facilities.
- Chalets.
- Camping areas.
- Caravanning areas.
- Youth camp/backpackers' inn.

13.3.7.4   Nature/environmental related activities

- Environmental education centre.
- Ecological interpretative kiosk or centre.
- Nature trails.
- Boardwalks.
- Bird hides.
- Eco-trails with interpretive signage (trees, animals, habitats).

13.3.7.5   Informal play activities/active recreation

- Jogging trails.
- Mountain bike trails.
- Roller blade and skate board arenas.
- Multi-purpose open spaces.

13.3.7.6   Events/social interaction

- Music festivals.
- Political gatherings.
- Cultural and traditional festivals.
- Weddings and receptions.
- Public meetings.

13.3.7.7   Paid for facilities/concessions

- Tea gardens and restaurants.
- Food courts/take away franchises.

- Conference facilities.
- Wedding halls/chapels/gardens.
- Theme park with rides.
- Possible leisure transport:
  1. Mini train ride.
  2. Tractor carriage.
  3. Horse buggy rides.
  4. Golf carts.
- Craft market/stalls at nodes.

13.3.7.8   Management

- Management offices.
- Security guard houses and kiosks.
- Public ablution facilities.
- Change rooms.
- Baby room, nappy changes.
- Medical aid.
- Maintenance yard and workshop.
- Staff parking area.
- Staff accommodation.

13.3.7.9   Miscellaneous

- Day care centre.
- Information kiosk.
- Curio/visitor's interest shop.
- Visitors parking.
- Bus and taxi drop-off area.
- Bus and taxi parking and departure area.
- Entrance features.
- Emergency access points and routes.
- Landscape features for orientation and legibility.
- Circulation hierarchy system for vehicles cyclists and pedestrians.

HIKING TRAIL
START
DISTANCE   : 4,5 KM
GATE CLOSES:
MAY - AUG : 7H00 - 18H00
SEP - APR : 5H30 - 19H00

CHAPTER 14

THE ACADEMIC APPROACH TO URBAN NATURE CONSERVATION

(This chapter focuses on the specialist issues of urban nature conservation. Ecological corridors are the main focus to link all urban nature areas with each other and to safeguard biodiversity as well as genetic diversity. It also looks at social needs and enrichment. A summary and additional information related to Tshwane nature conservation are included.) [1]

The objectives of urban nature conservation

Conservation interests and priorities must relate to those species that would be most under threat if we did not take active measures to ensure their survival.

Habitats or communities should be rated according to:
- **Extreme** or unusual environmental conditions that cannot easily be reproduced.
- **Threat** of severe damage that would lead to a drop in population numbers.
- **Specific** environmental conditions that have little environmental tolerance.
- **Complex** ecological processes, such as colonisation, that cannot easily be reproduced.

The target should be on habitats or communities that are most vulnerable and valuable, but viable and with a reasonable chance of survival if protected.

14.1   SETTING CONSERVATION PRIORITIES

Focus on conservation education. People learn to recognise things through reinforcement; recognising the plants and natural communities that we see around ourselves every day and learning how our own local environment functions.

Cole (1986) sets the following three main objectives for urban nature conservation:
- To conserve and press for the appropriate management of urban sites of intrinsic natural history value.

---

[1] Urban Nature Conservation – Toney Kendle and Stephen Forbes (Published 1997 by E & FN Spon, an imprint of Thomson Professional, 2-6 Boundry Row, London SE1 8HN, UK).

- To increase the habitat diversity of formalised areas of public open spaces.
- To create new temporary or permanent wildlife habitats on downgraded and derelict sites within the inner city.

It is those countries that have lost most of their natural countryside, such as England, that are among the most enthusiastic in supporting habitat creation of global conservation.

As long as wildlife remains endangered and under threat, we have the evidence that things are not well between man and nature and some changes have to be made such as:
- Focusing on regions with large areas of undisturbed habitat.
- Focusing on habitats which are a refuge for rare and threatened species.
- Focusing on species that have limited powers to cross intervening land barriers.
- Monitoring as an essential component of the conservation activity, especially where possible outcomes are uncertain.

14.2   STRATEGIC APPROACHES FOR NATURE CONSERVATION

Biodiversity loss is the main motivation factor for conservation strategy development. Species which have undergone significant decline may have too poor a genetic base, or too limited a range to ever be viable again as self-sustaining populations. Preserving the relationship between species is as important as preserving the species themselves. Conservation, through habitat protection, must therefore continue to form the keystone of biodiversity protection strategies.

Threats to biodiversity focus on development activities such as road building or mining. These are only significant because of the fragmentation. The root of most of the conservation problems that exist today is the change in the nature of agriculture, horticulture and forestry issues. These changes include direct habitat destruction and contribute to environmental change through drainage, liming and the increasing use of fertilisers and pesticides.

To designate land for a nature reserve is in itself inadequate to ensure protection of the species. Provision must be made for critical management inputs that also address the fragmentation problems. Even areas which were originally "natural habitats" that previously received no management may require intervention to maintain optimum specie balance in a small area, or to compensate for disrupted processes.

Technical analysis of the size and population levels of many reserves has also highlighted that many of the areas originally thought protected are simply too small to support viable populations of the species in them and that genetic paucity is likely to lead to decline.

The greatest threat to biodiversity in the coming decades must be pollution, particularly nutrient enrichment and climate change. Climate change has of course occurred many times in the past and species have adapted or migrated, but the rate of the expected change in the next century will be unprecedented, while the level of habitat fragmentation will of course present almost impossible adaptation challenges to species with slow dispersal mechanisms.

14.3   DIRECTIONS FOR FUTURE CONSERVATION STRATEGIES

The most important component for radical new approaches and mechanisms is a growing perception of the need and benefits of human intervention in natural processes and participation in conservation initiatives. Many habitat types once regarded as "natural" have actually been maintained by human activity.

With the incredible pervasiveness of factors such as pollution that influence specie distribution and survival even in the remotest areas of the world, it could be argued that strictly there are no "natural" ecosystems left.

The realities of nature conservation in this century call out for intervention on all levels. Fencing off reserves and keeping people out will sign their death warrants as surely as a bulldozer. Direct management of the species and valuable processes will become more and more necessary in all places. The scale and magnitude of this intervention may even extend as far as direct habitat recreation and specie translocation.

We must promote an ethic that sees human influences as a potentially positive and sustaining factor in the landscape; one that encourages each of us to explore the positive steps that we can take to protect nature. This is one of the key tenets of sustainability.

Key elements of future conservation strategies are:

- Link methods to recovery programmes wherever possible.
- Habitat restoration and similar intervention techniques, to overcome fragmentation and isolation effects and to accommodate necessary species displacements.
- Move away from isolated sites and try to ensure better environmental quality in the wider landscape.
- Environmental education and initiatives designed to gain greater public and political support for biodiversity protection. Focus on developing concerns and a positive attitude to nature.
- Exploration of methods of sustainable land use where human needs can be met with respect for and in partnership with nature.

The most important focus of such a new vision of the protection of nature has to be the town and city. Mainly, however, towns and cities are important because that is where people are and nature needs to be brought to them.

Conservation problems are caused by the cumulative decisions of all society; conservation battles will never be won by conservationists alone. Reaching the public is the most important job there is. Conservation work is dependent on public interest in wildlife; we need people to generate funds, labour and above all the political pressure that will help to conserve threatened habitats and endangered species. Above all, we need to remember that humans are the cause of the damage to the rainforests and the peat lands; ultimately it is only a change in the way that people behave that will be their salvation.

A great deal of conservation work has always been done for its *amenity value* – which means because of its importance to humans, not because of its importance to wildlife. We need to encourage people to come into contact with and to enjoy wildlife. In so doing, we aim to improve awareness of the value of nature, to encourage respect for wildlife, to promote and understand how nature works and more importantly of how people work in it.

The real conservation value of urban nature reserves and ecological landscapes therefore becomes more apparent. They exist for environmental education in its broadest sense. They are intended to make people care a bit more, to help them to understand a bit more clearly our necessary dependence on nature. Opportunities are recognised and seized that allow more positive involvement and connection with nature.

14.4   IDENTIFYING EXISTING URBAN SITES OF VALUE

In the UK the best known criteria for identification of nature conservation sites worthy of protection were outlined by Ratcliffe (1977). Aspects such as diversity are valid concerns, but on sites where the primary function is public enjoyment and education then sometimes areas with very low species diversity can still be successful.

Ratcliffe criteria for evaluation of nature sites
(Also see Figure 2.1 updated criteria by the author)

Size: Importance to nature conservation generally increases with size.

Diversity: Variety is better than uniformity; species richness is better than a poor species complement. Sites with a range of habitats are preferred (but rarity or interest need not coincide with diversity).

Naturalness: Sites which have been least modified by man are most valuable.

Rarity: Sites are more valuable if rare species or communities are present.

Fragility: Fragile communities are more valuable and deserving of protection. They may be vulnerable to internal changes, e.g. low population numbers causes die out, or successional change, or vulnerable to external change, e.g. by human action.

Typicality: One objective is to maintain examples of all habitat types, good examples are as important as rare ones.

Recorded history: Sites which are well researched or documented are more valuable.

The position in an ecological or geographical unit: This relates to landscape ecology, for example a wood which is contiguous with other wood is more valuable than one which is not.

Potential value: Sites with diminished importance, but not with irreversible decline, can have a potential value greater than present value.

Intrinsic appeal: This often applies more to species than habitats. Birds and flowers are more conspicuous and have greater appeal.

Problems that can be identified when sites of value are highlighted:

- Need for a value system that recognises local rather than national or provincial priorities.
- Need for accepting the diversity and real composition of urban nature.
- Challenges posed by early successional sites.
- Need for promoting positive conservation programmes.

Criteria for identification and designation of urban sites have been put forward by the London Ecology Unit (1985). Some of these criteria mostly relate to those sites which are significant for **biodiversity conservation** and apply to regionally important sites. These are:
- Richness in diversity.
- Rarity.
- Presence of ancient habitats.
- Size.
- Presence of non-creatable habitats.

Some of the criteria relate more to the **human value**. These are:
- Potential.
- Existing protection and opportunity.
- Public access.
- Aesthetic appeal.
- Proximity to urban areas.
- Presence in areas of deficiency.

The conservation plans on national and provincial levels aim to protect sites of importance from development or destructive activities. This concentrates on irreplaceable and unique habitats associated with rare species rather than those of regional or local interest. *The lack of designation for sites of local but not national significance was in fact often a weakness in planning applications, where an assumption was made that the sites were not that important.*

With the introduction of local nature reserves, the emphasis on locally rare habitats or on sites of great importance to local people is important. They are normally under the direct control of the local authority.

In the case of land in the hands of a private landowner, the authority has no control over what is done on these properties. They carry no penalties for destruction of land use changes and a site owner may, usually entirely legitimately, choose to destroy the wildlife value of an area in order to safeguard possible future planning applications. It is still within the law for landowners to change the management of a site and destroy the conservation interest on purpose, if they have intentions to plan development that will affect conservation issues.

The real conservation value of urban nature lies in its relationship to the people of the town or city, and in the potential this therefore presents for developing a land stewardship ethic. *The essential balancing act of the urban countryside evaluation process is therefore to match the distribution of the habitats identified with qualities such as the ease of access of local people, the size of catchment areas, the opportunities for recreation, the visual attractiveness of the landscape and so on* (Barker, 1986).

New techniques for identifying such areas include having local residents produce a map of their surroundings that highlights the features they value most. This assists planners in their process of protecting certain urban nature areas, but biodiversity may not necessarily be a priority.

Corridors and habitat links between reserves are desirable within urban areas as they may reduce the isolation and vulnerability of species.

14.5   THE ROLE OF CORRIDORS IN SPECIES DISPERSAL

The goal is to overcome the negative effect of land fragmentation, so that different reserves can buffer each other and localised extinction and random catastrophes can be compensated for by re-invasion of species from other areas. Effective corridors may thus allow several reserves to function ecologically as one larger unit.

A sophisticated analysis of what the nature of such a corridor could and should be is important. If habitat isolation really does pose a threat for biodiversity survival, the restorations of links must be approached on the basis of a detailed analysis of the dispersal behaviour of the key species.

It is clearly better to protect existing connections between habitats than to assume that they are unimportant.

Baker (1984) identified the following elements that should be in a strategic plan:
- Identify available wildlife.
- Identify corridors for wildlife in built-up areas.

Link nature areas (Corridor).

- Identify linkages between wildlife areas.
- Identify shortcomings, unavailable semi-natural habitats.
- Improve and rehabilitate areas where needed.
- Ensure public access and enjoyment of the wildlife available.
- Set a standard on adjacent building development to enhance wildlife habitat.
- Encourage local initiatives to achieve all the above.

Urban wildlife corridors: These are lengths of linear habitat or open space sites which are sufficiently closely connected to probably function as a route for wildlife movement. This can also be a connection between the town centre and the surrounding countryside (can include green road and railway verges, river and canal sides, parks and golf courses).

Tactical components of an urban conservation programme: Johnston (1990) considered how local authorities can improve the provision and management of urban nature areas according to the following:

Make land available

- Promote positive use of vacant land for the establishment of nature areas.
- Use planning tools to secure land for nature conservation.
- Require developers to incorporate nature areas into their designs.

Secure public access to nature areas

- Make areas safe by fencing, filling in dangerous holes, etc.
- Arrange appropriate leases and licences for present or potential nature areas.

Manage council land for nature conservation

- Train staff to undertake appropriate nature conservation management on all public open spaces.
- Employ specialist wardens/rangers.
- Draw up management agreements with others to manage land in accordance with the requirements of nature conservation.

Establish an ecology centre

- Provide a focus for environmental education and public information.
- Use the centre as a demonstration project.

Involve the community

- Enable local people to make positive use of available land.
- Consult widely on proposals.
- Respond positively to suggestions for potential nature areas where appropriate.

Allocate sufficient resources

- Establish, manage and protect nature areas.
- Employ qualified nature conservationists that can specialise in urban nature conservation.
- Establish a separate budget for urban nature conservation programmes and work.
- Consider giving grants – aid to voluntary organisations.

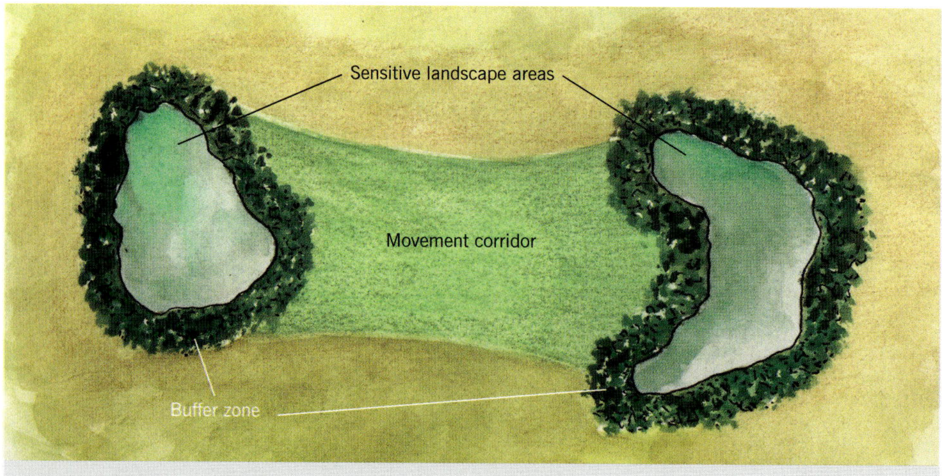

Figure 14.1: Buffer zone and corridor.

14.6 ECOLOGICAL RESTORATION AND HABITAT CREATION

The following are challenges to successful biodiversity protection within an urban context:
- The isolation of urban nature areas forms important ecological processes. This will lead to specie losses.
- The fragmentation of habitats.
- The size of the urban nature areas must be big enough. Many urban nature areas are too small to be viable and have no buffering capacity to survive.
- Pollution levels are a threat that small nature areas cannot handle.
- Micro habitat changes because of unfavourable impacts.
- Greater political and social commitment from all levels of society is needed.

Species need enhancement where suboptimal populations are boosted by situ propagation and re-introduction, or boosting resource availability, e.g. through nest box provision. Stretches of land adjacent to nature areas for improved buffering or habitat enhancement should be acquired. Corridors must be established to create links between isolated habitats and to allow specie migration (Jordan, Gilpin and Aber, 1987).

It is important to develop more opportunities for people to have contact with wildlife, rather than attempting to meet the difficult goals of rehabilitation of complex plant and animal communities.

Habitat restoration: This is an attempt to reproduce, as far as possible, a previously existing community of ecosystems. The species present should be capable of successful reproduction in order to maintain the community. It is important to analyse the reasons why the original habitat disappeared and determine whether these factors can be controlled in the future. The ease of restoration therefore depends on the degree and nature of disturbance.

Habitat creation: This is an artificial practise related to an urban environment and the following directions are proposed:
- Create a popular wildlife system for maximum human enjoyment. The focus is on a few species and not particularly diverse or botanically important.
- This is a specie-targeted programme.
- Aim for a system of species normally encountered in the region.
- The original biodiversity community will never be recovered, so it is better to manage a reduced diversity.

This type of work is of indirect value to nature conservation in that it can alleviate pressure on existing semi-natural habitats, bringing more people into contact with nature and encourage support for wider conservation objectives.

Rehabilitation: This is the re-establishment of the original biota and/or ecosystem through human intervention.

Recovery: This may apply when a disturbed site becomes partially restored without any human facilitation.

Re-vegetation, regeneration or reclamation: This is when a form of functional vegetation cover on a denuded site has been established, but it does not necessarily imply any resemblance to the original landscape.

Habitat extension: This is where existing habitats such as nature reserves are expanded or linked through acquiring additional land. This may be to provide a buffer zone that will protect the core habitat from adverse influences. It may also make small areas more viable. The "new" habitat needs to have a certain degree of functional similarity to the core landscape at the broad biome level.

Habitat extension may apply in circumstances where no efforts are made to introduce species, but where the management and land use patterns are matched with the requirements of the core plant and animal communities.

Habitat enhancement or enrichment: This is the deliberate management of diversification of an existing community. This is done through a variation in maintenance activities. It also involves deliberate planting of plant species or deliberate introduction of animal species.

Habitat diversification: This is increasing the specie richness (usually floristic richness) of existing habitats through the introduction of previously absent species.

Species recovery: This is the encouragement of targeted rare/endangered plant and animal species to extend their range or increase the population density within existing boundaries. This may also involve expansion of genetic stock, e.g. by controlled introduction of new genes from external populations.

This attempt usually puts single species back into a community where it once existed. The success depends on a realistic analysis of why the species first disappeared.

Another scenario is where the niche has been filled by an ecologically similar species which, once established, is strongly competitive. The outcome of the competitive relationship is far from clear, and there is evidence that "possession is nine-tenths of the law" (Gilbert, 1989) suggesting that the re-introduced species may never oust the competitor; they may co-exist or the original species may eventually die out again.

Reintroduction: This is when a locally extinct ecotype is replaced by a closely related stock from a different area.

Species replacement: This occurs when locally extinct species is replaced by one which may be taxonomically unrelated but which may have a functional similarity within the ecosystem.

Species eradication: Habitat restoration in situations such as island ecosystems where relatively undisturbed communities have been invaded by exotics that threatened the integrity of the entire biota.

Species introductions: An existing habitat is diversified by the introduction of plants or animals which would be expected to survive, but for which there is no evidence that they previously formed part of the community.

If species are introduced into a community where there is no existing niche, we would normally expect it to disappear, but some species may so modify the environment that they can reinforce their own survival and effectively create new niches.

Other perspectives: Ecological restoration is the process of repairing damage done by humans to the diversity and dynamics of indigenous ecosystems. The objectives are to upgrade the quality of existing natural areas and to augment the planetary inventory of natural areas.

Debates take place about whether the goal should be to restore to the stage before any human impact, to restore to the stage before the more heavily and rapidly degrading impact, or to restore to some assumed stage which would be the development of some of these communities assuming that no high-level degradation took place. The vision should be the harmonious co-existence of humans and nature.

14.7 ETHICAL AND CONCEPTUAL CHALLENGES OF RESTORATION ECOLOGY

Restoration is invariably more expensive than conservation, and the results are more uncertain. It is a problem when development uses restoration to compensate or mitigate for the loss of areas of nature conservation. Protecting existing habitats must always be the higher priority.

Wetland creation: The characteristics of wetland communities are so strongly dominated by water relations that creation of diversity is almost easy. Ponds and smaller water bodies are frequently created for no other purpose than to promote wildlife diversity in urban areas.

The role of water as a design element and as wildlife habitat in urban areas is restricted by safety and management considerations. Siting, size and depth influence water quality. Moffat (1986) recommends a depth of over 1 m to protect water quality, and of over 1.2 m to restrict the growth of aggressive emergent species such as *Typha* spp. and *Phragmites* spp. Shelving of banks allows establishment or colonisation of aquatic plants and assists in developing a zonation of species.

Trees: All the trees in a neighbourhood may help to modify the climate of the town beneficially through transpiration cooling and shade, shelter from winds. They may help to trap dust, clear pollution from the air and improve conditions for a range of other species.

Ecologically, the special qualities of trees mean that they are actually a habitat. They can be a home to many species with dependent animals or plants living on or in the roots, trunk, branches or leaves. From this perspective, individual trees could even be regarded as isolated landscape fragments with patterns of migration and colonisation between them.

Woodland: Urban forestry initiatives attempt to exploit the multiple benefits of woodlands to society. These include recreation opportunities, nature conservation, landscape improvement and timber production. More benefits are pollution control (including carbon fixation), noise reduction, and provision of educational resources, biofuels and even just simple, low maintenance land-bank filler, providing general environmental benefits on otherwise useless sites.

Strategic management issues in the urban countryside: An urban conservation policy will ensure that the needs of human users are addressed. This allows local residents to participate in management of the sites.

14.7.1   Choosing the appropriate management method and pattern

Management plans are seen as the cornerstone of conservation management programmes to ensure the necessary continuity of objectives and techniques over the long timescales involved. A management plan requires that the necessary information about the site, the objectives, the resources available and the proposed methods of working are specified.

An urban conservation management plan may differ from those prepared for established rural habitats as it needs to take account of what may be there in the future rather than only attempting to preserve what is.

The objectives of urban conservation may best be achieved by a programme of maintenance and inputs that are realistic, viable and favour maximum diversity within that particular biotype rather than specific groups of species.

We can predict that regular disturbances of some kind will be important for maintaining some of the unusual plant communities found in towns and cities. *The plant communities we see are largely the product of acute environmental disruption* that is far more severe in intensity than in rural areas. *Disturbance in closed rural grassland communities often encourages invasion of undesirable or exotic plants.*

14.7.2   The economics of urban vegetation management

Administrators will be keen to take on board the idea that natural is cheap because it means little or no management, but little or no management is not usually what conservation is all about.

Tractor-driven gang mowers on large level sites are one of the most cost-effective management systems available for land. Regular cuts are needed, but each cut is so quick per unit area that the annual costs are low.

Over the last few decades, conflicts between ecologists and horticultural maintenance staff have not been uncommon, where the latter is accused of insensitive or incorrect management of wild areas.

Horticulture is an industry that absorbs people from all walks of life. However, because of its relationship with gardening there are many people working who feel that they know what to do simply because they have had a garden and who make spontaneous decisions that are based on the eccentric priorities of gardening magazines rather than on sound management principles.

Cheap maintenance often equates with unskilled, easily programmed repetitive mechanised tasks, such as grass cutting, and not with infrequent but intensive tasks, such as scything or woodland thinning. In addition, aesthetic requirements, especially on small urban sites, may require constant intervention and management to maintain species diversity and the general attractiveness of the site.

14.7.3 Revenue opportunities from urban landscapes

Normally revenue is insufficient to cover the costs, but it is still a useful addition to the budget. Direct opportunities for income generation are by-products of landscape maintenance such as grass, timber, pruning and other green wastes. A concern is that grasslands may be so contaminated with airborne dust, other pollutants and even physical contaminants that they are unsuitable for feed.

The pressure on local authorities is to find a positive use for green waste. Pruning can be chipped and used as mulch and composting can lead to substantial cost savings for a local authority. Wood can be sold for firewood.

These reduce the financial scale of the management investment. Indirect financial benefits are tree screening, shelters that improve the energy balance in buildings leading to heating cost reductions, reducing airborne pollution which can lead to potential savings in healthcare, etc. According to Ulrich (1984), there are significant health benefits arising from contact with nature in cities.

The greatest financial return from urban nature is probably the influence on the desirability of living and working in these environments. According to Harris (1992), the benefit can arise when large companies are attracted to invest in environmentally positive regions.

14.7.4 Safety in the urban countryside

There is a phenomenal growth in urban fear and anxiety associated with the perceived risk of crime in urban nature areas. Women and the elderly are increasingly frightened of using some open spaces, which increases the sense of isolation and worry of those that do venture out. Parents are increasingly preventing children from playing outside, such that the health risks of increased inaction is beginning to cause serious medical concerns.

One possible solution is to consider the degree to which safety perception can be influenced by design. Sangster (1995) suggests the following design approaches to reduce or alleviate the anxieties:

- *Sightlines* – Ensure that paths have good longitudinal visibility, avoiding sharp bends.

- *Margins* – Paths should have open spaces on either side. Where the vegetation comes up to a path it should be cleared up to allow visibility. Open verges also are recommended for nature conservation.

- *Path widths* – They should be wide enough or have passing places so that people can pass comfortably.

- *Lighting* – In some circumstances this will be appropriate.

- *Thinning* – Differentially thin woodland to provide low stem densities and good visibility into the crop close to paths and roads.

- *Undergrowth* – Bushes and tall herbaceous vegetation are viewed with great suspicion by many townspeople. Mowed verges and low vegetation is preferred.

Wetland Education group Natali.

Designs are intended to prevent opportunities for strangers to enter within the local communities' territory without being obvious, making it harder for crime to happen. Sightlines are maximised; bushes and places of concealments are removed or replaced with spiny or prickly species.

A rich and stimulating environment encourages people, stimulates activity and increases the sense of safety. A team of ecological wardens can be made responsible for ensuring safety. Education and interpretative programmes can encourage public use. There are ways to accommodate many people without undermining the opportunity for privacy and the sense of getting away. Division of space into small, screened pockets may allow people to remain within shouting distance without them being constantly visible.

14.7.5   Community participation in urban land management

The particular educational focus of participative approaches in urban land management is:
* To produce an urban community that is better informed of how habitats work and of environmental issues.

* To develop a more positive attitude towards nature and support for the work of conservation agencies.

* To demonstrate to individuals the opportunity for positive change and to develop an awareness of how effective action can be taken at a local level.

The principles of community involvement

Three principals have emerged that when applied together, help make human environments more successful.
* People willingly take responsibility for their environment and participate both individually and collectively in its creation and management.

* A creative working partnership is established with specialists from one or more disciplines.

* All aspects of people's environmental needs are considered simultaneously and on a continuing evolutionary basis (Wates and Knevitt, 1987).

Motivational forces and psychological needs

Social needs: These include the needs of the individual for social interaction, for group affiliation, for companionship and love.

Stabilising needs: We have a need to organise the environment, to have a say in its form and content.

Individual needs: There is a need to be able to choose or make individual decisions about one's life.

Self-expression: Most people have the need for accomplishment and achievement, to be held in esteem by others.

Enrichment: People thirst for knowledge. Related to this is a need for self-realisation and personal creativity, plus a need for beauty.

User participation in the environment

When residents are given the major decisions and are free to make their own contribution to the design of the residential environment, the process and the environment produced stimulates individual and social well-being.

The higher up the ladder one gets, the more power is given to the user and the more fruitful the outcome is likely to be. Emotional engagement with one's environment leads to the motivation to care for it.

One element common to all successful schemes is the presence of an enabler, an individual who not only has the perception and enthusiasm to see the potential of the project, but who can communicate a vision that gives meaning to the work of others.

Community participation takes time and the group will only gain confidence by realising they can do it themselves.

The local authority as facilitator

Instead of the local authority acting as gate-keeper or supplier, professionals can become facilitators who help things happen rather than stopping them by:
- Cutting red-tape.
- Encouraging the voluntary provision of suitable temporary uses.
- Adopting a procedure whereby licences are granted speedily for the interim use of sites.
- Suggest suitable sites to tackle.
- Provide skips, equipment and technical advice.
- Dealing with requests from voluntary groups.
- Giving small grants for practical schemes.
- Establishing partnerships involving the public sector, with developers and private institutions, working closely with the voluntary sector (Cantell 1977).

Ensuring effective participation

The general criteria for the use of participation methods, extracted from various case studies and literature (Croft and Beresford, 1988; Hodge, 1995; Johnston, 1990) are as follows:
- There must be an understanding of people's needs for a feeling of relatedness to others and to the life of the community.
- Be proactive, linked with patience, persistence and commitment.
- Avoid a preoccupation with esoteric or obscure issues.
- The invitation to participate must be genuine.

- There should be small, but attainable goals for change.
- Provide well-focused initiatives.
- The problem must be with the time and effort in the eyes of all concerned.
- There must be attractive benefits to the community from the project.
- The terms must be clear.
- Conditions of responsibility in return for the benefits should be worked out by the community themselves.
- The individuals concerned must have the skills and information to enable them to participate effectively.
- The manager whether national government, local authority or landlord, must want participation and not indulge in it because of a sense of obligation.
- People should be involved from the earliest possible stages in the project.
- Involvement should progress to ownership of the project by the community.
- The manager should listen carefully to people's concerns, wants and needs.
- The resource implications of increased community involvement must be recognised and addressed with commitment.
- Opportunities for involvement must be without unnecessary barriers or bias.
- Social benefits are to have fun.

Volunteers generally prefer to implement than to maintain. Community members are not willing to do yet more hard work, unless there is an element of fun involved. Community involvement does require supervision, otherwise enthusiasm dwindles. People must be instructed and directed, particularly when performing tasks they are unaccustomed to.

Involvement is also very much a function of the level of funding: once funding dries up, then enthusiasm for community involvement dries up.

Groups fit well with democratic culture. If groups or committees are constructed for an inappropriate task, or with impossible constraints; if they are badly led or have ineffective procedures; if they have the wrong people, too many people, too little power or meet too infrequently; frustration will set in.

14.8   CONCLUSIONS

If a project fails because the group wasn't strong enough, or if a once successful community landscape falls into neglect for a period, that should not necessarily be seen as a bad thing. The process perhaps matters more than the end product, and it has to be that way, if we want to promote active caring by local people of their local places (Millward, 1987).

Some view community involvement in a greening project as a means of preventing vandalism completely. This is an over-simplified view of the situation. Participants respect the site more, but that doesn't stop others from nearby areas from doing damage. Often the best strategy is to immediately undo the damage done to restore the public image of the site, otherwise people will lose respect for it, further perpetuating the problem.

If after care of a site where the community was involved is not provided, it reflects badly on the organisations involved.

Voluntary organisations should willingly accept more responsibility for the creation and management of the environment.

Local government should learn to trust community organisations and should actively assist them in their formation and development. Government should help fund the services offered by community. All landscape projects should have simple maintenance manuals.

Environmental education programmes for the public should be expanded so that people can learn how the urban environment works and how they can take part in improving it.

14.8.1   Nature for people

Psychological value of nature for people in urban areas

We need to have sound information on the benefits of urban landscapes and nature for society. *Many parks seem increasingly tired and out of place. They are over-mature, poorly policed and poorly used. Decades of funding cutbacks have led to a gradual erosion of features that required intensive inputs.*

Attitudes towards green spaces are often perceived as locations for crime and moral degeneracy rather than positive experiences.

Urban green has potential value for humans on many levels. Urban nature areas in particular may embody the following values:

Personal benefits of participation of an urban wildlife area.

Emotional
*   Relief of escaping from the city.
*   Opportunities to identify with nature.
*   Sense of freedom.
*   A peaceful retreat to repair emotions.
*   Sense of pride and achievement.

Intellectual
*   Seeing nature at work.
*   Learning about the variety of flora and fauna.
*   Learning about local history.
*   New skills.

Social
*   Getting to know people better.
*   Pleasure from team and community spirit.
*   Becoming more responsible citizens.

Physical
* Appeals to the senses.
* Feeling fit.
* A safe place to exercise or play.

One of the main benefits of urban nature is therefore to provide an element that is missing from resident environments.

The following benefits of contact with nature have been identified for ethnic groups (Wong, 1997):
* Increased sense of identity and ownership of the country they live in.

* A sense of integration rather than isolation.

* A reunion with nature (many first-generation immigrants come from very rural backgrounds and move to completely urban inner-city experiences).

* The re-awakening of a sense of possibility, of widening horizons.

* Restoration and a relief from daily struggle.

* Empowerment, skills development and the enabling of the opportunity to participate in environmental care.

Psychological well-being and landscapes

Quality of life is of no less importance than health. The research evidence for the impact of urban nature on psychological well-being can be classed under five main headings (Rohde and Kendle, 1994):

* Emotional (e.g. through reduction in stress and increase in happiness).

* Cognitive (e.g. through reduction in mental fatigue).

* Developmental (e.g. through encouraging higher levels of mental activity, especially among children).

* Behavioural (e.g. through encouraging explorative and adventurous behaviour, which in turn can support or build self-esteem).

* Social (e.g. natural settings can facilitate contact, encourage conversation across social boundaries and even, in some cases, engender a broader social concern).

Patients had greater recovery from surgery when they had views of a tree from the hospital window (Ulrich, 1984). The mechanisms for this relationship are speculative, but are linked perhaps to the relationship between stress and the immune system (Antonovsky, 1979). The particular reasons why nature is believed to have these de-stressing and thus health-promoting qualities are not clear.

Values of urban wildlife

We must encourage wildlife within the urban fabric. *If urban communities do not care for nature on their doorstep, it is almost impossible to make them care for distant and abstract problems*. There is always the question of what urban nature means. An area will lose its naturalness if it is too closely maintained, modified or controlled by people. This distinction between the controlled and the uncontrolled is, after all, embodied in the term wildlife. There is the example of a jogger who can tell of his unexpected encounter with a fox in the local park with excitement still shining in his eyes many years after the event.

Green spaces are the setting for physical actions, such as jogging or walking the dog, but these are activities which could have taken place in the most concrete urban streets if necessary. Nature is a motivator for an activity which would not have happened otherwise.

Compared to the built environment, the natural environment is therefore characterised by variety and surprise. This triggers not only alertness and attention and captures the senses but also encourages thought and imagination.

People who value formal ornamental landscapes most strongly will often see wild areas as untidy, unmaintained or in some other way degraded. For others, the degradation is associated with too much human influence, when an area becomes manicured. Regardless of growing trends for wildlife gardens, the majority of people still choose to live with gardens that have a semi-formal design with ornamental plants.

Man-made landscapes differ from wild landscapes and the general public usually better understands the role of management of man-made landscapes than urban nature properties.

14.8.2   Conflicts between amenity and conservation

Inevitably, there may be conflicts arising between the wish to develop a site for conservation value and the need to integrate and allow for the pressures imposed by people. If recreation pressures ever threaten landscape quality in rural conservation sites, it is the recreation that should be curtailed.

The priorities may, however, be different in an urban site which contains habitats created almost solely for the purpose of allowing for human enjoyment. Some activities are unacceptable like excessive trampling or vandalism. The importance of zoning and the provision of tidy managed edges and components within a naturalistic landscape have been emphasised by Corder (1986). Also important are high standards of litter collection and interpretative information systems.

14.8.3   Education for urban conservation

Managing people's perceptions through education is as important as managing the actual landscape. The challenge is the need to encourage a wider understanding that there is a distinction between two approaches to environmental ethics:
- That which aims to preserve diversity and species.
- That which manifests as animal welfare or protection of individual species.

There are three distinct themes to an educational approach:
• Education **about** the environment (provide information).
• Education **through** the environment (using the outdoor as a teaching resource).
• Education **for** the environment (awareness for environmental issues).

In practise, education programmes frequently have multiple aims. Providing information alone is a particularly ineffective method of environmental education. More effective education, leading to attitude change, will only come about if we find a way to really captivate and inspire people. Above all, participation and the opportunities for direct action that leads to positive change seem to be among the most powerful motivating factors that exist.

The first step is that people must care enough to want to see nature and they must then see enough of it to care about it. The motivation, connection and inspiration are at the heart of urban nature conservation issues. Such policies must find ways in which everyone, regardless of cultural background, sex, age, disabilities and even personal preference, has opportunities to find a way to better relate to urban conservation issues. Potential benefits are safety, freedom to explore, high habitat density within a small area and the opportunity to become practically involved. Urban nature areas can therefore present an invaluable opportunity for participatory environmental education that integrates the three strands identified above.

The opportunity to see wild species in the heart of the city is a key component of strategies for environmental education. It is important to capture people's imagination by evoking the romance and the excitement of nature. Exploit the sense of adventure and the richness that contact with the wild can provide. This may be done by linking art, parties and picnics with nature conservation.

Nature must become recognised as an integral part of the fabric of urban life, but human life must also become reconciled as being part of nature. We must keep a clear vision of the relationship between people and wildlife – they need each other and urban nature conservation is the art that expresses that truth.

Educational group visiting Rooihuiskraal Reptile Park.

CHAPTER 15

FRIENDS GROUPS

(This chapter describes the history, functioning and contribution of friends groups and how friends groups can enhance urban nature areas. The role WESSA (Wildlife and Environmental Society of South Africa) plays in the running of friends groups and the tools to operate a friends group are also discussed.)

15.1   FRIENDS OF NATURE

According to Wikipedia, the Friends of Nature organisation was founded by three activists in Vienna in 1895. They were Karl Renner, a law student and future president of Austria, Georg Schmiedl, a schoolteacher, and Alois Rohrauer, a blacksmith. In the age of incipient tourism, the organisation succeeded in making nature accessible to broader population strata by providing requisite recreational and travel facilities. Even then, the organisation's activities were aimed at getting people to beautiful natural settings, awakening their love for nature and imparting knowledge about nature and culture. Parallel with the rise of the modern industrialised society and of commercial tourism, Friends of Nature developed a professional commitment to nature and environment protection and had a major share in advancing the theory and practice of alternative forms of ecological tourism.

The organisation was banned by the Nazis in 1933, but revived in 1945 (according to internet data on Friends of Nature).

The work of the Friends of Nature rests on the conviction that people's opportunities for personal development are inextricably linked with the protection of nature and the conservation of natural resources. The Friends of Nature have taken a stand for the conservation of an environment worth living in, for peace and international understanding, for the social and democratic rights of all people and for a meaningful organisation of leisure time. Building on their century-old tradition, the Friends of Nature are nowadays committed to the implementation of sustainable development, in particular to trans-boundary environmental solutions and to an environmentally and socially sound tourism industry.

The Friends of Nature is dedicated to the natural flora and fauna in their local areas. It is run for and by a group of people who are interested in the study and enjoyment of the conservation of wildlife and its habitat, natural or man-made.

With 600 000 members organised in approximately 3 500 groups, with 39 full-fledged offices and about 35 000 voluntary workers, the Friends of Nature is one of the biggest non-profit and non-governmental organisations worldwide. Apart from seminars and information material, they provide environmentally sound leisure-time and travel programmes for their members and run over 1 000 Nature Friends' Houses in Europe and overseas.

The International Friends of Nature (IFN), based in Vienna, is the umbrella organisation of the national Friends of Nature federations.

Friends of Nature (FON) is the oldest environmental NGO in China. They have been working for over a decade to promote environmental awareness about China's most pressing environmental problems. In particular, they have focused on protecting endangered species such as the Tibetan antelope and the Snub-nosed Monkey. They offer environmental education through camps, field trips, and most importantly, teacher-training. They also run awareness-raising campaigns such as photo exhibitions and publications. One of FON's greatest achievements is helping to foster a growing network of grassroots environmental NGOs throughout China. They believe that environmental education increases awareness, and awareness increases citizen participation. It is through the participation of all Chinese citizens that China can achieve the dream of an environmentally harmonious society.

Friends write newsletters to update information about the environmental situation in their local area. FON enjoys very close connections with journalists. Journalists play a vital role in expanding public awareness of environmental issues, and are thus crucial to the overall vision of FON.

FON has enjoyed unprecedented access to the policy-making process. FON has used this access to successfully promote the adoption and reform of laws pertaining to the environment, argued for the inclusion of the public and relevant experts in environmental impact assessments and raised the profile of environmental issues on government levels.

Friends of Nature believe that educating the young generations about the importance of environmental protection is one of the most effective ways to protect nature. Indeed, studies in other countries have shown that it is often children who make their parents more interested in the environment rather than the other way around. Friends of Nature have dedicated much of their time and resources to holding children's camps, fieldtrips, and public and school lectures aimed at raising elementary, middle and high school students' environmental awareness. Throughout the year, professionals in the fields of environmental protection and sustainable development are invited by Friends of Nature to give public lectures and thus spread a green culture.

As the average citizen becomes more affluent, they are becoming more interested in negative effects of rapid industrialisation and urbanisation. This is particularly true of emerging urban middle-class. These individuals and families are beginning to recognise that economic prosperity is meaningless if the water is not safe to drink and the air not safe to breathe. This growing awareness about the environmental and health costs of economic growth is particularly acute among young urbanites. Furthermore, more prosperous individuals and families increasingly want to spend their leisure time enjoying nature. This will not be possible, however, if we continue to develop economically without taking the environment into account. Friends of Nature are trying to help this middle class appreciate the beauty of nature and understand the environmental costs of economic growth. They are also conducting numerous campaigns aimed at persuading citizens to limit their consumption and to make the most environmentally-sound consumption choices possible.

15.2   ABOUT WESSA

Friends Groups in South Africa are community-based groups that are affiliated to Wildlife and Environment Society of South Africa (WESSA). Founded in 1926, WESSA is one of South Africa's oldest and largest non-government environmental organisations.

WESSA's vision is to be a highly effective and well-supported champion of the environment and they implement high impact environmental and conservation projects which promote public participation in caring for the earth.

Professional environmental staff is employed to work directly with the public, local, provincial and national government and with other environmental organisations for the protection of the environment. WESSA maintains a watchful eye on the South African environment through its extensive network of Regional Offices, Branches, Friends Groups and Environmental Clubs.

WESSA is represented on many national and regional conservation bodies and investigatory commissions, and is a founder member of the World Conservation Union (formerly the International Union for the Conservation of Nature – IUCN).

WESSA is a motivating force behind many of South Africa's most significant environmental decisions. These and other achievements are as a result the voices and actions of ordinary South Africans – people who have been willing participants in caring for the earth.

> "Tell people – and they may forget...
> show them – they may remember...
> but involve them and they will understand."
> *Confucius*

WESSA is a Section 21 company registered as an incorporated association not for gain.

VISION: To be a highly effective and well-supported champion of the environment.

MISSION: To implement high impact environmental and conservation projects which promote public participation in caring for the Earth.

AIM: To contribute to conserving the Earth's vitality and diversity by:
*   Promoting sound environmental values and sustainable lifestyles.
*   Integrating conservation and development.
*   Encouraging and generating individual and community action.
*   Enabling and growing a vibrant and active broad-based membership.
*   Securing the protection and wise use of natural resources.
*   Acting as an environmental watchdog.
*   Influencing policy and decision-making.
*   Responding to changing needs.
*   Fostering collaborative partnerships.

Friends groups in South Africa, affiliated with WESSA consist of community members who have banded together around a particular natural environment to ensure its conservation and environmental integrity.

The Friends scheme was established for people who
*   WORRY about what the quality of life will be for their children and grandchildren.
*   WONDER what one can do about environmental degradation and destruction that is going on all around us.
*   WISH to meet more people who feel the same way they do.
*   WANT to get involved.

15.3   FRIENDS GROUPS IN SOUTH AFRICA

15.3.1   What are friends?

Friends of Nature Areas are groups of concerned people who have banded together to work for the conservation of the natural environment of specific areas of their choice and to encourage greater public awareness of the value and wise use of these areas for present and future generations. No special qualifications or experience is necessary. All they ask of Friends is that they care about the environment and that they are prepared to be doers rather than just talkers!

15.3.2   Why be friends?

Our nature areas are part of our natural heritage and belong to all people of South Africa, yet many of them are not well known or really appreciated. Managing authorities do not have the money, manpower, time or expertise to make the public more aware of the value of these areas. The main aim of the Friends movement is to support local government by providing volunteer time and assistance to fill this gap. All activities and projects are therefore planned in liaison with the owner/ administrator of the area.

15.3.3 Some things Friends do:

- EDUCATE themselves and the public, by collecting and distributing information on the conservation-worthiness of their area – its unique and special properties, special lists, archaeology, history, etc.

- PROMOTE the natural assets of their area by establishing interpretive centres, producing information brochures, planning and constructing trails, conducting outings, and arranging talks, etc.

- HELP the management of the area to eradicate aliens and combat soil erosion.

- RAISE FUNDS to finance these and other approved projects.

15.3.4 How to set up a Friends group in South Africa with WESSA

- Register to affiliate with WESSA.
- Draw up a constitution.
- Register with SARS as a PBO (public benefit organisation).
- Your affiliation with WESSA will be a group membership with the following benefits:
  - Advice.
  - Publicity.
  - Support.
  - Respectability.

- WESSA can appeal on behalf of a party.
- If the turnover of funds in one financial year is more than R50 000, you have to audit all finances.
- All finances must always be available for public securitisation.
- WESSA manages your membership and all relevant requirements.
- Structure must include the following:
  - Chair person.
  - Secretary.
  - Treasurer.
  - Two or three members.

- You need to hold an AGM to elect a steering committee and present financial statements.

15.3.5 The landowner's role (local authority) in connection with a Friends group

- Continue to manage the facility and making of decisions. (Friends groups are a support function).
- Can ask the Friends to help.

- Can get a second opinion from the Friends group (they are local and have local knowledge, they live near the facility, they love the facility and want to help).

- Friends are not allowed to interfere with the management of the facility.

- Any contribution (fixed structures) from the Friends to a facility will be donated to the facility and will become part of the property (structures, bird hides, gabions, assets).

- The landowner must listen to concerns from the Friends group (liaise).

- The landowner must attend their meetings/gatherings to supervise and ensure cooperation by both parties.

- Friends' forum meetings can be held annually to create a platform to discuss issues and to get feedback on activities and information.

15.3.6   The role of the Friends group

- They are like a resident organisation that wants to get involved in the conservation of a specific nature area which belongs to a landowner.

- They want to support the landowner to enhance a specific nature area through funding and physical working projects (hands-on working groups).

- Friends groups represent all affective and interested role players to a specific nature area.

- Aims: "Friends are groups of concerned persons who have been brought together to work towards the conservation of a natural environment or specific areas of their own choice (volunteers). They are conservationists with a deep respect for nature; their aim is to try and heal the damage done by unsustainable development and utilisation, or to fend it off in the future by encouraging greater public awareness of the value and wise use of these areas for present and future generations."

- Activities:
    - Education and awareness campaigns.
    - Sponsorships and financial assistance.
    - Educational talks and visits (birds, flowers, grass, butterflies, etc.).
    - Working parties (alien and erosion control).
    - Tree planting.
    - Walk and Run for Wildlife (affiliation to WESSA).
    - Fund raising.
    - Research and surveys.

15.3.7   Benefits for the landowner (municipality)

- "Watchdog role" on irregularities (poaching, squatting, littering, alien plants, improper behaviour).
- Improvements to the property (structures like bird hides, path ways, notice boards, trails).

- Help to increase utilisation of the property (events, fund raising).
- Financial assistance.
- Mouthpiece for local communities.
- Press exposure for nature conservation areas.
- Identify and concentrate interested and affected parties.
- Support for nature conservation activities.
- Surveys and research.

15.3.8   Benefits for a member of a Friends group

- Knowledge and exposure to a special interest.
- Personal satisfaction for a drive to contribute to nature.
- Free access to facilities in some cases.
- Doing something useful for the environment satisfies a need for environmental service.
- Sharing and enjoyment of outdoor activities.

CHAPTER 16

FUTURE APPROACH TO URBAN NATURE CONSERVATION

(This chapter indicates what the future approach to urban nature should be. It explains the previous approach of nature conservation where pockets of nature areas were protected without considering the role of ecological corridors. It highlights the change to an approach of conserving an ecological function (including the ecological corridors). It shows the link between biodiversity and climate change and then highlights the issues that should be included in a biodiversity management system.)

16.1 KEY CONCEPTS IN BIODIVERSITY MANAGEMENT

South Africa has some of the oldest conservation areas in the world, but many of these were established for hunting purposes, not for conservation of biodiversity. Some reserves were selected on the basis of the unsuitability of the area for other purposes such as agriculture, or to protect a specific resource such as water catchments. As biodiversity conservation was not the primary reason for selecting or conserving areas, the result is a protected area network that is often not representative of biodiversity. Historical factors such as political values and opportunity costs instead of biological or ecological issues were considered.

How protected areas were often proclaimed in the past resulted in the establishment of pockets of conservation areas that do not make provision for ecological functions. This contributed to conditions under which some species became vulnerable or even extinct; a situation reflected in the number of Red Data species currently on record. We need to move from nature conservation (where pockets of nature areas were protected) to biodiversity protection (where the protection focuses on ecological processes, ecological infrastructure and ecological services).

Why is biodiversity important?

Natural resources provide the basic means for life, namely air, water, food and various other materials. All of us face the effects of global warming, which is the

Undisturbed nature area.

result of climate change. Biodiversity is the variability among living organisms from all sources, including aerial, terrestrial, marine and other aquatic ecosystems and the ecological complexes which they are part of. Biodiversity includes diversity within species and of ecosystems. An indication of biodiversity is the number of different species interacting with each other and with their environments.

Biodiversity ensures that ecosystems are more stable. The loss of many species means that the ecosystem becomes visibly degraded. Nutrient and energy pathways are disrupted and productivity decreases and the ecosystems are disrupted from the bottom up, from the primary producers up to herbivores and predators. Pressures on the natural environment (like development) mean that ecosystems are less able to adapt to changing natural conditions. The ability of species to adapt and survive depends on the mosaic of species that exists. Once the stocks of opportunistic species are depleted, the adaptive capability and resilience of the ecosystems are significantly lowered.

Maintaining biodiversity is the key to maintaining ecosystem resilience and adaptation. Ecosystem resilience and adaptation is necessary to help cope with climate change. We need to ensure that actions are taken to enhance and maintain processes and species that contribute to the resilience and adaptive capability.

Biodiversity is not just about nature reserves or parks – there is a level of ecological interaction. Specie richness or the diversity of living organisms is just one measure of biodiversity.

Adaptation is the adjustment of an organism to its environment. The ability of organisms to adapt to their changing environment can be, for example, through migration to more suitable habitat, or through evolutionary changes. It is important to note that, while ecosystems have the ability to adapt to change, the rate of change plays a key role in their resilience to such change.

Resilience is the change in order to reach and maintain an acceptable level of functioning and structure. Resilience is also the capacity of an ecosystem to tolerate disturbances without collapsing. A resilient ecosystem can withstand shocks and rebuild itself when necessary. Resilience is conferred by adaptive capacity. Species and habitats are able to offer a measure of resilience to change, up to a threshold level, beyond which the rate of change becomes detrimental to the species or habitat. Species diversity itself is valuable because the presence of a variety of species helps to increase the capability of an ecosystem to be resilient.

The most fundamental ecosystem service provided by biodiversity is primary productivity through the energy production processes of photosynthetic plants (absorb carbon dioxide and release oxygen). Primary production is the basis for all life on earth. The organisms responsible for primary production are from the lowest link of the food chain (plants, algae), supported by abiotic factors such as soil, air and water.

Sustainable development refers to the ability to continue a process. This should be development which meets the needs of the present without compromising the ability of future generations to meet their own needs (UN, 1987 Brundtland Commission). Natural capital or natural resources must be kept constant to be able to achieve sustainable development.

Open space edge is the zone between natural habitats and disturbed landscapes. The ecosystem in the natural habitat is affected from the edge (boundary) for a certain distance inwards. This is also referred to as buffer zones. The smaller the natural habitat, the bigger the impacts from the edge affect and vice versa. It is thus important to try and increase the natural habitat to a size that can minimise the edge effect.

Habitat fragmentation is where habitat islands are created because of human development. The total area of habitat is reduced and the potential for maintenance of biodiversity is reduced. Fragmented habitats may not be viable to support the species or populations present in these habitats.

Connectivity between fragmented habitats is important. Connectivity is the potential connection of open spaces occurring in close proximity to one another. Connectivity can add ecological values to the larger biodiversity environments. There can be various levels of connectivity from high (open spaces that are directly linked), medium (open spaces that overlap by the 50 m dispersal buffer) to none (open spaces that are isolated, interrupted by urban development and national and provincial roads). Connectivity can help to maintain processes through migration of organisms and the transport of energy and resources across habitats and ecosystems. This helps retain the broad processes and cycles.

Agencies responsible for land use planning routinely make decisions that result in the loss of irreplaceable biodiversity. Biodiversity issues should be incorporated in all levels of planning and decision-making.

16.2 CLIMATE CHANGE AND BIODIVERSITY

Concentration of the three greenhouse gasses carbon dioxide, methane and nitrous oxide has increased substantially. This increase is attributed to human activities. Temperatures will increase and precipitation will decrease. Extreme weather events like droughts and floods are predicted to occur. Droughts will have a negative effect on biodiversity and floods will have localised negative impacts in terms of soil erosion and water submersion.

The 4 areas where higher temperatures will have an impact on biodiversity are: direct, frequency (minimum/maximum), rate of organic matter turnover (short-term flush of nutrients and long-term decrease in nutrient supply and soil stability) and an increase in evaporative demand of the atmosphere.

Rising atmospheric CO_2 levels increases the efficiency with which plants use water, light and soil nitrogen and thereby increases plant growth. Burning of fossil fuels in vehicles and industrial furnaces produces oxides of nitrogen (NOx) as well as CO_2. All these changes will result in a decrease of the net primary production (plants that absorb CO_2 and release O_2).

Biodiversity resources can reduce the impact of climate change on us. Conservation of habitats will reduce the amount of CO_2 released into the atmosphere. Conserving species and drought resistant crops can reduce climate effects such as flooding. The conservation and sustainable use of biodiversity can strengthen ecosystem resilience. Biodiversity can thus be used to mitigate, or adapt, to climate change.

16.3   THREATS TO BIODIVERSITY

Development has historically enjoyed priority over conservation. Invasion of open spaces has been allowed to take place in close proximity to sensitive environments and wetlands through inappropriate land-use planning. Construction of roads and transport routes also fragmented habitats and linkages that were used by genetic flow between separated habitats. Ridges were also transformed by development.

Alien invasive species encroached into nature areas and latterly changed the composition of natural habitats. In Gauteng (South Africa) there are 129 invasive plant, 4 mammals, 5 birds, 3 reptiles, 1 amphibian and 4 invertebrates species present.

Informal settlements in proximity to sensitive areas expanded, for example, into wetlands and currently pose a threat to these areas. Wetlands are used as ablution and washing facilities and the absence of proper sanitation and waste facilities now lead to the destruction of these habitats. Uncontrolled veld fires threaten the already sensitive grasslands in the highveld areas of Gauteng (South Africa). In this province, 35% of the threatened plant species are collected and traded for horticultural purposes.

Eutrophication is also an issue in many water bodies, particularly wetlands, resulting in encroachment by reeds, problem water plants and exotics.

16.4   GUIDELINE POLICY FOR BIODIVERSITY PROTECTION IN AN URBAN ENVIRONMENT

16.4.1   The proposed 10-point policy that should be adapted by local authorities is:

- Expand existing protected areas.
- Improve the ecological functioning of all existing open spaces, parks and nature areas.

- Connect open spaces, parks and nature areas that have ecological function and importance (Corridors).

- Promote environmental awareness and education programmes.

- Keep a record of all information to monitor and evaluate biodiversity conservation and management.

- Maintain a network of green ways and nodes as well as blue ways and nodes that conserves a representative sample of biodiversity (maintain key ecological processes).

- Reduce pollution and waste in order to limit impacts on biodiversity.

- Control and eradicate alien invasive species.

- Integrate biodiversity protection measures with urban development projects.

- Integrate adaptation strategies related to climate change with biodiversity protection initiatives.

16.4.2 The proposed biodiversity strategy that should be implemented on local governmental levels is:

- Classify habitats in terms of ecosystem status (from critically endangered to least threatened).

- Establish new nature reserves, conservancies or protected areas.

- Expand the size and shape of existing nature reserves (maximise the cores and minimise the edges).

- Add ecological corridors.

- Create and expand buffer zones.

- Protect all Red Data species (address threats, weaknesses and current protection).

- Compile an action plan for the eradication of alien invasive species.

- Produce a best practice biodiversity manual for brown, grey and red nodes.

- Mainstream and integrate biodiversity in the integrated development plan (IDP).

- Design a biodiversity information management system.

- Compile an action plan for the protection of critical urban ecological systems (wetlands and riparian habitat).

16.4.3 The proposed action plan:

The focus is to identify priority habitats and priority areas. The status of each habitat and the area covered by these habitats is important. The habitats need to be prioritised as high, medium or low, with the focus on the high and medium habitats. The priority areas will focus on the expansion of existing formal protected areas.

The strategy will be managed by 3 disciplines namely: proactive/strategic planning, development impact management and conservation planning and management.

16.4.4   Proactive/strategic planning

All environmental strategic policy and plans should be in line with the focal areas and consideration of priority areas and habitats identified. Such policy and plans include the regional spatial development framework (RSDF), metropolitan spatial development framework (MSDF) and the city development strategy (CDS).

Regular reviews of the local conservation targets and priorities within the various habitat types needs to be conducted.

16.4.5   Establishment of a conservation forum

This forum will involve a diverse group of stakeholders. The stakeholders need to be updated on amendments, priority areas and threats, such as development proposals, etc. The forum thus should be represented by all major stakeholder groups, including non-governmental organisations, developers, association, conservancy groups and other conservation bodies.

The forum will discuss the following:
- Conservation priorities.
- Biodiversity issues (priority areas).
- Development impacts.
- Knowledge sharing.

16.4.6   Development impact management

Here the focus is on development that has a direct impact on priority areas (a specific priority area or those sites within 100 m of priority areas).

All development application, rezoning application or listed activities need to be looked at. If the site is a designated priority area, certain primary specialist studies have to accompany the development application. The application and recommendation for management of that area must be reviewed. These guidelines should be applied alongside existing land use management guidelines. The results of site-specific specialist biodiversity or ecological studies should be used to inform decision-making. All offset management plans or open space management plans and monitoring of implementation thereof must be done.

16.4.7   Conservation planning and management

The biodiversity protection unit is responsible for the management of the urban nature areas. They have to determine the current conservation status, ownership and zoning. They have to determine the disturbance in priority areas and habitats and the ecological function and importance of these areas. Priority areas owned by the local authority should be included into the protected areas network and managed accordingly. This unit will be responsible for the compilation, updating and implementation of a management plan for all priority areas. If a priority area is privately owned, mechanisms can be pursued with the landowner which may include expropriation of land, co-management agreements and transfer of purchase of development rights or declaration as a protected area.

16.4.8   Funding mechanism

There should preferably be a dedicated biodiversity programme budget to effectively allocate funds and track expenditures. The budget should be drawn up annually and should describe the annual conservation priorities and allocate funds accordingly. The conservation funds will need to include capital and operating costs associated with the management of these biodiversity priority areas.

CHAPTER 17

INVESTING IN ECOLOGICAL INFRASTRUCTURE

(This chapter explains what ecological infrastructure means, why it is important to invest in ecological infrastructure and how it should be addressed. It also highlights the importance of prioritising this responsibility in all sectors of society.) [1]

17.1   EVOLUTION OF THE APPROACH TO INVEST IN ECOLOGICAL INFRASTRUCTURE

A new approach to understanding and communicating the core intention of maintaining and restoring natural ecosystems that provide valuable services has emerged. This new model is referred to as "investing in ecological infrastructure".

Investing in ecological infrastructure has its foundation in simultaneously identifying critical services flowing from naturally functioning ecosystems, and identifying those organisations that would benefit from or have a key responsibility for investing in these naturally functioning systems. The ecosystem services that are prime factors for attracting investments are largely related to water and disaster risk reduction, with climate change adaptation elements in both of these. The interested primary stakeholders are government-related, although this should not discount the potential for private sector stakeholder involvement.

The shift in focus from communicating ecosystem services to communicating the concept of ecological infrastructure (i.e. the source of the service) was because potential investors found ecological infrastructure a far more tangible concept to grasp compared to ecosystem services. It allowed them to focus on very discrete elements in the landscape that required attention. The use of the term "infrastructure" has an immediate appeal for the identified stakeholders involved in national and local planning, as well as to those working with various forms of built infrastructure.

---

[1] Information in this chapter was extracted from a document compiled by the South Africa National Biodiversity Institute: SANBI (2014) *A framework for investing in ecological infrastructure in South Africa.*

This new focus on investing in ecological infrastructure captures the interest of government, at both a local and national level, as well as corporate investors.

17.2   WHAT IS MEANT BY ECOLOGICAL INFRASTRUCTURE?

Ecological infrastructure refers to naturally functioning ecosystems that deliver valuable services to people, such as healthy mountain catchments, rivers, wetlands, coastal dunes, and nodes and corridors of natural habitat, which together form a network of interconnected structural elements in the landscape. Ecological infrastructure is therefore the asset or stock from which a range of valuable services flow. The term "naturally functioning" refers to ecosystems that are in a natural, near natural or functional condition, whose basic ecosystem functions are predominantly unchanged, even though their composition and structure may have been modified.

Ecological infrastructure is the nature-based equivalent of built or hard infrastructure, and is as important for providing services and underpinning socio-economic development. It provides these services either directly to society (such as a coastal dune protecting a road from sea surge), or as part of a broader infrastructure system that includes built infrastructure (such as a natural catchment area functioning with a dam and pipes to provide water to a nearby settlement). Ecological infrastructure already exists in the landscape, although in some cases it might be degraded. However, as with all forms of infrastructure, ecological infrastructure needs to be maintained and managed and in some cases restored.

Degraded ecological infrastructure leads to reduced capacity and lifespan of dams, increasing the cost of their maintenance. It also increases the risk of flooding. The result is damage to infrastructure such as roads and bridges, which may even be washed away. All of this poses a significant risk to people. It is usually more cost effective to restore the ecosystems concerned than to keep repairing or replacing the built infrastructure. Investing in ecological infrastructure enhances investments in built infrastructure.

Key elements of ecological infrastructure are located in rural areas – catchments, corridors or tracts of natural vegetation. Restoring and maintaining ecological infrastructure contributes to diversifying rural livelihood options, on the one hand through direct job creation and on the other hand by strengthening economic sectors such as sustainable farming and ecotourism.

Rural communities often rely directly on ecological infrastructure for goods and services, for example getting their drinking water directly from a river, and tend to be most severely affected by declines in the quality of ecological infrastructure.

Well-managed ecological infrastructure can buffer human settlements and built infrastructure against the extreme events that are likely with climate change, playing a crucial and cost effective role in disaster risk reduction. For example, coastal ecosystems such as dunes, mangroves and kelp beds reduce the impact of storm surges on coastal settlements. In contrast, hardening the coastline puts people and property at greater risk.

Health riparian zones and wetlands help to reduce the impact of floods and droughts. In parts of the country, that become hotter and drier, it will help to curb excessive loss of water through evaporation. In parts of the country that become hotter and wetter, it will help to slow down flood waters. In both cases, ecological infrastructure can contribute to water security and thus to food security. Intact ecosystems also absorb and store carbon to varying degrees.

The term "restoration" is used to mean restoration of ecological functioning, rather than restoration to a pristine state. The level of ecological functioning to be restored should be agreed on based on the services that are required from the ecological infrastructure concerned. Restoration may include specific rehabilitation measures such as building gabions in wetlands.

The advantage of ecological infrastructure is that it already exists – we don't have to pay for constructing it. Ecological infrastructure must be maintained and managed especially when it has been severely degraded and needs to be restored. Key actions to unlock the potential of ecological infrastructure include:
- Scale up to invest in the restoring and maintaining of ecological infrastructure (focus on the highest value ecological assets).
- Build a natural resource management programme ("Working for Water" and "Working for Wetlands").
- Plan and managed ecological infrastructure networks (do not let their persistence change).

There are many cases where ecological infrastructure has common good or public good characteristics, where it is not possible to exclude people from benefiting from the services the goods provide. For example, multiple people benefit from a well-functioning catchment through fresh water it provides. As a result, a "free-rider" problem arises, where individuals tend to underinvest in the good. In addition, the ecological infrastructure may be on private or communal land, where the landowners themselves are often not receiving the full benefit of the service and will therefore tend to underinvest in it. In these cases where the market is unable to capture externalities, the public sector often has a role to play in ensuring optimal investment in ecological infrastructure.

The millennium ecosystem assessment (MEA) defines ecosystem services as benefits people obtain from ecosystems, and goes on to distinguish between four categories of ecosystem services – provisioning, regulating, cultural and supporting services (Millennium Ecosystem Assessment, 2005). Under this definition, ecosystem services are understood to flow from both naturally functioning ecosystems as well as highly modified ecosystems, such as irrigated monocultures. Given the understanding of ecological infrastructure within South Africa, ecological infrastructure underpins the delivery of a subset of ecosystem services – those delivered by naturally functioning ecosystems. One element of ecological infrastructure (e.g. a wetland) can deliver more than one service, for example, a wetland can support disaster risk reduction as well as water provision.

"Investment" refers to devoting time, effort, finances and/or making decisions in support of a particular undertaking with the expectation of a worthwhile result. Investing in ecological infrastructure involves maintaining functioning ecological infrastructure, as well as restoring degraded ecological infrastructure. This can be done through a range of approaches such as:
- Integrating ecological infrastructure into land-use planning and decision-making.
- Clearing invasive alien plants from catchments and riparian areas.
- Rehabilitating wetlands.
- Maintaining or restoring buffers of natural vegetation in riparian areas.
- Improving rangeland management practices.
- Establishing and maintaining protected areas or conservation areas.

Wherever possible, ecological infrastructure networks should be managed strategically, either as part of a larger system of built and ecological infrastructure, or as ecological infrastructure that provides a direct service.

Investing in ecological infrastructure improves the flow of services to society, thereby improving human well-being.

17.2.1 Some examples of the services and benefits flowing from investment in ecological infrastructure are:

17.2.1.1 Examples of interventions
- Clear invasive alien plants, especially in mountain catchments and riparian areas.
- Rehabilitate wetlands.
- Maintain buffers of natural vegetation along streams and rivers.
- Reinstate buffers of natural vegetation between development areas, rivers or wetlands.
- Improve rangeland management practices (grazing, fire management).
- Monitor compliance with effluent standards for agriculture and industry.
- Restore degraded coastal dunes.

17.2.1.2 Examples of benefits
- Increased water yield.
- Improved water quality through filtering of pollutants and toxins.
- Reduces flood damage.
- Improved soil quality.
- Increases base flow in dry season – assurance of water supply.
- Reduce sediment loads in rivers.
- Improve carbon balance.

17.2.1.3   Improved human well-being

- Decreased exposure to natural disasters (fire, floods, sea surge, etc.).
- Improved food security.
- Improved health.
- Safe and plentiful drinking water.
- Improve livelihood security.
- Adaptation to climate change.

The effects of climate change are expected to place additional pressures on already stretched water resources. Water quantity (annual yield as well as dry season flows) and quality (e.g. nutrients and sediment load) are both affected by catchment condition. Invasive alien trees remove a large percentage of total annual run-off water.

Poor vegetation cover results in soil erosion and subsequent siltation of built water infrastructure. Poorly functioning wetlands and the removal of natural vegetation buffers along river banks means that the natural function of filtering pollutants from the water cannot take place. Investing in the restoration and maintenance of important elements within catchments has the potential to increase dry season flows, improve water quality, reduce risk to life and property (including built water infrastructure) from extreme weather events and lengthen the lifespan of built water infrastructure and reduces maintenance costs.

The ability of landscapes to ameliorate or reduce the impacts of drought and flood events should be a critical consideration in disaster risk reduction and prevention. A catchment that is in good ecological condition can have a significant impact on flood damage. Natural vegetation slows the speed at which water runs down the gradient of the land surface, thereby increasing the infiltration of water into the soil. This reduces soil erosion. Wetlands act as sponges in river systems, holding back water during wet periods and releasing it at a slower rate into the system. Both of these have the effect of reducing the destructive energy of floodwaters.

Degraded foredunes and the hardening of coastal areas are key drivers of increased risks from sea storms along parts of South Africa's coast (The Santam Group *et al.*, 2011). Restoring dunes and preventing further inappropriate development along vulnerable coastal areas increases the ability of ecological infrastructure to reduce risk from sea storms. The existence of invasive alien trees, in particular pine *(Pinus)*, gum *(Eucalyptus)* and species of acacia, has been shown to be a key driver of fire risk in parts of the country (The Santam Group *et al.*, 2011). Controlling and/or eradicating these trees should be seen as a critical component of managing fire risks. Investing in disaster risk reduction and management is of interest to both the public, such as municipal duties related to disaster risk management and the private sector, such as the insurance industry (The Santam Group *et al.*, 2011).

Investment in ecological infrastructure supports built infrastructure. It can lengthen the life of existing built infrastructure, and reduce the need for additional built infrastructure, often with significant cost savings. For instance, a degraded catchment with poor vegetation covers results in increased erosion. Downstream dams silt up, leading to reduced storage capacity and dam lifespan, increasing the cost of infrastructure maintenance.

A degraded catchment also increases the risk of flooding, which could result in damage to infrastructure such as roads and bridges, and poses a significant risk to people. Restoring the ecosystems concerned as well as maintaining built infrastructure, is often a more cost effective response than solely repairing or replacing the built infrastructure.

It is becoming increasingly clear globally that naturally functioning ecosystems will assist society's adaptation to climate change. Ecosystem-based adaptation is likely to become an increasingly significant driver of investment in ecological infrastructure, as it becomes better understood and supported. Some ecosystems also have a role to play in climate change mitigation as carbon sinks. Peat-containing wetlands, for example, provide one of the most important long term carbon stores globally (Parish *et al.*, 2008). South Africa has more than 30 000 ha of peat lands (Grundling and Grobler, 2005).

17.3   ROLE PLAYERS IN INVESTING IN ECOLOGICAL INFRASTRUCTURE

Ecological infrastructure often has a strong "public good" element, where the benefits of investing in ecological infrastructure accrue largely to the broader public, making it difficult to isolate direct returns on an investment to a private sector investor. For example, downstream communities benefit from improved water quality and flood attenuation services provided by upstream wetlands, while upstream landowners have no real incentive to invest in the maintenance of a wetland on their property.

The state has a central and often lead role to play in ensuring optimal investment in ecological infrastructure landscape elements. This may take the form of a direct investment of public funds in restoration, maintenance or conservation of ecological infrastructure, even if this infrastructure is located on private or communal land. In some cases it may be more appropriate for the state to provide subsidies, incentives, or create new regulations which indirectly ensure private sector investments in ecological infrastructure.

Land-use decisions made at the municipal level affect the existence and state of ecological infrastructure, such as the maintenance of healthy wetlands that provide a disaster risk reduction role for human settlements. The enforcement of buffers along river stretches on agricultural land by provincial agricultural departments also has a direct impact on river health and water quality.

The private sector has a critical role to play in investing in ecological infrastructure both as an investor and as a landowner. There are a number of motivations for private sector investment in ecological infrastructure. One of the main motivators is to manage risk. In some sectors, investing in ecological infrastructure serves as a direct investment in risk reduction to a business, such as in the case of insurance companies playing a collaborative role in reducing their exposure to flood or fire risk. In some cases, a company or entire sector may recognise the importance of the ecosystem services that are critical in their supply chain or the production of their own products – such as clean, readily available water – and invest in the supply of these services. Investing in ecological infrastructure is also an investment in a more stable society, through helping to address poverty and socio-economic disparities. Much corporate social investment is built on this premise.

17.4   CONSERVING BIODIVERSITY

The process of mainstreaming spatial biodiversity priorities into traditionally non-biodiversity sectors is not only a technical exercise. It requires investing time and resources into building relationships within other sectors, learning and speaking the language of these sectors and supporting champions within the sectors. This experience should be built on when mainstreaming spatial ecological infrastructure priority areas into land-use planning and decision making.

Natural resource management programmes aim to restore ecosystem functions and improve the provision of ecosystem services, while creating jobs and alleviating poverty. Programmes such as Working for Water focus on controlling invasive alien plant species which have a negative impact on water resources, biodiversity and the productive potential of land. Working for Wetlands drives the conservation, rehabilitation and sustainable use of wetland ecosystems and Working for Land deals with the restoration of degraded landscapes.

Investing in ecological infrastructure does not require the development of a range of new mechanisms or instruments, but rather the integration of ecological infrastructure into existing practices and programmes of work and institutional structures, such as planning, mapping, restoration and partnerships between the state and private landowners.

17.5   GUIDELINE EXAMPLES FOR INVESTING
IN ECOLOGICAL INFRASTRUCTURE

Particular objectives around water service delivery, disaster mitigation or climate change adaptation, the desired state of ecological infrastructure, as well as any additional socio-economic desired benefits should be clearly defined.

A map of prioritised ecological infrastructure supporting water services may identify different landscape features compared to a map of priority ecological infrastructure for disaster risk reduction.

Investment in ecological infrastructure requires people from different disciplines working together (such as the building, engineering, environmental and water sectors), each drawing from their own knowledge and communities of practice.

Existing programmes (Working for Water and Working for Wetlands) as well as mechanisms of funding (the municipal infrastructure grant) can assist to invest in ecological infrastructure.

It is important that job creation and poverty alleviation goals are factored into programme design when planning for investment in ecological infrastructure. Focus on projects where there are clear socio-economic benefits as well as ecosystem service provision benefits, such as Working for Water projects that focus on labour intensive practices in order to increase job creation.

Relevant stakeholders should be involved in integrated adaptive planning, implementation and monitoring of the project where appropriate. This should include stakeholder engagement in the development of goals, outcomes and the implementation and monitoring plan. This may mean that it takes longer to set up a project. Appropriate resources, time and money should be allocated for this and appropriate skills should be incorporated into the project team.

Baseline data should be collected and additional data should be gathered throughout the project to track improvements in the state of restoration measures, infrastructure and the services that would be improved.

Each potential source of funding for investing in ecological infrastructure requires a unique approach. The role of leveraging contributions from landowners who are custodians of ecological infrastructure requires specific attention in order to provide effective incentives, create and maintain contractual agreements, and in some cases, penalise disinvestments.

CHAPTER 18

THIERRY REVERT'S STORY

(This chapter summarises what happened to Thierry Revert. Thierry tells the story when he attended the first Earth Summit in Rio de Janeiro in June 1992. Thierry told this story in person to the author when they first met in 2012).

How to change the world

My early activism advocating that human beings must live in total respect of the Great Spirit and nature comes from my initiation by the Hopi Indians in Arizona in the US in the mid-1970s.

These two and a half months of being immerged in understanding how the universe really works changed my whole view of the world. As a Westerner, I viewed the ideology of science, the market, consumerism and money as the main preoccupations in modern life, as well as the constant exposure to brainwashing from the media and marketing agencies that try to sell us something at any cost.

For the next 20 years (1970s to 1990s) I spent most of my activist life speaking out on the dangers of our economic growth paradigm on our future. I became finely acquainted with the principles of sustainable development through the Bruntland Commission in the mid-1980s.

This came in the middle of a period dominated by the Reagan-Thatcher era. They were the uncontested champions of the so-called free market economy only to cement the overwhelming power of the financial private and public institutions. They were now free to create money and capital to feed the greed and obsession with ownership of the multinational corporations.

These excesses unveiled the dark side of a materialist and colonialist domination of the world by the US-UK axis, and with it, activists started to reveal the massive abuses committed against mother earth and all its creatures, including humans.

These abuses were supported by the "Gunho" approach of policing the world through wars and conflicts designed to secure the natural resources to feed the huge demand for consumer goods and the pursuit of an American dream, symbolised by the Coca Cola global takeover of our thirst. We have now realised that we are living under a total illusion and lie.

Based on this background and my residence in South Africa from 1981, along with the release of Mandela and the end of Apartheid, I decided to attend the very first Earth Summit in Rio de Janeiro over 12 days in June, 1992.

It was also the first time that the "green activism" brand started to raise its head all over the world. Most of the movements decided to converge in Rio, to show discontent with mainly the United States under George Bush Sr. who was denying any of the visible degradations that greed capitalism was generating all over the world.

We were probably 10 000 protesters who took to the Rio streets with various slogans to demonstrate the discontent and frustration of all nature lovers.

Brazil was under military rule at the time and on the first day of the marches, the police was to arrest the first two or three front rows of activists and we were trucked under heavy guard to a jail outside the city.

The jail consisted of 4 large cells, containing 30 to 40 people each. These cells were facing each other with a space in the middle. Policemen on duty stood watching a crowd of unhappy and vocal individuals who had been stripped of all bags, laces, belts and ID documents.

As the mood started to mellow, some of the jailed leaders decided to take the opportunity to democratically discuss the formulation of a Civil Society Manifesto for the Earth Summit.

We were reluctantly given paper and pens (only the convenors of such an exercise who were speaking Portuguese with the wardens) and the discussions started, all in English.

After much deliberation 22 points were put down on the Manifesto. We were released after 48 hours of detention. Our leaders decided to take the Manifesto and present it to the main building where the official guests and attendants were gathering.

Upon arrival, our small group (now identified as troublemakers) was stopped at the foot of the stairs of the conference centre by police and asked to disperse.

After lengthy discussions with the police officers, a person with a badge indicating that he was an important person came out and asked us the reason for our noise and gesticulation and we requested his permission to present the Manifesto to the organisers so they could table it at the plenary, on behalf of Civil Society.

He accepted after we demanded to have a receipt from him that this would be done and he declared that he would hand it directly to the secretary general, but without any guarantee that it would be considered.

We stayed for a while and tried to negotiate a pass as official attendants, but were declined. We only followed the congress from neighbouring places which were displaying on-coming reports of the various commissions.

It was to our surprise that at the end of the Earth Summit when the final document (discussed by the whole congress for more than a week) was published and officially called the Agenda 21, that the 21 points reflected the points that we discussed and agreed upon while being incarcerated for 2 days as a group of "persona non grata".

For the story, the only point not reflected in the official Agenda 21, was a point indicating that capitalism should be eradicated from the planet and be replaced by a New world governance to discipline the rich nations on matters affecting the planet and the people. This was to be implemented immediately with adequate and appropriate institutions for its enforcement.

To this day, the failure to implement sustainable development is still attributed to the fact that there is no global agreement on the Earth Charter or the New Rights of Mother Earth.

This whole story tells us that a bunch of unruly, undisciplined and loud group of activists can collectively think creatively and clearly to put together world class documents that can change the world.

After getting information from various delegates inside the process, we found that mostly the US delegation opposed the famous point 22, which is the one that should guide the current economic growth model based on the GDP measuring system. The neo-liberal political and ideological framework of the US must be reformed, if not completely eradicated from operating on the planet

The debate is still raging, but 22 years later, the uncontested proof that the US/EU/Westernised promise of prosperity for all, has failed miserably and that we have to repair the massive damages and cope with the current disasters and crises. This time we must definitely listen to the protesters in the first row and ensure that the proposals for another type of new world order are duly considered for a sustainable future.

18.1   THE CONTENTS OF THE AGENDA 21 DOCUMENT THAT CAN BE DOWNLOADED FROM THE INTERNET [1]

United Nations Conference on Environment and Development
Rio de Janero, Brazil, 3 to 14 June 1992
AGENDA 21
CONTENTS

Chapter Paragraphs

1.   Preamble 1.1–1.6

---

[1] Small Island Developing States Network (SIDSnet) has formatted this document for MS-Word from the original version available for downloading from the United Nations Department of Economic and Social Affairs (DESA) at: http://www.un.org/esa/sustdev/agenda21.htm. Reproduction and dissemination of the document - in electronic and/or printed format - is encouraged, provided acknowledgement is made of the role of the United Nations in making it available.

***Section I: Social and Economic Dimensions**

2. International cooperation to accelerate sustainable development in developing countries and related domestic policies 2.1–2.43.
3. Combating poverty 3.1–3.12.
4. Changing consumption patterns 4.1–4.27.
5. Demographic dynamics and sustainability 5.1–5.66.
6. Protecting and promoting human health conditions 6.1–6.46.
7. Promoting sustainable human settlement development 7.1–7.80.
8. Integrating environment and development in decision making 8.1–8.54.

***Section II: Conservation and management of resources for Development**

9. Protection of the atmosphere 9.1–9.35.
10. Integrated approach to the planning and management of land resources 10.1–10.18.
11. Combating deforestation 11.1–11.40.
12. Managing fragile ecosystems: combating desertification and drought 12.1–12.63.
13. Managing fragile ecosystems: sustainable mountain development 13.1–13.24.
14. Promoting sustainable agriculture and rural development 14.1–14.104.
15. Conservation of biological diversity 15.1–15.11.
16. Environmentally sound management of biotechnology 16.1–16.46.
17. Protection of the oceans, all kinds of seas, including enclosed and semi-enclosed seas, and coastal areas and the protection, rational use and development of their living resources 17.1–17.136.
18. Protection of the quality and supply of freshwater resources: application of integrated approaches to the development, management and use of water resources 18.1–18.90.
19. Environmentally sound management of toxic chemicals, including prevention of illegal international traffic in toxic and dangerous products 19.1–19.76.
20. Environmentally sound management of hazardous wastes, in hazardous wastes 20.1–20.46.
21. Environmentally sound management of solid wastes and sewage-related issues 21.1–21.49.
22. Safe and environmentally sound management of radioactive wastes 22.1–22.9.

Section III: Strengthening the role of major groups

23. Preamble 23.1–23.4.
24. Global action for women towards sustainable and equitable development 24.1–24.12.
25. Children and youth in sustainable development 25.1–25.17.
26. Recognizing and strengthening the role of indigenous people and their communities 26.1–26.9.
27. Strengthening the role of non-governmental organizations: partners for sustainable development 27.1–27.13.

28. Local authorities' initiatives in support of Agenda 21 28.1–28.7.
29. Strengthening the role of workers and their trade unions 29.1–29.14.
30. Strengthening the role of business and industry 30.1–30.30.
31. Scientific and technological community 31.1–31.12
32. Strengthening the role of farmers 32.1–32.14.

Section IV: Means of implementation

33. Financial resources and mechanisms 33.1–33.21.
34. Transfer of environmentally sound technology, cooperation and capacity-building 34.1–34.29.
35. Science for sustainable development 35.1–35.25.
36. Promoting education, public awareness and training 36.1–36.27.
37. National mechanisms and international cooperation for capacity-building in developing countries 37.1–37.13.
38. International institutional arrangements 38.1–38.45.
39. International legal instruments and mechanisms 39.1–39.10.
40. Information for decision-making 40.1–40.30.

* * * * *

* For section I (Social and economic dimensions), see A/CONF.151/26 (Vol. I); for section III (Strengthening the role of major groups) and section IV (Means of implementation), see A.CONF/151/26 (Vol. III).

* For section II (Conservation and management of resources for development), see A/CONF.151/26 (Vol. II); for section III (Strengthening the role of major groups) and section IV (Means of implementation), see A/CONF.151/26 (Vol. III).

* For section I (Social and economic dimensions), see A/CONF.151/26 (Vol. I); for section II (Conservation and management of resources for development), see A/CONF.151/26 (Vol. II).

CHAPTER 19

LITERATURE

19.1   BOOKS

Allen, G.M. 1942. *Extinct and vanishing mammals of the western hemisphere, with the marine species of all the oceans.* American Committee for International Wild Life Protection, Massachusetts: Cambridge,

Antonovsky, A. 1979. *Health, Stress and Coping.* San Francisco: Jossey-Bass Publishers.

Bailey, F.A. 1889. *Birds through an Opera Glass.* Montana: Kessinger Legacy Reprints

Bain, M.B. and Stevenson, N.J. 1999. *Aquatic Habitat Assessment. Common methods.* Maryland: American Fisheries Society.

Barnes, K.N. 2000. The Eskom Red Data Book of Birds of South Africa, Lesotho and Swaziland. Birdlife South Africa, Randburg.

Branch, B. 1992. Bill Branch's field guide to the snakes and other reptiles of southern Africa. Struik Publishers, Cape Town.

Broadley, D.G. 1990. Fitzsimon's snakes of southern Africa. Jonathan Ball & A.D. Donker Publishers.

Bumstead, P. 2004. The Art of Birdwatching. Simply Wild Publications Inc. ISBN 0-9689278-2-3. OCLC 56329274.

Carpenter. 1997. Freshwater Ecosystem Services. In Nature's Services, G.C. Daily (ed.). Island Press. Washington D.C.

Cocker, Mark 2002. Birders: Tales of a tribe. Grove Press. ISBN 0-87113-844-1

Corder, M. 1986. Naturalistic techniques and the urban local authority. In R. Brooker and M. Corder (eds), Environmental Economy, E & FN Spon, London, 113-37.

Cronk, J.K. & Siobhan Fennessy, M. 2001. Wetland Plants: Biology and Ecology. Lewis publishers.

Davies, A & Ruth Miller 2010. The Biggest Twitch: Around the World in 4,000 Birds. A & C Black. ISBN 1-4081-2387-8.

Dunlap, Thomas R. 2011. In the Field, Among the Feathered: A History of Birders & Their Guides, Oxford University Press, ISBN 0199734593. p 47.

Eliasch, J. 2008. Climate Change: Financing Global Forests. The Eliasch Review. The Stationary Office Ltd., London.

Moreleta Kloof Nature Reserve.

FISRWG (10/1998). Stream Corridor Restoration: Principles, Processes, and Practices. By the Federal Interagency Stream Restoration Working Group (FISRWG), (15 Federal agencies of the US gov't). GPO Item No. 0120-A; SuDocs No. A 57.6/2: EN 3/PT.653. ISBN-0-934213-59-3.

Forman, R.T.T., 1995. *Land mosaics: the ecology of landscapes and regions*. Cambridge University Press, Great Britain.

Gilbert, O.L. 1989. *The ecology of Urban Habitats*. Chapman & Hall, London.

Ginn, P.J., McIlleron, W.G. & Milstein, P. le S. (1989). *The complete book of southern African birds*. Struik, Cape Town.

Harris, L.D. and Silva-Lopez, G. 1992. In P.L. Fiedler and S.K. Jain (eds). *Conservation Biology*, Chapman & Hall, London and New York.

Hockey, P.A.C., Dean, W.R.J. & Ryan, P.G. 2008. *Roberts Birds of Southern Africa*. 7th Edition, 3rd Impression. ISBN: 978-0-620340-53-3.

Johnston, J.D. 1990. Nature areas for city people, Ecology Handbook, 14, London Ecology Unit, London.

Jordan, W.R. Gilpin, M.E. and Aber, J.D. 1987. *Restoration Ecology: A Synthetic Approach to Ecological Research*. Cambridge University Press.

Del Hoyo, J. 1992. Handbook of the Birds of the World: Complete Series.

Keddy, P.A. 2002. *Wetland Ecology: Principles and Conservation*. Cambridge University Press.

Kendle, T. and Forbes, F. 1997. *Urban Nature conservation.* E & FN Spoon, an imprint of Thomson Professional. 2-6 Boundry Row, London SE1 8HN, UK.

Law, J. and Lynch, M. 1990. Lists, Field Guides, and the Descriptive Organization of Seeing: Birdwatching as an Exemplary Observational Activity in *Representation in Scientific Practice*. M. Lynch and S. Woolgar (eds.). Cambridge: MIT Press. pp. 267–299.

Lewis, D. 2012. *The Feathery Tribe: Robert Ridgway and the Modern Study of Birds*. Yale University Press. ISBN 0-300-17552-3.

London Ecology Unit 1985. Nature conservation guidelines for London, Ecology Handbook, 3, London Ecology Unit, London.

Lowrey, T.K. & Wright, S. 1987. *The Flora of the Witwatersrand. Volume I: The Monocotyledonae*. Witwatersrand University Press, Johannesburg.

Loney, B. & Hobbs, R.J. 1991. *Management of vegetation corridors: maintenance, rehabilitation and establishment*. In Nature Conservation 2: The role of corridors. Saunders, D.A. & Hobbs, R.J. (eds). Pages 299-311. Surrey Beatty & Sons Pty Limited, Australia.

Maclean, G.L. 1993. *Roberts Bird Book of southern Africa*. 6th Edition. The Trustees of the John Voelcker Bird Book Fund, Cape Town.

Mayor of London, 2011. The London Plan, Spatial development strategy for Greater London. Cover the third version of the London Plan. ISBN: 9781847814517. Preceded by the London Plan: Consolidated with alterations since 2004.

Mitch, W.J. & Gosselink, J.G. 2000. *Wetlands*. Third edition. John Wiley & Sons Inc., New York.

Millennium Ecosystem Assessment. 2005. *Ecosystems and Human Well-being: Synthesis*. Island Press, Washington, DC.

Moffatt, D. 1986. The natural approach to open space. In R. Brooker and M. Corder (eds.) *Environmental Economy*. E&FN Spon, London, 79-112.

Moss, S. 2004. *A bird in the bush: A social history of bird watching*. Aurum Press. P. 102-103, ISBN 1-85410-993-6.

Nellemann, C. and Corcoran, E. (eds). 2010. *Dead Planet, Living Planet – Biodiversity and Ecosystem Restoration for Sustainable Development*. Birkeland Trykkeri AS, Norway.

Oliver George Sheffield. 1941. Friend Earthworm: Practical Application of a Lifetime Study of Habits of the Most Important Animal in the World.

Snetsinger, P. 2003. Birding on Borrowed Time. American Birding Association. ISBN 1-878788-41-8.

Primack, R.B. 1995. A Primer of Conservation Biology. Sinauer Associates, U.S.A. 277 pages.

Ratcliffe, D.A. 1977a. *A Nature Conservation Review* (2 vols), Cambridge University Press, Cambridge.

Ratcliffe, D.A. 1977b. *The Nature Conservation Review*. Cambridge University Press, Cambridge.

Richardson, J.L. & Vepraskas, M.J. 2001. *Wetland Soils: Genesis, Hydrology, Landscapes and Classification*. Lewis Publishers.

Peterson, R.T. 1934. *A Field Guide to birds*. Caliban Books, Pittsburgh PA. ABAA (Wilkinsburg, PA, USA).

Samways, M.J. 1994. *Insect Conservation Biology*. Chapman & Hall.

Sangster, M. 1995. *Planning and designing new woodlands for people*. In R. Ferris-Kaan (ed.) The Ecology of Woodland Creation, John Wiley & Sons, Chichester, 17-26.

Sibley, D.A. 2000. *The Sibley Field guide to Birds of Eastern North America*. Random House Inc.

TEEB – The Economics of Ecosystems and Biodiversity for National and International Policy Makers. 2009. Chapter 9: Investing in ecological infrastructure. Available at: http://www.teebweb.org/LinkClick.aspx?fileticket=9NUqttjb3bo%3d&tabid =1019&language=en-US [Accessed 10/05/10].

TEEB 2011. The Economics of Ecosystems and Biodiversity in National and International Policy Making (ed.) Patrick ten Brink. Earthscan, London and Washington.

The atlas of southern African birds. Volume I: Non-passerines. BirdLife South Africa: Johannesburg. 374-375.

Tiner, R.W. 1999. *Wetland Indicators. A Guide to Wetland Identification, Delineation, Classification, and Mapping*. Lewis Publishers. U.S. Army Corps of Engineers, 2004).

Wates, N. and Knevitt, C. 1987. *Community Architecture. How People Are Creating Their Own Environment*. Penguin, London.

Weidensaul, S. 2007. *Of a Feather: A Brief History of Birding*. Harcourt, Orlando.

Williams, M. 1994. *Butterflies of southern Africa. A field guide*. Southern Book Publishers.

Young, T. "Creating Community Green space: A Handbook for Developing Sustainable Open Spaces In Central Cities". California League of Conservation Voters-Education Fund, 2000.

19.2   ELECTRONIC SOURCES

BirdLife International. 2009. Species factsheet: *Haematopus moquini* [Online]. Available: www.birdlife.org. [4 December 2009].

CIFOR. 2002. Review of forest rehabilitation initiatives – Lessons from the past. Available at: http://www.cifor.cgiar.org/rehab [Accessed 12/05/10]

FAO. 2005 Helping Forests Take Cover. RAP PUBLICATION 2005/13. http://www.fao.org/docrep/008/ae945e/ae945e05.htm

International Union for the Conservation of Nature (IUCN). 2009. IUCN Red List of Threatened Species. Version 2009.2 [Online]. Available: www.iucnredlist.org. [3 November 2009].

Low, A.B. & Rebelo, A.G. (eds.) 1996. Vegetation of South Africa, Lesotho and Swaziland. Pretoria: DEAT. This publication is available online.

SANBI. 2010. Threatened Species: A guide to Red lists and their use in conservation. Threatened Species Programme, Pretoria, South Africa. 28 pp.

Soman, S., Beyeler, S., Kraft, T.E., Thomas, D. and D. Winstanley. 2007. Ecosystem services from riparian areas: a brief summary of the literature. Report prepared for the Scientific Advisory Committee of the Illinois River Coordinator Council. Springfield, Ill. 14pp. http://www.standingupforillinois.org/pdf/cleanwater/RiparianAreas.pdf

SiyaQhubeka Forests. Changing old Paradigms in Plantations under FSC Principles and Criteria – Success Story by FSC [Online]. Available: http://www.siyaqhubeka.co.za/news/general/fsc.pdf. [2 March 2010].

U.S. ARMY CORPS OF ENGINEERS. 2004 Identifying Wetlands: A Tutorial. http://el.erdc.usace.army.mil/wrap/tools.html

UNDP. 2006. United Nations Development Programme, Human Development Report 2006. UNDP, New York. Available online at: http://hdrundp.org/en/reports/global/hdr2006/. [Accessed May 2010].

UNEP. 2001. GLOBIO. Global methodology for mapping human impacts on the biosphere. UNEP/DEWA/TR.01-3. Available online at: http:// www.globio.info/download.cfm?File=region/polar/globioreporthires.pdf [Accessed on the 20 January 2009].

UNEP. 2010a. Sick water? The central role of wastewater management in sustainable development UNEP/GRID-Arendal, Arendal, Norway. Available online at: http://grida.no/publications/rr/sickwater/

UNDP. 2006. United Nations Development Programme, Human Development Report 2006. UNDP, New York. Available online at: http://hdr.undp.org/en/reports/global/hdr2006/. [Accessed May 2010].

USDA_NRCS. 1999a. "Buffers, Common Sense Conservation," Internet URL: http://www.nhq.usda.gov/CCS/BufrsPub.html. Accessed 15 April 2004.

WHO. 2007. The World Health Report. A Safer Future. Global Public Health Security in the 21st Century. WHO, Geneva, Switzerland. Available online at: http://www.who.int/whr/2007/whr07_en.pdf [Accessed on the 20 January 2009].

"Which Bird Seeds are Best?" from National Wildlife Magazine 1/31/2010.

19.3   E-MAIL

Miller, 1998. 3206 Croul Hall Earth System Science Assistant Researcher UC Irvine www.ess.uci.edu/~miller Irvine, CA 92697-3100 sdmiller@uci.edu (949) 824-6174

Sondergaard and Jeppesen 2007. Department of Bioscience, Aarhus University, Vejlsøvej 25, PO Box 314, DK-8600 Silkeborg, Denmark

19.4   JOURNALS

Acerman, M. 2000. Wetlands and Hydrology. Conservation of Mediterranean Wetlands, number 10. Tour du Valat, Arles (France).

Anser, J.P. *et al.* 2005. Selective logging in the Brazilian Amazon. Science 310: 480-482

Bala, G. *et al.*, 2007. Combined climate and carbon-cycle effects of largescale deforestation. Proceedings of the National Academy of Science of the USA 104: 6550-6555.

Barker, G. 1984. Urban nature conservation abroad, The Planner, 70(6), 21.

Benayas, J.M. R, *et al.* 2009. Enhancement of biodiversity and ecosystem services by ecological restoration: a meta-analysis. Science 325: 121-124

Bonan, G.B. 2008. Forests and climate change: forcings, feedbacks, and the climate benefits of forests. Science 320: 1444-1449.

Burnett, M.R., August, P.V., Brown, J.H. & Killingbeck, K.T. 1998. The influence of geomorphological heterogeneity on biodiversity. I. A patch-scale perspective. Conservation Biology, 12, 363-370.

Cantell,T. 1997. Urban wasteland, Civic Trust, October.

Cordell, H. Ken; Herbert, Nancy G. 2002. The Popularity of Birding is Still Growing (PDF). Birding: 54–61.

Cooper, C.B. & Smith, J.A. 2010. Gender patterns in bird-related recreation in the USA and UK. Ecology and Society 15 (4): 4.

Costanza, R., d'Arge, R., de Groot, R., Farber, S., Grasso, M., Hannon, B., Limburg, K., Naeem, S., O'Neill, RV., Paruelo. J., Raskin, RG., Sutton, P., van den Belt, M. 1997. The value of the world's ecosystem services and natural capital, Nature, vol. 387, p. 253.

Costanza, R., 2008. Ecosystem Services: Multiple classification systems are needed. Biological Conservation 141, 350–352.

Croft and Beresford 1988. A third approach to city regeneration, Town and Country Planning, 57(2), 82–4.

Dunne, P. 2007. Big Day Big Stay. Birder's World, 21(5), 18–21.

Fuller, R.A., Warren, P.H., Armsworth, P.R., Barbosa, O. & Gaston, K.J. 2008. Garden bird feeding predicts the structure of urban avian assemblages. Diversity & Distributions 14, 131–137. DOI:10.1111/j.1472-4642.2007.00439.x

Hetherington, P. Invest in greenbelt land: Planners eye green belts for housing. Guardian, 2002.

Hill A.R. 1996. Nitrate Removal in Stream Riparian Zones, Journal of Environmental Quality. 25: 743–755.

Kotzé, D.C., Klug, J.R., Hughes, J.C. & Breen, C.M. 1996. Improved criteria for classifying hydric soils in South Africa. S. Afr. J. Plant Soil. 13(3):67–73.

Lal, R. 2008. Carbon Sequestration. Philosophical Transactions of the Royal Society B 363: 815–830

Menne, W. 1992. Future of new Kniphofia in jeopardy. PlantLife, 7:7–8 Rowntree, K.M., and Wadeson, R.A. (1998). A geomorphological framework for the assessment of instream flow requirements. Aquatic Ecosystem Health and Management, 1, 125–141.

Ong, J.E. 1993. Mangroves – A carbon source and sink. Chemosphere 27: 1097–1107.

Richard, Lowrance, Ralph Leonard, and Joseph Sheridan. 1985. Managing Riparian Ecosystems to Control Non-point Pollution, Journal of Soil and Water Conservation 55: 87–91.

Richardson, Scott. Feeding Time. Pantagraph [Bloomington, IL] 31 January 2010. Print.

Ryan, P.G., Dorse, C. and Hilton, G.M. 2006. The conservation status of the spectacled petrel Procellaria conspicillata. Biological Conservation, 131(4):575–583.

Sali, M., Kuehn, D., & Zhang, L. 2008. Motivations for Male and Female Birdwatchers in New York State. Human Dimensions of Wildlife 13 (3): 187–200. doi:10.1080/10871200801982795.

Samways, M. & Hatton, M. 2000. Palmnut Post, Vol 3, No 2, 9–11. SANBI (2011). Payments for Ecosystem Services in South Africa: A discussion document. South African National Biodiversity Institute, Pretoria.

SANBI (in prep). The Case for Biodiversity Stewardship. Scientific and technical submission prepared for Department of Environmental Affairs. South African National Biodiversity Institute, Pretoria.

SANBI (South Africa National Biodiversity Institute) (2014) A framework for investing in ecological infrastructure in South Africa.

Saveriades Alex. 2000. Establishing the social tourism carrying capacity for the tourist resorts of the East Coast of the Republic of Cyprus. Tourism Management 21 (2000) 147–156

Schaffner, Spencer 2009. Environmental Sporting: Birding at Superfund Sites, Landfills, and Sewage Ponds. Journal of Sport and Social Issues 33:206-229

Shelby, B. Heberlein, T.H. 1984. A Conceptual Framework for Carrying Capacity Determination. In Leisure Science Vol. 6, No 4, pp. 433–451

Sterba, James B. Crying Fowl: Feeding Wild Birds May Harm Them and Environment, Wall Street Journal, December 27, 2002.

Tjørve, K.M.C. and Underhill, L.G. 2006. Population increase of African Black Oystercatchers *Haematopus moquini* on Robben Island, South Africa. Ostrich 77(3):229-232.

Ulrich, R.S. 1984. View through a window may influence recovery from surgery, Science, 224, 420–1

U.S. House. Representative John Porter of Illinois speaking on National Wild Bird Feeding Month. 103rd Cong. Congressional Record (23 February 1994). Volume 140.

Van Rooy, J. 2000. Introduction to bryology in southern Africa. 8. Moss diversity and endemism. PlantLife, 23, 31–32.

Van Wilgen, B.W., Reyers, B., Le Maitre, D.C., Richardson, D.M. & Schonegevel, L. 2008. A biome-scale assessment of the impact of invasive alien plants on ecosystem services in South Africa. Journal of Environmental Management 89: 336–349.

Wong, J.L. 1997. The cultural and social values of plants and landscapes. In J.A. Stoneham and A.D. Kendle (eds, Plants and Human Well-Being, The Federation to Promote Horticulture for Disabled People, Gillingham.

Zhao, B. *et al.*, 2005. Estimation of ecological service values of wetlands in Shanghai, China. Chinese geographical science 15: 151-156

19.5 PAPERS READ AT CONFERENCES

Cole, L. 1986. Urban opportunities for a more natural approach. In A.D.Bradshaw. D.A. Goode and E. Thorpe (eds), Ecology and Design in Landscape. The 24th Symposium of the British Ecological Society, Blackwell, Oxford, 37-54.

Rutherford, M.C., Midgley, G.F., Bond, W.J., Powrie, L.W. & Rebelo, A.G. 2001. Vulnerability of the plant diversity of South Africa to projected climate change. Paper presented at the 27th annual conference of the South African Association of Botanists.

19.6 RESEARCH PROJECTS

Adams & Dove, 1989. Wildlife reserves and corridors in the urban environment. A guide to ecological landscape planning and resource conservation. National Institute for Urban Wildlife, U.S.A.

Allanson. B.R. January 1995. An Introduction to the Management of Inland Water Ecosystems in South Africa: WRC Report TT 72/95: Pretoria.

An introduction to birdwatching (PDF). Texas Parks and Wildlife Department. 2003.

Armitage N., Rooseboom A., Nel C., *et al*: The Removal of Urban Litter from Storm Water Conduits and Streams: WRC Report No. TT 95/98

Barker, G. 1986. An Introduction to Nature Conservation in Urban Areas, unpublished report. Nature Conservancy Council, Peterborough.

Barling and Moore. 1994. Role of Buffer Strips in Management of Waterway Pollution: A Review. Abstract Rural Water Corporation 590 Orrong Rd. Armadale, Victoria 3052 Australia and Centre for Resource & Environmental Studies Institute of Advanced Studies. The Australian National University, Canberra, ACT 0200, Australia

Cadman, M., Petersen, C., Driver, A., Sekhran, N., Maze, K. and Munzhedzi, S. 2010. Biodiversity for Development: South Africa's landscape approach to conserving biodiversity and promoting ecosystem resilience. South African National Biodiversity Institute, Pretoria.

Carrying Capacity: Defining, measuring and evaluating carrying capacity – members of the Environmental Planning Laboratory of the University of the Aegean, Greece, Athens, December 2001

Chittenden, Nicks, de Villiers & Cape Metropolitan Council. Defining, Mapping and Managing MOSS in the CMA. Cape Metropolitan Council, September 2000.

Chittenden, Nicks, de Villiers & Cape Metropolitan Council. CMOSS Phase II: Mapping. City of Cape Town, 2001.

Collins, N.B. 2005. Wetlands: The basics and more. Free State Department of Tourism, Environmental and Economic Affairs – South Arica)

Cook, C. 2000. Unpublished report on the current conservation status of amphibian species in the Gauteng province.

DACEL, Development guidelines for ridges, compile by Michele Pfab Scientific services. Contributions from: Marianne Forstyh (Invertebrates), Dean Peinke (Mammals), Craig Whittington-jones (Birds, reptiles, amphibians). 19 April, 2001

Dallas H.F., Day J.A., Musibono D.E., *et al.*: Water Quality for Aquatic Ecosystems: Tools for Evaluating Regional Guidelines: WRC Report No 626/1/98

DEAT: March 2003, A conceptual introduction to the nature and content of the water quality management and assessment components of a catchment management strategy, Water Quality Management Series, Sub-series No. MS 8.1.: Pretoria

DEAT: March 2003. A guideline to the water quality management component of a catchment management strategy: Water Quality Management Series, Sub-series No. MS 8.2.: Pretoria

DEAT: March 2005. River Health Programme (2005). State-of-Rivers Report: Monitoring and Managing the Ecological State of Rivers in the Crocodile (West) Marico Water Management Area: State-of-Rivers Report Number 9: Pretoria

Department of Water Affairs and Forestry (DWAF). 1997. White Paper on a National Water Policy for South Africa. DWAF: Directorate Communication Services, Pretoria.

Dickens. C, *et al*. 2003. Guidelines for Integrating the Protection, Conservation and Management of Wetlands into Catchment Management Planning: Water Research Commission: TT 220/04: Pretoria

Dosskey, *et al.*, 1997. Postal and Carpenter. 1997, Field, *et al.*, 2006 in Soman 2007. Ecosystem Services from Riparian Areas. Environmental Resources and Policy Program. Southern Illinois University, Carbondale.

Dudley, N. & Stolton, S., eds. 2003. Running pure: the importance of forest protected areas to drinking water. Gland, Switzerland, WWF/World Bank Alliance for Forest Conservation and Sustainable Use.

Durban Metropolitan Council. Development Planning Service Unit: Environmental Branch. Durban Metropolitan Open Space System. Durban Metropolitan Council. 1999.

DWAF. August 2002. Proposed First Edition – National Water Resource Strategy, Pretoria

EPA. 1997. U.S. Environmental Protection Agency, Washington, D.C. 20460, EPA/630/R-96/012, February, 1997

Ethekwini Municipality. Durban Environmental Services Management Plan. Ethekwini Municipality, 2002.

Field, C.V., Schmidt, G.A., Koch, D. and Salyk, C. 2006: Modeling production and climate-related impacts on 10Be concentration in ice cores. J. Geophys. Res., 111, D15107, doi:10.1029/2005JD006410.

Gauteng Department of Agriculture, Conservation and Environment. Directorate of Nature Conservation. Departmental Policy: Red Data Plant Policy for Environmental Impact Evaluations. Gauteng Department of Agriculture,

Conservation and Environment. Directorate of Nature Conservation: Scientific Services. 2001.

Gauteng Department of Agriculture, Conservation and Environment: Directorate of Nature Conservation. Departmental Policy: Development Guidelines for Ridges. Gauteng Department of Agriculture, Conservation and Environment: Directorate of Nature Conservation: Scientific Services 2001

Gets, D. 1987. Capacity to absorb tourism – concepts and implications for strategic planning. Annals of Tourism Research 10(2), 239 – 261

Grobicki A., Males R., Martinez I., Matika S. *et al.*: Integrated catchment Management in an Urban Context, The Great and Little Lotus Rivers, Cape Town: WRC Report No864/1/01

Grundling. P.L. & Grobler, R. 2005. Peatlands and mires of South Africa. Stapfia 85, zugleich Katalogeder OÖ. Landesmuseen Neue Serie 35: 379–396.

Hansen J.E., Sato M., Lacis A., Ruedy R., Tegen I., Matthews E. 1998. Climate forcings in the industrial era. Proceedings of the National Academy of Science of the USA 95: 12753–12758.

Holness, S. & Skowno, A. (2013). Mapping ecological infrastructure for the greater uMngeni Catchment: Technical Metadata. Report for WWF South Africa.

Hockey, P. 2009. Resurgent African black oystercatcher. Africa Birds & Birding, 14(6):46-53.

Hodge, S.J. 1995. Creating and managing woodlands around towns, Forestry Commission Handbook, 11, HMSO, London

Huwyler, F., Käppeli, J., Serafimova, K., Swanson, E. and Tobin, J. 2014. Conservation Finance: Moving beyond donor funding toward an investor-driven approach. Credit Suisse, in collaboration with WWF and McKinsey & Company.

International Union for the Conservation of Nature (IUCN). 2001. IUCN Red List Categories and Criteria Version 3.1. IUCN Species Survival Commission, Gland, Switzerland and Cambridge, UK.

IPCC 2007. Climate Change 2007: Synthesis Report. Contribution of Working Groups I, II, and III to the Fourth Assessment. Report of the Intergovernmental Panel on Climate Change, IPCC, Geneva, Switzerland.

Jacobsen, N.H.G. 1988. Proposal for the deregulation of the reptiles and amphibians of Gauteng province.

Kerlinger, P. 1993. Birding economics and birder demographics studies as conservation tools in Proc. Status and Managem. of Neotrop. Migr. Birds. eds. D. Finch and P. Stangel (PDF). Rocky Mountain Forest and Range Experiment. Station, Fort Collins, CO. USDA For. Serv. Gen. Tech. Rept. RM-229. pp. 32–38.

Kit Cambell Associates. Rethinking Open Space: Open Space Provision and Management: A Way Forward. A research report prepared for Scottish Executive Central Research Unit. Edinburgh: Scottish, 2001.

Kotzé, D.C., Marneweck, G.C., Batchelor, A.L., Lindley, D.S. & Collins, N.B. 2005. WET-EcoServices. A rapid assessment procedure for describing wetland benefits. Mondi Wetlands Project.

Kearns, C.A., Inouye, D.W. & Waser, N.M. 1998. Endangered mutualisms: The conservation of plant-pollinator interactions. Annu. Rev. Ecol. Syst. 29, 83-112.

King J.M., Scheepers A.C.T., Risher R.C., *et al.*: River Rehabilitation: Literature Review, Case Studies and Emerging Principles: WRC Report No. 1161/1/03

Ko, J.Y. *et al.* 2004. A comparative evaluation of money-based and energy-based cost-benefit analyses of tertiary municipal wastewater treatment using forested wetlands versus sand filtration in Louisiana. Ecological economics 49: 331-347

Kotzé, D.C. & Breen, C.M. 1994. Wetlands and people. What values do wetlands have for us and how are these values affected by our land-use activities? WETLAND-USE booklet 1. Share-Net. Umgeni Valley.

Kotzé, D.C., Breen, C.M. & Klug, J.R. 1994. Wetland-use. A wetland management decision support system for the Kwazulu/Natal Midlands. WRC Report No. 501/2/94. Water Research Commission, Pretoria.

Kotzé, D.C., Ellery, W., Beckedahl, H., Winstanley, T., Marneweck, G., Batchelor, A., Collins, N.B., Russell, W., Walters, D., Braack, M. & Cowden, C. Wetland Rehabilitation Manual. Mondi Wetlands Project.

Lindenmayer, D.B., Steffen, W., Burbidge, A.A., Hudghes, L., Kitching. R.L., Musgrave, W., Stafford, Smith, M. and Werner, P.A. (in Press) Conservation strategies in response to rapid climate change: Australia as a case study. Biological Conservation.

Malan H.L., Day J.A.: Development of Numerical Methods for Predicting Relationships between Stream Flow, Water Quality and Biotic Responses in Rivers. WRC Report No. 956/1/02

Maia, J. Giordano, T., Kelder, N., Bardien, G., Bodibe, M., Du Plooy, P., Jafta, X., Jarvis, D., Kruger-Cloete, E., Kuhn, G., Lepelle, R., Makaulule. L., Mosoma, K., Neoh, S., Netshitomboni, N., Ngozo, T., Swanepoel, J. 2011. Green Jobs: An estimate of the direct employment potential of a greening South African economy. Industrial Development Corporation, Development Bank of Southern Africa, Trade and Industrial Policy Strategies

Martin, A.P. 1997. African Black Oystercatcher *Haematopus moquini*, in J.A. Harrison, D.G. Allan, L.G. Underhill, M. Herremans, A.J. Tree, V. Parker and C.J. Brown (eds.).

Measey, G.J. and Tolley, K.A. 2009. Investigating the cause of the disjunct distribution of *Amietophrynus pantherinus*, the Endangered South African Western Leopard Toad.

Natural Resource Defence Council: www/nrdc.org Palmer C.G., Berold R.S., Muller W.J.: 2004: Environmental Water quality Management in Water Resources Management. WRC Report No. TT 217/04, Water Research Commission, Pretoria

Nel, J., Colvin, C., Le Maitre, D., Smith, J. & Haines, I. 2013. South Africa's Strategic Water Source Areas. CSIR Report No: CSIR/NRE/ECOS/ER/2013/0031/A. Report for WWF South Africa.

Novotny, 2005. Department of Ecology and conservation Biology. Faculty of Science, University of South Bohemia, Czech Republic.

Pegram, G.C., Görgens. A.H.M., Quibell. G. August 1999. A Framework for Implementing Non-Point Source Management Under the National Water Act: WRC Report No TT 115/99, DWAF Report No WQP 0.1: Pretoria.

Parish, F., Sirin, A., Charman, D., Joosten, H., Minayeva, T., Silvius, M. & Stringer, L. (eds). 2008. Assessment on Peatlands, Biodiversity and Climate Change: Main Report. Global Environment Centre, Kuala Lumpur and Wetlands International, Wageningen. 179pp.

Pegram, G.C., Görgens. A.H.M. September 2001. A Guide to Non-point Source Assessment: WRC Report TT 142/01: Pretoria

Powledge, Fred. 1 January 2006. The Millennium Assessment Bio Science 56 (11): 880-886

Poynton, J.C. & Roberts, D.C. 1985. Urban open space planning in S.A.: A biogeographical perspective. South African Journal of Science, 81, 33-37.

Pullis La Rouche, G. 2003. Birding in the United States: a demographic and economic analysis. Addendum to the 2001 National Survey of Fishing, Hunting and Wildlife-Associated Recreation. Report 2001-1. (PDF). U.S. Fish and Wildlife Service, Arlington, Virginia.

Reid, P.C. et al. 2009. Impacts of the Oceans on Climate Change. In: D.W. Sims (ed) Advances in Marine Biology, Vol. 56, Burlington: Academic Press. 150 pp.

Robinson, J.C. 2005. Relative Prevalence of African Americans among Bird Watchers. General Technical Report PSW-GTR-191 (PDF). U.S. Department of Agriculture–Forest Service, Pacific Southwest Research Station. Albany, California.

Rohde, C.L.E. and Kendle, A.D. 1994. Human well-being and nature in urban areas, English Nature Science, No. 22, English Nature, Peterborough.

Rogers, J. 2002. Birdfeeding: Another viewpoint. Alberta Naturalist 31: 1-11.

Rosenberg, D.K., Noon, B.R. & Meslow, E.C. 1997. Biological Corridors: Form, Function and Efficacy. Bioscience, 47, 677–687.

Rountree, M. W. and Batchelor, A. L. (in prep). A classification system for wetland management in South Africa.

Roux, D.J. May 2001. Development of Procedures for the implementation of the National River Health Programme in the Province of Mpumalanga: WRC Report No. 850/1/01: Pretoria

Scherman P-A., Palmer C.G., Muller W.J. February 2003. Use of Indigenous Riverine Invertebrates in applied Toxicology and Water Resource-Quality Management: WRC Report No. 955/1/03

Sethuram Soman, Ph.D. Candidate Environmental Resources and Policy Program. Southern Illinois University, Carbondale; Suzanne Beyeler, Illinois Natural History Survey. Steven E. Kraft, Professor Dept. of Agribusiness Economics Southern Illinois University, Carbondale; David Thomas, Chief Illinois Natural History Survey and Derek Winstanley, Chief State Water Survey May 2007

Scott-Shaw, C.R. 1999. Rare and threatened plants of KwaZulu-Natal and neighbouring regions. KwaZulu-Natal Nature Conservation Service: Pietermaritzburg.

Scotland: Planning Advice Note: PAN 65: "Planning and Open Space", 2003.

Site selection criteria used by Strategic environmental focus for a report to identify a recreation resort for the City of Tshwane August 2004 – SEF REF No. 1314

Society for Ecological Restorations (SER, 2004). Non-profit organisation founded 1987, 285 West 18th Strat Suite 1, Tucson, Arizona 85701 USA

Society for Ecological Restoration International (SER). Science and Policy Working Group. 2010. CBD Information Note for SBSTTA 14, www.ser.org & Tucson: Society for Ecological Restoration International.

Tarboton, W.R. 1997. The status and conservation importance of birds in Gauteng Province.

The Santam Group, the WWF, UCT, CSIR, and the United Nations Environment Programme Finance Initiative. 2011. Insurance in a changing risk landscape: Local lessons from Southern Cape of South Africa.

Toad. Conservation Genetics Online First: DOI 10.1007/s10592-10009-19989-10597.

United Nations. "World Urbanization Prospects, The 1999 Revision, 2001.

Wishart M.J., Davies B.R., Stewart B.A. *et al*: February 2003: Examining Catchments as Functional Units for the Conservation or Riverine Biota and Maintenance of Biodiversity: WRC Report No. 975/1/World Bank (2012). Managing disaster risks for a resilient future: The sendai report. World Bank, Washington DC

WRC. 2008b. Wet-sustainable use: A system for assessing the sustainability of wetland use. Report to the Water Research Commission by author D. Kotzé1. Series Editor: H Malan2, 1 Centre for Environment, Agriculture and Development, University of KwaZulu-Natal; Freshwater 2, Freshwater Research Unit, University of Cape Town.

19.7   STATUTES AND LEGISLATION

Conservation of Agricultural Resources Act 43 of 1983 (CARA)
Environmental Management Protected Areas Act, 2003 (Act 57 of 2003)
Forestry Act No 122 of 1986 (Section 75)
National Environmental Management Act, No. 107 of 1998
National Water Act, 1998 (Act 36 of 1998)
Policy (Department of Agriculture, Conservation, Environment and Land Affairs). Directorate of Nature Conservation. Development Guidelines for Ridges. Compiled by: Michele Pfab. Scientific Services. Contributions from; Marianne Forstyh (Invertebrates), Dean Peinke (Mammals), Craig Whittington-Jones (Birds, Reptiles, Amphibians) 19 April 2001

19.8   THESES AND DISSERTATIONS

Eber, S. 2000. A comparative study of land cover change in the Magaliesberg mountain area, Gauteng, South Africa. Doctoral thesis. In progress.

Grobler. 2000. From MSc. investigation of plant communities associated with urban open spaces in Gauteng. University of Pretoria.

Jordaan, M.J.S. 2005. Die Jordaan-familie: 'n Historiese ontleding van hulle genealogie en die vestiging van 'n toerismeroete. PhD. Universiteit van die Vrystaat.

Millward A.M. 1987. Community Involvement in Urban Nature Conservation, unpublished Phd thesis, Aston University, Birmingham, UK.

Sali, M.J. 2005. Bird watching in New York State: a study of motivations and gender, PhD. graduate. SUNY College of Environmental Science and Forestry.

19.9   WEBSITES

webpage on feeding birds
(Centre for International Forestry Research)
United Nations Environment Programme, GRID Arendal.

Boxes for Tawnies: a, Home-made Tawny Owl box; b and c, Home-made Tawny Owl box made to modified Dutch letterbox design; d, Barn Owl at nest box; e, Owl box; f, Barn Owl nest box.

CHAPTER 20

ADDENDA

20.1   ADDENDUM A (OWL BOXES)

We take a look at examples of what others are making or buying to put up for their local owls. Two of the box samples are for the Tawny Owl and the Barred Owl (*Strix varia*) which has similar nesting requirements.

BOXES FOR TAWNIES

Home-made Tawny Owl box (See p. 342, a)

- Dimensions: 35 cm x 35 cm (sides); height at back 55 cm, at front 45 cm. Entrance 15 cm diameter.
- Materials and construction: timber and nails
- Attachment: nailed/screwed back batten

Home-made Tawny Owl box made to modified Dutch letterbox design (See p. 342, b).

- Dimensions: 45 cm x 30 cm (width by depth front to back); height at back 66 cm, at front approximately 60 cm. Upper part of box is about 41 cm front to back.
- Materials and construction: Shiplap panel screwed to batten frame. Floor and side panels have to be removable for access.
- Attachment: single batten fixed in place with exterior grade timber fix wood screws.

This is a really nice nest box. This sample was placed in a tree in a garden that was overgrown with bushes and hedges and undergrowth. There were tawnies in the area, and for some time the owner had a chimney-style box out for them, but it wasn't used. He decided to run up a Dutch letterbox to see if the owls were tempted to move in.

The special feature of this box is the interesting semi-protected ledge. The box faces east, away from the prevailing westerly wind with an approach that's clear of branches.

Home-made Tawny Owl box made to modified Dutch letterbox design (See p. 342, c)

- Dimensions: 400 x 360 x 570 mm (OD), 360 x 320 x 530 (ID). This gives a roomy internal diagonal of 475 mm.
- Materials and construction: Recycled bedroom floorboards.

General owl box (See p. 342, e)

General owl box that also can accommodate Tawny Owls. A design lately used on properties.
- Dimensions: 600 x 400 x 300 mm (l x w x h); 24 x 16 x 12 in. Weight: 15 kg.
- Materials and construction: timber, assembly appears to be with nails.
- Tree attachment: nailed back bar.

Why attract owls to one's garden?

There are several advantages of attracting owls to your garden or homestead:
1. Importantly, they can assist with the control of rodents and insects.
2. The presence of owls means that no pesticides need to be used, resulting in financial savings.
3. It is extremely gratifying to listen to the lovely calls of owls at night.

Which species?

Barn owls will frequently make use of owl nest boxes, indicating perhaps that they are limited by suitable nest sites. Artificial nest boxes will also be used by Spotted Eagle-Owls, African Wood-Owls, Pearl-spotted Owlets and African Scops-Owls. Barn Owls and Spotted Eagle-Owls in particular live in close association with humans and they therefore often accept artificial nest boxes attached to the walls of buildings and trees.

Some important aspects about attracting owls to one's garden

1. Obviously only species that occur in the surrounding area will adopt a nest box in your garden. It is also important that nest boxes and their location imitate the species' requirements in the natural environment.

2. Nest boxes should be firmly attached to a wall or tree trunk in a quiet area, such as a seldom used outbuilding away from human disturbance and inaccessible to predators. It is perhaps better not to attach the boxes to walls of houses, as the owls may make a noise and mess and attack people and pets when defending their chicks.

3. The boxes should be erected on the shady side of a building or tree.

4. The boxes, especially the roof, must be waterproof.

5. A piece of wood just below the box's entrance is useful for the birds to perch on when arriving at the nest.

6. Barn Owls may make regular use of a perch site, which can then result in an accumulation of white wash on the floor. The only way to prevent this is to remove anything that may provide a perch for the owls, or make the perches unattractive to them, or prevent access to these perch sites.

7. Do not use harmful pesticides in your garden and buildings and, if necessary, seek environmentally friendly methods to control insects and rodents.

8. Swarms of bees may pose a hazard to barn owls as they sometimes take over their nest boxes, causing the birds to abandon their eggs or chicks. A swarm of bees can be discouraged from settling in by burning a mosquito coil at the entrance to the box. Do not use harmful poisons, as this will harm the owls and their chicks. An alternative is to paint the owl box with three coats of boiled linseed oil and, once dry, spray the outside of the box with baythroid (cyfluthrin).

Nest box designs

There are two simple nest box designs for Barn Owls and Spotted Eagle-Owls (see below).

Spotted Eagle-Owl nest box

Scrap wood can be used to build a simple, open nest box with a roof. The base should be 45 cm x 45 cm and the roof supported by four pieces of wood about 45 cm in length. Attach sides, 10-15 cm high, around the base and to the roof supports (this will reduce wind chill and help keep the eggs and chicks safely in the box). To help prevent the eggs from rolling around, place a layer of sawdust on the base of the box. Seal the wood with a good quality exterior varnish.

Barn Owl nest box

The Barn Owl prefers a large, enclosed box in which to lay its eggs and rear its chicks.

Figure 20.1: Spotted Eagle-Owl nest box.

Materials:
- 1 x 2 700 mm x 457 mm x 21 mm length of pine.
- wood glue.
- 20 brass screws (4.5 mm x 30 mm).
- 3 mm wood drill bit.
- Yacht varnish.

Cut the 2 700 mm length of pine into six pieces (A-F), as illustrated.

Assemble the box, joining the sides (D and F), front (A) and back (C) to the base (E) using glue and screws.

Attach the roof (B) to the structure in the same way, using glue and screws.

Varnish the exterior of the box three times, sanding lightly between each coat. Place the nest under the eaves of a roof or in the fork of a tree where it is shaded and secluded.

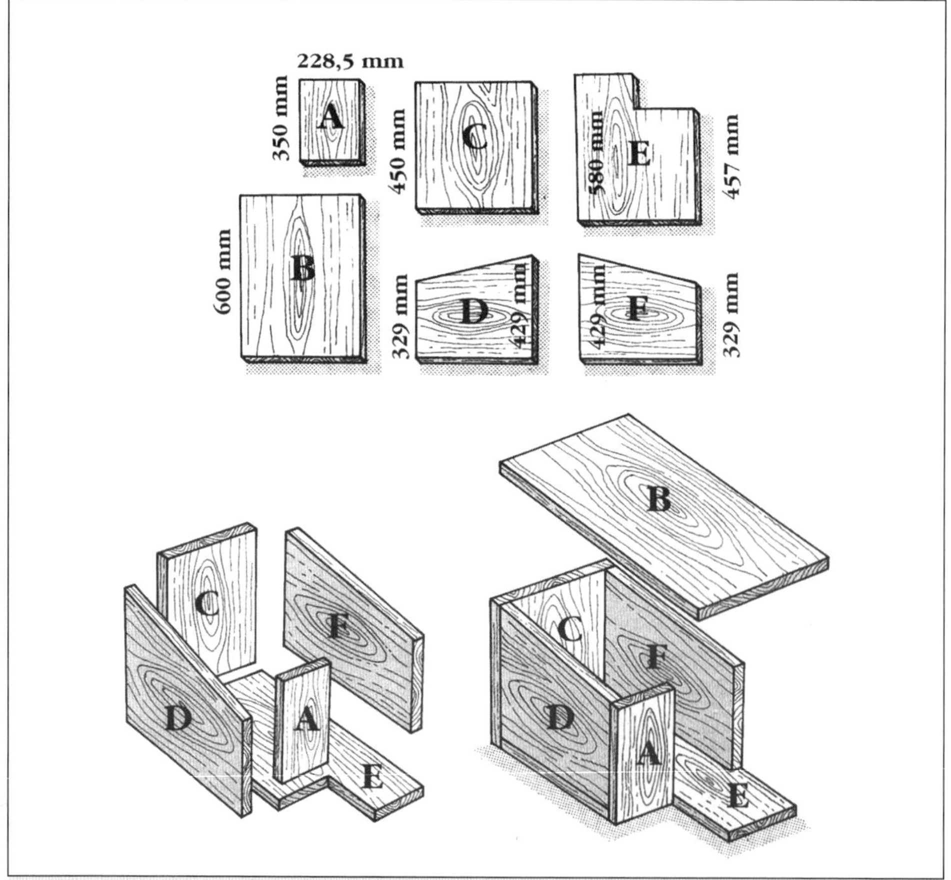

Figure 20.2: Barn owl nest box.

Source of information

Much of the information (and sketches) in this addendum was obtained from:
Tarboton, W. and Erasmus, R. 1998. *Owls and owling in southern Africa*. Cape
Town: Struik. Trendler, R. and Hes, L. (1994) *Attracting birds to your garden
in southern Africa.* Cape Town: Struik.

20.2   ADDENDUM B (BIRD FEEDERS)

Birds won't know the difference between a fancy, store-bought bird feeder and one
that's homemade, so save your money and make one out of an empty household item.

Whether you are an avid ornithologist or simply looking for children's holiday ideas,
this project is simple and easy. Once you have made it, you can sit, relax and watch
the birds that fly in to eat from the feeder.

Plastic bottle feeder

You will need:

- Empty plastic bottles.
- Craft knife.
- Wooden skewers or old wooden spoons.
- Craft paint.
- Hooks for hanging the feeders in the trees.
- Bird seed.

Here's how:

1. Wash and dry the bottles thoroughly.

2. Use your craft knife to cut openings in the sides, back and front. In the containers we followed the shapes in the sides of the bottle and left the back and
front closed.

3. Leave a small flap of plastic at the bottom of the openings for the birds to rest on.

4. Make a hole in the front and back for the wooden spoon or skewer. You can put
fresh fruit on these for the birds.

5. Paint attractive designs onto the bottles and leave to dry. Designs can match
your outdoor garden theme or be completely neutral to the surroundings.

6. Insert a hook into the cap and hang from a tree in the garden.

Don't forget to add bird seed so that plenty of feathered friends can come to visit
your feeder.

Article courtesy of http://www.home-dzine.co.za.

Plastic jar feeder

In spring, many birds visit your garden and it's always fun to feed them. This is a really simple bird feeder that you can make easily.

Here is a list of the things you will need.
*   A small plastic jar like a peanut butter jar.
*   75 mm of dowel (round wood).
*   200 mm of wire or string.
*   Waterproof glue or hot melt glue.

Kids should have their parents available to help with the cutting so that they do not cut themselves!

Wash out a small empty plastic peanut butter container or something similar. Remove the label using hot soapy water. If you let it soak a while, it will come off a lot easier.

Cut a 25 mm hole so the bottom of the hole is about 25–38 mm up from the bottom of the container.

Make a small hole just below the 25 mm-hole, big enough for the piece of wood dowel.

Poke the 12 mm-dowel into the small hole and glue it in place. Poke another small hole in the middle of the lid for the wire or string to go through.

Run the string or wire through the hole in a loop and tie it off big enough, so it won't pull out.

Put the lid on the jar and there you have it, a bird feeder.

Some people don't like bird seeds sprouting in their flower gardens, here's a little tip you can share with them. Spread the bird seed out on a cookie sheet and bake in an oven at 250° for 30 minutes.

Article courtesy of http://www.runnerduck.com/kc_plastic_birdhouse.htm

20.2.1   Make your own bird feeders

Engaging the entire family in constructing and designing new homemade bird feeders is a great way to bring everyone together. It's also an ideal addition to any landscape.

They can be as small or large as you please, and the children can even help paint and decorate them to feel part of the entire process.

First, you must decide where the new bird feeders will be placed. Do you have an ideal tree you can attach them to, or will they need to stand alone?

Figure 20.3: Plastic bottle feeders.

Bird feeders: a, carton feeder; b, Cape Sparrow feeder; c and d, bird feeders for sun birds; e, Dark-capped Bulbul feeding on fruit.

Also, ensure you know which types of birds are in your area and how to construct a feeder that will attract those you want to your garden.

For a quick and easy solution, have a look at this children's homemade bird feeder by Chris from Hampshire.

20.2.2   Kids homemade bird feeder

Homemade bird feeder

Kids had great fun making this neat little homemade bird feeder. It can be made from an empty juice or milk carton so it's a good way to recycle them! (Figure 3, a).

This is an interesting project and such a feeder will start to attract birds to your garden. Chris was so proud of his creation and it's lovely to see how he enjoyed it.

What you need:
- A milk or juice carton.
- Paint and a paint brush.
- String or garden wire.

Making the bird feeder:
- Cut out most of the sides of the carton remembering to leave plenty of space at the bottom for the bird food.

- When you paint your feeder, it is recommended to use more natural colours, it should blend with its surroundings so it won't frighten off the birds (the blue is the sky and the green are leaves).

- Once the paint has dried, use a pen to poke a hole though the fold at the top of the carton and then thread a piece of string or garden wire though it.

- Fill the bottom of the homemade bird feeder with seed, then let your child hang it outside and wait for the birds to come and feed.

20.3   ADDENDUM C (EARTHWORMS)

20.3.1   Vermicomposting

Vermicomposting uses earthworms to turn organic waste into very high quality compost. This is probably the best way of composting kitchen waste. Adding small amounts of wet kitchen scraps to a large compost pile in the garden day by day can disrupt the decomposition process so that the compost is never really done. But it works just fine with vermicomposting.

Many gardeners use vermicomposting systems for all their garden and kitchen waste, many more use both types of composting, and thousands of households without gardens use neat and unobtrusive worm boxes indoors to compost their kitchen scraps (as well as newspapers and cardboard boxes), reducing their garbage by up to a third and providing their own organic soil for pot plants and container gardens on balconies and roofs.

See *Friend Earthworm: Practical application of a lifetime study of habits of the most important animal in the world* by George Sheffield Oliver (1941) – one of the all-time classics on the earthworm. Dr Oliver was one of the first to harness the earthworm to the needs of the farmer and gardener, making highly fertile topsoil for optimum crop growth and producing a constant supply of cheap, high-grade, live protein to feed poultry. He devised simple yet elegant and effective systems to bring costs and labour down and productivity up to help struggling farmers make ends meet. Oliver had an observant and critical eye and understood nature. His ideas on the nature of modern food and health (or the lack of it) are only now being confirmed, half a century later. A delightful book. Full text available online at the Journey to Forever. Other titles include *My Grandfather's Earthworm Farm, Eve Balfour on Earthworms, Albert Howard on Earthworms* and *The Housefly* by Roy Hartenstein.

20.3.2   Vermicomposting and plants

Vermicomposting consists mostly of worm casts (poop) plus some decayed organic matter. In ideal conditions worms can eat at least their own weight of organic matter in a day. In fact it seems they don't actually eat it, they consume it. What they derive their nourishment from is all the micro-organisms that are really eating it. Their casts contain eight times as many micro-organisms as their feed! These are the micro-organisms that best favour healthy plant growth. The

Worm casts – the best soil there is.

casts don't contain any disease pathogens – pathogenic bacteria are reliably killed in the worms' gut. This is one of the great benefits of vermicomposting. Worm casts also contain five times more nitrogen, seven times more phosphorus, and eleven times more potassium than ordinary soil, the main minerals needed for plant growth, but the large numbers of beneficial soil micro-organisms in worm casts have at least as much to do with it. The casts are also rich in humic acids which condition the soil, have a perfect pH balance and contain plant growth factors similar to those found in seaweed. There's nothing better to put in your garden!

> "Worms seem to be the great promoters of vegetation, which would proceed but lamely without them, by boring, perforating, and loosening the soil, and rendering it pervious to rains and the fibres of plants, by drawing straws and stalks of leaves and twigs into it, and, most of all, by throwing up such infinite numbers of lumps of earth called worm-casts, which, being their excrement, is a fine manure for grain or grass."
>
> Rev. Gilbert White of Selborne, 1777

> "All the fertile areas of this planet have at least once passed through the bodies of earthworms."
>
> Charles Darwin.

20.3.3   The red worms

These worms are not the usual big burrowing earthworms that live in garden soil. They are called red worms, tiger worms, brandlings, angle worms, manure worms or red wrigglers. They occupy a different ecological niche, living near the surface where there are high concentrations of organic matter, such as on pastures or in leaf mould or under compost piles.

Two breeds are used in vermicomposting: *Eisenia foetida* or *Lumbricus rubellas*. Many garden centres now supply them and in most countries they can be bought by mail order from worm farms. Some sellers advertise special high-performance breeds or specially developed hybrids. They'll be one of these two breeds because there's no such thing as a hybrid-worm.

You'll need 1 000 worms (500 g) to start a worm box, maybe twice that if you want to process your garden wastes too. They breed very fast in the right conditions, but starting with more will give the system a good start.

20.3.4   Breeding

Worm populations double each month. In ideal conditions they can reproduce much faster than that: 500 g of worms can increase to 450 kg (one million worms) in a year, but in working conditions 500 g will produce a surplus of 80 kg in a year.

When the vermicompost is harvested, hatchlings and capsules (cocoons or eggs) are usually lost.

Mature red worms make two or three capsules a week, each producing two or three hatchlings after about three weeks. The hatchlings are tiny white threads about 12 mm long, but they grow fast, reaching sexual maturity in four to six weeks and make their own capsules. Three months later they're grandparents!

This rapid breeding rate means the worm population easily adjusts to conditions in the worm box according to the feed supply and the proportion of worm casts to feed and bedding. Their casts are slightly toxic to them and as the box gets full, they'll rather leave if there's anywhere for them to go or they'll die off.

If you only want the vermicompost for the garden, it doesn't much matter if the worms die off, as long as you've kept some aside to set a new box going. It also makes it easier to harvest the castings, and you'll have a higher proportion of pure castings.

If you want to produce excess worms to extend your worm system to sell as fishing bait, or to feed to poultry or fish (they really thrive on worm feed), you'll need to separate them from the vermicompost before the proportion of castings gets too high. (See below, 20.3.9)

20.3.5   Worm boxes

This section mainly applies to using worms to compost kitchen wastes. For garden wastes, the same basic principles apply, with a few cautions: see below, (20.3.11 **Garden waste)**.

There's a good range of specialised worm composting units that you can buy: Can-O-Worms, Worm Factory, Worm-a-way, Eliminator, Worm-A-Roo, Tiger Wormery and others.

You can also easily build one yourself. Many people advise it, saying that wood is better than plastic. The commercial models are usually made of plastic, which doesn't "breathe", while wood is porous and allows for better ventilation.

20.3.6   Dimensions

The size of the unit should be geared to your household's production of kitchen scraps.

One or two people usually produce about 2 kg of food waste a week: use a 600 mm x 600 mm by 200 mm deep box. For three people, make it 300 mm deep. For more, 600 mm x 900 mm x 300 mm deep. Two 2-person boxes might be better, because bigger boxes can be too heavy to move when they're full.

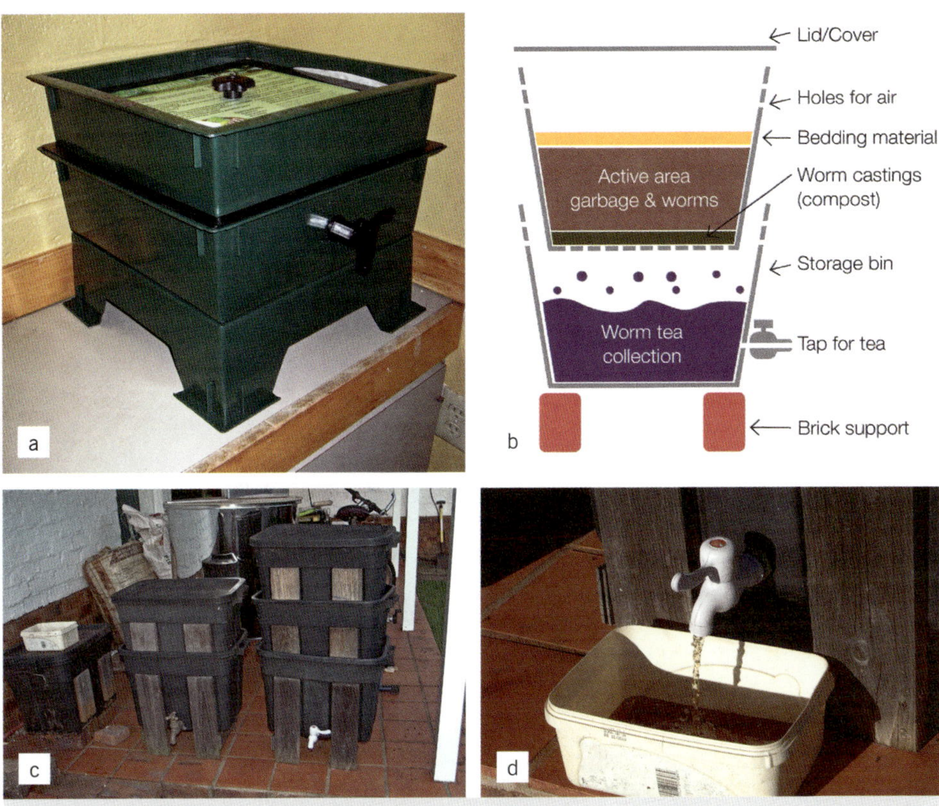

Figure 20.4: Worm boxes/bins: a and b, earthworm bins; c, layout of an earthworm bin; d, harvesting eartworm tea.

Use exterior-grade 12 mm plywood. Don't use chemically-treated wood. Treat the wood with a non-toxic wood preservative or paint it with vegetable oil, or linseed oil. Use galvanised nails. Drill at least a dozen 12 mm holes in the bottom for aeration, and arrange it so that two opposite sides are 12 mm deeper so that the bottom stands off the ground. Stand the box in a tray, because it will probably leak a bit.

Once filled, cover the surface with black plastic sheeting (a garbage bag) slightly smaller than the surface area: this will keep the moisture in, and the worms will work right up to the surface. If this makes it too wet, use a couple of newspapers instead. Make a lid for the box. Keep it anywhere convenient.

20.3.7   Bedding

Fill the box with moist bedding for the worms to burrow in and to bury the food scraps in. You need about 3 kg (dry weight) for a 600 mm x 600 mm x 400 mm box. Worms will eat the bedding as well as the food scraps, so you'll need to top it up in a few months.

Any inert, non-toxic, fluffy material that holds moisture and allows air to circulate will do. Don't use anything that will decompose too rapidly when you moisten it and get hot, like manure that's not aged enough or hay, especially alfalfa hay. Mixed bedding is better, but no need to be too complicated: 2/3 corrugated cardboard and 1/3 sphagnum is a good mixture, or sphagnum peat moss, shredded leaves and sawdust or just cardboard and/or newspaper.

- Cardboard cartons (corrugated): cut them up into strips 25 mm wide and about 75 mm long. Don't use the shredded cardboard sold for insulation because it's treated with toxic chemicals.

- Newspaper: Tear it into 25 mm-strips – it's easy to tear with the grain. Black ink is non-toxic, avoid glossy paper.

- Shredded computer paper.

- Autumn leaves: spread them thickly in the driveway and drive over them with the car a few times to break them up, or shred them with a lawnmower. Or moisten them, sprinkle some lime, ground limestone or wood ash over them and bundle them up in a garbage bag, tie the top closed, and in a few months they'll have broken down enough to be excellent worm bedding. Or just use them as is, though it'll take a bit longer for the worms to break them down.

- Aged manure, or composted manure: Cow, horse and rabbit.

- Sphagnum: Use Canadian peat moss, soak it in water for 24 hours, squeeze it out and sprinkle some lime on it.

- Coir (coconut fibre): Comes in compressed bricks, soak in water and they swell up – no need to add lime.

- Chopped-up straw or other dead plant material, spoiled hay, yard clippings, dried grass clippings, any plant material aged beyond the green stage.

- Sawdust, wood shavings: From non-aromatic wood, avoid treated wood, about a quarter to a third of the bedding mixture.

Add a couple of handfuls of soil or sand. It helps the worms grind up the food in their gizzards. Sprinkle a bit of lime, ground limestone or wood ash over the bedding (not too much!). Ground limestone is best.

Worm bedding and feed can be wetter than compost material: 75%, compared with 65% maximum for compost. Dry bedding usually needs a bit less than three times its weight in water (a liter of water weighs 1 kg, a litre weighs a kilogram).

Once it's all suitably shredded, mixed and moist, put it in the box and add the worms (about 500 g – 1 000 worms). Leave it for two or three days to let the worms settle in before adding wastes.

20.3.8   Feeding

No metal, foil, or plastic. Use vegetable and fruit scraps, coffee grounds (including paper filters), tea bags (remove the staple), eggshells (best dried and crushed first, then sprinkled over the surface), stale bread, houseplant trimmings. Chop up big chunks. Some people advise against citrus and also onion and garlic, others use them: try small quantities first. Not too much vegetable oil, be cautious at first with dairy products, meat and fish. Small amounts chopped fine, well-dispersed and well-covered with bedding should be okay. Broken chicken bones are okay, bigger bones won't break down but shouldn't cause problems either – they'll be picked clean.

It's best to collect food scraps in a small bucket with a lid and add them to the worm box every couple of days (or more often in hot weather – don't let it rot). Bury them in the bedding in a corner of the box. Next time, bury the new scraps near the first scraps. You can have about nine burial sites in a 600 x 600 mm box: by the time you've used the ninth one, you can go back to the first site again, the worms will have cleared it.

You'll be surprised how much feed you can put in that box – the worms and micro-organisms reduce it more than you'd think possible.

The box will need emptying every 3-6 months. Best tool for burying feed: A three-pronged hand-cultivator (hand-fork).

20.3.9   Harvesting

If it is mainly the worm casts you want to use as garden compost, any of the following methods will do. If you value production of worms as well as casts, use the light separation method or a wire mesh screen.

Some hassle – light separation.

Dump the finished material from the box onto a big piece of plastic (e.g. an opened-out garbage bag) on the floor or on a table under a 100W light, or outside in the sun.

Form it into eight or nine mounds. Worms are sensitive to light and immediately burrow beneath the surface. Wait a few minutes, and meanwhile put fresh bedding in the box.

A hand brush and dustpan are useful for this. Lightly brush the top off each mound until the worms are revealed, then wait for them to burrow deeper and do it again. Eventually you're left with a squirming mass of worms all trying to get under each other to avoid the light. Quickly put them in the new bedding in the box with a fresh supply of feed.

This leaves you with a rich harvest of worm castings and a lot of capsules, which you lose (the hatchlings won't survive in garden soil), but the worms in the bin will soon replace them. Store the castings for a week or two before using them in the garden.

Children love this – you can usually talk them into doing it for you.

Worm spaghetti!

Less hassle – sideways separation

Shift all the material in the box to one side and fill the other side with fresh bedding; put your kitchen scraps and feed only in the fresh bedding side. In the next week or two the worms will migrate from the finished vermicompost into the fresh bedding. In the meantime the capsules will hatch and most of the hatchlings will also move across, so you won't lose them, which is an advantage over the dump-and-sort method.

Even less hassle – vertical separation

Get a piece of nylon or mesh window screening a bit bigger than the surface of the box and lay it flat on the surface of the vermicompost. It should be big enough to flatten against the sides and leave some overlap at the top. Fill the box up with fresh bedding on top of the screen and continue feeding it with kitchen scraps. The worms will migrate up through the screen into the new bedding as the food runs out below.

When the top part is ready for harvesting, use the overlap to lift the screen from the box, vermicompost, worms and all. Set it aside and empty the box it will have a very high concentration of worm castings and few if any worms, hatchlings or capsules.

Dump the wormy material that was on top of the screen into the bottom of the box and put the screen back on top of it, with fresh bedding on top of the screen.

Harvesting earthworms.

Check the condition of the screen each time you empty the box, and replace it before it gets rotten enough to rip just as you're removing it, spilling everything back into the box.

No hassle

This method will give you lots of trouble-free castings, but no extra worms. Go on feeding kitchen scraps to the box for up to four months, and then start a second box prime it with fresh bedding and a supply of worms from the first box. Just leave the first box until the second box is full, by which time the first box will contain a very high proportion of fine castings, and very few worms.

To make sure there are enough worms for both boxes, you can prepare the second box about a month earlier, adding some worms to it every time you add feed to the first box.

Screening

The vermicompost might need screening, especially if you've used rough stuff (sticks, etc.) in the bedding that takes time to break down. A circular gardener's sieve with a 5 mm mesh will work best. Try to get one with stainless steel mesh as it'll do the job much quicker, the worm castings won't stick to the mesh and it won't rust.

This is also a good way of separating the worms from the finished vermicompost, though capsules and hatchlings are lost.

20.3.10   Problems

Flies and smells: There shouldn't be any, but sometimes it happens. Worm casts have a pleasant, earthy smell, like forest soil. If the worm bin starts to smell, there's too much feed in it, more than the worms can process – you've overloaded the system. Stop feeding the worms, add more dry bedding, a little sprinkled lime, and stir the bin with the hand-cultivator (hand-fork). Repeat until the smell vanishes.

Fruit flies (actually vinegar flies) can get into the box, but they do no harm. Lots of them mean too much feed – cut down the feeding rate and cover the surface with a damp newspaper.

The bin can also have an influx of soldier fly maggots, up to an inch long (they're a favourite with fishermen). Vinegar fly larvae are much smaller. The maggots actually benefit the composting process, but if you don't like them, add more bedding and lime and stir as above, or put a chunk of bread soaked in milk on the surface. In a couple of days it will be infested with larvae; take it out and get rid of it (give it to a fisherman or a chicken).

20.3.11   Garden waste

Outdoor boxes can be bigger. The simplest way of all is a 30 mm-deep trench in the soil about 600 mm wide or more with 200 mm of bedding and/or compost to put the worms in. Red worms can't survive long in ordinary garden soil so they won't crawl away. Add garden wastes as they come, putting it in a different part of the trench each time, and cover with a sprinkling of soil and lime. Bury kitchen wastes at the bottom, under the garden wastes.

Fresh garden wastes might get hot, but the worms will have a place to escape to until it gets cool enough for them to handle.

To keep moles away, line the trench with 12 mm chicken wire or wire mesh.

You can also make a four-sided wooden box with four 450 mm by 900 mm boards (or nail narrower planks together), treat it with vegetable oil or linseed oil and stand it on a layer of bricks on top of the soil. Put 150 mm or so of bedding in the bottom and put the worms in it. Add wastes to the corners in succession. Shake the soil off clumped roots. Chop up big bits with the edge of a spade. Add more bedding as necessary. Bury kitchen scraps.

20.3.12   Using vermicompost

Dig it lightly into the topsoil around your plants. In composting growing beds or preparing new beds, vermicompost generally goes about twice as far as ordinary (aerobic) compost, so use half as much. Each garden is different (and so is each gardener!), some people have good results simply dumping large amounts of the stuff on top of their beds. Vermicompost gives seedlings a really good start in life.

Results from vermicompost.

In pots and containers, don't use pure vermicompost. About 25% of the growing mixture seems to be about ideal, but experiment, it might vary according to what you mix it with.

You can also use vermicompost to make "compost tea" liquid fertiliser. Mix two tablespoons of vermicompost with a litre of water and let it stand for a day, shaking it occasionally, then sprinkles under the plants. One-litre drinking water bottles make good sprinklers: drill a few small-diameter holes in the lid, point and squeeze.

For transplants, especially bare-root transplants, spray them with an even more diluted solution of "tea", or stand them in it for a while. It'll help to prevent transplant shock. (Liquid seaweed solution is excellent for this.)

Don't let the vermicompost dry out before using it. It loses a lot of its value and resists wetting. If you store it, don't use an airtight container. In this case it will stay active for a year or more.

20.4　ADDENDUM D (ORGANIC COMPOST) MAKING COMPOST

20.4.1　Good compost

It's easy to make good compost. Quite a lot of people make some kind of compost, but you couldn't say it is "good". It's no more trouble making a really good product

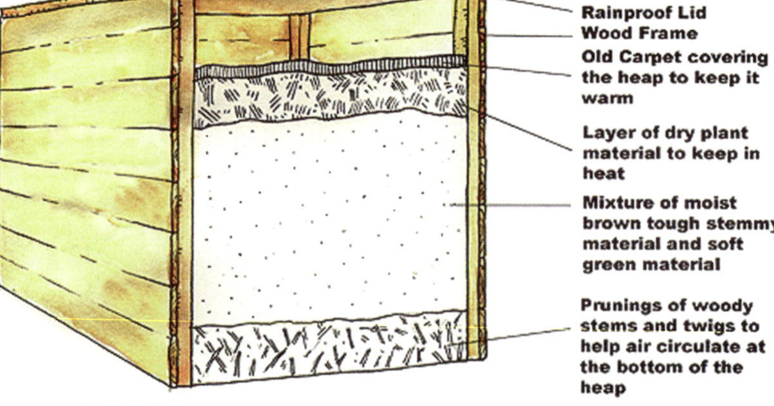

Figure 20.5: Composting: a, turning compost; b, compost bin; c, filling a compost bin; d, compost bin layout.

– in fact it's less trouble, because good compost reduces almost every other kind of gardening problem. So why not get it right in the first place? This guide is about making GOOD compost.

There's a lot of discussion about all the technicalities involved in what constitutes "good" compost, but we reckon good compost is either compost that gets HOT – 60 °C (140 °F) or more, or it is made for you by special earthworms.

20.4.2   How not to fail

It's a common mistake to use too much water – it's probably the most common reason for failures. (Others are not enough nitrogen and more rarely, no aeration.) The overall moisture content of the assembled pile should be about 60–65%. They say it should be as moist as a wrung-out sponge, which is a good guide if you've put everything through a shredder so it's homogenised and the particle size is small, but with the usual rough compost materials it's not very useful.

This is typical advice: "Spray the mixed materials with a hose until wet like a sponge but not soggy. Fork it into the bin, spray more water to make sure it is wet enough."

Beginners read such things and end up with a disaster. When the stuff starts to decay it disintegrates into a slimy, stinking sludge, like what happens to grass clippings if you leave them in a big pile: it gets very hot, and then it dies into a dark green gunge – much worse if there's manure and kitchen scraps in it! It's difficult to repair the damage and get it working properly. That's often the end of that particular beginner's composting efforts.

Compost materials are often much wetter than they look at first. Fresh green leaves can be 95% water, but they don't *look* wet. Kitchen wastes are usually more than 85% water. Spreading fresh greens out and letting them wilt for a day loses a lot of the water and probably quite a lot of the nitrogen too, unfortunately.

Manure is a lot easier to handle if it's on the dry side, which also loses a bit of the nitrogen.

20.4.3   Greens and browns

Compost materials are assembled in the correct proportion of "greens" (nitrogen-rich) and "browns" (carbon-rich) to achieve an overall carbon/nitrogen ratio of 25-30:1. Put simply, fresh green matter such as grass clippings, vegetable wastes, fresh leaves, etc., contain a lot of nitrogen. So does manure, blood meal, kitchen scraps, alfalfa meal, and hay. Fallen leaves, straw, sawdust, shredded newspaper and cardboard, wood chips browns contain high proportions of carbon.

Instead of thinking in "greens" and "browns", think in terms of "wets" and "dries". In fact wets are usually green and browns are often dry. You can make sure the browns are dry-collected fallen leaves when the weather's dry, for instance. Presume your compost materials will always be too wet and always have lots of dry browns on hand to balance it with. Too much carbon? We'll deal with that in a minute.

The advantage of dry browns is that you can store them indefinitely, unlike wet greens. With a bit of foresight and effort you can always have a few garbage bags filled with dries ready for when you need them. Make a big effort in autumn to collect enough leaves for the whole year.

20.4.4   Hints

20.4.4.1. Not enough water is better than too much water.

Too much water is usually a disaster, but if there's not enough, the pile will heat up and then stop. Empty it out, loosen it all up with the compost fork, add more moisture, and put it back in the box again, no big deal. Soon you'll learn how much water is enough. If your pile is too wet, try emptying it, fluff it out, add more dry stuff and some dry greens if you have such a thing (blood meal, peanut cake, alfalfa meal) and rebuild it. It might work.

20.4.4.2. Too much nitrogen is better than not enough nitrogen.

If there's not enough the pile will just sit there forever, nothing happens for a year or two. If there's too much the pile will heat up well and simply blow off the excess with the steam in the form of ammonia gas, until the balance is right. But isn't that a waste of precious nitrogen? No – nitrogen is only costly when you buy it from a chemical company (see below, 23.4.7). Again, this way you'll soon learn how much is enough.

20.4.4.3.   Roots: Shake as much soil as you can off clumped roots before putting them in the compost

Many people put much too much soil in the compost with the roots, and it clogs everything up. Always have *some* soil sprinkled throughout the pile. It helps to inoculate the compost with the beneficial soil micro-organisms that make the process happen, especially if you're not using animal manure. Clay particles in the soil help to spread a thin film of moisture throughout the pile, which is just what you want.

20.4.4.4.   Useful additions

Lime or ground limestone, the finer ground the better. Liquid seaweed emulsion, such as Maxicrop, SM-3 or equivalent all the minerals for all the soil bugs, in easily digestible forms. Compost or compost siftings from the previous batch to inoculate the pile. Sprinklings of ground rock powders are useful.

20.4.4.5.   Newsprint

Modern printing inks are almost always non-toxic and biodegradable, particularly black ink, so don't be shy of using shredded newspaper (very "brown").

20.4.5   Compost containers

If you have really big supplies of organic wastes, make windrows, 2 400 mm at the base, 1 500–1 800 mm high, with sloping sides, and as long as you like. Otherwise prefer boxes or bins to heaps. If you're expert enough you can make a steep-sided heap, even a sheer-sided one, otherwise it degenerates into a mound, which is not efficient unless you're making an expert Biodynamic compost heap, that is.

Boxes and bins have sheer sides, and protect the compost from the elements. There are endless different designs.

Here's how to make a wire mesh bin.

Make a "tube" of chicken wire, 900 mm in diameter. Leave about 200–250 mm overlap, and connect the ends with four twists of wire each. You'll need about 3 m of 900 mm-wide mesh, and two more pieces each 900 mm long – total 4.95 m.

Line the bin with a garbage bag, or two bags, with the bottoms cut off, to keep the moisture in. Have the liner flush with one end and overlapping the other (that's the top).

Make a 900 mm square of four bricks, one at each corner, with a fifth in the middle, and put a 900 mm square of tough wire grille, such as pig fencing, on the bricks. Put

A chicken wire compost bin. When cooked, you can open the wire mesh and work on the pile (centre).

one of the two 900 mm square pieces of chicken wire on top of that. Stand the mesh bin on end on top of this aerated base. Now you can fill it with compost material.

When it's full, depending on the weather, you can close it loosely with the garbage bag overlap, again to keep the moisture in. When it starts steaming, open the bag, if it seems to be getting dry, close it again.

Cover the top with the second 900 mm square piece of chicken wire and clip it on to dissuade wildlife. If it's in the open, cover the top with a garbage bag to keep the rain out.

You'll need two of these bins you always need at least two compost bins/boxes: when one's full, you start filling the next one. By the time that one's full, the first one is done and can be emptied.

20.4.6   Assembling the materials

It's easier to make good compost if you have enough materials to fill the box at one go. If not, see below, 20.4.8 . Basically, anything that was once alive or part of something alive can be composted. This is the recipe: the assembled pile should have 60–65% moisture content, good aeration, acid-alkaline level about neutral (pH 7) or slightly acidic (pH 6–6.5), carbon/nitrogen ration 25–30:1.

First, collect all the greens together and mix them thoroughly with a compost fork. If anything's too big to mix, chop it up into 100–150 mm lengths with the edge of a spade or a chopper.

Up to 10% of the material can be rough material like small sticks and prunings. They probably won't break down but they'll help with aeration and prevent the material packing down and clogging up too much.

Assemble all the ingredients in a sort of big pancake (1 500–1 800 mm diameter) in front of the open box (leave yourself enough room around it to work).

Put wet greens on top of dry browns. Use a 25 l bucket or a basket. Spread out two buckets of browns (pack it in) and then one bucket of greens on top.

Do that twice, then add some sprinklings: A handful of ground limestone or wood ash (sprinkle it like icing sugar on a sponge cake), some bone meal if you have it, a handful or two of soil and a couple of handfuls of compost (unless you're using the siftings from the previous batch – mix with the browns if they're dry enough). Scuff over the surface to bury the sprinklings a bit, then add liquid (see below, 20.4.7) 1–2 litres, with a sprinkling can. If you must use a hose, set the nozzle to a fine mist.

Repeat this whole layering process two or three more times or until you've used all the materials.

Now work from the edge of the layered pancake: Rake off about 30 cm with the compost fork, mix it up well and fork it into the box, spreading it evenly and tamping it down firmly (but not too tight). Layering it and then mixing vertical slices this way gets it thoroughly mixed and evenly distributed. Then do the next 300 mm and continue until it's all in. Sweep up fines as you go, sprinkling them into the box with a shovel.

Aeration

Compost needs air from underneath. You can put the box on the soil, if it's good soil that breathes well. Even then, loosen it well with a fork to a depth of about 300 mm. An advantage of this is that if the pile is too wet, some of the excess water might drain off into the soil (or it might not.)

Alternatively make a base like that for the wire mesh bin described above: Make a 900 mm square of four bricks, one at each corner, with a fifth in the middle and

Figure 20.6: a, Turning compost; b, Compost bin; c and d, Making compost.

put a 900 mm square of tough wire grille such as pig fencing on the bricks. Put a 900 mm square piece of chicken wire on top of that, and stand the box on this base.

When filling the box, stand a 1 500 mm length of bamboo or a broomstick upright in the middle until the box is full. Then shake it from side to side a bit and pull it out. Or make vertical holes every 150 mm or so across the top with a piece of rebar and push it right down until you hit the wire mesh at the bottom. Now your compost can breathe easily.

Put a lid on the box when it's full, not airtight, but wildlife-proof and waterproof if it's in the open.

That's it. By the next day, the temperature should be above 50 °C, and it should climb to 60 °C or higher. You can turn it after a week or two when the temperature's fallen to about 40 °C, or just leave it for another couple of weeks instead.

Get a soil thermometer, or any long thermometer that will reach the centre of the pile to monitor the temperature. Or just put your hand in – if it is too hot to keep it there, it's fine.

20.4.7   Adding liquids

The best form of liquid addition for compost is what some composters primly call Household Compost Activator. Other people call it urine. Don't be coy about it this is what *should* happen to urine rather than wasting it by flushing it down the toilet. Develop a self-righteous attitude about not wasting it – but don't shout about it too loud, modern city people like neighbours and so on can be funny about these things, what they don't know won't hurt them.

First, urine is sterile. Second, it contains the drainage of every cell in the body it's crammed with minerals and vitamins. Third, it contains a lot of nitrogen that's one reason that it's silly to buy nitrogen (there are others).

It shouldn't prove too difficult to arrange to have a few litres of Household Compost Activator set by when it's time to make the compost. You can use it neat, or mix it 50-50 with water, and add a capful of seaweed emulsion while you're at it. Use a sprinkling can.

More about nitrogen: Well-made compost piles often end up containing more nitrogen than they started off with – up to 25% more. It's provided by free-living nitrogen-fixing bacteria that thrive in a compost pile and "fix" nitrogen from the copious supplies in the air.

20.4.8   Batches

Smaller gardens won't provide enough material to fill a 3.5 m³ cube compost unit at one go, it comes in dribs and drabs. So do kitchen scraps. You could just throw it all in a compost bin as it comes, but it'll probably be too wet and clog up, or it won't get hot, or only quite hot (mesophilic) rather than very hot (thermophilic), which is better than nothing. It's worth organising the process by gearing garden wastes to kitchen scraps and then processing it all in batches until the bin is full.

Kitchen scraps

Get a smallish (250–300 mm) plastic bucket with a lid and a tray that it can stand in. Drill some holes in the bottom. Put 75 mm of dry stuff in the bottom, add your kitchen scraps on top as they're produced. Keep the bucket in the kitchen. No meat/fish, etc. or cooked food until you're more experienced (eggshells are fine). If you're a big family you might need a bigger bucket.

Don't let it get too wet, don't let it rot – if liquid starts coming out the bottom, empty it (every few days, depending how much you cook).

Meanwhile collect garden wastes and odds and ends of greens – they'll keep for a while if you spread them out somewhere to dry in a layer a few inches deep.

For the first batch, put 100 mm of dry stuff in the bottom of the compost bin. Mix up greens and kitchen wastes, add some manure if you have it. Then mix it up with twice the quantity of browns/dries, add sprinklings of lime or wood ash, bone meal, some dry compost, as above (*Assembling the materials*) and a bit of liquid if necessary. Dump it in the bin, spreading it evenly. Pack it down quite tightly.

Add 25–50 mm of browns plus a sprinkling of compost or topsoil on top. The first batch might not have the bulk to get hot, which normally eradicates the smell of the kitchen scraps (and anything else) and a layer of browns on top will help keep flies away. As further batches increase the bulk, it should heat up well. Put a lid on the bin.

Once it cools down it should be turned – empty the bin, fluff everything up thoroughly with the compost fork, add liquid if necessary and put it back in the bin. If it doesn't get that hot the second time, never mind, just leave it there for a few weeks.

20.4.9   Animal manure

Many people say it's not essential to use animal manure to make good compost and it's true. Some people actively avoid it. It is better to use manure if you can get it. All natural topsoil is derived from a mixture of animal and plant matter – nature never attempts to raise plants without animals. It is important that some portion of what is recycled into the soil should have passed through animals. This is one of the reasons we recommend using urine as an activator.

Manure from any animal that is not a carnivore will do, plus poultry. The Biodynamic School Of Organic Growing – ace compost makers – swears by cow dung, ascribing special qualities to it. In Hong Kong, manure from the herd of feral water buffalo

Animal manure.

was used and it was excellent. A fifth of the total amount of compost material is enough manure, don't use more than a quarter.

Beware of manure from factory-farmed livestock that's fed commercial feed laced with antibiotics. You can use it, it will probably work alright and the antibiotics will break down in the heat, but why put stuff in your compost that will kill the very critters that do all the work for you?

20.4.10   Sifting

If you have a shredder, you can shred the materials before you load the box, shred them again a week later and maybe again a week after that and then you won't need to sift the compost. Otherwise it'll need screening.

There are many different screening systems. Simplest is a 1 500–900 mm wide piece of 16 mm or 19 mm wire screen wire-stapled to a light wooden frame. Stand it at an angle against a wall and throw the compost at it with a shovel (aim high). Or use it placed horizontally to the ground, supported at each end at a height of 900–1 200 mm, shovel the compost onto it and rub it through the screen with your hands (use gardening gloves) or with the back of a garden rake.

Store what goes through the screen for a few weeks to let it cure before using it in the soil. When applying it to the soil, hoe it lightly into the top few inches where it'll do the most good. The earthworms will do the rest. No earthworms? Don't worry, they will soon be there!

You'll be left with up to a quarter of the pile in siftings. It makes a very good mulch, or you can add it to the browns for the next lot, or mix it with kitchen scraps and greens for batch composting.

20.4.11   Cold weather

An overseas person who said he'd made "lots of compost" wrote: "In northern climes especially, you're more in need of adding heat to the pile some of the year...

Sifting the finished compost.

The problem here in Wisconsin is it just gets too cold in winter. I know, I've tried it, it froze solid in the winter. Somewhere I've seen plans for a solar-heated outhouse, and solar-heated compost bin, which would probably be the ticket."

That is just not how compost works. If it's correctly prepared, the biological activity will heat it up, no matter how cold the weather is. Adding extra heat from outside is no use.

Finally he admitted: "I don't think my compost piles ever heat up much. Not enough nitrogen for one thing, here in town. I suppose if you had a large batch of materials mixed up properly with the correct ratios, it might have a chance, but you can't do that with the daily wastes." Yes, you can.

Elaine Ingham, President, Soil Foodweb Inc., wrote: "The definition of properly composted material, when applied to thermal compost, is that it has reached a temperature throughout the material for long enough that weed seed, human pathogens and most of the plant pathogens and pests have been killed... Many people do not understand that the bacteria and fungi growing in organic matter raise the temperature. If all you do is physically heat compost, you don't get the same reduction in pathogens. This is a biological process. Competition with aerobic bacteria and fungi, inhibition by other bacteria and fungi, and consumption of disease-organisms by protozoa and nematodes are all part of the process of making good compost and getting rid of the pathogens. If you just steam heat organic matter, you don't get the same benefits of the growth of the competitive, inhibitory and consuming interactions that happen when the full food web is present." Sustainable Agriculture Network Discussion Group, 5 November, 2002.

"Even in Alaska in the middle of the winter my compost pile reaches 140 degrees or more. If it gets too hot, beneficials, such as worms, simply move (crawl) out of harm's way. Turn the pile every 4 or 5 days, folding ouside materials to the inside and versa visa, like kneading bread. Keep it moist, not soggy, and be glad you're making 'post! Nice work!" Marion, message to the Gardening Organically Internet mailing list, 26 September, 2002.

We've made compost outside in the usual way at temperatures of -15 °C (5 °F) with no difficulty, the compost rose to 65 °C (150 °F) as usual.

20.5   ADDENDUM E (HONEYBEES)

Why honeybees are important

Many plants are dependent on pollination by honeybees. Bees use beeswax to form hexagonal cells called honeycombs. The bees use the hexagons to store food in the form of honey and pollen. A healthy honeybee hive usually has around 20 000–

Honeybee (photograph: Hein Waschefort).

50 000 bees during summer. Almost all of these will be female workers, along with a queen and a few hundred male drones.

Honey is made using the nectar of flowering plants and is saved inside the beehive for eating during times of scarcity. Nectar – a sugary liquid – is extracted from flowers using a bee's long, tube-shaped tongue and stored in its extra stomach, or "crop." While sloshing around in the crop, the nectar mixes with enzymes that transform its chemical composition and pH, making it more suitable for long-term storage. When a honeybee returns to the hive, it passes the nectar to another bee by regurgitating the liquid into the other bee's mouth. This regurgitation process is repeated until the partially digested nectar is finally deposited into a honeycomb.

Once in the comb, nectar is still a viscous liquid – nothing like the thick honey you use at the breakfast table. To get all that extra water out of their honey, bees set to work fanning the honeycomb with their wings in an effort to speed up the process of evaporation.

When most of the water has evaporated from the honeycomb, the bee seals the comb with a secretion of liquid from its abdomen, which eventually hardens into beeswax. Away from air and water, honey can be stored indefinitely, providing bees with the perfect food source for cold winter months. Honey's colour, taste, aroma and texture vary greatly depending on the type of flower a bee frequents. Clover honey, for example, differs greatly from the honey harvested from bees that frequent a lavender field.

Just how important are honeybees to the human diet? Typically, according to the U.S. Department of Agriculture, these under-appreciated workers pollinate 80% of our flowering crops which constitute $^1/_3$ of everything we eat. Losing them could affect not only dietary staples such as apples, broccoli, strawberries, nuts, asparagus,

Honeybees.

blueberries and cucumbers, but may threaten our beef and dairy industries if alfalfa is not available for feed. One Cornell University study estimated that honeybees annually pollinate $14 billion worth of seeds and crops in the U.S. Essentially, if honeybees disappear, they could take most of our insect pollinated plants with them, potentially reducing mankind to little more than a water diet.

Bees are of inestimable value as agents of cross-pollination and many plants are entirely dependent on particular kinds of bees for their reproduction (such as red clover, which is pollinated by the bumblebee and many orchids). In many cases the use of insecticides for agricultural pest control has created the unwelcome side effect of killing the bees necessary for maintaining the crop.

Such environmental stresses plus several species of parasitic mites devastated honeybee populations in the United States beginning in the 1980s, making it necessary for farmers to rent bees from keepers in order to get their crops pollinated and greatly affecting the pollination of plants in the wild.

Usually a honeybee can visit between 50–1 000 flowers in one trip, which takes between 30 minutes to four hours. Without pollen, the young nurse bees cannot produce bee milk or royal jelly to feed the queen and colony. If no pollen is available to the colony, egg laying by the queen will stop.

Many homeowners believe dandelions and clover are weeds, that lawns should be only grass to be mowed down regularly, and that everything but the grass should be highly treated with pesticides. This makes a hostile environment for bees, butterflies and other pollinators. Many bee poisoning problems could be prevented by better communication and cooperation among the grower, pesticide applicator and the beekeeper.

When most people think about honeybees and what they contribute to our society, they likely think only of honey. Honeybees, however, have a much larger impact in our lives through agriculture. Not only do they provide pollination to fruit and vegetable crops, but they also pollinate crops we grow and feed to animals which we then eat or use for dairy products. Without a healthy honeybee population, and the beekeepers who keep them, our lives would change dramatically in a very short period of time.

As honeybees play a very important role in our lives and our quality of living, attention must be paid to the fact that beekeepers are finding it more difficult to keep their bees healthy than ever before due to many different circumstances. Some of these circumstances are controllable and others are not. We must seriously reconsider the chemicals and pesticides we use in our yards and in agriculture.

Too often, we neglect to think of the indirect consequences of our actions. Unfortunately, many cities and towns prohibit even one or two hives of honeybees to be kept. Large scale beekeepers can find it difficult to find areas to keep their bees because people exhibit ill behaviour towards keeping bees anywhere near their homes. The fact is that honeybees will almost never sting people away from their hive. It is wasps and hornets that are aggressive and seem to sting people for no reason. If you see colonies of honeybees in your area, you should not complain but appreciate the fact that someone is willing to keep and care for them, provide the pollination services needed to sustain our standard of living and that they do all this for very meagre or no profits.

20.6 ADDENDUM F (EVALUATION OF AN URBAN NATURE AREA)

20.6.1 EVALUATION TO DETERMINE THE NATURE CONSERVATION STATUS OF A PROPERTY (CITY OF TSHWANE METROPOLITAN MUNICIPALITY)

20.6.1.1 Description of the site (please attach a map of the area):

Date of evaluation:

Write down the full answer for each question and then give a point for the answer according to the following criteria:

1. = bad
2. = poor
3. = average
4. = good
5. = excellent

20.6.1.2 Biological status:

a) What is the availability of water habitat on this property? (5)

b) Does this habitat make a contribution to the representation of habitat for urban nature conservation? (5)

c) Are there Red Data species involved? (Please list them.) (5)

d) What is the coverage (size in ha) of this potential conservation area? (5)

e) Will it make any contribution to urban nature conservation/ local biodiversity? (5)

f) What is the status of species diversity? (5)

g) What is the invasive alien species status of the site? (5)

h) What is the rehabilitation status of the site? (5)

20.6.1.3　Availability of the land:

a) What is the council-owned status of the land? (5)

b) What will the expenditure costs be if council need to obtain the land? (5)

20.6.1.4　Development status:

a) What is the impact of the current development (excavations, roads, buildings, power lines, housing, and landfill) on the conservation status of this site? (5)

20.6.1.5   Utilisation potential of this site for urban nature conservation:

a) What is the potential for outdoor recreational activities that will enhance urban
    nature conservation?   (5)

b) What is the environmental education potential for this site?   (5)

c) Will it make a contribution to feeding and breeding habitat for endemic
    species?   (5)

d) Is this site in line with the conservation plan of the CTMM?   (5)

e) Will residents get involve with activities on this site? Can a Friends group or
    stakeholder make a contribution?   (5)

                                                                        Total: (80)

Name of evaluator:
Position of evaluator
Signature of evaluator:

20.7   ADDENDUM G (TEMPLATE FOR AN ECOLOGICAL MANAGEMENT PLAN)

20.7.1 Table of contents:

20.7.1   Introduction

20.7.3   Definitions

Ecological management plan

Nature reserve

20.7.4   Introduction to the environmental management plan (EMP)

In terms of new legislation, specifically the national environmental management: Protected Areas Act, 2003, a nature reserve is required to have an ecological management plan which encompasses biological diversity aspects, socio-economic development, cultural-historical and development aspects.

In terms of Section 31 of the Act, the minister must follow the prescribed consultation process with regard to the proclamation of any nature reserve. The ecological management plans for all nature reserves must therefore be compiled by following such a consultative approach and must include aspects of the IDP objectives of local municipal authorities.

Upon proclamation of the nature reserve in the Gazette, the minister must invite public comment and consult all affected parties surrounding or occupying the area.

The ecological management plan will strive to achieve the following objectives:
- To ensure that a nature reserve is proclaimed as a nature reserve subject to current legislation.
- To list the unique biological, socio-economic, cultural-historical and development characteristics of the area.
- To provide an accurate inventory of natural resources within the area.
- To provide an inventory of management and visitor-related infrastructure and services.
- To list norms and standards with regard to the management of this protected area.
- To prescribe management actions which comply with the prescribed norms and standards.
- To set performance indicators by which compliance can be gauged for adaptive management purposes.

Each section of the ecological management plan should contain the following aspects:
- Ecological filing system references.
- The vital attributes or special features being dealt with under each section.
- Historical information with regard to previous management strategies.
- Management principles, norms and standards.

- Current areas of concern regarding noncompliance with legislation.
- An action plan to deal with and rectify legislative deficits.

The current document should be regarded as a draft document for review by the Provincial Authorities.

20.7.5 Geographical location and demographic profile

20.7.5.1 Demographic overview
20.7.5.2 Economic overview

20.7.6 History of the nature reserve

20.7.6.1 Short history and reasons for proclamation

Nature reserves should be read together with the maps/addendums of the area.

20.7.6.2 Proclamation

The farm in question and the portion.

20.7.6.3 Current conservation importance of the nature reserve.

20.7.7 Vision, mission and objectives

20.7.8 Governing legislation

20.7.8.1 Declaration according to the national environmental management: Protected Areas Act

According to Section 23 (1) (a) and (b), the MEC may only proclaim an area as a nature reserve to protect the area if the area has
- significant natural features or biodiversity;
- is of scientific, cultural, historical or archaeological interest; or
- is in need of long-term protection for the maintenance of its biodiversity or for the provision of environmental goods and services;

Additionally, the area must:
- provide for a sustainable flow of natural products and services to meet the needs of a local community;
- enable the continuation of such traditional consumptive uses as are sustainable;
- or to provide for nature-based recreation and tourism opportunities. *(National Environmental Management: Protected Areas Act, Chapter 3 p11)*

Notwithstanding the provisions of the section quoted above, Section 23 (5) states as follows:
- An area which was a nature reserve immediately before this section took effect must for the purposes of this section be regarded as having been declared as such in terms of this section.

20.7.8.2   Vital attributes with regard to legislation:

The conclusion with regard to the proclamation of a nature reserve is as follows:

Section	Criteria	Compliance
23 (b)	Biodiversity status, scientific value, cultural and historical value, provision of ecosystem services.	
23 (c)	Sustainable flow of natural products and services to meet community needs (see harvesting of thatch grass and exotic plant control).	
23 (d)	Continuation of traditional uses as is sustainable.	
23 (e)	Provision of nature-based tourism and recreation benefits.	
23 (5)	Previous proclamation.	

20.7.8.3   Supporting legislation

Subject to the national environmental management: Protected Areas Act, there are other sets of legislation that are all used in the management of nature reserves:
- The Protected Areas Act No 57 of 2003.
- The Biodiversity Bill.
- The Nature Conservation Ordinance 12 of 1983.
- The Conservation of Agricultural Resources Act, No. 43 of 1983.
- National Environmental Management Act, No 57, 1998.
- The Veld and Forest Fire Act (Act 101 of 1998).
- Mountain Catchment Areas Act, 1970 (Act No. 63 of 1970).
- The Fencing Act (Act No 31 of 1963).
- The Criminal Procedure Act.
- The Public Finance Management Act.
- PSCBC Resolutions.
- The Extension of Security of Tenure Act, No 62 of 1997.
- Basic Conditions of Employment Act.
- The Employment Equity Act, No 55 of 1998.

All of the management decisions and actions implemented on the reserve must conform to all of the above-mentioned legislation.

20.7.9   Management authority

According to Section 38 (2) of the National Environmental Management: Protected Areas Act:

> "The MEC, in writing – (a) must assign the management of a nature reserve to a suitable person, organization or organ of state, and (b) may assign the management of a protected environment to a suitable person, organization or organ of state...."
> *(National Environmental Management: Protected Areas Act, Chapter 4, S38 (2) p30)*

20.7.9   Chapter 2: (Resource inventory)

20.7.10.1 Climate

Vital attributes

Management guidelines

1.   Weather data must be collected on a daily basis.
2.   Weather stations should be stationed in representative areas on the reserve.
3.   The full range of weather conditions should be monitored per station.
4   Weather data should be downloaded from monitoring stations at least twice per month.
5.   Data collected from the stations should be stored in a central database on station, both electronically and on hard copy.

20.7.10.2 Topography

Vital attributes

Management guidelines

1   A detailed topographical map should be available for the proclaimed reserve as well as all future extensions of the area.
2   The correct game species should be stocked on the reserve, according to their specific habitat requirements.
3   Correct stocking rates should be applied in order to prevent overgrazing on steep gradients with corresponding soil loss and accelerated erosion.
4   The burning regime on the reserve should take topography into account and avoid denudation of vegetation on steep slopes for extended periods of time.
5   Roads should be correctly placed with correct run-off structures to ensure that water is not channeled with corresponding erosion of the soil profile.

Community benefit

20.7.10.3 Geology

Vital attributes

Management guidelines

1.   A complete geological map of the existing nature reserve.
2.   Copies of the map must be placed on file in the ecological filing system.
3.   All maps should be verified by a qualified geologist.

4   Geology should be taken into account when planning new infrastructure zonation

20.7.10.5 Soil

Vital attributes

Management guidelines

1.   Detailed soil maps should be available for the existing NR.
2.   Soil forms should be used as a major determinant of sensitivity indices when conducting EIA's for development purposes and zonation exercises.
3.   Development of infrastructure should not take place on alluvial deposits.
4   Roads should not be planned across sensitive soils that are prone to accelerated erosion.

        In cases where existing roads transverse sensitive soils, adequate water flow control structures should be installed to ensure that erosion does not take place and those ecological processes are not disturbed.
5   Soil tests should be conducted on agricultural lands and adjacent benchmark sites to determine the degree of disturbance and rate of recovery during the rehabilitation process.

20.7.10.5 Hydrology

Vital attributes

Management guidelines

1.   Eradicate alien vegetation in and around the natural streams.
2.   Eradicate alien vegetation in the catchment within the reserve.
3.   Prevent and control soil erosion within the reserve.

Community benefit

20.7.10.6 Fauna

Vital attributes

Management guidelines

1.   Manage and conserve the habitat for the flagship species.
2.   Manage and conserve habitat for other fauna occurring on the reserve.

Community Benefit
The ensured future survival of the ecosystem functions for future generations through regulated research and education ventures.

20.7.10.7   Flora

Vital attributes

Management guidelines

1.   Manage and conserve vegetation and habitat processes in the reserve and the greater area around the reserve.
2.   Manage the burning programme to conserve and assist vegetation and system dynamics.

Community benefit

20.7.10.8   Alien biota

Vital attributes

The following exotics have been identified: (EG)
* Jacaranda – *Jacaranda mimosifolia*
* Black wattle – *Acacia mearnsii*
* Blue gums – *Eucalyptus sisal*
* Prickly pear – *Optutia ficus indica*

The following weeds have been identified: (EG)
* Large thorn-apple – *Datura ferox*
* Black jack – *Solanum sisymbrifolium bidens*
* Wild asparagus – *Protasparagus iaricinus*
* Chaff flower – *Achyranthes aspera*

Management guidelines

1.   Eradicate alien, exotic plants and animals.
2.   Prevent the spread of alien biota.
3.   Use most effective methods and equipment to eradicate alien biota.

Community benefit

20.7.10.9   Heritage phenomena

Vital attributes

Management guidelines

1.   Manage and conserve the natural occurring heritage phenomena as they occur on the reserve.

Community benefit

20.7.11   Chapter 3: (Management objectives)

23.7.11.1 Ownership and Municipal regions

Vital Attributes
Geographical positioning of Reserve and Land Portions

Municipal area:
(Farm name and number)   Portions
Biodiversity Objectives

....

Ownership of land
Demographic constitution

23.7.11.2 Boundaries and fences

Vital attributes

Biodiversity objectives
- Restrict and prohibit unauthorised access for vehicles in the reserve to protect the vegetation, soils and fauna species occurring in the reserve.
- Restrict and prohibit unauthorised access of people doing illegal plant harvesting or illegal hunting within the reserve.

Management principles:
- Boundaries should be clearly marked by means of a game proof fence.
- Fencing should comply with the minimum standards as stipulated in the Fencing Act as well as the Nature Conservation Ordinance (12 of 1983 and the GDACE policy on fencing for the types of game to be contained within such fences.
- The current minimum height of the fence for jumping game is 2.4 meters.
- The correct fences for dangerous game such as rhino and predators such as cheetah should be erected if and when such species are introduced to the protected area.
- Fences should be regularly inspected and maintained on a daily basis.
- Cavities under fences should be filled to avoid game species from escaping.
- Sections of boundary fences that are stolen should be replaced immediately.
- "No entry" notices should be placed along the boundary to demarcate a protected area and to inform local communities of regulations.
- Flow control structures should be placed along water courses to ensure that fences are not removed by storm water drainage.
- Sections of boundary fences should be kept free of vegetation in order to reduce the risk of fire damage and to prolong the durability of the fence.

Management guidelines

1. Maintain the boundary fence in good condition.
2. Fence of the remainder of the reserve not currently fenced off.
3. Training of staff in compliance and enforcement.

Community benefit

23.7.11.3 Access routes

Vital attributes

Management guidelines

1.   Ensure that signage on the access roads are correct and informative.
2.   Keep the access roads within the reserve in good condition.

Community benefit

23.7.11.4 Roads

Vital attributes

Management guidelines

1.   Keep the roads within the reserve in good condition.
2.   Control and limit erosion on the roads within the reserve.
3.   Limit the number of roads to the minimum necessary for management purposes.

23.7.11.5 Management infrastructure

Vital attributes

Management guidelines

1.   Maintain the infrastructure needs.
2.   Develop compatible infrastructure where needed.
3.   Training of staff in compliance and enforcement.

Community benefit

23.7.11.6 Visitor infrastructure

Vital attributes

Bookings at Nature Reserve.

Management guidelines

1.   Maintain all infrastructures in good condition.
2.   Clean facilities for use by visitors.
3.   Maintain gardens and other areas around buildings.

Community benefit

23.7.11.7 Waste management system

Vital attributes

Management guidelines

1.   Remove waste as per schedules as and when needed.
2.   Prevent and control environmental pollution at all times.

Community benefit

23.7.11.8 Security system

Vital attributes

Management guidelines

1.   Ensure that all communication devices on the reserve are in good working order.
2.   Ensure that the security alarm system is working at all times and is activated at all times.
3.   Regular patrols of the areas and around the buildings.

Community Benefit

23.7.11.9 Fire management

Vital attributes

Management guidelines

1.   Planned fire breaks around the reserve to protect it from uncontrolled and accidental fires.
2.   Planned burning of block burns to create a mosaic burning pattern over an extended cycle.

Community benefit

23.7.11.10 Veld and game management

Vital attribute

Management guidelines

1.   Managing the vegetation for the ecosystem functions and ecosystem health.

Community benefit

23.7.11.11 Ecological projects

Vital attributes

Management guidelines

1.   Regulate informative research projects on natural occurring fauna, flora and ecological aspects.

Community benefit

23.7.12   Chapter 4: (Visitor services and interpretive plan)

23.7.12.1 Visitor facilities

Vital attributes

Management guidelines

1.   Maintain all infrastructures in good condition.
2.   Clean facilities for use by visitors.
3.   Maintain gardens and other areas around buildings.

Community benefit

23.7.12.2 Environmental education

Vital attributes

Management guidelines

1.   Maintain all environmental education infrastructures in good condition.
2.   Clean facilities for use by visitors.
3.   Maintain gardens and other areas around buildings.

Community benefit

23.7.12.3 Neighbour relations policy

Vital attributes

Management guidelines

1.   Maintain good neighbour relations.
2.   Identify best practices.
3.   Sustain regular communication.

Community benefit

23.7.12.4 Management of heritage phenomena

Vital attributes

Management guidelines

1. Manage and conserve the natural occurring heritage phenomena as they occur on the reserve.

Community benefit

23.7.13   Chapter 5: (Development plan)

23.7.13.1 Sensitive areas

Vital attributes

Management guidelines

1. Ensure EIA compliance.

Community benefit

23.7.13.2 Management impacts

Vital attributes

Management guidelines

1. Monitor impacts.
2. Identify problem areas.
3. Implement solutions.

Community benefit

23.7.13.3 Listed activities

Vital attributes

Management guidelines

1. Comply with all listed activities according to legislation.

Community benefit

23.7.13.4 Commercialisation

Vital attributes

Management guidelines

1. All activities should be compatible with a nature reserve.

Community benefit

23.7.13.5 Zonation plan

Vital attributes

Management guidelines

1.   Zone sensitive areas.

2.   Zone areas with visual impact.

3.   Zone areas that will enhance light or noise impacts.

Community benefit

23.7.13.6 Capital development plan

Vital attributes

Management guidelines

1.   Identify projects that are compatible to the nature reserve.

2.   Address visitor' needs.

Community benefit

23.7.13.7 Registered land claims

Vital attributes

Management guidelines

Community benefit

23.7.13.2 Proposed settlement options

Vital attributes

Management guidelines

Community benefit

22.7.14   Executive summary (give a brief explanation of this document)

22.7.15   Appendices (relevant information that will assist this document)

20.8   ADDENDUM H: INDICATIVE LISTS (SUSTAINABLE UTILISATION CRITERIA)

Physical-ecological indicators

Issues	Sustainability indicators	Sustainable tourism indicators	Tourism carrying capacity indicators
1. Natural environment and biodiversity			
Ecosystems Ecological destruction, natural open spaces, habitat loss	• Total size of nature area • % of nature area • In good condition • Heavily degraded	• Change in vegetation cover due to tourism activities • Change in biodiversity due to recreation activities • Change of critical areas due to tourism development	• Type of nature areas (wetland, mountain, etc.)
Loss of fauna and flora	• Number of endemic and threatened species • Area occupied by endemic or threatened species	•	
Overcrowding			• Number of visitors per square meter of accessible nature areas
Protection	• % of area under protection • Type of nature area protected • % threatened nature protected		

Issues	Sustainability indicators	Sustainable tourism indicators	Tourism carrying capacity indicators
2. Cultural heritage			
		• Loss or degradation of built structures and other archaeological or historical sites due to tourism development	
3. Tourist infrastructure			
		• Total number of beds • % occupancy	• Visitor and staff accommodation
4. Air quality			
	• Pollution level		• Pollution level
5. Noise pollution			
	• Pollution level		• Pollution level
6. Energy			
Energy consumption	• Amount of electric power and petrochemical fuels • Energy consumption from renewable and non-renewable sources	• Annual and monthly consumption	• Local capacity for energy supply
CO_2 emissions	• Total CO_2 emissions per year and per capita	• CO_2 emissions from visitor related activities	
7. Water			
Water consumption	• Consumption/ resident/day • Renewable water resources	• Consumption per bed per tourist/day • Consumption during peak season/annual consumption	• Consumption related activities/total consumption • Total available resources

Issues	Sustainability indicators	Sustainable tourism indicators	Tourism carrying capacity indicators
Water quality Water management	• Water samples • Waste water treatment/ total	• Drinkable water? • Annual cost of water supply/ number of tourists	
8. Waste production	• Daily production per capita • % composition of waste (organic, plastic, metal, etc)	• Waste production per tourist • % composition during peak season	• Waste production in peak period/ day/annual
9. Land use	• Urbanised/total land • Green area ratio per person (sq. m/ per capita) • Eroded land/total land	• No. of houses • Loss of agricultural, forest, wetland, etc. • % of natural area spoiled by activity/facilities	• Urbanised land for tourism/total urbanised land • Density of tourism development (No of beds) • Rate of erosion
10. Landscape (loss of aesthetic values)		Average and maximum height of construction Architectural aspects	
11. Transport and mobility	Road density (road length/ total area) Telecommunication networks	Average traffic per day/ season Public transport Accident levels	Distances and time to travel Waiting time to use facilities Number of parking places

CHAPTER 21

LIST OF ABBREVIATIONS

AOU	American Ornithologist Union
BIDs	Business Improvement Districts
BMP	Best Management Practices
BOD	Biochemical Oxygen Demand
BTO	British Trust for Ornithology
CARA	Conservation of Agricultural Resources Act (Act 43 of 1983)
CBD	Convention on Biological Diversity
C-Plan	Conservation Plan
CO_2	Carbon dioxide
CoT	City of Tshwane
CSIR	Council for Scientific and Industrial Research
DACEL	Department of Agriculture, Conservation, Environment and Land Affairs
DDT	Dichlorodiphenyltrichloroethane
DEA	Department of Environmental Affairs
DWAF	Department of Water Affairs and Forestry
EIA	Environmental Impact Assessment
EMP	Environmental Management Plan
EPA	Environmental Protection Agency
FAO	Food and Agricultural organization
FISCRWG	Federal Interagency Stream Corridor Restoration
FON	Friends of Nature
GLOBIO	Modelling human impacts on biodiversity
GDARD	Gauteng Department of Agriculture and Rural Development
Ha	Hectare
ICLEI	International Council for Local Environmental Initiatives
IDP	Integrated Development Plan
IFN	International Friends of Nature
IPCC	Intergovernmental Panel on Climate Change
IUCN	International Union for Conservation of Nature
KNP	Kuscenneti National Park
KPI	Key Performance Indicators
LBAP	Local Biodiversity Action Plan
LBSAP	Local Biodiversity Strategy and Action Plan
LDA	Limited Development Area
MA	Millennium Ecosystem Assessment
MFMA	Municipal Finance Management Act

NGO	Non-Governmental Organisation
NEMA	National Environmental Management Act (107 of 1998)
NEMBA	National Environmental Management: Biodiversity Act, 2004 (Act 10 of 2004)
NEMPAA	National Environmental Management: Protected Areas Act, 2003 (Act 57 of 2003)
PEDs	Special Park Districts
PNE	Protected Natural Environment
RSPB	Royal Society for the preservation of Birds
SABCA	South African Butterfly Conservation Assessment (May 2007 – April 2011)
SANBI	South African National Biodiversity Institute
SANParks	South African National Parks
SEA	Strategic Environmental Assessment
SER	Society for Ecological Restorations
SIDSnet	Small Island Developing States Network
SPDs	Park Enhancement Districts
SPCA	Society for the Prevention of Cruelty to Animals
SNR	Special Nature Reserve
TEEB	The Economics Of Ecosystems and Biodiversity
TOSF	Tshwane Open Space Framework
UNDP	United Nations Development Programme
UNEP	United Nations Environmental Programme
UNFCCC	United Nations Framework Convention on Climate Change
WESSA	Wildlife and Environment Society of South Africa
WHO	World Health Report
WRC	Water Research Commission
WWF	World Wide Fund for Nature

INDEX

Nature conservation 1, 2, 7, 20, 41, 112, 115, 124, 138, 190, 278, 279, 280, 283–285, 287, 288, 290, 297, 305, 307, 375, 382, 386
Nerium oleander 153
Northern Pygmy Toad 209

O
Oleander 153
Open space 2, 3, 4, 19, 36, 83, 84, 85, 87, 89–93, 95, 97, 99, 100–108, 110–116, 137, 161, 182, 183, 190, 227, 229, 230, 273, 274, 278, 283, 284, 290, 309, 310, 311, 312
Open space alienation 112
 categorisation 91
 conservation 112
 funding 113
 general 111
 in public trust 112
 land use management 113
 network 90, 93, 95, 98, 99, 100, 108, 110, 114, 115, 182, 211
 policies 111
 resource management 114
 value 111
Orange-breasted Rockjumper 249
Organic compost 38, 43, 361
Oribi 249
Owl boxes 32, 43, 343

P
Passenger Pigeon 76
Peacock Moraea 76
Pepper Tree 155
Peregrine Falcon 209
Pheidole megacephala 35
Pied Barbet 28
Pink Tamarisk 155
Pinus pinaster 155
Place-making 90, 92, 108, 109, 111, 113, 114, 115
Pollution 2, 10, 13, 14, 51, 62, 77, 81, 87, 90, 119, 121, 122, 133, 138, 140, 178, 187, 189, 195,

213, 214, 219–223, 225–229, 232, 236, 237, 239, 240, 241, 244, 245, 251, 259, 261, 263, 265, 270, 278, 279, 285, 288, 289, 311, 388, 393
Pom-pom weed 149, 151
Populus canescens 155
Porcupine 66, 68
Protected area 89, 93, 94, 95, 116, 126, 131, 135, 206, 264, 268, 269, 307, 310, 311, 313, 318, 380, 381, 382, 386
Protected species 71, 72, 73
Public Open Space 90, 93, 97, 99, 102, 183, 278, 284
Puff Adder 32

Q
Queen of the Night 150

R
Rana angolensis 209
Rapid response assessment 131
Recreational activities 4, 9, 100, 129, 182, 186, 268, 270, 273, 377
Red Data species 10, 41, 71, 87, 95, 118, 119, 125, 126, 127, 129, 195, 208, 268, 272, 307, 311, 375
Red node 83, 93, 108–111, 115, 311
Red way 83, 93, 108, 109, 115
Rehabilitate 4, 20, 21, 96, 99, 112, 113, 143, 175, 197, 199, 219, 251, 283, 318
Rehabilitation 21, 41, 94, 97–101, 106, 119, 127, 132, 134, 138, 139, 145, 182, 205, 214, 215, 285, 317, 321, 376, 384
Restoration ecology 287
Ridges 9, 10, 13, 19, 20, 41, 84, 85, 87, 91, 95–97, 109, 119, 120, 124–126, 187, 195, 205, 206–212, 219, 271, 272, 310, 316, 320
Riparian forests 187
Riparian zones 93, 100, 159, 181, 182–184, 189, 210, 317